THE SCIENCE OF POLITICS.

PART I.

THE THEORY OF HUMAN PROGRESSION.

THE THEORY

OF

HUMAN PROGRESSION,

AND

NATURAL PROBABILITY

OF A

REIGN OF JUSTICE.

"The charm that exercises the most powerful influence on the mind is derived ess from a knowledge of that which *is* than from a perception of that which *will be*, ven though the latter be nothing more than a new condition of a known existence."
-Humboldt's *Cosmos*.

BOSTON:
SANBORN, CARTER AND BAZIN.
PORTLAND:
SANBORN & CARTER.
1856.

STEREOTYPED AT THE
BOSTON STEREOTYPE FOUNDRY.

DEDICATION.

TO

MONSIEUR VICTOR COUSIN,

PROFESSOR OF PHILOSOPHY AT PARIS.

SIR:—To you I beg leave to dedicate the following Essay on Human Progression, with those sentiments of esteem and admiration which I share in common with so many of my countrymen.

The truth I endeavor to inculcate is—That *credence rules the world*—that credence determines the condition and fixes the destiny of nations—that *true* credence must ever entail with it a correct and beneficial system of society, while false credence must ever be accompanied by despotism, anarchy, and wrong—that before a nation can change its *condition*, it must change its credence; that change of credence will of necessity be accompanied sooner or later by change of condition: and consequently, that true credence, or in other words *knowledge*, is the only means by which man can work out his well being and ameliorate his condition on the globe.

To no one could I dedicate a work intended to elucidate these principles so appropriately as to yourself—to you, Sir, who have labored so earnestly and so well to give to your countrymen a correct system of Ethical Philosophy, and, through them, to communicate to Europe a scheme of natural morals which must ere long bear a rich and most beneficial harvest.

The question is often asked, What is the *use* of philosophy? —nor is the answer difficult. Next to religion, philosophy is, of all known causes, the element that most powerfully tends to determine the condition of a country. It is a *power*—a power so vast that we are scarcely likely to over-estimate its effects; and, though it must ever be unable to solve the great questions in which our race is involved, it may, by uprooting political superstitions and false religions, exercise an influence that no calculation can compute. The theories of one generation become the habitual credence of the next; and that habitual credence, transformed into a rule of action, is ere long realized as a palpable fact in the outward condition of society. And thus it may be truly said—As the philosophy of a country *is*, so its condition *will be*.

In aiding so powerfully as you have done to substitute a rational philosophy for the sensationalism that previously prevailed, you have conferred a boon on France and on the world; and your eloquent appeals for the principles of natural duty will, no doubt, find a response in the hearts of your countrymen, that must carry them onward to even a higher and more stable glory than they have ever yet attained.

France has yet to read her great lesson of new philosophy to the continent of Europe; and every student of the world's thoughts and the world's actions must rejoice that you, Sir, have been her instructor, and that you have laid on her those *moral* obligations, of which to propagate the principles must open up to her a new and glorious career.

Accept, Sir, the dedication of this work as a tribute of respect from your sincere admirer,

THE AUTHOR.

CONTENTS.

INTRODUCTION.

CHAPTER I.

ON THE ELEMENTS OF HUMAN PROGRESSION.

SECTION I.

SECTION II.

SECTION III.

SECTION IV.

CHAPTER II.

ON THE THEORY OF MAN'S INTELLECTUAL PROGRESSION.

SECTION I.

SECTION II.

CHAPTER III.

ON THE THEORY OF MAN'S PRACTICAL PROGRESSION.

SECTION I.

SECTION II.

SECTION III.

CHAPTER IV.

CONCLUSION.

APPENDIX.

THE

THEORY OF HUMAN PROGRESSION.

INTRODUCTION.

PRELIMINARY EXPLANATION OF THE NATURE OF POLITICAL SCIENCE.

BEFORE attempting to exhibit an argument to establish the possibility of a science of politics, and to prove also the probability that such a science may reasonably be expected to evolve at this period of man's progressive acquisition of knowledge, it is necessary to define exactly what we mean by a *science of politics.*

Science is nature seen by the reason, and not merely by the *senses.* Science exists in the *mind,* and in the mind alone. Wherever the substantives of a science may be derived from, or whatever may be their character, they form portions of a science only as they are made to function logically in the human reason. Unless they are connected by the law of reason and consequent, so that one proposition is capable of being correctly evolved from two or more other propositions, called the premises, the science as yet has no existence, and has still to be *discovered.* Logic, therefore, is the universal *form* of all science. It is science with *blank* categories, and when these blank categories are filled up, either with numbers, quantities, and spaces, as in the mathematical sciences, or with the qualities and powers of matter, as in the physical sciences, mathematics and physics take their scientific origin, and assume an ordination which is not arbitrary. Science, then, wherever it is developed, is the same for the human intellect wherever that intellect can comprehend it. It abolishes diversity of credence, and reëstablishes unity of credence.

We have then to ask, "What is the *matter* of political science?" Of what does it treat? What are its substantives? What is the general character of the truths it professes to develop?

1. It treats exclusively of *men.*

2. It treats exclusively of the *relations* between man and man.

3. It treats exclusively of the relations of men *in equity.*

Equity or justice is the *object-noun* of the science of politics, as number is the object-noun of arithmetic; quantity, of algebra; space, of geometry; or *value* of political economy.*

* It must be observed that *equity* or *justice* is not itself capable of definition. If it were so, it could not be the object-noun of a *science,* as no science ever defines its object-noun. For instance, *unity, quantity, space, force, matter, value,* are all incapable of definition; but *forms* of unity, *forms* of quantity, *forms* of space, *forms* of force, *forms* of matter, *forms* of value, are capable of definition.

Politics, then, is the science of EQUITY, *and treats of the relations of* MEN *in equity.*

The fundamental fact from which its propositions derive a *practical* importance, is the following: —

"Men are capable of acting equitably or unequitably towards each other."

To obliterate all unequitable (or unjust) action of one man towards another, or of one body of men towards another body of men, is therefore the *practical* ultimatum of the science of politics.

Politics, then, professes to develop the *laws* by which human actions ought to be regulated, in so far as men *interfere* with each other.

Human actions may be viewed under various distinct aspects: —

1. In their *physiological* aspect. In this aspect, to kill a man is to inflict such an injury on his bodily frame as causes the cessation of his functions.

2. In their *economical* aspect. In this aspect, to kill a man is to destroy a mechanism which possessed so much *value;* and, consequently, to inflict a greater or less injury to society, according to the value of the person killed. Men *cost* a considerable expense to

On this subject we have some observations to offer hereafter; but if the reader should suppose that a science ought to define its object-noun, he has only to refer to the mathematical sciences, not one of which ever attempts to offer a definition of its noun-substantive major. Were a geometrician to offer the smallest speculation as to what space *is*, he would have departed altogether from the province of geometric *science*. *Spurious* definitions of *value* are occasionally set forth; that is, we are told not what value *is*, but what it *does*, a mode of definition altogether illicit.

rear, and the destruction of the object reared is, or may be, the loss of the cost and profit.

3. In their *political* aspect. In this aspect, to kill a man may be a *crime*, or a *duty*, or *neither*, (an *accident*, for instance.) If by accident, the physiological fact is the same, the economical fact the same, but the *political* fact is essentially different from *intentional* killing.

4. In their *religious* aspect. In this aspect, to kill a man may be either a *sin* or a righteous act; and in this aspect the killing involves all the three previous modes, as intention is taken for granted.

Politics then, in its *position*, is posterior to political economy, and anterior to religion. It *superadds* a new concept to economics, and religion again superadds a new concept to politics. Political economy in no respect can be allowed to discourse of *duty*, nor can politics be allowed to discourse of *sin*. Economy superadds the concept *value* to physiology, and the physiologist has exactly the same case to deny the *value* of the economist that the economist has to deny the *equity* of the politician, or the politician to deny the religious quality of actions posited by the divine. The four regions are perfectly distinct; distinct in their noun-substantive major, distinct in the end of their inquiries, distinct in their method, and distinct in their practical signification and importance, although all meeting in the organized, intellectual, moral, and religious being, MAN.

Into politics, therefore, no action can be allowed to enter which is not at the same time *intentional*, and the action of one man, or one body of men, on another man, or body of men.

The substantives, then, that enter the science of politics, are

Man, *Will*, *Action;*

and the general problem is to discover the laws which should regulate the voluntary actions of men towards each other, and thereby to determine what the order of society in its practical construction and arrangement ought to be. Men *have* social rules of action; and, from the condition of men on the surface of the globe, men *must* have social rules of action, whether those rules are right or wrong. A practical necessity exists for some kind of determination; but it is plain from history, that in many cases the practical rules have been altogether erroneous and criminal. It is therefore necessary to discover what the rules ought to be; for the rules determine the political *condition* of society.

In politics, as in every other science, it is necessary to classify the *forms* of the matter with which we reason; thus geometry classifies the forms of space into lines, angles, and figures.

Actions, then, are classified into *duties* and *crimes.* But as duty and crime are thus viewed *subjectively*, it is necessary to determine the objective characteristics of a duty and a crime, so as to be able to determine the character of the action itself, without inquiring into its motives. The only requisite would then be to ascertain whether it was or was not *intentional*, for this intentionality can never be laid aside.

Again, it is not only necessary to take into consideration man, the *subject*, with whom lies the whole question of human *liberty*, but the earth, the *object*, with which lies the whole question of human *property*.

The same division that enabled us to classify human actions, will enable us to exhibit the aspects in which the *earth* is considered.

1. The earth may be viewed as involved in physical science. In this aspect, it is involved in astronomy, mechanics, chemistry, &c.

2. The earth may be viewed as involved in economical science. In this aspect, it is a *power of production* — a power capable of producing wealth.

3. The earth may be viewed as involved in political science. In this aspect, the power of production has superadded to it the concept, *property*. Economy can no more discourse of *property* than it can discourse of *duty* or *crime*. *Property* is a quality altogether incapable of being apprehended in the object itself by means of sensational observation, exactly as the *criminality* of an action can never be apprehended in the physiological characteristics of an action.

4. The earth may be viewed as involved in religion. "The earth is the Lord's, and the fulness thereof." The difference between the political and the religious mode of viewing the earth as property, is this: In politics, the *power of production* is viewed as property; in religion, the *substance* is viewed as property. Politics in no respect treat of the *substance*, although the feudal system — according to which the king derived his rights from God — assumed the proprietorship of the *substance*, exactly as the correlative system, the *papacy*, claimed for its head the spiritual vicegerency of God, and assumed the power of forgiving sin.

The feudal system has transmitted, on this subject of property, a superstition strictly analogous to that of *slavery*. The slave was an *object*, not an *agent*,—a thing, not a being; he was *property*, and could not possess property. In course of time, however, he passed from the objective and superstitious mode of estimation, and became transformed into a political agent and *power*. The earth has not yet been transformed into *a power;* but the whole analogy of scientific progress would, we think, lead to the belief that it will come, ere long, to be viewed in this light.

It is quite evident that the earth cannot function in political economy until it is transformed into a power of production having *a value*. And, to carry it forward into the science of politics, all that is requisite is to apply the axiom, "an object is the property of its creator;" so that when political economy has determined, by a scientific method which is *not* arbitrary, what value is created and *who* creates this value, politics takes up the question where political economy had left it, and determines, according to a method which is not arbitrary, *to whom the created value should be allocated.*

We have thus the substantives *man*, *will*, *action*, *duty*, *crime*, *property;* but as action of one man upon another necessarily implies an agent and an object, a doer and a sufferer, the *same* action may be regarded in its relation to the agent and in its relation to the object. Thus the action which is called *a crime* in the agent, is called *a wrong* in respect to the person against whom the crime is committed; and again, whatever *duty* lie upon one man, gives birth to a coëxtensive and correlative *right* in all other men. If one man is bound not to murder or to defraud, another man has a coëxtensive and correlative *right* to be unmurdered and undefrauded; and herein lies the whole theory of human *rights*. Thus the terms present themselves in the following manner:—

Agent or Person acting.	*Person acted upon.*
A duty.	A right.
A crime.	A wrong.

Finally, then, the principal substantives of the science of politics are—*man*, *will*, *action*, *duty*, *crime*, *rights*, *wrongs*, and *property*. And *equity* or *justice* is the object-noun of the science *in* which the relations have to be determined.

From the previous considerations it is evident that political science, if it can be exhibited as really and truly a branch of *knowledge*, must assume to determine, not merely the laws that should regulate *an individual*, but any number of individuals associated together. If an action be criminal for an individual, it is no less criminal for ten individuals, or a hundred, or a thousand, or a million. If it be a crime for one man to seize another man and reduce him to slavery, the criminality of the action is in no respect diminished if a whole nation should commit the action with all imaginable formalities. If it be a crime for one man who is more powerful than another to deprive that other of property without his consent, the action is no less criminal if a thousand or a million deprive another thousand or million of their property without their consent. Science can acknowledge none of these arbitrary distinctions. If there be a rule at all, it must be general; and therefore political science must assume to determine the principles upon which political societies ought to be constructed, and also to determine the principles on which human laws ought to be made.

And as there cannot be the slightest doubt that God has made *truth* the fountain of *good*, it may perhaps be fairly expected, that if ever political science is fairly evolved and really reduced to practice, it will confer a greater benefit on mankind, and prevent a greater amount of evil, than all the other sciences.

Political science is peculiarly *man-science;* and though, as yet, the subject is little or no better than a practical superstition, we propose, in the present volume, to exhibit an argument, affording, we think, sufficient ground for believing that it will, at no distant period, be reduced to the same form and ordination as the other sciences.

Of course, any thing like a unity of credence is at present altogether out of the question. Such a unity is neither possible nor desirable. It *could* only be a superstition — that is, a credence without evidence. To produce conviction, therefore, is not so much our hope, as to endeavor to open up the questions that really require solution. And here we must be allowed a remark on the subject of politics, taking the term in its general signification. Perhaps no subject, except religion, absorbs so large a share of the attention of Britain, and perhaps no subject has so small a portion of English literature devoted to its exposition. At the utmost, there are only a very few works which can be called dissertations on the principles of political ethics. This paucity of special works is certainly one of the most curious facts in the history of literature. The word *politics* is in almost every man's mouth; the subject involves interests of the utmost magnitude; questions of politics are continually in debate; the greatest assembly in the kingdom assembles yearly to discuss practical measures, which are necessarily founded on *some* theoretic principles, (right or wrong;) and yet, perhaps, no subject of ordinary interest could be named that has so small a quantity of literature devoted to the exposition of its more general truths.

The current literature of politics is one of the wonders of the world, but the *book* literature is of the scantiest character. Some of it is said to be *antiquated*, (Milton and Locke, for instance — a very great mistake, as we propose to show hereafter,) and some of it never even approaches the main questions. Under these circumstances, therefore, perhaps no apology is requisite for an endeavor to systematize the subject.

The first question in every branch of knowledge is its *method.* So long as the method is in dispute, the whole subject is necessarily involved, not only in obscurity, but in doubt. Without method there can be no standard of appeal, no process of proof, no means of determining otherwise than by opinion, whether a proposition is true or false. But even if opinion *were* the rule, this could not exclude the necessity for theoretic principles. *Whose* opinion is to be taken as the rule? Is it the opinion of the emperor, as in Russia? or the opinion of the free population, as in the United States? or the opinion of the whole male population, as in France? or the opinion of a small portion of the population, as in Britain? Whatever system may be practically adopted, that system necessarily involves a theory; and the question is, "Is there any possibility of discovering or evolving a natural theory which is not arbitrary?" Is there, in the question of man's political relation to man, a truth and a falsity as independent of man's opinion as are the truths of geometry or astronomy? A truth there must be somewhere, and in the present volume we attempt to exhibit the probability of its evolution.

Our argument is based on the theory of progress, or the fact of progress — for it is a fact as well as a theory; and the theory of progress is based on the principle, that there is an order in which man not only *does* evolve the various branches of knowledge, but an order in which man *must necessarily* evolve the various branches of knowledge. And this necessity is based on the principle, that every science when undergoing its process of discovery is *objective*, that is, the object of contemplation; but when discovered and reduced to ordination it becomes *subjective*, that is, a means of operation for the discovery and evolution of the science that lies logically beyond it, and next to it in logical proximity.

If this logical dependance of one science on another could be clearly made out for the whole realm of knowledge, it would give the outline, not only of the classification of the sciences, but of man's intellectual history — of man's intellectual *development* — where the word development means, not the alteration of man's *nature*, but the extension of his knowledge, and the consequent improvement of his mode of action, entailing with it the improvement of his condition.

And if the law of this intellectual development can be made out for the branches of knowledge which have already been reduced to ordination, it may be carried into the future, and the future progress of mankind may be seen to evolve logically out of the past progress.

Let us then consider the aspects in which a science of politics may be viewed.

1. In the probability of its evolution, based on the logical determination of its position in a scheme of classification.

2. In its constituent propositions, and the method it employs for their substantiation.

3. In the history of its doctrine (not the history of its *books*) — in the history of the past reduction of its theoretic principles to *practice*, and in the application of its principles to the present condition of society; thereby attempting to estimate what changes ought to be made, and what, in fact, ought to be the one definite form of political society.

The present volume professes to treat of the first of these divisions.

In attempting to classify the sciences, and to show that they evolve logically out of each other, we do not profess, in the slightest degree, to discourse on the matter of the sciences themselves, further than their primary propositions are concerned; but on their form, their position, their actual development, (as commonly acknowledged,) and on the lesson which, as a whole, they must ultimately teach.

With regard to the classification of the mathematical sciences, we have not the slightest misgivings. We believe that the order in which they are presented will be found correct; and as logic has not usually been considered as the first and simplest of the mathematical sciences, we have said rather more on logic than might otherwise have been necessary.

With regard to the inorganic physical sciences, the mode of classification is by no means so evident. The method according to which they must be classed, *if we knew their characteristics*, is apparent enough; but that difficulties attend the application of the method, so as to locate the various suites of phenomena in an unobjectionable scheme, must certainly be admitted. The difficulties will no doubt be ultimately removed; but they must, in the first place, be removed by the acquiescence of men of science before the mere logician can profess to arrange the materials, and to schematize the branches of knowledge according to their essential characteristics.

Thus it belongs to the physicist to determine whether there is, or is not, a material substance called *light;* but it does not belong to the physicist to determine whether the mechanical phenomena of light are, or are not, to be confounded with its chemical phenomena. Let light be what it may, the mechanical (including the geometric) phenomena of light fall necessarily *before* the chemical phenomena. Again, it belongs to the physicist to determine what *sound* is; but the mechanics of sound (vibration) must be logically separated from the music of sound, (tone, &c.,) inasmuch as the music might be studied without even the knowledge that the sound was accompanied by, or produced by, vibration; and, on the other hand, the vibrations might be observed and measured by a deaf person, who could have no knowledge of tone, and to whom the vibrations would be only *motions*.

Chemistry, again, treats of the *qualitative* characteristics of matter, and it may be viewed in one sense as a science complete in itself. But if such a major *power* could be discovered as would produce the phenomena logically in the observed conditions, then chemistry, from being a science in itself, would become only the *classification* of a science, and the *power*, whatever name it might receive, would assume the precedence, because the qualitative relations would be made to function under the influence of the power.

Every function, of whatever character, or wherever found, we assume to present itself under the form of

An Agent, *An Object*, *A Product;*

and this division belongs, in no respect, to any one particular science, but to all, — that is, it is *a necessary form of thought*, and being so, it belongs to the metaphysician. Now, if a science be viewed as a complete function, it must range all its substantives under one of these heads. Every thing of which science treats must be ranked either as agent, object, or phenomenon; and no science can be considered as completed, even in part, until it has made such a logical ordination as will make the phenomenon to result logically from the operation of the agent on the object. But while a science is undergoing its process of discovery, this logical ordination of its parts is illegitimate, and cannot be made on sufficient grounds; so that the development of the constituent propositions of a science is necessary before its various portions can be classified in such a manner as to satisfy the requirements of the reason.

Under these circumstances, we have given only a general estimate, sufficient to direct the line of argument without trespassing on special departments, or intruding opinions on subjects that lie beyond our province. To construct an argument that should be *in the main* correct, is all we could hope to achieve.

CHAPTER I.

ON THE ELEMENTS OF HUMAN PROGRESSION

SECTION I. — REMARKS ON THE MATTERS INVOLVED IN POLITICAL SCIENCE.

A DISTINCTION must necessarily be drawn between the science of politics itself, and its application to *Man*.

The science is purely abstract and theoretic. It professes only to determine the trueness or falsity of certain propositions which are apprehended by the reason; and the reason may take into consideration this trueness or falsity, without dwelling on the fact that man is a *moral* being, who ought to *act* in accordance with such principles as are legitimately substantiated. In this sense the science of politics is as purely abstract as geometry, which determines the general relations of figures, without in the slightest degree attempting to pronounce whether there are any real material objects to which its truths can be *applied*.

But when we have admitted the fact, that man is a moral being, the theoretic dogma becomes transformed into a practical rule of action, which lays an imperative obligation on man to act in a particular manner, and to refrain from acting in another manner. The theoretic truth determines the relations of moral beings, and consequently determines what ought to be their conditions with regard to each other; the practical rule determines what man may, or may not, do *justly*, and consequently what the political construction of civil society ought to be.

The science of politics then treats of *equity*, and of the relations of men *in* equity. And the general questions which the science has to solve are, —

1. What are those actions which men may do *equitably?*

2. What are those actions which men are by equity *bound* to do?

3. What are those actions which men cannot do *equitably?* that is, what are those actions which, though they may actually be done, are not, and never can be, *equitable?*

Political science, therefore, discourses of human *actions;* and these actions classified with regard to the agent, are divided into *duties*, *crimes*, and negative actions. But when the moral motives of the agent are left out of account, the actions themselves are investigated as to their characteristics, and they may then be treated of in their relation to the two great categories of political science, *liberty* and *property*.

Under the heads of *liberty* and *property* all questions of politics may be discussed, bearing in mind always that political science treats exclusively of the *relations* of men. The questions then assume the form of, —

1. What are the equitable relations of men in the matter of *liberty?*

2. What are the equitable relations of men in the matter of *property?*

Both of these objects, *liberty* and *property*, may be treated of under the head of human action, (the moral laws of property being nothing more than rules which prescribe or prohibit certain *modes of human action*,) but the division conveniently expresses a distinction of the *objects* upon which action may be exercised. Thus, an exposition of the laws of liberty should determine the moral rules that preside over the actions of men in the matter of mutual interference; while an exposition of the laws of property should determine the moral rules that preside over men in their possession of the earth.

But politics, taking into consideration only the relations of *men*, cannot take cognizance of any duty which would still be a duty if only one man were in existence. The duties of religion that relate to the Creator are beyond and above the sphere of politics; and so also are the duties of benevolence, which belong to another category than equity.

It is only as men may act towards each other *equitably or unequitably* that we consider their relations. An act of benevolence is not, strictly speaking, either equitable or unequitable. The recipient has no equitable claim to the bounty; and what the donor gives, he gives not to satisfy the law of equity, but a higher law, which applies to him as an individual, but which it is impossible to apply (by law and force) to a society. The relations of men in society must first be constructed on the principle of equity, and then each individual may exercise his benevolence as occasion may require. Were there no equity, there could be no benevolence, because no man could know what was his *own*, or what he had *a right to give.**

Liberty, like slavery, poverty, depravity, purity, beauty, &c., is one of those concepts that men have idealized, and made into nouns-substantive, for the purpose of using them with greater facility in language. As such, it is incapable of definition, not being composed of any more simple concepts. In this sense it is an *object*, and may be reasoned with like any other noun. But it also signifies *a condition*, namely, the condition in which a man uses his powers without the interference of another man. It differs from *freedom* in the circumstance of amount. Freedom appears to signify the *absolute* condition in which interference by human *will* is altogether removed; in which case there would be a perfect equality of political rights, and the law would recognize no difference whatever between the individuals of whom a state was composed. Liberty, on the contrary, appears capable of indefinite variation, from the smallest amount that the most oppressed slave has, to the utmost and most perfect amount, which then becomes *freedom*.†

For instance, the kings of England *gave* lands (which belonged to the *crown*, that is, to the *nation*) to private individuals. The question then is, Had the incumbent monarch a right to alienate those lands in perpetuity from the nation?

† Such, at all events, would seem to be the sense usually affixed to the two terms. But, in that case, the word *freedom* would ad-

Licentiousness is compatible with liberty, but not with freedom. For instance, a slaveholder has far too much *liberty* — that is, he is at liberty to perform acts of licentiousness; but where there is freedom, there can be no surplus liberty; for the moment the equilibrium of equity is disturbed by the licentious exercise of power, that moment freedom has vanished, and liberty becomes relative. One man then comes to have *too much* liberty, and another man *too little.*

The powers of man involved in the general term liberty, are the powers of feeling, thinking, speaking, writing and publishing, and acting. The sum total of these is implicated in the fact of *life;* so that, if the life be taken away, the whole of the powers are taken away. Politically speaking, therefore, to take away life is to take away the sum total of liberty, and to destroy or obliterate a free agent.

Liberty, in its most extensive signification, involves the whole powers or conditions of men which can be affected by the agency of other men; but liberty has also a more restricted signification, which confines it to liberty of thought, speech, publication, and action. In the former sense, *life* is involved in liberty; in the latter sense, life assumes a separate standing, and becomes a category by itself. And again, the *moral* feelings may be interfered with by slander or defamation; and this gives rise to another category of politics, namely, *reputation.*

vantageously supplant *liberty* in several passages of the New Testament, such as Rom. viii. 21; 2 Cor. iii. 17; Gal. ii. 4; v. 1, 13, &c., where absolute freedom, or *emancipation,* seems to be spoken of.

Life, *liberty*, *property*, and *reputation*, are then viewed as the *possessions* of men; and the laws which should regulate men in their mutual action on each other, with regard to life, liberty, property, and reputation, have to be determined by political *science*.

With regard to *life*, we do not believe that any principle whatever can be found in *natural* knowledge that would justify the taking away of life, save in defence of self or others. For life, therefore, there can only be a negative theory of very limited extent. All that can be said on the subject must necessarily resolve itself into one or two propositions. Laws may take lives, but laws cannot create axioms of the reason; and without these there can be no principle to determine otherwise than superstitiously *when* a life ought to be taken. That the laws by which lives have been taken away have been only formal superstitions, is plainly evident from the changes which the laws have undergone. The laws have no other basis than vague opinion, directed by human passion; and the day appears to be not far distant when capital punishment will be either abolished altogether, or confined to the case of the murderer, if it be determined that Scripture commands or implies the execution of him who has taken away the life of his fellow.

The genuine essence of all liberty is *non-interference*, and to secure universal non-interference is the first and most essential end of all political association.

But interference may be from the government and law, quite as much as from the individual, and interference *by law* is incomparably more prejudicial to a community than any amount of casual interference that would be likely to take place in a civilized country.

SECTION II.—ON THE MODE IN WHICH MEN HAVE MADE LAWS.

LIBERTY presents itself under the form of liberty of *thought*, liberty of *speech*, liberty of *publication*, and liberty of *action;* and political liberty evolves chronologically in the order of thought, speech, publication, and action. To secure this liberty *by law*, and to make it exactly equal for all individuals in the eye of the law, is the great end of political civilization.

Thought is now (in Britain) almost emancipated from state interference, although the time was, and not so very long since, when men attempted to control each other in their thoughts. Religious superstition has ever played the most prominent part in this species of interference, and the priest of by-gone days was the licentious tyrant of the mind, who would have forced uncredited conviction by the fagot and the flame. Not only was freedom of speech controlled, and punished by the rack, the dungeon, and the lingering death of infamy, but the very thoughts were scrutinized; and unless a man *renounced* his creed, he was tortured by the ruthless arm of power, and carried to the stake as the living offering of bigotry to the demon of superstition.

Feeling is not under man's control, and therefore

they have allowed each other to escape from *profession* upon that subject, at the same time taking advantage of the nerves for the infliction of as much pain as man could reasonably devise. What is technically called torture (in the art of inflicting pain) is also abolished, and some obscure principle of retribution is now substituted, which sometimes shuts a man up in a prison, sometimes transports him to the southern hemisphere, sometimes fines him a sum of money, and sometimes allows him to escape altogether, because the legal punishment is felt to be disproportioned to the crime.*

Speech is still, and properly enough, made a matter of superintendence. A man may *injure* another by his speech, and consequently speech does come within the limits of politics. Immense changes, however, have taken place in the laws that relate to the expression of thought, more especially on political subjects. Freedom of speech, and of public speech, and in any number of speakers or auditors, is one of the first essentials of true liberty. Wherever it is not enjoyed, liberty is a shadow and tyranny is a substance. France has yet to learn this essential lesson of liberty,

* "In France, the average values have been from 0·477 to 0·665 for the six years previous to 1831. Thus the chances are only 477 to 1000 that the individual will be condemned when accused of crime against persons; 665 when the crime is one against property. The principal cause of this inequality appears to be, as has been frequently remarked, that we are averse to apply punishment when it has a certain degree of severity, or appears severe in proportion to the crime; this is especially the case with crimes against persons." — QUETELET'S *Treatise on Man*, Book IV. Chap. ii.

and until the French either obtain or take the freedom of speech that they have not now, and never have had, they must be in a state of political subserviency to the executive power, that should make a nation blush with shame, where so many cultivated men have turned their attention to the public affairs of the state. That France should submit to restriction on public discussion, is one of the best evidences that something more than revolution is required to make a people free.

Freedom of discussion is the great turning-point of liberty, the first great field of battle between the nation and the rulers. If the nation gain the day, its progress is onward towards freedom; but if the rulers gain the day, the nation must submit to tyranny, and must groan under the licentious hand of a self-constituted government. So soon as freedom of speech is prevented, no other resource than revolution can possibly remain, and the men who might not speak with tongues must have recourse to weapons of more powerful argument. Where there is freedom of discussion, there is always hope for the nation. The government may enforce its privileges for a time; but so certainly as freedom of discussion is preserved, so certainly must those privileges be curtailed, one after another, and freedom of action must eventually complete the evolution.

Writing and publication are as essential as speech. The censorship is an abomination altogether incompatible with freedom, and every country that tolerates it must lay its account, not for the reformation of reason, but for the revolution of violence — not for change effected by the *intellect* of the country, but for change effected by the explosion of pent-up passions seeking to destroy rather than to reconstruct.

England has almost achieved her emancipation in the matter of thought, speech, and writing; but very considerable changes still remain to be effected before liberty of action can be said to be achieved. There are actions which are naturally *crimes*, and which never can be any thing else than crimes — robbery and murder, for instance. Such actions are criminal anterior to all legislation, and independently of any human enactment whatever. They are unjust from their nature, and we can predicate, *à priori*, that they are unjust, as well as prove, *à posteriori*, by their effects, that they are eminently prejudicial.

Such actions, and such actions *alone*, is the government of a country *competent* to prohibit, and to class as crimes. But let us observe what takes place in actual legislation. No action can be *less* criminal than the purchase of the productions of one country, and the transport of those productions to another country, for the legitimate profit of the trader and the convenience of the inhabitants. The government, however, passes a law that such transport shall not be allowed, and that the man who still persists in it shall be called a criminal, and treated as such. The government thus creates a new *crime*, and establishes an artificial standard of morality, one of the most pernicious things for a community that can possibly exist, as it leads men to conclude that acts are wrong only *because* they are forbidden, and also enlists in favor of the offender those feelings which ought ever to be retained in favor of the law.

The restriction would be a crime if it were only a restriction, and *prevented* the international exchange of produce. But what are its effects? It calls into existence a set of men who devote themselves by profession to infringe the law. The act of transport is perfectly innocent and highly beneficial; but so soon as it is prohibited by law, the man who engages in it is obliged to use the arts of deception and concealment, and from one step of small depravity to another, sinks lower and lower, until he at last employs *violence*, and does not hesitate to *murder*. The *act of transport* in which the smuggler is engaged is one of the most legitimate modes of exercising the human powers. Every kind of advantage attends it. First, it is profitable to the foreign seller. Second, it is profitable to the merchant. Third, it is profitable to the carrier. Fourth, it is profitable to the home consumer; for if the goods were not more highly esteemed by him than the money, he would not purchase them at the price. And fifth, it is injurious to no one. The first three profits are *money* profits; the fourth, the profit of convenience and gratification. But the moral effects are no less beneficial. First, the man who is engaged in lawful trading is well employed, and likely to be a peaceful and good citizen. Second, the fact of purchasing from a foreigner gives the trader an interest in that foreigner, and eminently tends to break down those national antipathies which have descended from the darker ages. The buyer and the seller are a step further from *war* every bargain they conclude in honest dealing; and the iniquitous doctrine, that a "Frenchman is the natural enemy of an Englishman," must every day find its practical refutation in the substantial benefits of trade. First, then, the prohibitory law sacrifices all these benefits, and the law of restriction diminishes them to the full extent of its restriction. But what takes place? The contraband trader is created by the prospect of gain arising from the increase of price. This increase of price, instead of being a benefit to the *legal* trader, is his curse. It is neither more nor less than a premium held out to the smuggler to evade the custom and to *undersell* the legal trader, thereby tending constantly to reduce his profit, as well as to diminish his sale. But this is not all. It is a premium to the reckless to *break the law;* and the man who lives in the habitual breach of the law soon becomes a ruined character and a ruined MAN.

There are, perhaps, few courses of life that end so certainly in ruin as the smuggler's and the poacher's; and yet, barring the *law*, the acts in which they are engaged are perfectly innocent and perfectly legitimate. The man who takes to smuggling or to poaching as the means of gaining his bread, is almost as certainly beyond recovery as the drunkard or the thief. It has been our lot to see some of these characters, and to observe the influence of their pursuits, and we can say no otherwise than that we have been shocked to see men of energy and great natural endowment destroyed by the temptations which the law had so superfluously placed in their way. When once the habit of breaking the law is established, the distinction is overlooked that would not otherwise have been forgotten, namely, that there is a *right* and a *wrong* independently of the law; and the man who commenced by shooting a hare in his cabbage-plot finishes by shooting a keeper, and expiating the offence on the gallows.

We do not mean that a man has a right to shoot every where and any where, but we mean that the act of shooting the game — the *legal* crime — is *not* a crime, and never can be such; and that the consequences are in a great measure the fruits of the *law*, and must be charged against it.*

Let us take another case. The Creator, in his bounty, has distributed rivers over our country; and the rivers of Scotland, at a certain season, teem (or did teem till the sea nets were established) with abundance of food in the shape of salmon, which are thus brought, as it were, to the very door of the inhabitants. The uncultivated moors of the same district abound with wild birds, to an extent perhaps unequalled in the world. It might be supposed reasonable that these gifts of Providence should be of some service to the stated inhabitants who labor; and as corn land is not so plentiful in the north as in the south, Providence appears to have thrown the salmon and the grouse into the scale to furnish the necessary food for man. But what has the law done? To shoot a grouse is not merely a trespass on the occupier of the land, but a *crime*, a criminal act, a thing that must be *punished*, a deed for which the half-starved Highlander

* Since the above was written, some partial changes have been made with regard to hares, preparatory, we hope, to the total abolition of all game laws whatever.

can be hailed to prison, and shut up as an offender against the laws of his country, when that country had reduced him to the verge of starvation. And to spear a salmon, a fish from the sea that no man may ever have seen, and cannot possibly *recognize*, is also attended with pains and penalties for killing the fish that Heaven had sent for food.

Let us consider that Providence has made some animals susceptible of domestication. A man takes the trouble of rearing a lamb or a bullock; and by every principle of equity they are his — at least he has the claim of preference, which no other man has a right to invade. Were any man to take this sheep or ox for his own use, we see at once the impropriety of the action. First, it is an interference with another man without a justifying reason; and second, were such interference allowed generally, the domestication of animals would cease, and food would become so much the less abundant.

In this case, there is a breach of equity involved, and the taking is a crime. But, on the other hand, Providence has made other animals incapable of domestication, and distributed them over the country, apparently for the very purpose of affording *food*, and this in the very districts that are not so highly favored with the cereal productions of the soil. Such, in Scotland, are the salmon and the grouse; and these, at one period, were so abundant as to afford a staple article of food, and even now are sufficiently numerous to feed a large portion of the population from August to December. And what has the law done with regard to these bountiful gifts of Providence? The law has made it a *crime* for the poor man to touch them. The poor man now can never *legally* have either a salmon or a grouse; and in the very parishes where those animals are sufficiently numerous to feed the whole resident pauper population, the poor may take their choice between starvation and expatriation.

Now, in the case of the animals that are not capable of domestication, there is an important distinction to be observed. To shoot one of these animals is not a breach of *equity*—that is, the wild one is no man's *property*, while the domesticated one must practically be regarded as such; and therefore, as the wild animals could not be regarded as *property*—for property must be recognizable—the law has made it a *crime* for the poor man to take them for his use. And the privileged classes, not content with all the land, and nearly all the offices of the state, have usurped the fowls of the air, and the fish of the sea, that never owned a master save the Lord of heaven and earth.

It may be considered that the question is of no great importance; neither perhaps is it, compared with the weightier question of the *land;* but we have taken it as an illustration (the first that happened to occur) of the principle of legislation as regards *action.* As regards action, England is not a free country, and the sooner the nation is convinced of the fact, the better for the community. And by free country, we mean a country in which every man has a legal right to do every thing that is not *naturally* a crime. Where a man can do what is a crime, freedom is no more. But the law may be the criminal as well as the nation; and injustice from the law is quite as unjust, and ten times more detrimental, than injustice from the individual.

With regard to the *crime*, the real *criminality* of the action, measured either by reason or by Scripture, and with regard to the detriment, measured by the consequences, let us ask the following question, and let any man answer it on his conscience: Here are animals provided by nature in abundance — they cannot follow even the laws of *property* established in all analogous cases, inasmuch as they are not recognizable, and cannot be claimed as ever having been in possession. These animals are distributed widely, and spread throughout the country in a manner to afford a convenient supply to the various districts. The fish arrive from the sea in their highest condition, and afford good and wholesome food. The birds are of the poultry kind, distinguished for the quality and quantity of their flesh, and for their powers of reproduction, — characters that have always drawn a line of demarcation between them and the birds of prey, and pointed them out for *food*. These animals are distributed by nature throughout the habitable districts where cultivation must be limited, and where animal food must be required, both from the scarcity of corn and from the nature of the climate. Such, at least, is the judgment of Providence, as manifested in the works of creation, and in the harmony which is every where perceptible between the productions of a region and their suitability to man. These districts (from the monopoly of the land) are now inhabited by a race reduced to the lowest state of poverty, and in many cases to a degradation that would class them with the savages. Let us ask, which is the *crime?* That these people should take the animals which nature has provided, or that the privileged classes of the country should pass a *law* to prevent their touching a single one of them under the pain of fine and imprisonment? And be it remarked, these animals are not *property*, even by the wording of the enactment, which does not punish for interference with property, but for interference with animals, which the privileged classes wish to monopolize for other purposes. Hundreds of tons of fish, and thousands of boxes of birds, are annually taken away *for sale* from these districts, and yet not one of the poor of the *inhabitants* may touch a feather, nor finger a scale, without being guilty of a *crime;* and from one year's end to the other, the mass of the population have not the *legal* right to take one single meal from a bird without danger of imprisonment, nor from a fish without danger of a fine. Is it a crime, or is it not, that the privileged classes should pass such a law? And is it a crime, or is it not, that the nation should allow such laws, and such privileged classes, to continue?*

* "We are inclined to believe that the real value of game in this country is not in general fully understood. It is usually looked upon as kept chiefly for amusement, and its commercial importance is little thought of. Yet its direct value as a marketable commodity is very considerable; and its indirect value, as enhancing landed property, is so great that it is not easy to form an estimate of it. The prices of ordinary game are pretty well known in Scotland. In England they are still higher, and there is always a ready demand. The value of a brace of grouse is, on an average, 6s. in England; pheasants, 6s.; partridges, 3s.; hares, 2s. each; woodcocks from 6s. to 10s. a pair. The average value of a Highland

Again, the manufacturers of certain articles, who are certainly not guilty of crime, or even of the shadow of offence, are not allowed to carry on the necessary operations except under the lock and key of the state officials; and the regulations are of so stringent a character, that if they were not partially relaxed by the exciseman, the business could scarcely be carried on without incurring penalties from *the law.*

The soap manufacturer is certainly engaged in the

red deer is not less than £5. So much for the direct value of game; and when we consider its importance indirectly, we are first led to think of the Highland moors which it has rendered so profitable. For the following facts on this portion of the subject, we are indebted to an able letter on the Game Laws by Lord Malmesbury. A vast number of moors are now let for £400 or £500 a year, which formerly brought nothing to the proprietor, as they are unfit even for sheep. Large tracts, which formerly let as sheep farms, are now converted into deer forests, and pay at least one third, and even one half, more than they did formerly. Five hundred deer may be kept on a space of ground that will feed twelve hundred sheep. Taking the sheep at the average price of 18s. each, these would be worth £1080; but the deer would realize nearly double that sum — namely, £2000; for the average price of stags in summer, and hinds in winter, is fully £4. From a long standing knowledge of the Highland moors, Lord Malmesbury is of opinion that they are yearly advancing in price, and becoming a more important kind of property. He saw a list last year of one hundred and six moors let for shootings, the rent of which could not be averaged at less than £300, which makes a total of £31,800. There were twice as many more let at an average of £100, and a third portion unlet, whose value may be fairly stated at £17,000; the whole making together a rental of £70,000 on the Highland shootings. He adds, that this may be looked upon as a clear gain as far as respects the grouse moors, and an increase of two fifths on deer ground called "forest." — *Journal of Agriculture.*

production of an article that benefits the community; and even the distiller (for whom as much cannot be said) is entitled to carry on his business on the same footing as every other man. The legislators make a pretext of revenue; and revenue of course is necessary, although not to the extent to which revenue is raised in Britain. But when the necessity of revenue is granted, is it at all necessary that the man who is engaged in the lawful manufacture of an article required by the community, should be obliged to give notice to a state official that he is about to perform this, that, and the other process of his manufacture, and be esteemed a criminal worthy of punishment if that notice is forgotten or neglected? *

All these restrictions are the remnants of the more exclusive privileges claimed and enforced by the privileged classes of other times, and the remnants of that political superstition which, next to religious superstition, every man ought to lend his aid to destroy.

The pretext that revenue is necessary, is one that would scarcely be entitled to attention, were it not accompanied by the injustice and detriment that follow in its train. Revenue, so far as necessary for the ac-

* "The duty on paper is levied with a multiplicity of detail known only in the department of the excise. The duty is taken upon every single ream; and every single ream has to be weighed, and stamped, and cut, and made up, and labelled, and endorsed, and certified, and entered in a particular and special manner; and if there is the slightest infraction of the excise regulations, the board is immediately down upon the manufacturer for a penalty."

Tax on soap, 1848, - - - - - - £795,981

Tax on paper, - - - - - - - 578,704

tual requirements of a state, need form a very trifling portion of a nation's expenditure. The whole cost of the administration of justice, and of every other valuable service that the state really requires, is a mere trifle in comparison to the actual revenue, and *to the still greater cost occasioned by the enactments of the legislature.* But as revenue may be derived from two sources, the privileged classes have taken care that it shall be derived from that source in which they are not so immediately interested.

We have spoken of the liberty of human *action;* and one of the forms of that action is *labor.* The material objects of the creation possess a *value of exchange;* that is, people are willing to pay for them. But labor also possesses a value of exchange, and people are willing to pay for *it* as well as for the material objects that constitute the globe and its inhabitants. Let it be observed that labor is essentially private property. It has a value, and the land has no more than a value.

Let it also be observed that the land is *not* essentially private property, and that naturally one man has as much right to the land as another.

Labor on the one hand, and land on the other, are susceptible of taxation.

The privileged classes, in the earlier stages of society, had all the land and all the labor. The lord was the lord not only of the land, but of the labor of those who were engaged in the useful arts of industry. In the course of time the serfs obtained a small portion of their rights, and towns were formed where the citizens could carry on their labor with a certain degree of advantage to themselves, and with a certain degree of emancipation from the licentious will of the lord. Taxation could consequently be on the land of the lord, or on the labor of the townsman, for all the townsman's *capital* was originally the produce of his labor.*

If we consider the various states of Europe, from Russia to England, we shall find the lord and the laborer to occupy various stages of the political scale of evolution, by which the laborer at last succeeds in withdrawing his industry from the interference of the lord, and from the taxation of the state.

Let it be observed, that when the *land* is taxed, no *man* is taxed; for the land produces, according to the law of the Creator, *more* than the value of the labor expended on it, and on this account men are willing to pay a *rent* for land. But when the privileged classes had monopolized the land, they called it *theirs* in the same sense in which labor is supposed to belong to the laborer; and, although the absurdity of the proposition is sufficiently apparent, the laborer was glad enough to escape with even a small portion of his liberty, and to rejoice that he could call his life and his family his own.

But then the lords of the land were the rulers and the makers of the laws, and the imposers of taxation, and it was not *reasonable* to suppose that they should tax the land. The king required money, and various persons about kings in all ages require money, and of

* Probate and legacy duties, 1843: —

Legacies, - - - - - -	£1,223,342
Probates and administrations, -	922,839
Taxes on the inheritance of *land*, -	0

course the only choice in the matter of taxation is between *labor* and the *land*.

To tax labor, then, becomes a matter of the most palpable necessity, and those who have been divested of almost every single particle of earth or sea that could be of any benefit to them, must also be made to bear the burdens of the state, and to pay for the support of a government that was of little use to the community, and that only existed by the right of the strongest, or the consent of superstition.*

The principle of taxing labor is only a remnant of the serfdom of the darker ages, and it has been continued in this country by the ingenious device of what are termed *indirect taxes*, by which labor is taxed, although the laborer is only made acquainted with the fact by the distress that periodically oppresses him.

* *Immediately* a bad government is of no use to the community, but *mediately and prospectively* the most stringent despotism in the world is of the highest importance and of the greatest value. Man must apparently progress through *centralization;* and a bad government, provided it centralizes, is the foundation of after changes most beneficial to mankind. The good part of the Russian government is its centralization; and, notwithstanding the antipathy manifested against that government, we have little hesitation in maintaining, that on the whole it is doing good to the population under its rule. It is gradually subjecting savage tribes to the ordinary course of homogeneous law; and, though the laws are bad, and the administration worse, the *phase* is one which the nomadic tribes and the semi-barbarous population must pass through before they arrive at political freedom. In the general history of man it seems requisite that central monarchy should destroy the privileges of multiple aristocracy; and Russia is gradually effecting this great change. The sympathy manifested towards the Poles is questionable, inasmuch as the great majority of Poles were ruled by individual aristocrats instead of by *laws*.

The man who is poisoned without his knowledge does not die the less certainly for his ignorance, and the people who are taxed do not suffer the *less* because the taxes happen to be imposed in such a manner that the unthinking and the ignorant do not perceive those taxes in the price they pay for almost every article of consumption. All the *real* harm is done to a country as effectually by indirect taxation, as if every penny were paid out of the day's wages to the tax-gatherer of the state. But the rulers know full well that if the tax-gatherer were to present himself at the pay-table of the laborer, at the counter of the shopman, at the office of the merchant, and at the ship of the seafaring carrier, the doom of labor taxation would be sealed, and the country would not tolerate so glaring an injustice. And the indirect system of taxation is employed, not that it prevents the community from suffering, but that it prevents the community from dwelling on the *cause* of their suffering, and thereby retards a revolution against the privileged classes.

Such are the circumstances that led to the establishment of customs and excise; and the total and complete abolition of those two branches of interference is one of the necessary changes that must take place before this country can be free, and before this country can enjoy that commercial liberty, without which a periodical crisis must necessarily be the lot of the laborer, the merchant, and the manufacturer.* It is

* "Simultaneously with the relaxation of the restrictive policy of the United States, Great Britain, from whose example we derive the system, has relaxed hers. She has modified her corn laws, and reduced many other duties to moderate revenue rates. After ages

true that the total abolition of the customs appears chimerical at present; yet, if we consider the history of the changes that have already taken place, and seize their abstract form, (the only form that contains real instruction,) we have sufficient ground to hope, not only for the abolition of every species of tax upon labor, but for the recovery of each man's natural *property.* So certainly as this country continues to progress, so certainly must every restraint be removed from every action that is not a crime; and the customs' laws can no more be perpetuated, if the present liberty of discussion continues, than restraints upon discussion could be perpetuated after men had learnt to think for themselves, and to form their convictions according to the evidence before them.

of experience, the statesmen of that country have been constrained by stern necessity, and by a public opinion having its deep foundation in the sufferings and wants of impoverished millions, to abandon a system, the effect of which was to build up immense fortunes in the hands of the few, and to reduce the laboring millions to pauperism and misery. Nearly in the same ratio that labor was depressed, capital was increased and concentrated by the British protection policy.

"The evils of the system in Great Britain were at length rendered intolerable, and it has been abandoned, but not without a severe struggle on the part of the protected and favored classes to retain the unjust advantages which they have so long enjoyed. It was by the same classes in the United States, whenever an attempt was made to modify or abolish the same unjust system here. The protective policy had been in operation in the United States for a much shorter period, and its pernicious effects were therefore not so clearly perceived and felt. Enough, however, was known of these effects to induce its repeal."—*President's Message*, 1846, (*United States.*)

The great source of the evil that weighs so heavily on the unprivileged classes of society is to be found in the doctrine, "*that rulers are competent to legislate for every thing and for any thing.*"

This doctrine appears to be universally adopted in states that are just beginning to emerge from a condition of barbarism. Thoughts, words, and actions are all legislated for, without even an inquiry into the right of the ruler to promulgate a law upon the subject of his enactment. The right is *assumed*, and the ruler has the *power* to enforce the law. The multitude, who are obliged to devote their attention to the means of their livelihood, offer a passive acquiescence, and endeavor to carry on as well as they can, until they find the operation of the law so prejudicial that they can bear it no longer, and then a struggle ensues, by which liberty is advanced a step; and the multitude return to their toils. In course of time, however, it is found that the remaining laws are as prejudicial to the advanced stage of society as those which were abolished were prejudicial to its earlier stage. A new struggle ensues, and liberty is advanced another step. Knowledge increases, and trade increases, and still it is found that the laws are so prejudicial that they must be abolished. This process goes on for centuries; and law after law is repealed, because the actual conditions of the people can permit their existence no longer. In this process of evolution, we perceive laws going one after the other, in proportion as knowledge increases; but it is quite evident that such process cannot continue indefinitely; and it becomes an interesting question to inquire, how it happens that such a process should be necessary, and what is its natural termination.

The process is necessary, because legislators had overstepped the boundaries of legislation, and interfered with matters beyond their province. Instead of confining themselves to the prohibition (or rather to the *proclamation* of the prohibition) of every action by which one man *injured another man*, they legislated for men's thoughts, and enacted laws about religion, and persecuted by law those who differed from the sect that happened to be in power.

This persecution, a few centuries since in England, and not a century since in Spain, was at its *utmost possible extreme;* that is, men inflicted all the *possible* pain that they could on their fellow-creatures of a different creed, and finished by committing them to the flames.

In course of time, however, knowledge increased, and men thought it scarcely right to proceed to the utmost *possible* extreme; and a modification of the *auto da fé* was introduced in the shape of imprisonment, fine, banishment, &c., &c.

The Protestant creed introduced a very important change in the credence of the country in this matter of religion.

The Romanists always professed to slaughter men to the glory of God; and so long as the *theological* propriety of immolation was current in the minds of men, there was little chance of their seeing the character of their actions. The Protestants, on the contrary, abandoned the high ground of sacrifice to the *Deity*, and substituted the more rational idea of sacrifice to the *king*. The unfortunate Covenanter, who was shot or decapitated, was not an offering to the Deity, but an offering to the king; and the difference was of immense importance to the country, although of no particular consequence to the Covenanter. So soon as persecution (legislation for men's *thoughts*) was conceived to be for *man*, and not for God, men began to inquire whether, after all, the king had really the right to legislate to such an extent. And as knowledge increased, they began to relax their principles a little, and to think that the deprivation of civil privileges would be punishment sufficient for the offence of thinking differently from the sect in power.

The modification still goes on, and measure after measure is abolished, until at last the professors of different creeds almost begin to think that they can inhabit the same country without persecuting each other on account of their religion.

Catholic emancipation was one of the insignificant measures that concluded the evolution with regard to that sect. The repeal of the Test and Corporation Act was another insignificant measure that brought up the rear of a system of persecution that had been waxing weaker and weaker for a century or two.

Both of these measures were hailed as the glorious evidences of Britain's impartiality, and certainly the measures were necessary, (if freedom be necessary;) but, after all, they were no more in comparison to the measures that had preceded them, than the nursery tales and the popular superstitions are to the gorgeous pagan credences from which they had their birth.

The last remnant of this religious superstition that

once played so prominent a part in Britain, is now to be found in the taxation of nonconformists; and the church-rates, and the official distinction between the various sects, are the last representatives of that system of legislation that lit the fires of Smithfield, and sent Claverhouse and his dragoons to murder the hill-side peasant, and to torture the differently thinking Presbyterian.

But what, after all, is the principle that has so modified the laws of Britain? Whence comes it that men should have so singularly changed their opinions in the course of a century or two?

It is perfectly evident that justice does not vary from age to age. Justice is the same from the beginning of the world to the time that man shall change his constitution. An act of justice can no more alter its character (without a revelation) than the diameter of the circle can alter its relation to the circumference. What was just yesterday is just to-day, was just a thousand years ago, and will be just a thousand years to come.

How then does it happen that so strange a modification should have come over the credence of our race, and how does it happen that men should legislate so differently?

The credence has changed with the acquisition of knowledge, and the legislation has changed with the credence.

Men have discovered that legislators have no right to legislate for credences, and thus the last remnants of such legislation are obliged to appear under another name, and to assume a false guise, that they may be allowed to continue a few years longer.

Legislation, with regard to thought, never was just, and never can be just; and the abstract form of the change is nothing more than that the legislators have so far been driven off a ground that they never had a right to occupy.

For the man animal, *food* is the first necessity; but for the man mental, credence according to evidence is the first correct law of his intellectual nature. Food is one of the conditions of *existence;* and, until it can be procured in tolerable quantity, and with some degree of certainty, a community cares little about the mind, and allows the question of free thought to remain in abeyance.

When a community begins to emerge from barbarism, and legislation assumes a definite form, *every thing* is legislated for. Food, thought, speech, action, property, and in all their various forms, are all made subjects of enactment; and men thus endeavor to improve the world that God made, by passing laws to amend the order of nature. The first necessity for the community is to have some small opportunity of procuring food, and when the necessary conditions are obtained, (which involve some degree of liberty,) men turn their attention to other subjects, according to the character of their theological belief. The religious impulses of our nature require satisfaction, perhaps, before any other portion of the mental constitution; and as men must have some kind of theological credence, right or wrong, they believe any thing rather than remain in doubt. And as, where there is no evidence, there can be no truth and no error, but mere arbitrary superstition, the state has generally established some form of credence by law, and committed the care of the supersitition to the priest. But there does happen to be a true religion as well as an indefinite number of superstitions; and, after the revival of learning, when the truth began to break on men's minds, that religion was not a matter of mere arbitrary church authority, but a real matter of truth and falsehood, in which life and death were involved, the Christianity of the Bible came into collision with the established superstitions of the papal priesthood, and a struggle was commenced, which began by the maximum of persecution, and ended, in this country at least in the maximum of liberty of thought.*

* "But we shall next consider the state of religion in England. From the days of Wickliffe there were many that differed from the doctrines commonly received. He wrote many books that gave great offence to the clergy, yet being powerfully supported by the duke of Lancaster, they could not have their revenge during his life; but he was, after his death, condemned, and his body was raised and burnt. The Bible, which he translated into English, with the preface which he set before it, produced the greatest effects. In it he reflected on the lives of the clergy, and condemned the worship of saints and images, and the corporeal presence of Christ in the sacraments; but the most criminal part was the exhorting all people to read the Scriptures; when the testimonies against those corruptions were such, that there was no way to deal with them but to silence them. His followers were not men of letters, but being wrought on by the easy conviction of plain sense, were by them determined in their persuasions. They did not form themselves into a body, but were contented to hold their opinions secretly, and did not spread them but to their particular confidents. The clergy sought them out every where, and did deliver them, after conviction, to the secular arm, that is, to the fire."—BURNET'S *History of the Reformation*, abridged, p. 14.

But it is not one single shade more *right* now than it was two or five hundred years since, that men should think and believe for themselves *without the interference of the legislator.* The legislator never had a particle of right to interfere in matters of faith, which right he does not possess to the full extent in the present day. And the real essence of the change is to be found, not in the alteration or improvement of the laws, but in the *total exclusion* of legislation from the province of *thought.* The legislator was altogether out of his sphere; and *every law* was necessarily unjust, whether mild, moderate, or severe. No matter what the character of the enactment happened to be, it was an injustice and a licentious invasion of the natural rights of man; and as such, the only question that could legitimately be taken into consideration respecting it was its *abolition.*

It must not be supposed, however, that a country is in the same circumstances before a law has been called into existence, and after its abolition. Before the law is enacted men are *naturally* free, but when the law has been abolished, men are *legally* free. A country, arrived at complete freedom after the various transformations of superstition and injustice, is a very different thing from a country where legislation has only commenced. The actual laws that exist in both cases might perhaps be the same; but in the one case they are the stepping stones to an indefinite series of legislative acts, and in the other case they are the permanent records of a nation's final judgment. England, *before* men legislated for thoughts, and England *after* men have legislated for thoughts, and *abolished* such legislation, is in very different circumstances; inasmuch as it may now be reckoned a matter of *ascertained truth*, that legislation for matters of belief is preëminently *prejudicial*, as well as unjust. And the probability of new legislation on the subject can scarcely be contemplated, unless some very unexpected change take place, altogether out of the order of the scheme of progress that may naturally be anticipated.

But if legislation can be out of its sphere in the matter of thought, it can also be out of its sphere in the matters of speech, action, and property.

Next to liberty of thought comes liberty of speech, writing, and publication.

Speech and publication are very extensively legislated for, and the countries of continental Europe appear all, or nearly all, to admit the unlimited right of the legislator to interfere as much as he pleases with the natural rights of the community in the sphere of *the expression of thought.*

Where rulers govern by power, and not by the *enlightened* choice of the nation, they are a party *opposed* to the nation. On the one hand is the nation and the national interest; and on the other hand is the government and the interest of the individuals connected with it. The more power the rulers have, the less liberty the people have; and the more land and privilege the rulers have, the less wealth have the population. Now wealth and power are exactly what men are desirous of possessing; and as rulers are men, it is not to be wondered at that they dip their fingers into every man's dish, equitably or unequitably, and monopolize the best things that happen to be going. The land, of course, either in kind or in some other form, falls to the lot of the rulers and their coadjutors — the nobles and the priests. The cultivation of the land, (the labor,) instead of also falling to the lot of the privileged classes, becomes the portion of the people.

But excessive privileges are much easier maintained against a weak people than against a strong one; and as the people can only be strong by knowledge, virtue, and combination — knowledge, virtue, and combination are in little favor with despotic governments. Political knowledge (that is, the knowledge of their rights and interests) is carefully excluded from the mass of the population; and as political knowledge grows out of discussion about social welfare, as well as out of the thoughtful toil of the author, both discussion and authorship are subjected to partial or total prohibition. The most frantic blasphemies will find a readier license for publication than a sober treatise on the public welfare; and a philosophical denial of all right and wrong whatever will be more tolerable than an inquiry into the foundations of the rulers' *privileges.* The most infamously immoral production is less likely to be scrutinized than a dissertation on political economy; and an association for murdering, torturing, and expatriating the population,* would be more readily authorized than an association for forwarding the rights of the people.

Any thing in the shape of superstition (that is, *uninquiring* credence) is esteemed proper enough; but the moment men begin to inquire and to seek for

* An inquisition, for instance.

reasons, that moment is the government alarmed, and that moment must means be put in operation to stop the course of knowledge.* Governments, like those of Russia, Austria, and Italy, *can* only exist by means of superstition; and the question with them is, not as to the propriety of allowing men to obtain knowledge and to express their thoughts, but as to the propriety of *the existence of the government;* and every restrictive measure that affects the free expression of opinion, is only an act of self-defence against the nation. The government must either give up its privileges, or keep the people in slavery with regard to expression of opinion; and the stringent laws of the continental powers, relative to every kind of political meeting, are no more than measures of precaution, analogous to those practised by the pirate who scuttles his prize (with its crew) as a measure conducing to his *safety.*†

* "Thus the universities governed by ecclesiastics persuaded the poor bigot Philip III. to pass a law prohibiting the study of any new system of medicine, and *requiring* Galen, Hippocrates, and Avicenna; they scouted the exact sciences and experimental philosophy, which said they made every medical man a Tiberius; and so they scared the timid Ferdinand VII. in 1830, by telling him that the schools of medicine created materialists, heretics, and revolutionists; thereupon the beloved monarch shut up the lecture rooms forthwith." — FORD's *Spain.*

† The pirate is *rationally correct;* that is, his act *does* conduce to his immediate safety, for dead men tell no tales, and sunk ships cannot appear in evidence. And despotic governors are also *rationally correct;* that is, an ignorant and superstitious population has less power and less desire for liberty than a population that thinks for itself, and has free opportunity of expression. The remote consequences, however, are sometimes overlooked. When the truth is discovered, the pirate is hanged, and the ruler guillotined.

The *objects* of a despotic government must necessarily be distinguished from its *means*. The objects are WEALTH AND POWER; the means, TYRANNY AND SUPERSTITION. Tyranny is power without right, and superstition is credence without evidence. The means of a despotic government, therefore, are power without right, and credence without evidence. The governor of a country, in the earlier stage of legislation, is the strongest man in the country; and, by conversion, the strongest man in the country is the governor. Now, one strongest man, who has the opportunity of taking a thousand weaker men in detail, is stronger than the whole thousand *if he can prevent them from combining*. This is the concise explanation of the theory of a despotic government. A noble, a chief, even a bishop, may become a sovereign, and remain so as long as he has power or dexterity to prevent the people from combining. As soon as they combine, he is no longer the strongest, and his wealth as well as his power is in a fair way to depart. It therefore becomes a matter of serious consideration for him to discover and put in practice those means that tend to secure his power, and prevent his enemies (his subjects) from combining.

In the first place, he must have more wealth; and, as he cannot have it by his own honest industry, he must have it by the industry of others, or by the monopoly of those natural objects which other men must possess as the conditions of their existence.

Land is the great source of wealth; forests and fisheries are also tolerable; mines and minerals are capable of yielding a revenue; and, in addition to these, comes the taxation of labor.

These sources of wealth, therefore, must be turned to account, and the governor, of course, does not neglect them. Wealth is power for the ruler, as knowledge is power for the people; and the more wealth the ruler has, the more power has he for taking advantage of his subjects. Wealth, therefore, is both a means and an end — a means of getting more wealth and of getting more power. Wealth gives birth to a standing army, and a standing army gives birth to more power, as it enables the ruler to apply his principles more extensively and with greater security.

But if a people were to combine against any standing army that is likely to exist, the ruler would no longer be a ruler, and the army would no longer be an army. It therefore becomes a matter of serious thought for the ruler to obviate the tendencies towards combination.

There are two or three kinds of combination.

1st. The combination of national antipathy. This combination may exist where there is abundance of ignorance. The Indians might combine against the whites on the continent of America, and, though the combinations were partial, they did a great deal of mischief in by-gone times. The Tyrolese might combine on the same principle, and so might the Poles, the Swiss, the Greeks, &c. It must not be supposed that these are contests for *freedom*. On the contrary, they are contests against a foreign tyranny in favor of a domestic one. Such combinations are interesting as matters of history, but of very little importance to the progress of real freedom.

2d. Religious combination. This also is a matter

of *sentiment*, and by no means advances freedom as a matter of necessity. The crusades were singular exhibitions of this kind of combination carried out on a large scale. The wars of the *Ligue* also exhibit a double combination of ruffians on both sides, who perpetrated astonishing crimes for the advancement of their religious party.*

The Presbyterians of Scotland, and the Puritans of England, HAD HOLD OF THE TRUTH; and, though they had scarcely yet learnt to view it in its true light, they progressed immensely towards freedom. They did confound civil and religious liberty; but notwithstanding, it is to them, under God, that we owe the preservation of the cause of liberty in this country, when the continent, and especially France, either extinguished the little liberty that had begun to illuminate the people, or so impeded its progress that they have still their convulsions before them. The extinction of Protestantism in France rendered a physical force convulsion necessary before the obstacles to the prog-

* Absurd as the crusades were in themselves, they were of the highest value to Europe; in fact, it seems that whatever the temporary evils attendant on any one part of human condition, or of human manifestation, that condition was a phase of progress, calculated to leave society in a better state than it found it. This principle is applicable also to the first French revolution. It was a fearful scene when viewed individually. But if we look to the condition of France before the revolution, and again after the revolution, we cannot deny that its effects were of the greatest value to the country. Those who attend merely to the revolution and its horrors, are like those who go to see a criminal executed without asking the reason of his execution, or inquiring into the reasonableness of the laws which demand his execution. The French revolution was produced *by the laws of nature*. Who made those laws?

ress of society could be removed; and if full liberty of thought had been accorded, instead of the revocation of the edict of Nantes, in all probability the progression of society would have taken place by the gradual removal of abuses, instead of being arrested until the bulwarks of despotism were no longer strong enough to retain the expansive energies of the population. To suppose that the French revolution could have been prevented by any of the individuals who happened to figure in it, is to suppose that causes are no causes, and effects no effects. But France has still her work to do; and, although none of the past frenzy can be again anticipated, as the causes do not exist to produce it,* France has yet to shake off despotism,

* The atrocities of the first French revolution were *French;* the atrocities of the last were *Parisian.* In the former case there was not only insurrection in the towns, but there was the most fearful of all convulsions — a rural insurrection. The atrocities of the last revolution, &c., were very partial. They were confined to a few of the lowest population in Paris; and, no doubt, there are in Paris, at the bottom of society, persons who would do any thing. There is no possibility, however, of instituting a comparison between the frenzy of the late revolution and that of the former. It is perfectly absurd, and only shows how panic and party feeling will blind the judgment and make the tongue rave nonsense.

To those who speak so loudly and so long of the horrors of insurrection, we propound a question: "Which is the worst, the most atrocious, the most base, and the greatest reproach to a nation,

"1st. The atrocities that accompany a political insurrection? or,

"2d. Women poisoning people by scores for the sake of obtaining burial fees?" In the paper, yesterday, we read an account of a woman thus disposing of eight of her offspring.

The first is *French.*

The latter is *English.*

The demoralization going on in Britain is such, that if ever there

and to form a government that shall rule otherwise than by a standing army and a system of officials.

In the convulsions of France we have a third kind of combination; namely, combination to overthrow an evil that presses on the feelings, thoughts, and interests of men. The population suffered from a common evil; and when that evil was *exposed*, they combined to overthrow it. The combination, however, was not of a *high* character. It was a mere reaction under *pressure*. To get rid of the pressure was nearly the sum and substance of the combination; and disunion and licentiousness followed when the pressure was removed.

But there is another kind of combination, and a far more important one for the welfare of the world — the combination of knowledge and reason. Knowledge is credence based on sufficient evidence; and reason is the power of perceiving consequences, and of inferring antecedents. Without reason man would only be a higher kind of ape; as it is, he is a spirit and an immortal.

Man has an intellect, as well as a bodily frame, and this intellect has its laws and its requirements. Observation is its food, reason is its process of digestion, and truth is its circulating fluid, without which it degenerates and dies. Truth makes the mind strong, ignorance makes it weak, and error infects it with

were any thing like an insurrection, it is impossible to predict the extent to which frenzy might be carried. The demoralization of the population is England's greatest danger; and, if not met in time by means of moral and intellectual training, it may produce the direst evils, and make England a manufacturing hell.

disease. Knowledge is not only power — it is *strength* — strength of the mind, health, and life, and strength. To obliterate this strength, therefore, is the object of the despotic ruler. If the people are strong, the despot must be weak; but the legitimate ruler is so much the stronger as the people are stronger. When the rulers and the nation are in opposite scales, the less weight the people have, the more easily are they outweighed; but when both are in the same scales, the heavier they both are the better for both, and the worse for those who are opposed to them. In a free country, where law was absolutely supreme and really equitable, every man would feel the ruler to be a portion of himself, and would lend his arm or his aid to further the ends of justice. The ruler of a free country should be the pure administrator of the law — the first magistrate of *equity*, to whom every man was bound by the righteous bonds of justice, and by the sentiments of reverence implanted in our nature to elevate our race above the creatures that surround us.

In a despotism, superstition takes the place of knowledge, and the fear of suffering helps to procure an unwilling obedience.

The ruler is the wolf, the people are the flock, and the lawyers * and priests † are the foxes who prepare the flock for slaughter.

* England, happy in the integrity and mildness of her judges in the 18th century, and in our own times — during the Stuart reigns, was cursed by a succession of ruffians in ermine, who, for the sake of court favor, violated the principles of law, the precepts of religion, and the dictates of humanity." — CAMPBELL'S *Lives of the Chancellors.*

† In speaking lightly of the priests, we do not speak lightly of

When the priesthood lose their influence, an army must be resorted to, and physical tyranny and centralization must do the work of superstition. At all hazards, the people must be kept *down*, or the game of despotism is lost.

The simplest plan of a despotism is to make the people believe that the ruler is a distant relation to some of the deities of the country. A greater or less degree of this method appears to be common in infant stages of society, but a small advance of knowledge suffices to disturb so convenient a doctrine; and this is partly the reason why so dire an antipathy should be manifested by the rulers of various countries to the introduction of the gospel as contained *in revelation*. Russia, Austria, and Italy are little better than pagan countries, and the rulers are partially or altogether believed to have some special connection with the object of worship, and to rule by right divine.* The

men holding a sacred office. The priest — that is, the sacrificer and the mediator — does *not* hold a sacred office. Every human priest is an antichrist. In the Christian religion there is but one Priest, and his sacrifice is offered, so that there remains no more offering for sin. "It is finished!"

The *only* real Priest has ascended into heaven, and to those who wait for him he will come a second time unto salvation. *All* other priests are antichrists.

The present priests, including the Roman sacrificers and mediators, must be classed with alchemists, astrologers, and necromancers, partly deceived, and partly deceivers. Next to that of becoming the object of worship, (like the Grand Llama,) the *office* of priest is the most wicked that it is *possible* for man to fill.

* "Emperors, kings, and other superiors have their power from God, because they are the substitutes of God on earth."

pope, of course, is a kind of partial divinity, from being the high priest of the Roman superstitions; and, in Russia, "God and the emperor" are much on the same footing as God and the pope. Both the pope and the emperor are blasphemously associated with the divine Majesty, and the authority of Heaven is supposed in some obscure way or other to attach to the persons of those worthies. France has passed the theological view of government, and the priest is no longer a jackall to the king. Superstition has lost its hold; and though the women must still have some kind of religion, the men have got beyond the point of believing merely on authority; and as, unfortunately, they have been denied the truth, they have sunk into passive infidelity. Superstition and the ruler are no longer allied in their thoughts, and an innumerable multitude of officials must be called into existence to keep them from indulging in political disturbances.

Mere superstition, however, is insufficient to enslave a people that has commercial intercourse with other

Ques. — "How must subjects behave towards their sovereign?

Ans. — "Subjects must behave towards their sovereign like faithful slaves towards their master.

Ques. — "Why must subjects behave like slaves?

Ans. — "Because their sovereign is their master, and has power over their property as well as over their life.

Ques. — "Are subjects bound to obey also bad sovereigns?

Ans. — "Yes, subjects are bound to obey not only good, but also bad sovereigns." — *The Duty of Subjects towards their Sovereign, for Instruction in Reading, in the Second Class of Elementary Schools.* Milan: 1824.

Such are the deliberate blasphemies inculcated by order of the Austrian government.

nations. So long as the country can be surrounded with a barrier, and free communication prevented, superstition may do its work tolerably well, and a nation may remain in much the same state for an indefinite period.* When, for a thousand years, the sun

* We have only to look at Spain to see how effectually superstition eradicates even an aspiration after freedom. Let it be remembered that, a few centuries since, Spain was second to no country in Europe in the extent of her political power. What is she now, and what has superstition made her? "The masses care no more for a *constitution* than the Berber or Oriental; with them this thing of parchment is no reality, but a mere abstraction, which they neither understand nor estimate. The people do not want their laws to be changed, but to have them fairly administered; the laws are good in theory, but worm-eaten in *practice*, by bribery and corruption. Confer a spick-and-span patent Benthamite *constitution* on Spaniards, and they will take it without thanks; annul it, and they will respond by a patient shrug. Their only idea of government is *despotism*." — Ford's *Spain*, p. 862.

Mr. Ford adds, that though despotism may be odious in *theory*, it never pressed harshly on the nation in *practice*. This is rather a singular way of reading Spanish history; and we would ask, if despotism have not pressed hard, what is it that has pressed so hard? If despotism has not pressed hard on Spain, what was it that burnt 30,000 of her inhabitants, and imprisoned and expatriated an immense multitude of her industrious population? Of course the Roman superstitions were at the bottom of the persecutions, but the despotism was the efficient agent in carrying out the diabolical instigations of the monks and priests. Where there is not a despotism, the power of the priest is annulled. He can no longer procure the death or the exile of those who differ in belief. And wherever the priest is found, there will be found an ally and a supporter of despotic power. Superstition ruined the credence of Spain, and despotism ruined the country. The two walk hand in hand, like the invisible pestilence and the loathsome disease that shows that pestilence to the world.

rises every day upon *similar conditions*, it is by no means wonderful that change should not take place. In the political, as well as the physical world, the *conditions* must be changed before we can look for a change in the phenomena. Change the conditions, and some change or other will be exhibited in the consequent results. For those who have the land and the privilege, *every* change is dangerous; and the invariable tendency of the privileged classes to oppose change is only a prudent exercise of foresight.

One of the most important changes in the condition of a people is free intercourse with strangers. Interchange of thought and opinion takes place, information is given and received, new arts are learnt and communicated, and something analogous to a chemical effervescence takes place between the two people, who are thus mutually excited to a state of social ferment. But not only are nations stimulated by intercourse with others; it appears to be a law of animal development, that the mixture of races produces a higher and better type than either of the originals, and the finest races are those in whose elements the original types have almost disappeared. Races of men may, at the same time, be so mingled as to produce a lower type, and this law also extends to the lower animals; but while two races, already low, may be injudiciously crossed, to the detriment of the progeny, there seems little reason for doubt that the intermixture of national blood, where the races are of a higher character, is conducive to the physical perfection of mankind. The races of western Europe, that now take the preëminence in the world, are complex, and the result of many amalgamations. The south of Britain, especially, which produces men probably inferior to none on the whole surface of the globe, is peopled by a race resulting from many tribes who successively invaded the shores, and left a greater or less impress on the character of the inhabitants.* The Spaniard and the Frenchman are also the results of mixed blood; and, though the *kingdom* of Spain has sunk to insignificance from the effects of superstition and tyranny, the Spaniard is a high type of the human species, and only wants *truth* and *freedom* to enable him to play a distinguished part in the destinies of the world. When England and France were as superstitious and as enslaved as Spain, Spain was perhaps the most powerful kingdom in Europe; but since Spain did not progress in freedom, she has naturally sunk into every kind of licentiousness; and the Spanish race, with all its immorality and recklessness of blood-

* "The Saxons and Normans having sprung from the same Teutonic stock, the mixture of races, aided by the common services and sympathies of religion, became a matter of much greater facility than the same process in other countries. And this mixture we know has ever given the most powerful impetus to the progress of civilization. *Perhaps no race of men ever ceased to be barbarous and stationary without mingling blood with another race.* On the other hand, such interfusion has rarely if ever occurred, without imparting benefit to both sides — energy, knowledge, enterprise, and advancement in the arts of life. These causes combined, as well as others that might be mentioned, gradually gave prevalence to the Saxon language, and ultimately produced the 'Commons of England,' before whose ascendancy Norman feudalism must 'hide its diminished head;' while the '*Englishry*,' whom it so long trampled down and spurned, are now the most illustrious and the mightiest nation on the globe." — *North British Review.*

shed, is a living evidence of what kings and priests can do with a nation, when the nation does not destroy their influence in time. Had Spain established freedom of thought, instead of torturing and expatriating her industrious inhabitants, she might now have been a second England, with wealth and power beyond any other continental country. Freedom of thought is now evolving in Spain; and if a moderate tyranny could be established, to consolidate the disjointed elements of the country, Spain might still progress. But freedom of thought is now necessary; and if any attempt be made to curtail it, the progress of revolution may go on for years and years, until worn out by anarchy, and the credences of the rising generation running counter to the old superstitions, some bold adventurer may seize the reins of government, and exhibit Spain in an entirely new aspect. That the present rulers will continue is almost an impossibility.

SECTION III. — THE COMBINATION OF KNOWLEDGE AND REASON.

[*Knowledge is Credence based on sufficient Evidence, and Reason is the Power of perceiving Consequences, and of inferring Antecedents.*]

THE combination of knowledge and reason is the great moving power destined to emancipate the world. It is the only ground of hope for the unprivileged classes, but, at the same time, it is a sure ground of hope, and the more rapidly knowledge increases, the more rapidly will its all-powerful influence be made apparent to the world.

The first great condition of true knowledge is *the Bible*. Without this, man knows nothing. He neither knows what he is, nor what is his destiny; and though he may guess at some of the important truths in which the race is involved, he gropes in obscurity as to the most essential. Without the Bible, superstition and infidelity reign universally.* But God never made man to be either superstitious or an infidel; and

* "It will be better to avoid all religious discussions whatever, on which the natives are very sensitive. There is too wide a gulf between, ever to be passed. Spaniards, who, like the Moslems, allow themselves great latitude in laughing at monks, priests, and professors of religion, are very touchy as regards the articles of their creed; on these, therefore, beware of sportive criticism. *The whole nation in religious matters is divided into only two classes — bigoted Romanists or infidels;* there is no *via media.* The very existence of the Bible is unknown to the vast majority, who, when convinced of the cheats put forth as religion, have nothing better to fall back on but infidelity. They have no means of knowing the truth, and even the better classes have not the *moral courage* to seek it; they are afraid to examine the subject; they anticipate an unsatisfactory result, and therefore leave it alone in dangerous indifferentism. And even with the most liberal, with those who believe every thing except the Bible, the term *hereje*, heretic, still conveys an undefined feeling of horror and disgust, which we tolerant Protestants cannot understand. A Lutheran they scarcely believe to have a soul, and almost think has a tail. . . . . . . One thing is quite clear; that however serious and discouraging the blows recently dealt to the pope, the cause of infidelity, and not of Protestantism, has hitherto been the sole gainer." FORD's *Hand-book for Spain*, p. 168. It would say very little for Protes-

as soon as either of these forms is stamped upon a nation, every kind of error is let loose, and the erroneous credence in the matter of religion extends to the temporal affairs of the state. There is but one *truth;* and if men go wrong in the most important item, we cannot wonder that they should err as to the moral principles by which they should be guided in their actions towards each other. If they know not their duties to their Creator, how can it be expected that they should fulfil their duties to their fellows? *

Independent of all considerations of a hereafter, the

tantism if it *did* gain where there is *no evidence.* The process by which Romanists pass to infidelity is very easily explained. Popery is a *positive* credence; that is, it maintains a great many positive propositions. When these are examined, the *evidence* on which they ought to be based is found wanting, and the inquirer properly abandons them, thereby sinking into a *negative* state. He should, however, return to the God of nature until he finds evidence for a *positive* creed.

"From the state of matters in this country, it will not be long in all probability before the fruit of this religious toleration begins to appear. There is already much secret infidelity, and that will now no longer be concealed, so that we shall have an *infidel party.* There will also be a considerable body who hold pertinaciously by the forms, ceremonies, miracles, and worship of Rome, whom you may call the ***Romanist party;*** and there will be a third, which I trust by God's blessing may be a rapidly increasing party. Though small in its beginnings, you may call it the *evangelical party.*" —*Letter from Italy, Witness,* March 8, 1848.

* In saying that without the Bible man knows nothing, we do not mean that science or philosophy are to be learned from the Bible. All natural knowledge may be learned without the Bible; but suppose a nation were possessed of all natural knowledge, and yet had not the Bible, what doubts and mysteries would remain to overwhelm the inquirer? Besides, man, as man, is a worshipping

Bible has an eminent effect in regulating the conditions of men in this world. Religious superstition is essentially *tyrannical.* It interferes with men's thoughts and actions in almost every country of the globe, and freedom appears to be scarcely possible wherever it has a decided hold on the community. Superstition is the basis of bigotry, and bigotry is the basis of persecution. Destroy the superstition, and both bigotry and persecution will soon fall to the ground.

The Bible strikes at the root of persecution, by removing the false credence on which it is based; and wherever the Bible gains an ascendency over the priestcraft of a superstition, we may be certain that, sooner or later, all persecution will disappear, and liberty of

creature, and all history informs us that where the revelation of TRUTH was unknown, men plunged madly into superstition. The Bible saves from this great whirlpool of destruction; and by enlightening man on his nature and destiny, and by revealing more clearly and specifically the wonderful benevolence of the Creator, and the constant interest taken by the Divine Being in the affairs of this world, the Bible enables man to *settle* his credence, and to *classify* his knowledge upon a system unknown to those who have not the truth. When, above all our philosophy, there remains an infinite void or an infinite unknown, we doubt, and speculate, and wander in obscurity. But when revelation opens up the highest truths that involve our race, and teaches what we must do *to be saved,* all other knowledge ranges itself lower down in the scale, and assumes a definite position, instead of floating loosely amidst the vague mysteries of the imagination. Philosophy, however clear, is but the deceitful moonlight that mocks with its illusions; and though much may be seen and known even by the moonlight, the calm and steady rays of *day* are requisite before the spell of the fancy is dissolved, and before the form and color of creation can be seen in their reality.

thought be established. The Bible sanctions no persecution, but teaches men that they are made of one flesh, and that they are personally responsible to their Creator.

Next to the Bible is the knowledge of material nature. An endless variety of phenomena are constantly occurring around us, and these, by a law of our mental constitution, are referred to *causes.*

These *causes* have ever played a most prominent part in the history of mankind, and the fancy has ever thrown around them that mysterious mantle of the imagination by which they were clothed with personality. From necessary forms of rational thought, they became transfigured, each and all of them, into conscious existences, that willed and acted for themselves, and produced the multifarious phenomena of nature. The child asks us, not "What?" but "Why?"* And infant nations, who never belie the great principles of our nature, whether moral, intellectual, or sensual, whether good or evil, rushed from the exhibition of the phenomenon to the cause creator that produced it — endowed that cause with all the attributes of mind, and filled the world with half material spirits, demons and demigods, and all the vague mythologies of mysterious influences that spring from the unhallowed heart of man, which, naked and shamed, has sought refuge in the dark caverns of superstition. As *man* was, so were the *causes:* fierce warrior deities with the warlike nations — emblems of thought, "sitting on

* A child never thinks of measuring a phenomenon, but asks, "What *produced* it?" "*Why* did it take place?"

a lotus leaf, immersed in the contemplation of their own divinity," among the mystic speculators of the sunlit lands — demons of carnage, figured in the tiger fetish of the oppressed progeny of Ham — Molochs, Baals, or Saturns — fates, furies, or destinies; while the classic poesy of Greece and Rome deified the sentiments of the human mind, and pictured them as beings presiding over nature, though steeped in all the vices of mankind.

Still, wherever there was intellect there was *beauty.* False as were the credences, we cannot now turn to them without recognizing the glorious attributes of reason with which mankind has been endowed. Nor can we wonder at the spell of fascination, when we find the mere abstractions of our thought presented in the form of a Hebe, a Venus, or Minerva. Dark as were the times of ancient paganism, there was a beauty of imagination that speaks home to the intellect of man, and leaves a sad regret. Let us not forget, however, that *we* behold, not as actors in the scene, but as the spectators at those gladiatorial shows, where the contest of man with death was the absorbing drama for the onlooker, while the victims in the arena poured forth their blood and perished.

It was reserved for the corruption of Christianity to throw the *darkest* shade. It is said that "the shadow is nowhere so dark as immediately under the lamp;" and the true light of Heaven was converted, not into the lamp that lightens, but into the lamp that casts a shade. Piety died away, and theology took her place. Creeds and confessions were substituted for living virtue. Christians forgot to fix their eyes on Heaven, and deified the symbols of religion.

The wisdom that is from above is *not* a creed, but *a principle of life imbued with truth;* and when the church forgot the life, the truth vanished from the symbol, and left the dead remains of unspiritual knowledge. The shadows were dark before, but now night shrouded in a veil.

Now was the night of degradation. Now was man seen, not in the energies of his pride, not in the brilliant colors of his fancy, not in the heroism of a noble heart, that had framed its country for its God, and rushed to death self-sacrificed — but in the drivelling wretchedness of priestcraft, and in the sensuality of worse than pagan Rome. Now indeed was darkness. Truth had few worshippers — tradition had her hosts. Virtue was gone, and man was content with ceremony. Causes were no longer deities; and all that had remained of beauty was drowned in the senseless legend of the monkish tale.

Causes now were demons and demi-demons. The atmosphere of earth was filled with spirits of malignity. Demons and devils stared from out the ordinary phenomena of nature.* Tempests had their witches, winds had their wizards, and *saints* were prayed to for

* "Such were the words which Paracelsus addressed to his contemporaries, who were as yet incapable of appreciating doctrines of this sort; for the belief in enchantment still remained every where unshaken, and faith in the world of spirits still held men's minds in so close a bondage, that thousands were, according to their own conviction, given up as a prey to the devil; while, at the command of religion as well as of law, countless piles were lighted, by the flames of which human society was to be purified." — *Hecker's Epidemics of the Middle Ages*, p. 100.

protection. Now was death triumphant. Death of all that was noble, death of all that was true, death of all that was brave. Now was the reign of ignorance, and now was the priest man's deity. Now was "the heel bruised," and now was truth transformed into a LIE. Lies in the life, lies in the heart, lies on the tongue, lies in the creed, lies in the ceremony, lies in the vow, lies in the church, lies at the altar, and lies to the lips of the last expiring agonies of man. O, mystery of iniquity!

But the *causes* did not fall alone. As the causes fell, so fell man. Man and his deities are linked by a chain that nothing severs but death; for as the object of our worship is, so shall we be, more and more nearly.

While we look to the night of intellect and virtue that followed the teaching of the priest, let us also look to one incident that shows the depth of human degradation. Man had anciently deified *the cause*, and created, according to a necessary law of our nature, a something that should afford an explanation of phenomena. The priest now creates not a cause, but *a phenomenon.*

So long as man takes *the fact* in nature, and seeks to assign *a cause*, he follows the true path; and that path is abstractly correct, however absurd may be the fancied explanation. The priest, however, who turned *every thing* into a lie, forsook even this great principle of our intellect, and took *a cause* and worked *a miracle.* He sought no longer to personify, but to *simulate.* And the vulgar miracles of the papal heresy were *simulated facts*, wrought for the purposes of deception. His bleeding idols and moving pictures, and all the other stock-in-trade of lying priestcraft, were imitations of phenomena; while wooden virgin Marys and human saints were supposed to preside over the operations of the elements.

To suppose that any thing else than vice, abomination, and *tyranny* could exist with such a system, is out of the question. All the history of man teaches us, that where there is a corrupt priesthood, there is a corrupt people. And if the people are corrupt—if from the king on the throne to the peasant who tills the field, lies and superstition form the sum and substance of theological credence, where in all the world can *liberty* be expected to come from? Does liberty grow out of lies? or out of *truth?* Out of ignorance and vice? or out of knowledge and virtue? And if it *does* grow out of truth, there is but ONE TRUTH; and that truth is the condition of man's welfare, and the only price at which true freedom can be purchased.

It may be supposed that we dwell too strongly and too long on the superstitions of the Roman heresy. Not so. These superstitions have more political influence for the destruction of freedom, than all the other causes that act on the states of central and southern Europe. Read the history of *any* country where Romanism has been the prevailing superstition; read the best accounts of the present condition of *any* Roman Catholic countries—and then say if you can find any thing whatever that can be called even an approach to *liberty*—to an *equitable* condition of society. Take France before the revolution, (and even forget the ameliorating influence of time in softening down the asperities—an influence that makes us look with almost calm indifference at deeds however dark, provided they are far enough removed,) and ask what Romanism had done for France? See brute carnality pursued *intentionally*, see despotism not even arrested at the *oubliettes*, see a peasantry taught lies by the priest, while the farmers of the taxes ground them into madness and desperation, the state corrupt in every function, the best and the most industrious part of the population expatriated or destroyed, and liberty of thought uprooted by the sabres of the soldiery. When at last (without the aid of what is called *Protestantism*) the very people, who from infancy had been taught to reverence the priest and his mysteries, could no longer believe his lies, what could be expected? When every thing had been so corrupted that France was rotten to the core, and there remained no single bond that could keep the nation together as a society; and when the very light of reason, that professed to teach *nothing*, destroyed the superstitions of the priest, and unhinged the credence of the nation; when the priest was found a deceiver and the ruler a despot, and men's reason told them that it was so, even without the Bible; and when *all* religious credence was swept away in the reaction of the poisoned intellect —what could we expect? And can it be supposed that Russia and Austria have nothing of the kind in store? Will ignorance remain there forever, and teach men that, though they have a reason, they must not exercise it, but be, like the beasts of the field, subject to their master? Some may think that "to-morrow shall be as to-day, and much more abundant." "God forbid!" must be the prayer of every freeman.

The degradation of the *causes* of natural phenomena entailed some of the most horrid cruelties that have stained the history of the world. GOD was dethroned from the realm of *nature*, as well as from the realm of *religion;* and when virgins, saints, old bones, and bits of wood became the objects of men's *worship*, witches and sorcerers were the minor deities of nature, and the *causes* of phenomena. The priest, however, had the *power*, and, as he dealt in miracles himself, the witches trenched too closely on his domain, and he removed them by a process more frantically cruel than that by which he himself was afterwards removed by the few insane atheists of France. The terrible crimes that were committed, under the pretext of punishing witchcraft, show us that nature as well as religion was provided with an inquisition by the priest; and the multitudes of sorcerers who were immolated in the middle ages, were as much the victims of nature misinterpreted, as the martyr Christians were the victims of a false theology. Truth, in either case, would have prevented the commission of the crimes.

Not only, however, does popery destroy the elements of *freedom;* it uproots that most pure and most holy of all man's natural sentiments — patriotism. Some have come to speculate about the country that produces most food, most population, most machinery, and most, &c., &c., as if *that* were necessarily the *best* country. Granted, if man were to live forever. But as threescore years and ten are the time of man's days upon earth, he who *has* a country has but *one.* All trade, all fairness, all peace, all good will to all the nations in the world; but yet there is a country for which something else is reserved. It is not merely the country of our *birth;* that is an accident that goes for nothing in the case of birth *abroad.* It is the land of our fathers, the land of our hopes, the land of our language, the land of our affections, and the land of our heart. It is the land that we should stand with or fall with. Were there ten thousand Tamerlanes ravaging the earth, we might look on as spectators; it might, or it might not, be our duty to interfere. But *our* land is the land of our sanctuary, on which foeman's foot is the impress of pollution; and, so long as there beats a patriot's heart, there will be found the patriot's sword. Nothing in the history of the world ever struck patriotism dead, save the blasphemous doctrines of Rome. Search all history for a thousand years, read tales and legends, and records of all that has come down of papal Roman history, and say if you can find one single Roman *patriot.* Ask if there be one man in all that city, and that state, whose heart has beat for Rome, and whose hand grasped a *patriot's* brand on the threshold of his fathers. Saxons and Franks, Northmen, Genoese, Pisans, Venetians, Sicilians, Burgundians, Flemings, Spaniards, Moors, Normans, Europeans, Africans, and Asiatics, all the races that ran to seek a country, or staid to defend one, have left a name in the annals of the age. And where amidst them all is the *Roman?* Rome fought, but not with Romans. She who buys and sells souls, and purgatorial fires, and redemption with a bloodless sacrifice, bought and sold men, and hired the arms of hirelings.

Rome taught men that they might fight here to-day, there to-morrow, and sell their swords for gold. Men fought because it was their *trade*, and worked for the employer that gave most wages — wretches without a country, fit emblems of their instructor. Patriotism was disbanded, save with the peasant cultivators of the soil, who still could fight for their homes, like the tiger for his lair.

Whatever may be said of the material benefits of countries, one thing is certain — a country where there is no patriotism is not safe for a day. Patriotism is a country's true strength; for where there is no patriotism there is no bond of union. When France was patriotic, and trusted her frontier to her peasantry, all the armies of Europe could set no foot upon her soil. But when men fought for the *emperor*, and not for their country, France was humbled in the dust. Ten grains of true patriotism would have saved Spain, Italy, and Germany from Napoleon; but, alas! "they had them not," and, what is more, never will have, and never can have, till Roman priestcraft is destroyed.

But time rolled on, and night was drawing to a close. Broken gleams of light flickered here and there, to give warning of the coming day. Day broke at last, and nature was emancipated from the mystic folds of superstition. The great turning-point of modern times was, when the doctrine of *constant repetition of similar phenomena in similar conditions* was substituted for the dread of unseen, and too often *malevolent*, agency.

Man learned at last to bend his eye on the phenomenon, accurately to observe the *conditions*, and accurately to measure the *change*. Physical truth was the result of this operation, so simple, now we know it, yet of such vast importance to the welfare of the world. Superstition here received its blow of death; and, just in proportion as the inductive philosophy (in physical science) was received and cultivated, so was man emancipated from the terrors of unseen agency, and the phenomena of nature were fixed on a stable basis, that invited man constantly to further inquiry.

But what had become of the *causes?* The immense revolution that had taken place in man's view of nature, was accompanied by another revolution that went far to destroy the priestcraft of Rome, and to bring man back to the spiritual worship of his Creator. The Bible had been resuscitated, and some at all events had learned to love the pure beauty of religion as taught by God, and to forsake the doctrines of devils as taught by man. Instead of stocks, and stones, and graven images, and the remnants of the human frame, men learned to bow the knee to Him who sitteth on the throne of righteousness, and to confide in the God of heaven, who had sent his Son for the redemption of the world.

The *causes* were now no longer beings, but *the laws by which the one God carries on the government of the material world.* No wonder that Rome will have no *science.*

But has this view of nature a *direct* bearing on the political condition of mankind? No doubt of it whatever. Those who have advocated the utilitarian theory are true benefactors to their country; and, though we may take occasion to advert to the cases in which that theory has been carried altogether out of its legitimate province, we of course accept it to its utmost extent in those matters that come within its range. But what is the utilitarian theory, and what is its connection with inductive philosophy?

Let us suppose men legislating on a *theological* principle, (no matter what,) and carrying out their laws by force. Let us suppose an inductive philosopher beginning at the effects of these laws, carefully collecting the statistics of the things he can observe, and arranging them into an exhibition of *facts*. Let us suppose that these facts (as it is most likely they would) show the *results* of the legislation to have been eminently detrimental to the great body of the population. Suppose he publishes these details. Of course those who legislate on a *theological* principle care nothing about consequences; for if the *principle* be correct, the legislation is a duty at all hazards. Now, what is to be *done?* Of course, if the populace are not quite so certain about the principle as the legislators are, they might begin to suspect a mistake in the rulers' method of proceeding, and perhaps they might weigh the statistics against the theology, and give the preference to the former. This is very likely. Now, what course have the rulers? Either to abandon their legislation, or to *expel the philosopher, and prevent all further inquiries of the kind.* But suppose the inductive mode of judging of legislative acts should happen to procure free course, it is quite impossible that *facts*, mere *facts*, should not tell on the country in the long run, and that reasonings upon those facts should not spring up in every man's mind, and cause him to throw all his weight into every change in which he could see his own, and the interest of his fellows, involved.

But suppose a new light were to break upon the nation. Suppose men should happen to reflect that *facts* come from the operations of the laws of God, and suppose the thought should strike them that God is a *benevolent and a just* God — that he made a *good* world, gave it *good* laws, and that social evils spring from man's injustice to his fellow, and from the *wrong* way in which things have been divided. Suppose the idea should go abroad that God is no respecter of *persons*, but that perhaps the welfare of a peasant is of as much value in the eyes of Him who doeth all things well, as the welfare of a king. Now, suppose to these reflections were joined another or two, that God made man's *reason*, and made man to hate pain and flee from it; and also that man's nature obliges him to live in society, and that societies may make mistakes, as the child does who puts his finger into the flame, and that the pain is to teach him to beware in future. Were such notions to go abroad, it is perfectly evident that the inductive philosophy, when it found out evils and suffering attending legislative acts, would come, backed with the authority of Him who made the laws of nature, and it would lead to the belief that the welfare of the great masses of the population was never sacrificed to procure the wealth of the few, without God's displeasure being always made manifest in the suffering that ensued. *Not* that this suffering was a miraculous interference, but the result of the ordinary laws which God has made for the government of the world.

Suppose, however, *one* more principle should be admitted, namely, that "that which is *just* is *beneficial*, and for the good of the greatest number." Suppose men should reflect that induction requires time and knowledge before it can be brought to perfection, and that God endowed man with an *à priori* principle of *justice*, to enable him to steer clear of injuring his fellow, even where the inductive evidence should not be at hand. Suppose the results of this *justice* and of this *induction* should happen to turn out always and invariably coincident, and although pursuing different paths to reach the same end, yet the end arrived at never was different.

Were all this admitted, (and though it takes many words to tell it, perhaps it might be seen all at one view,) it is plain that the inductive method of examining the *condition* of the country would have the most direct and the most powerful influence on the legislation of the country. Where suffering was considered not the mere accident of chance, nor the work of a malevolent spirit, but the voice of a just and benevolent God, telling men to amend the order of society, and to return to those elementary principles of justice that he had implanted in their mind — surely we can see that the progress of this nation must be very different from the progress of that nation from which inductive philosophy was banished, and where men legislated *for themselves* and pretended to be legislating for God.

Next to a rational view of nature comes a true philosophy of the mind and of the mental operations. It might be supposed that this could have little influence on the political condition of a nation; and if all the great truths relating to man were not so inseparably linked together, that error in the one usually involves or implies error in the other, perhaps, taken alone, it might be of no great importance. But from some cause or other, speculative errors about *man* have usually involved speculative errors about *God*, and speculative errors about God have usually unhinged the whole framework of human *duty*, and obscured the distinction between right and wrong. This subject the reader will find discussed in the first volume of M. Cousin's "History of the Moral Philosophy of the Eighteenth Century," where he traces, with a grace peculiar to himself, the doctrine of "no causes but physical causes" to the "*sensation*" school of mental philosophy.*

Of M. Cousin's work, it is perhaps impossible to speak too highly, and we rejoice to see so eminent a man, and so candid a reasoner, speaking out for the *natural* principles of *duty*, declaring his honest conviction, that, as a philosopher, he finds a law of justice written in the constitution of man. At the same time, we cannot but hope that those who adopt that philosophy will not confine themselves to the general idea of a just and righteous God made manifest through the glorious works of nature and of mind, but continue in the onward path of truth, and really investigate with the same candor the authenticity of the

* The doctrine of no causes but physical causes, is said to have produced, perhaps, the most frightful exclamation that ever crossed the lips of man, — "Nous pouvons faire ce que nous voulons, il n'y-a pas de Dieu!" said to have been uttered by the rabble at Arras, as the executioner's cart tracked its way with blood. Fit doctrine to fit deed.

BIBLE. For ourselves we cannot speak as if the Bible were not a revelation, or even as if it were a collection of *doubtful* documents; and therefore we cannot speculate as if there were a question *as to whether God has revealed himself directly*, *as well as by necessary inference from his works. Christianity* is never to be found in nature, although *religion* is; and THE CHRIST, the Son of the living God, equal and one with the Father, forms as necessary a part of all true acceptance with God, and of all present religion, (now since the fall,) as the most clear acknowledgment of the Creator. When we confine ourselves purely to philosophy, and ask what may be learnt by the unaided exercise of the reason, we do well, so long as we do not advance our results to *the exclusion* of revelation; but when we form a system of philosophy from nature, however perfect that system may be, we suggest that it is not *logical* to predicate any thing whatever about the reality or unreality of a revelation, with only that philosophy for the premises. Nothing whatever is capable of being the premises of the question of revelation, except the *evidence* on which any particular revelation is stated to be founded. And although the attributes of the Deity are made evident through nature, we must never from that leap to the conclusion, that God has *not* made known his *particular acts*, which could never be inferred, as we can infer his attributes. "God that made the world and all things therein, seeing that he is Lord of heaven and earth, dwelleth not in temples made with hands; neither is worshipped with men's hands, as though he needed any thing, seeing he giveth to all life, and breath, and all things; and hath made of one blood all nations of men for to dwell on all the face of the earth, and hath determined the times before appointed, and the bounds of their habitation; that they should seek the Lord, if haply they might feel after him, and find him, though he be not far from every one of us. For in him we live, and move, and have our being; as certain also of your own poets have said, For we are also his offspring. Forasmuch then as we are the offspring of God, we ought not to think that the Godhead is like unto gold, or silver, or stone, graven by art and man's device. And the times of this ignorance God winked at; but now commandeth all men every where to repent: because he hath appointed a day, in the which he will judge the world in righteousness *by that Man whom he hath ordained;* whereof he hath given assurance unto all men *in that he hath raised him from the dead.*" — PAUL'S *Address to the Athenians.*

But what, after all, is the sum and substance of our argument concerning the combination of knowledge and reason? Merely this, that *correct credence* is absolutely essential to the human race, before that race can know and work out its own well being.

The elements of this correct credence are, 1st. The Bible. 2d. A correct view of the phenomena of material nature. 3d. A correct philosophy of the mental operations.*

* We do not, in this place, enter on the subject of moral science, having to treat it more specially hereafter. A correct philosophy of the mental operations would of course include the science of equity, but a science of equity there cannot possibly be, so long as there is a *sensational* philosophy; and therefore we have affirmed.

1st. The Bible. There is but one truth, and, if the Bible system be true, every other system must be erroneous, and must lead to a course of action prejudicial to mankind. The question is not as to the necessity of all men becoming, what is sometimes termed *religious*, but as to the general acceptance or rejection of that system of revealed knowledge which is contained in the Bible alone; and, when we consider how vast an amount of information is there afforded us respecting man, man's nature, and man's destiny, we see at once, that if all that information be correct and be rejected, men shut themselves out from the light, and plunge wilfully into vague and hopeless darkness. So far from the Bible being in opposition to the reason of mankind, the Bible is the great emancipator of the reason; the first great influence that delivers man from the empire of passion and superstition, and leaves him free to exercise those faculties with which the Creator has endowed his intellect. Sceptics may frame their sophisms, and point incredulous to its insoluble mysteries; but HISTORY dashes their sophisms into the dust, and shows us the great evolution of freedom and civilization taking place under the shadow of revealed truth, while the mass of the earth's inhabitants struggle helplessly onward in a vain endeavor to deliver them-

that a correct mental philosophy is essential to human welfare. At the conclusion of the volume, we shall endeavor to show how a genuine philosophy may become possible, and possible in such a manner as to cast aside dispute. Philosophy, strictly speaking, can never assume a satisfactory form until the whole of the direct sciences are completed, and then philosophy will become purely *critical.*

selves from the evils that inseparably accompany superstition. No truth can be more certain, than that the welfare of the human race is wrapped up in the universal acceptance of the Bible as the Word of God, and the only true source from which man must draw the first great facts in which all the children of men are irrevocably implicated.

2d. A correct view of natural phenomena. In this, two things are implied: 1st. A knowledge of natural phenomena, (science;) and, 2d. The attribution of those phenomena to their true cause. If God be the Creator of the universe, God is also the physical Governor of the universe; and as such we must regard the occurrences of nature as the results of the laws established by him. And when once men shall really awake to the conviction, that the social evils of the community (poverty and want,* with the accompaniments of

* That poverty and want have a direct tendency to produce *crime*, is a fact which may be ascertained inductively in the same manner as any general fact or principle is ascertained and established in the physical sciences. If prevention be better than cure, it is most certainly better than *punishment*, which has proved itself, in the general history of the world, to be the clumsiest and most inefficient means of preventing crime that has ever been employed towards a population. There is a vast difference between the man who is by habit and repute a criminal, and the man who is led to commit crime under certain circumstances of social distress. Almost every man in the world is of such a nature that he would commit crime in certain circumstances; and this very fact should point out the necessity of reforming the circumstances, as well as endeavoring to restrain the offenders by threats of consequent infliction. So intimately is crime connected with the physical condition of the population, that it may almost be said *to fluctuate with*

crime, ignorance, and disease) arise from an infringement of certain invariable laws, no more uncertain in their nature than those which regulate the fall of a stone or the motion of a planet, we may reasonably

the price of provisions and the demand for labor; and the only sure mode of reducing it to a minimum, is to remove those political obstacles which prevent the cultivator and the laborer from reaping their natural reward, or which prevent them from employing their labor on the earth, which God has given as a storehouse for food, but which the laws of men reduce to sterility by the common system of landed property. How many thousands of criminal Irishmen might be made useful members of society, by allowing them to cultivate the land, according to the law of God's word and of God's nature, *for their own profit!* Let any one compare the following statement of Irish crime with the price of provisions in Ireland at the respective periods, and deny, if he can, the same inductive relation of cause and effect which forms the essence of all physical science:—

"OUTRAGES.—*Ireland, October,* 1847.—Returns have just been issued (pursuant to an order of the House of Lords, dated June 28) stating the number and kind of outrages reported by the constabulary in Ireland, from the month of June, 1845, to the month of May, 1847, inclusive. This return is intended as a continuation of the sessional paper, No. 279 of 1845. The results of this latest document show a fearful and extraordinary increase of crime in Ireland. Thus the total number of outrages specially reported to the constabulary force in Ireland, during the month of July, 1844, was 552. In June, 1845, the number was 896, and in July, 1845, it was 708. In September of the same year it was 552; in August, 1846, it was 478; while in the following month it had increased to 829. In October, the number of offences again increased to 1482—(nearly *three times* as many as during the corresponding period of the preceding year;) in November last it was 1761; and in the concluding month of the year, no less a number than 2666—(upwards of *four times* as many as in December, 1845.) Of that number, 1389 were cases of cattle stealing; 14 homicides, (in one month;) 22 cases of

expect that men will bend their eye on the phenomenon, endeavor to ascertain the conditions and forces that result in good or evil, and thus to discover a natural science of society that may open a new era in the history of civilization. Induction is no less applicable to the phenomena of men than it is to the phenomena of matter; and, although there are disturbing causes that render the study more complex and more difficult, we can have no reason for supposing that the same stability that prevails in the inorganic world, does not also prevail in the social world of men, and entail many effects which are too often attributed to the voluntary volitions of the mind. Not that there are no phenomena in the social world which cannot be accounted for by physical laws — for this would obliterate man's moral nature; but that certain social conditions are for the most part accompanied by certain social phenomena, which may be studied in the same manner as the facts of any other science, and made the basis of social action and of human legislation.

firing at the person; 25 aggravated assaults, &c. Thirty-five of the offences were of an agrarian character. In the first month of the present year, (1847,) the number of offences reported by the constabulary in Ireland was still further augmented, for it amounted to 2885 — (1276 in Munster alone.) In May it was 2647, of which number 1446 were cases of cattle stealing; while in the May preceding there were only 69 of these offences reported. The return from which these results are extracted does not come lower than the month of May. During the two years included in the account, (June, 1845, to May, 1847, both inclusive,) the total number of outrages reported by the constabulary in Ireland amounted to no fewer than 29,302, or at the rate of more than 40 outrages every day in the year." — *Witness*, October 30, 1847.

Thus every religion and every political system may be judged of inductively (by an examination of the condition of the people where it prevails) as well as dogmatically, by an inquiry into its own inherent nature; and we may, as politicians, pronounce the utter condemnation of idolatry, on account of its fruits of ignorance, vice, crime, and detriment to the social condition of mankind; while, as theologians, we exhibit its falsity and error, and condemn it because its credence is unsupported, and therefore superstitious. It is true that this view may, by certain classes, be esteemed a low one; but all truth is worthy of attention, much more especially that which affects the social condition of men, because these effects, that may be observed by the natural exercise of our faculties, must be considered as the results of God's laws operating in the world. It is no mean advantage to truth, that she has always the benefit (the common worldly benefit) on her side; neither is it a small argument against any erroneous system, that we may point to its deadly fruits, and show the demoralizing influence of its operation.

But if idolatry may be judged of by its fruits, so may *despotism*, so may slavery, so may restrictive laws, and so may all those inventions of worldly legislation, by which a small benefit is conferred on the few at the expense of the mass of the population. And these effects, whatever their kind, belong to a natural and inductive science of society, the great principles of which remain the same in all ages and in all conditions, however much, or however little advantage may have been derived by a nation from their contemplation.

3d. A correct philosophy of the mental operations.

Whenever we approach what is termed *metaphysical philosophy*, we feel that we approach a quagmire, over which a dense mist seems to hold its perpetual habitation.* The footing is all unsound, or at least suspicious, and the little light there is, is only sufficient to confuse and perplex us. If we attempt to advance, two ultimate and hitherto impassable objects present themselves to view. On the one hand is the bottomless pit of scepticism, and on the other is the commanding but inaccessible height of absolute truth. Some, wearied with vain endeavors to scale the precipice, have at last, as if despairingly, advanced beyond the brink, and sunk into the unfathomable void; while

* In speaking thus of *metaphysical philosophy*, we do not speak of that genuine philosophy which consists in the enumeration and discussion of the primary elements and propositions of human credence, but of that spurious speculation that endeavors, by a subtle use of language, and of half-formed thought, to uproot the foundations of truth. Let us suppose that every man in the world immediately gives his assent to the *necessary and universal truth* of an axiom, (no matter what.) Some philosophers say, "But your axiom is only a subjective conviction; now prove to me its objective truth." The most definite reply to this objection, and one which the sceptic may fail to get over with all his ingenuity, is this, "Give me a definition of objective truth." Axioms are, it is true, incapable of proof; but why? because they are the standards of all other propositional truth whatever. The idealist, on the other hand, accepts *truth*, but confuses the question of *reality*. The fact we believe to be, that if *truth* and *reality* were fairly defined, and not jumbled together in a kind of mysterious way, both the sceptic and the idealist (the Berkleyian) would at once be convicted of introducing a *new term* into their conclusion, and making a palpable logical fallacy.

others, startled at the plunge, have flattered themselves that, by some mighty effort of their own faith or imagination, they could compensate for the reality, that could only be obtained by setting the foot on the summit and casting the eye over universal nature.

Between scepticism on the one hand, and the dogmatism of unsupported faith on the other, philosophy has slowly swayed backwards and forwards, leaving man as little farther advanced in ontology as he was five hundred, or a thousand, or two thousand years since.

To suppose, however, that philosophy is the useless jargon that some writers appear desirous of representing, because it has failed to solve the great problem, namely, "How can objective existence be *rationally* substantiated?" is surely to look at history with only one eye. Philosophy *has* failed; that is, the human intellect has failed; that is, man as man has failed; that is, in fact, that after all the mental toil of the greatest, the problem appears insoluble, and seems to teach us that humanity cannot arrive at objective truth by its own unaided efforts; neither, we candidly confess, does it appear to us to be of the slightest importance whether it can or cannot.

Grant that scepticism in philosophy is the ultimate result of all investigation; let us only be consistent, and make that scepticism *universal*, and the bugbear of scepticism disappears forever. Let us write a plus or a minus, a sign positive or a sign negative, before *all* our knowledge, and what difference can it possibly make? Knowledge remains the same in all its relative proportions; and all that man has really ascertained to be true, remains as permanently stable, and as really capable of application, as if ten thousand syllogisms had proven that *knowledge* was *truth*, and that the axiomatic credence of mankind was really veracious. Scepticism, whatever be its dangers, is only dangerous when partially applied, and when we apparently undermine one branch of knowledge by insisting on *rational proof*, while at the same time we admit as much, and perhaps infinitely more, without any process of proof whatever, but merely because we are constrained to believe. When one man shall have demonstrated to another man his own existence, (and the most sceptical of the sceptics admits the existence of the *me*,) it will then be time to substantiate objective existence, by a process of proof that can have no difficulties, when once the proof of the one *me* is furnished to the other. If we will be sceptics, let us be consistent; and let us write our sign negative, not merely before objective knowledge, but before the existence of that *me*, whose existence is absolutely as incapable of every approach to rational proof as is the existence of an external world.*

* It is commonly supposed, that philosophic scepticism has some mysterious power to unhinge the very framework of *morals*. Now suppose that, after all, *the whole* of man's knowledge should be proven subjective, what difference can it make? Suppose a subjective man is arrested by a subjective policeman, tried by a subjective jury, and condemned to subjective imprisonment — is the *pain* the less *real* because it is subjective? Or, to extend the argument, suppose the whole system of morals should be subjective, and that there shall be a subjective day of judgment, and a subjective eternity. What difference could the mere mode of ex-

When, however, we take the existence of the *me* for granted, and then insist that other objective existence should produce a proof of which it is incapable, our scepticism is not only dangerous but fatal, and the tangled web of sophistry is made to envelop certain subjects, as if they, and they only, were shrouded in obscurity. To proceed in this manner is no more rational than it would be to take objective existence for granted, and then to reflect on the *me*, and imperatively to demand its rational proof. Rational proof there is none, either in the one case or the other; for the *me* is as really *objective* to all our *consciousness*, as is matter or universal mind. We are *conscious* of mental *phenomena* alone; and the *me* is as far removed from immediate appreciation, as is any other substantive existence that our race admits with persevering universality. Let us only make scepticism (philosophic scepticism) *absolutely universal*, and the foundations of real knowledge are laid anew, and the glorious edifice of science acquires its fair proportions, and becomes the settled home of man's intellect, where he may dwell in peace and safety, having buried scepticism in a grave of its own digging.*

pression make? If scepticism were *practical*, it would save from terrestrial consequences and terrestrial pain; and, if it cannot do so, it makes the most groundless assumption when it proposes to abolish future punishment. Even if *matter* were only an idea, it is plain that *pain* is to be avoided, even if it *were* only subjective; and consequently if criminality of action brings pain, it is plain that the most certain of all knowledge is *morals*. The *moral* law is abiding, whatever view may be taken of *matter*.

* There is one argument which appears to us valid against all

For ourselves, we believe that scepticism may be fairly met, and fairly vanquished by the most strict rules of logic. Its stronghold is in the ambiguity of terms, and in the use of terms which it has no logical right to use. Let us, however, without descending into abstract disputations, take it up on *the fact.*

philosophers who admit the *me*, and require rational proof of the existence of the *not me.* Let us grant that all the external material world may come to be viewed by that philosopher as an assemblage of the sensations or phenomena of the *me.* This may, perhaps, be possible; but these philosophers use arguments and *write books.* Now, for what purpose are these books written? Surely not to convince the *me*, for the *me* is supposed convinced already, but to convince some other *me*, that is, some *objective* mental existence which can never, even by the utmost stretch of scepticism, be confounded with the *me* personal. An argument is to convince *a mind;* and assuredly that mind never made a sensual impression on the sceptic. Nothing in the shape of a sensual impression, nothing in the shape of observation, nothing in the shape of phenomenal affection, could ever be experienced by the sceptic of that *mind*, whose existence he takes for granted when he endeavors to convince it. Every philosopher who writes a book or uses an argument, appears to us to admit objective existence in a manner that is not liable to the reply usually given to his admission of the material world. *That*, we have granted, may be phenomenal; but when he acts for the conviction of a judgment by publishing an argu ment, will it, or can it, be advanced that that judgment is phenom enal? Is it not absolutely and essentially *another me*, perfectly distinct and perfectly distinguished from every thing that the *me* who writes can possibly predicate of itself? We can easily imagine a sceptic viewing men's *bodies* as phenomena, and classing them among the modifications of himself; but when he endeavors to convince their judgments, he thereby substantiates external existence objective to himself, and utterly incapable of ever being reduced to that *modification of the* ME, that forms the essential groundwork of the sceptical philosophy.

Scepticism says, "You have no proof for the objective truth of your subjective convictions." We deny the *fact*, and allege that an argument based on the calculation of probabilities would establish, beyond the smallest possibility of doubt, the objective veracity of the subjective laws of reason. The mathematical sciences are, every one of them, — namely, arithmetic, algebra, geometry, and statics, — purely subjective; every one of their primary *propositions* is an axiomatic truth taken for granted, *self*-evident, incapable of question, purely abstract, and that does not pronounce on the real existence of any concrete reality whatever. Now how comes it, that when these subjective sciences are applied to matter, an entity with which *they* have nothing to do, they are invariably as correct as when merely contemplated by the reason? How, if the subjective convictions and subjective processes of the reason are not correct, can an astronomer predict the return of a comet? — and the comet *does* return, to other men's perceptions, years after he is dead. Scepticism is the greatest imposition that ever fooled man's reason, yet it must be *fairly* met.

Never, perhaps, was the absence of a definition productive of so much fruitless toil, as when men set to work on philosophy. It had been well if philosophers had definitely laid before them the object they were about to pursue, and satisfied themselves that the means of arriving at their end were really within their reach. What is the object of philosophy? What is philosophy? What does a man propose to expound when he teaches philosophy? These are questions usually evaded by some oblique dissertation on the general form of knowledge, the nature of things, &c., &c., and the definite object to be pursued is never ascertained. For a long period philosophy was *ontology;* that is, the knowledge of being, entirely and exclusively objective in its character, entirely and exclusively subjective in its means of operation. That is, men endeavored to substantiate both the reality and the form of the universe in their own minds, without the connecting link — *evidence* — that renders one form of thought *knowledge*. There was no evidence, therefore there was no knowledge. With such a system the abstract sciences *alone* are possible, as in them the evidence is subjective, and supplied by the rational constitution of the mind.

The Baconian philosophy broke up ontology, by supplying the connecting link that must unite the object and the subject. That link was *evidence*, and that evidence was only possible by means of *observation.* Philosophy now separated into two parts — one of which was *metaphysics*, the representative of the ancient philosophy; and *science*, the new philosophy that arose from the new method of founding knowledge on evidence.

The new philosophy has advanced with wonderful strides, enlightening man's intellect, and dispersing innumerable benefits, which reproduce themselves in an infinity of forms, and hold out hopes of great and permanent advantage to our race. The old philosophy remains much where it was, as regards its nature, but in a very different position as to the extent of the ground it occupies.

At one period the ontological method of making

science (that is, the method of making science *without evidence*) was universal. It was applied to physics as well as to metaphysics, and its domain was supposed to extend over every thing that could become the subject of human knowledge. Not only was there a scholastic theology, but a scholastic series of assertions with regard to the essence of matter, all explanatory of observed phenomena. Alchemy, astrology, &c., completed the circle, and reduced to art the principles of dogmatic assertion. During the reign of this system, it is worthy of remark that diversity of credence and contradiction of statement were just as prevalent in matters of physical science, as they now are in matters of politics and philosophy.

When, however, a new *method* was discovered, diversity of credence and the ontological system retired from all those regions where real knowledge was acquired; and, as the new philosophy extended its domain, the old philosophy was curtailed in its sphere of operation, and restricted to those subjects that have not yet been reduced to scientific ordination. Thus the region of conflicting belief was one of indefinite boundary, or rather one whose boundary was constantly fluctuating and retiring before the advance of real knowledge. The history of real or positive knowledge might almost be termed the history of the retrogression of philosophy; and just as the new method was enabled to substantiate its propositions in such a manner, that all who investigated the evidence arrived at the same unity of credence, was philosophy constrained to abandon its ground, and to retire to those heights where it now enjoys but a precarious authority.

Let us now firmly lay hold of the fact, that philosophy at one period pretended to explain the phenomena of the external world, and that philosophy has now been driven from every part of that region that has been occupied by positive science.

Can nothing be learned from this fact? We think that something can, and it is this: That philosophy, after retrograding from every region of thought to which man may apply his attention, shall at last resolve itself into the science of human thought, and pronounce nothing whatever on any subject that is not merely and exclusively human thought. If we consider knowledge, we shall find that it implies three things; the object, (that is, the universe;) the subject, (that is, the human mind;) and the connecting link between them, that is, *evidence*. Now, if we consider that philosophy has abandoned one portion after another of the object, just in proportion as positive science has occupied that portion, we can see that, if the process continues, the whole of the object must ultimately be abandoned, and the subject alone become the object of contemplation. And if so, then will philosophy teach only psychology,* that is, the science of mental phenomena, which we can have no reason to

* Psychology, taking that term extensively to signify mental science. Of course, mental science has its divisions. First, there is inductive psychology, the *observational* part of mental science; and, second, there is the science proper of *thought*. The latter alone is entitled to the name of philosophy; the former is the natural history of mind. All the direct sciences must be evolved *before* there can be a science proper of thought. On this subject, however, we shall remark towards the close of the volume.

doubt may assume somewhat of the same ordination that prevails in those sciences that have the material world for their foundation.

Let us now for a moment reflect upon our argument, and endeavor to seize the point at which philosophy broke away from the path of legitimate inquiry, and lost itself amid the shifting quicksands of doubt, denial, and contradiction.

Let us place both the vulgar multitude and the philosophers before us, and examine their various occupations.

The multitude, in all ages and in all places, have admitted the existence of the mind, the existence of the external world, and the existence of Deity. These appear to be the common facts which those who do not enter on philosophic inquiry admit and act upon as matters requiring neither proof nor specific investigation. They are the common and general groundwork of human credence and of human action; and their certitude is never shaken in the popular mind until some philosopher shall have promulgated some abstract speculations as to the evidence on which those propositions are received. The multitude, then, believed and acted on their belief, taking the three great facts we have mentioned as the most common and ordinary truths, without which the whole economy of thought must be overturned, and laid in inextricable confusion.

The philosophers, however, were desirous of rendering some intelligible account of the phenomenon presented by the multitude, and clearing their minds of mere ordinary belief, endeavored to give a rational explanation of the theory of human credence. Their object was not to accept these great facts, and thence to proceed to specific knowledge, but to lay anew the rational evidence on which these facts themselves were to be admitted.

This intention appears at first sight to be praiseworthy, and the process may seem not altogether illegitimate.

Let us however posit the universal fact, that before man can *reason*, three substantives must be given or taken for granted, and that two propositions must also be given, involving those three substantives as the terms, before man can by any possibility arrive at a proposition established by rational, that is, by logical, proof. Let men therefore pursue their inquiry as far back as the most subtle intellect can possibly reach, there must necessarily be found at the bottom of all real or of all hypothetical reasoning, three substantives and two propositions, which, if accepted, may lead to real knowledge, and, if rejected, must land us without further difficulty in scepticism, absolutely universal, obliterating all truth, all possibility of knowledge, and all existence of whatever kind or character, subjective or objective.

Such being the case, we may unhesitatingly assert, that, at the bottom of all knowledge whatever, there must be found some substantive existences absolutely incapable of rational substantiation, and some propositions absolutely incapable of rational demonstration. Without these it is impossible for man *to reason.*

Any man, therefore, who admits any rational knowledge whatever, does thereby necessarily admit certain undemonstrable propositions, and the existence of certain substantives which he has necessarily taken for granted.

The specific difference, then, between real knowledge and philosophy appears to be this: Real knowledge, or positive science, accepts the ordinary belief of the multitude, and, pursuing it forwards, endeavors to determine its limitations, becoming at every step less and less general. Philosophy, on the contrary, commencing at the ordinary belief of the multitude, pursues its course backwards, endeavoring at every step to become more and more general. The ultimate termination of this course must ever necessarily be, either to accept some propositions as primary and unproven, or to maintain a consistent scepticism, which absolutely obliterates the possibility of rational knowledge. To show how this difference is manifested, we have only to inquire upon what terms the primary substantives of the sciences are accepted by science and philosophy.

The geometrician, for instance, accepts *space*, without the smallest inquiry into its nature. His object is to limit, define, and exhibit the relations of spaces. Philosophy, on the contrary, going backwards, might discourse forever on the nature of space, without eliciting one truth that should be of the smallest importance to mankind. The sister substantive of space, namely, *time*, is also accepted by the man of science, whose only object is to measure it accurately; that is, definitely to determine the limitations of its portions. The physical sciences, again, accept *matter*; and without the smallest speculation as to what matter really *is*, they each, in their several branches, endeavor to determine definitely its various forms, and accurately to specify its manifestations. Philosophy, on the contrary, endeavors to go backwards from the ordinary credence, and to furnish some explanation as to what matter is or is not, for some have attempted to obliterate it altogether.

The two substantives, *space* and *matter*, are sufficient for our purpose. Positive science, accepting space, and pursuing the inquiry *forwards* — investigating first the forms of spaces, and then the necessary relations that exist between those forms — furnishes us with geometry. While by accepting matter, and inquiring only into the forms of its manifestation, and the relations that are observed to exist between those forms, we are, by the exercise of the human reason, at last presented with the sciences of astronomy, mechanics, chemistry, physiology, &c.; where we know not whether most to admire the power and wisdom of God as displayed in the objects themselves, or his goodness in endowing man with an intellect to comprehend them.

Against this, what has philosophy to place in the opposite scale? Starting from the very same point, only pursuing her fancied investigation backwards, what are the treasures she has amassed on her way, and what the results she has presented to mankind? A thousand years of speculation as to whether matter be a substance or a shadow, an existence real or ideal; and, notwithstanding that the most acute minds have devoted no small time to the speculations, not one single hair's breadth of progress has ever been made towards the determination. Every discussion as to the nature of matter or of space, may be raised to-day as well as two thousand years ago; and, for all that we can possibly have reason for anticipating, may be raised at any future period of man's existence on the earth, with just as much and just as little probability of ever terminating in any other proposition than "space is space, and matter is matter."

We conceive, then, that the moment at which philosophy wandered and went astray was, when it attempted to discuss the objective truth or falsehood of the primary credences or convictions of mankind. These primary convictions, in their general form, are at the bottom of all human *knowledge;* but whether human knowledge have or have not an external, real, and objective counterpart, which would remain if man and man's intellect were annihilated, neither philosophy nor any other natural method can possibly determine. Whether *knowledge* be *truth* is (to philosophy) an insoluble mystery; neither has any reason ever been exhibited to the world for supposing that the means of solution are at all within the reach of man.

But if it be impossible for philosophy to solve the question of objective existence, and if all the various sciences accept, without inquiry, the primary substantives of which they respectively treat, what conclusion must we come to as to the character of knowledge? and what object must we allocate to philosophy to constitute it a possible branch of knowledge?

First. All human knowledge, obtained by the natural exercise of the faculties, is real only in so far as it is phenomenal. That is, knowledge, being only a form of *thought*, exists *in the mind*, and it is beyond the reach of the human faculties to ascertain certainly whether the mental propositions which constitute knowledge coincide with actual and external realities. That they do so, is a matter, not of knowledge, which can be rationally substantiated, but of primary, unproven, and unprovable *credence.**

Second. If every portion of what is commonly understood by the objective universe be made the subject of some one particular *science*, (which always *accepts* its primary substantives, and inquires only into the modes of their manifestation,) and if ontological or metaphysical philosophy be rejected from every portion of that object which positive science comes to occupy, then can philosophy no longer attempt to pronounce *à priori* upon what is, or what is not, but must confine itself exclusively to thought, and to thought alone; thereby changing its character from metaphysics to a proper science of *thought*. This, then, we believe to be the true province of philosophy, not to inquire into the truth or falsehood of the primary convictions of the intellect, but to observe and record what those primary convictions are, to enumerate them, to

* The fallacy of philosophic scepticism is, not in viewing knowledge from the subjective point of view, which is in fact a legitimate process, but in supposing that this mode of viewing knowledge entails any consequences whatever affecting morals. Crime may be viewed by the philosopher in its subjective aspect — that is, in the *mind;* and the punishment that follows crime may *also* be viewed in its subjective aspect — that is, in the pain experienced by the criminal. But is the *pain* one single atom less an evil because it happens to be viewed subjectively?

determine the forms of their manifestations, and to pursue with regard to human *thought* the same kind of inquiry that the mathematical sciences pursue with regard to numbers, quantities, and spaces, and more nearly still, the same kind of inquiry that the physical sciences pursue with regard to matter and its manifestations.

One of the most valuable distinctions that has ever been made in philosophy, and one that we believe will ultimately incline mankind to clearer views of the true province of philosophy, is the distinction between the *matter* of knowledge and the *form* of knowledge. This distinction will, we have no doubt, ultimately strike at the root of metaphysical speculation. For what, after all, is ontology? An attempt to construct the universe out of the general convictions of the understanding. Now, let us suppose that the human mind, so far from being an unwritten tablet, formed merely for the reception of impressions, is, as it were, organized up to the highest possible point, so that it universally and invariably stamps a form on those impressions, which form is in nowise dependent on the external objects, but due to the constitution of the mind itself. This form will every where be present in every portion of knowledge. What then? Shall we thence conclude that we may, by some more than usually subtle process of mental analysis, reconstruct a mental universe harmonious with that without us, merely by excogitation? Shall we not rather still adhere to the belief that, be the mind as complex as it may, it could of itself originate not one single iota of knowledge, unless the substantive groundwork of that knowledge were furnished to it from without?* Observation, psychological or sensational, can alone furnish us with *a fact*, and a fact in one form or other must lie at the bottom of every chain of reasoning not purely hypothetical. Let us grant to the utmost possible extent that the form of knowledge is determined by the constitution of the intellect itself; yet the substantive and concrete element, the primary matter of knowledge, whether relating to the *me* or the *not me*, must be derived exclusively from observation, and never can by any possibility be more than guessed at by the mere metaphysician. Ontology, however, has always aspired to determine the matter as well as the form of

* In affirming that *observation* is the origin of all knowledge, we mean the *chronological* origin, not the *logical* origin. The doctrine that makes all knowledge to consist of transformed sensation — in other words, the sensationalist doctrine — is perfectly untenable. It cannot be consistently maintained, even in a conversation that lasts but a few minutes. The sensationalist, whatever he may argue, is under the constant necessity of using terms to which he can assign no physical correlative. He *argues* as a sensationalist, and in so doing exhibits himself an intellectualist. He cannot help it — no man ever could. Sensation, however, is necessary *to call the mind into activity;* and thus all knowledge may be said to originate, not *in* sensation, but *through the sensations.* Were there no sensation, there is no reason to suppose there would be knowledge; but when once there *is* sensation, the mind, from its internal constitution, posits things altogether and essentially distinct from sensation, or from any possible transformation of sensation. It is very singular that sensationalism, which is commonly supposed to lead to absolute *materialism*, does actually lead to absolute *idealism.* Instead of substantiating matter, it obliterates it, and leaves nothing but the phenomenon; the substances, *mind* and *matter*, being both extinguished. — See Morell's *Hist. of Philosophy.*

knowledge, and never till it abandons the vain attempt, can we hope to see philosophy regenerated, and reconstructed, as it may be, into perhaps the most interesting of all human sciences. The form of knowledge, and not the matter, is the true object of philosophy.*

* In saying that philosophy should confine itself to psychology, we do not mean that it should confine itself to the mere record of what takes place in the mind. This is the *natural history* of thought, and the natural history is only the basis of the *science*. Every branch of knowledge has a natural history as well as a science; and if we confound the two, as the Scotch psychologists did, we must either leave a large number of questions unexplained, or dogmatize through thick and thin, and attempt to suffocate the questions instead of answering them. All knowledge is necessarily divided into *real-ology* and *thought-ology*, (if the expressions may pass,) and we maintain that the knowledge of *reals* is *not* the knowledge of thought, and that the knowledge of *thought* is *not* the knowledge of reals. Now, philosophy may take its choice, either to discourse on reals — God, Nature, Man — or to discourse on thought — perceptions, abstractions, relations; but it cannot be allowed *under the same name* to discourse on both, unless that name be coëxtensive with *knowledge*, and embrace all that can be known. If philosophy be a *peculiar*. branch of knowledge, it must, like every other branch, *select its object*, and to that object it must be confined. It is perfectly illegitimate for any science to pretend to discourse on the *subjective* intellect that is in operation. If this be allowed, truth and falsehood are immediately overthrown and blended in one mass of inextricable confusion. Who would allow a geometrician, *as such*, to discourse on the trueness or falsity of the primary axioms of geometry? The only circumstance that renders geometry *possible*, is the subjective truth (necessary and universal) of those axioms, and the circumstance that they are *incapable* of such questioning, and are the essence, the most abstract form, and the universal standard of all geometric truth. If we pretend to make the axiom objective, and to inquire into its truth, we may be philosophers, or any thing else, but most certainly we

We conclude, then, our argument with regard to the combination of knowledge and reason. We mean not that men must combine knowledge and reason, but that the great masses of the unprivileged classes must combine together on the same knowledge, and on the same principles, that they have rationally deduced from that knowledge. It has been said, that "for men to be free, it is sufficient that they will it:" never was there a greater mistake, or one so utterly at variance with the great facts of history. Perhaps no sentiment is stronger in the human breast than the

are no longer geometricians. And so it is with all other sciences whatever, even those that relate to *thought*. If we make thought *objective* for the purpose of studying it, and we *can* only study it by making it objective, we must speak of thought, the *product*, analyze it, classify its forms, and exhibit their relations; but most certainly we have nothing whatever to do with the intellect that is thinking about thought. If we turn from thought, the product, to the intellect that thinks, and wish to know the intellect, then we must make *intellect* objective, analyze it, classify its faculties, and exhibit their relations; but here again, as every where else, we must not confound the object that is thought about with the subject that thinks. The *subjective* intellect can never legitimately be taken into consideration. Philosophy appears to us to wander about without a resting-place for the sole of her foot: first, she speaks of the absolute reality, and then of the absolute idea, and changes backwards and forwards in such a way, that really it requires no ghost to tell us, that questions investigated upon such a methodless principle must ever remain insoluble. If philosophy be as extensive as knowledge, then knowledge is composed of the various scientific and historical branches, with their relations, and there is no *peculiarity* about philosophy. But if, as we imagine, philosophy is a peculiar *branch* of knowledge, it must necessarily select its object, like all other sciences, and if it assume to be the *scientia scientiarum*, then its object is *knowledge* and not *reality*. If its object be knowledge, then

love of liberty. For this men have panted, prayed, fought, struggled, rebelled, and endured every kind of hardship, and every kind of cruelty. And yet they are not free. To be free, it is first necessary that men should know wherein true freedom consists; namely, in the absolute supremacy of equal and impartial law, made without respect of persons or classes, and administered with uprightness and regularity. Nor is this all. True freedom is the very highest point of political civilization; and to suppose that mere *will* can ever lead to that point, is to suppose that men may

to knowledge it must confine its discourse, every speculation about *reality* being altogether illicit. Thus, if philosophy profess to treat of God, it is theology, and must never attempt to discourse on the *idea* of God. All speculations about absolute *ideas* are (however interesting, and however useful) *illegitimate;* they have no more business there than speculations on the *idea* of substance have in treatises on mechanics. And if philosophy select the idea, and not the reality, as its object, it may discourse on absolute ideas, but must refrain from discoursing on theology. This mode of distinctive investigation is the great first principle of method, and the great means of the progression of knowledge; and when the day comes that the separate branches have been completely investigated on a principle of independent inquiry, and the sensationalist has exhausted the world without, and the philosopher the world within, and the Christian doctor has attained to a perfect knowledge of Scripture, the three regions may again blend into *one*, and show the wondrous harmony of the universe — of that creation which came spotless from the hand of the Lord, but has so long exhibited the discord and diversity of sin. Whether that day may come ere the new heavens and the new earth shall be the place of man's abode, we know not, nor have the means of ascertaining; but that the constant progress of man's intellectual perception is towards that final *unity*, we can learn, as certainly as we can learn that the political progress of men is towards a condition of *equality*.

overleap the conditions of their nature, and reach the goal without the struggles of the race. True freedom, however simple in its theory, is the highest, and probably the most complex, form of combined society. It is the whole body of society acting on the principles of knowledge, and carrying truth into practical operation. *Will* can never achieve this.

True freedom supposes *a condition of society* which is incompatible with ignorance and error — a condition negative in its principles, positive in its institution and establishment — a condition that has never yet been attained, even in a tolerable degree, by any nation under the dominion of superstition, and never yet completely attained even by the most enlightened states, — a condition to be attained not by one great tumult, but gradually evolved and perfected with the lapse of years. It is the result and ultimate end of a great progress, which makes its way with knowledge, sometimes advancing with peaceful steps, sometimes overturning the barriers that stand in the way amid the din of revolution. It is the condition of society where *will* is excluded, and law is made on an objective reason, which convinces man's judgment that it is equitable. It is a condition first to be defined in its abstract form by the man of thought, and then to be striven for by the mass of the population; a condition that supposes great advancement and infinite benefit to mankind, but a condition that must be purchased, and purchased only on those terms which are prescribed by the laws of man's constitution.

The political history of our race teaches us that

there are three conditions of society involving a cause on the one hand, and an effect on the other.

The causes are Knowledge, Superstition, Infidelity. The effects, Freedom, Despotism, Anarchy.

Knowledge and Freedom.
Superstition and Despotism.
Infidelity and Anarchy.

Such are the conditions of our nature. Man may make his election of the cause, but God has determined the character of the consequent.

No fact stands out more prominently from the condition of the various nations, or from their history, than that those conditions, and the great actions of men in the figure of society, depend upon *their credences;* that is, on the convictions of their intellect; that is, on the propositions they hold to be true. What makes one nation press ardently forward in the pursuit of liberty, while another sits dead and stupid under the iron rule of the despot? *Thought*, mere thought, impalpable and invisible thought, a something which can neither be seen, felt, nor handled; but which fixes man's destiny, raising him if correct to the dignity and energy of freeman, dooming him if erroneous to vice, degradation, and slavery. The history of the world has to be re-written on a new principle, and this unseen element has to be exhibited as the cause of the condition of the nations. Climate, circumstance, and race may all go for something or for much; but, far more influential than either, is *credence.** What

* Mr. John Macgregor (who, by the way, takes upon him to call a far greater man than himself *a canting hypocrite* — Oliver Crom-

makes Africa slumber on in her barbarous dream of semi-brutality, as if her sons were forever doomed to claim kindred with the beasts of the field? Her credence, her bloody superstitions, her errors of thought. And what makes Asia the perpetual home of despotism, of cruel exaction and licentious tyranny, of fabled wealth to the ruler, and grinding poverty to the culti-

well, to wit) begins his dissertation on the "Natural Resources, &c., of the Nations of Europe," with the following passage: "The geographical position of a country has always been admitted as of the first importance in regard to its prosperity and power."

Mr. Macgregor also informs us, "that the science of statistics is that of *truth;*" but we will undertake to affirm, that the science of statistics never did, and never can, lead to such a doctrine as Mr. Macgregor's. Will any man in the world rank the geographical position of England as so very superior to that of Turkey? or that of North America to that of South America? or that of Prussia and Holland to that of Spain and Portugal? Yet Turkey, South America, and Spain, are going to wreck and ruin; although Turkey was very powerful at one period, and Spain was the first kingdom in Europe. And is the geographical position of Switzerland, without even a seaport, so very superior to that of Ireland? Yet Dr. Bowring's report on Switzerland would lead to the conclusion that the country was *prosperous*, and not desolated by hunger fever. Mr. Macgregor himself states, "with, however, nearly every natural element of power and advantage for commerce, there is scarcely any country in Europe or Asia so ill cultivated as, or where industry is farther in arrear than in, Asiatic Turkey."

The prosperity of a country does *not* depend on its position, but on *the character of its inhabitants*, on their credence, their knowledge, their institutions, and the freedom of their government. The geographical position of the United States has not altered since 1776, yet since that time the country has made a progress unequalled in history. Suppose North and South America were to change *inhabitants*, would the *position* be of any imaginable consequence? Position, indeed!

vator of the soil? Asiatic superstition; that is, the common and every-day thought of the millions who inhabit Asia. And what has fixed the destiny and determined the present position of the countries of Europe? Credence. Why is Spain in a constant struggle between despotism and anarchy? Because the mind of Spain is struggling between superstition and infidelity. Why is Italy worn out? and why is she the home of all that is little and despicable in the eyes of Englishmen? Because her credence has ruined the mind of the population. And why, with every advantage of earth, ocean, and sky, are the fairest portions of the earth, the shores and islands of the eastern Mediterranean, inhabited by degenerate races, who dare not strike one blow for liberty, but lie grovelling in vice, without a thought for the regeneration of their country? Because their credence has degraded them. And why is Russia a vast conglomeration of slave plantations, with one great slave owner for a master? Because the minds of Russians are enslaved by the greater despot — superstition. And why is England the mightiest of nations, with a power and an influence that are felt in every quarter of the globe? Because the mind of England is the most enlightened, and because knowledge has made her powerful. What makes Turkey's weakness and England's strength? Not climate, not geographical position, not any physical advantage to which so much of the difference is usually attributed — but *credence;* the credence of England is correct, and the credence of Turkey is erroneous. Sooner or later men must learn the great fact, that the social and political condition of a nation is absolutely dependent on that nation's credence. Correct credence is knowledge, and knowledge alone is capable of regenerating the political condition of mankind. Change the credence of a nation, and you change the whole current of its future progress. Let the most darkened and benighted spot on earth, the far-away South Sea island, where the fierce idolater could feast on his captive victim, and the unhappy mother could think it no crime to destroy her new-born offspring; where man was, if we may so speak, a demon worse than a beast of prey; let that spot be but visited by the knowledge of the true God, the first great element of truth — let the truth be but received — let the idolater *change his credence*, and you have changed the whole order of society. Even let the truths of the gospel descend savingly but into the hearts of a few, if the truth obtain an intellectual assent with the population, instead of a perpetual record of crime and abomination, we shall see man's reason emancipated, and the whole figure of society transformed, as it were, beneath the miracle-working hand of the Most High.

SECTION IV. — THE USE AND OPERATION OF THE COMBINATION OF KNOWLEDGE AND REASON.

We now turn to the *use* of combination. Why should men combine, and for what object should they combine?

First. There are certain evils which belong to the race of mankind, and which afflict humanity more or less in every quarter of the globe. Some of these evils are of such a nature as to appear under circumstances of extreme aggravation in certain conditions of society; while, in other and better conditions, they are kept under some beneficial restraint by the direct intention and continued effort of society. In the existence of these evils is to be found the reason of combination; and the object of combination is to remove as much as possible, or at all events to diminish, such of these evils as affect the political condition of men, or the condition of men in society.

The first great master evil, and the one to which most others may be traced, directly or indirectly, is the innate corruption and depravity of man, which makes him prefer falsehood to truth,* vice to virtue, and the

* In saying that man prefers falsehood to truth, we do not mean that man's *intellect* prefers falsehood. The intellect, were it not impelled in a wrong direction by the sentiments, would naturally seek truth, and truth only; and, were it left unbiased by the will, would form its propositions regardless of all save the evidence before it. From the complex nature of man, however, and from the corruption of the moral portion of the mind, it happens that propositions altogether unfounded are received as true, apparently for the purpose of filling up the general scheme or chart of knowledge, which must be filled up either with truth or falsehood, but, at all events, filled up. Hence all nations, at one period or other, have had a false religion, and a false scheme of ethics. Whatever metaphysic difficulties assail the question, it is an *historical fact*, that the human race has preferred, and still does, throughout the greater part of the globe, prefer, falsehood to truth on the subject of religion and morality; and a false religion is the source from which

gratification of passion to the enlightened and rational exercise of his natural faculties. Whatever view may be taken of the theological question of natural depravity, we hold it an historical fact of the very first magnitude, and of the most indubitable veracity, that the human race, as such, has always, and in every known region of the earth, "done the things which it ought not to have done, and left undone the things which it ought to have done." With regard to man's *nature*, we shall enter into no disputation; but, with regard to men's *actions*, we view them through the common medium of history, and we hesitate not to see the practice of injustice more or less prevalent in every country of the earth, and, at the same time, to accept that explanation of the fact which is furnished in such plain terms by the words of divine revelation. History informs us that the actions of men are wicked; and surely there can be no absurdity in giving credence to Scripture, when it informs us that their hearts are so likewise. With the depravity of the heart, politics has no concern; but so soon as that depravity comes to manifest itself in action, and to appear in the form of fraud or violence, the necessity of a system of politics is immediately substantiated. Men are wicked, and therefore inclined to do wrong; but they are also rational, and may combine systematically to prevent the wrong from being done.

Among the evils that prey upon humanity, there are some which men inflict upon each other. These may

error on almost all other subjects flows as naturally as water from a fountain. There cannot possibly be any hope of political regeneration so long as a nation adheres to a false religion.

generally be reduced to the class of violence or of fraud; and the prevention of violence and fraud is the first great end of political association. The possibility of violence and fraud naturally originates some kind of government, the character of which appears to be determined much more by the condition of the population as regards knowledge, than by any direct intention on the part of the rulers, or of any body of men whatever.

The evils that would arise from the unrestrained passions of mankind form the general groundwork or reason for the establishment of some rule, order, or government, which the mass of the population, for the most part, acquiesce in, whatever be its character. When a government is established, we have the more or less perfect formation of a state; that is, of an association of individuals supposed to be acting together for their common advantage. [It will be altogether unnecessary for us to go back to the formation of governments amongst nations scarcely emerging from barbarism. The character of such governments is a matter of little or no importance, neither would any change merely in the form of government be attended with any particular advantage. The first great necessity for such nations is the acquisition of knowledge. Give knowledge, and civilization will follow of its own accord, just in proportion as that knowledge is more or less complete, and more or less generally disseminated. We confine our remarks to those nations that have undergone some considerable process of consolidation, and arrived at some definite form of constitution. such as the nations of modern Europe; in each of which we have a government varying in character, according to the moral and intellectual condition of the population.]

The ostensible reason for the existence of a government, we suppose to be "the necessity of preventing individual fraud or violence." Were there no tendency in the individual to fraud and violence, the first great end of political association would cease to exist.

If, then, the government be established for the prevention of fraud and violence, — that is, for the prevention of injustice, — what is the use of that other combination of which we have spoken, namely, the combination of knowledge and reason?

1st. The progress of mankind is a progress from ignorance, error, and superstition, towards knowledge.

2d. Governments being established in the earlier stages of society, — that is, during the reign of ignorance, error, and superstition, — have always, and in every known case, been more or less despotic; that is, have systematically assumed powers to which they were not justly entitled.

3d. The progress of political society is a progress in which these unjust powers have been gradually curtailed and abolished, in proportion as the nation has progressed from ignorance and superstition, and advanced towards knowledge.

The use, then, of the combination of knowledge and reason is (*not* to combine against individual injustice, this being the province of the government, but) to reduce the powers of the government and the laws of the country within those bounds of justice beyond which they cannot be other than despotic.

The first great fact that we learn from history with regard to governments is, that they are all (whatever be their form) despotic in their character during the earlier periods of society, and that they lose their despotic character only when the nation progresses in knowledge, and combines for the advancement of its liberties.

In all the countries of Europe we may observe the powers of the government undergoing a gradual but sure process of curtailment; while, on the other hand, the liberties of the people are expanding in a corresponding ratio, and becoming systematically established by law. In Russia, the process exhibits only the first faint symptoms of commencement; while in England the process is tolerably complete, (as regards personal liberty;) the interval between these two being filled up by the other European countries. The progress of liberty, then, is an *internal* progress, by which the internal constitution of the country is altered and amended.

What, then, is the combination of which we have spoken, as if it were capable of working out the great evolution of liberty and justice?

It is the combination of the nation, or of the enlightened portion of the nation, against the laws of the nation, and against the unjust powers of the rulers.

Liberty is advanced not by the warfare of one nation against another nation, but by the warfare (physical or moral) of the unprivileged classes against the unjust laws, and against the unjust privileges that prevail within the nation itself; and this warfare can only be carried on efficiently by the mass of the population combining to extort those measures that have been theoretically shown to be right, or those measures that on good grounds are presumed to be beneficial.

The common notion almost universally adopted in the earlier stages of society, and still prevalent in some of the countries of Europe, is, that the ruler rules by his own will, as if he were the lord or supreme director of the nation. Instead of laws being made on an objective reason that establishes their *equity*, they are the expressions of the will of those who happen to be in power; and the gradual destruction of this doctrine, with its evil consequences, is the result of knowledge disseminated throughout the population.

When we look back on the history of England, or of any other country that has made considerable progress, we see that all the great changes that have taken place in the political condition of the population have been preceded by changes in the *theoretic credence* of the population, and that the amended order of society has resulted directly from a new and more correct order of thought. And we may also see that these beneficial changes have seldom, if ever, originated with the rulers themselves, but have been extorted from them, sometimes by force, and sometimes by the moral influence that the man in the right has over the man in the wrong.

Without alluding to the explosion of the "divine right of kings," &c., (which enabled the rulers to practise flagrant iniquities without being brought to judicial trial,) we may refer to two modern instances of the combination of knowledge and reason, by which the people of Britain obtained changes of vast extent, by a moral power which overcame the will of the rulers and of the privileged orders, who were linked to support the abuses. We refer to the emancipation of the negroes, and to the repeal of the corn laws.

We have selected these two instances because they represent two great classes — of evils on the one hand, and of argument on the other.

The laws of Great Britain declared that it was lawful for one man to possess another man as his property; and this principle was carried into practical operation by the seizure and reduction to slavery of vast numbers of Africans, who were thenceforward viewed as mere laboring animals, denied education, denied religion, and denied those rights of family which Nature has established as the first of her social laws.

In this negro slavery we have a vast system of fraud and violence, established and continued by authority of the British government; that is, we have the power which had been conferred on the government for the purpose of preventing violence and fraud, turned altogether away from its legitimate exercise, and made the instrument of supporting a system of glaring injustice and flagrant iniquity. We have that greatest of all political evils, injustice, established and maintained by law; that is, in fact, *the despotism of false law.*

Here, instead of the government and the law being the means of *protection*, they give systematic countenance to the injustice; and, by legalizing crime, they deprive the man who is oppressed (the negro) from endeavoring to recover by his own effort the natural rights with which the Almighty had endowed him.

And how was slavery abolished? What were the efficient means that led first to the abolition of the traffic, and afterwards to the authoritative declaration, that slavery should no longer be countenanced by law; that is, that the system itself must cease in the British dominions? Was it by the natural mode? by the method which Nature teaches, when she tells us to resist every attack upon our liberty? Alas! the negro knew little about liberty, and his ignorance was, perhaps, as much the true cause of his slavery as was the color of his skin. What was it that abolished negro slavery? It was the moral influence of knowledge, reason, and religion. The trade had been sanctioned by long use; the interests of the wealthy and powerful were linked to maintain it; the laws of the empire had declared it legitimate, and the government was opposed to its abolition. More than this, not one single man who had the means and the opportunity to make himself heard on behalf of the negro, had one farthing of pecuniary interest in procuring the negro's emancipation. Those who argued had no suffering to impel them, save the suffering of just and generous hearts; no interest to lead them on, save the interests of humanity and the good of the oppressed.

What, then, were the motives and the means that led to so great a political change as the emancipation of a race from slavery?

First. Certain individuals learnt to think aright on the subject, and to give utterance to their thoughts. The battle was then commenced. On the one hand was reason, involving the principles of natural equity; and on the other was *the despotism of the law*, the power of the government, and the pecuniary interests of the wealthy and influential.

Sooner or later, correct thought makes its way, and the more rapidly and surely, the more a nation has abandoned superstition.

The theoretic argument or credence adopted by the advocates of liberty was, "That man is made free by God, and can never be made rightfully a slave by man." The argument in its most essential character was one of mere *justice*, not of economical benefit or prejudice, profit or loss. A moral agitation was commenced, the few were transformed into the many, and the progress of opinion (of *credence*) was such, that every possible argument that could be adduced on the opposite side was brought forth from the lying chambers of selfishness. Every thing in the shape of an argument — every thing that could be made to pass for one, though halt, lame, or blind, was pressed into the service of casuistry, for the purpose of perpetuating injustice.*

* "The question now is only the continuance of this abominable traffic, which even its friends think so intolerable that it ought to be crushed. Jamaica has imported 150,000 negroes in the course of twenty years, and this is admitted to be only one tenth of the trade. Was there ever, can there be, any thing beyond the enormity of this infamous traffic? The very thought of it is beyond human endurance. It is allowed, however, that the trade is infamous, but the abolition of it is resolvable to a question of expediency; and then, when the trade is argued as a commercial case, its advocates, in order to continue it, *desert even the principles of commerce; so that a traffic in the liberty, the blood, the life of human beings, is not to have even the advantages of the common rules of arithmetic which govern all other commercial dealings.*" — *Pitt's Speech*, April, 1792.

The theoretic credence, however, gained ground, and was powerfully aided by a more accurate knowledge of the enormities that Britons practised on Africans under shelter of British law. Authentic information was obtained and disseminated, and at last a great combination of knowledge and reason was brought to bear against the iniquity. Political justice, however, is a plant of slow growth; and years of debate, of contest between truth and falsehood, were necessary, before even the trading in human blood, the buying and selling of man, who was made in the image of the Creator, ceased to receive the sanction of the most enlightened and freest state in the world. And here we cannot fail to remark one circumstance that has almost invariably accompanied every political change which had for its object the destruction of an injustice. We mean the outcry about the *evils that would follow* No sooner has any one, more enlightened or more impartial than his neighbors, insisted on an act of justice, (which, after all, let it never be forgotten, is only *the refraining from injustice*,) than all the evils in the category are immediately prognosticated, as if the doing of God's will were to let loose hell to ravage the earth.*

* To Mr. Alderman Watson belongs the unenviable honor of having presented this kind of argument in a form that may serve as a model for those who seek to prevent change, and as a type of the argument by which economists have so often endeavored to evade justice, by advancing the most glaring absurdities and the most unblushing lies. "Mr. Alderman Watson said, that the natives were taken from a worse state of slavery in their own country to one more mild. The abolition of the trade would ruin the West

When the emancipation of the African was spoken of, and when the nation of Britain appeared to be taking into serious consideration the rightfulness of abolishing slavery, what tremendous evils were to follow! Trade was to be ruined, commerce was almost to cease, and manufacturers were to be bankrupts. Worse than all, *private property* was to be invaded, (property in human flesh,) the rights of planters sacrificed to the speculative notions of fanatics, and the British government was to commit an act that would forever deprive it of the confidence of British subjects. These evils at home were, of course, to be accompanied by others abroad much more tremendous. The West India islands were, of course, to be ruined past all possible hope of recovery; the blacks were to insurge and to destroy the white population; a moral hurricane, ten times more dreadful than the winds of heaven, was to sweep across the Caribbean Sea; blood was to flow like water; the emancipated slave was to celebrate the first moment of his liberty with rape, rapine, and murder; evils unheard of and inconceivable were to astonish the earth; the very heavens were to fall. And why? Because British subjects

Indies, destroy our Newfoundland fishery, which the slaves of the West Indies supported, by consuming that part of the fish which was fit for no other consumption (!); and consequently, by cutting off the great source of seamen, *annihilate our marine*." — *Debate, H. C.*, 1791. Such were the arguments used, and successfully used, in the British House of Commons, for perpetuating a system, the cruelties of which have probably never been surpassed, whether we consider their severity, their extent, or the length of their duration.

were no longer to be permitted by British law to hold their fellow-men in slavery on British ground.*

With regard to the emancipation of the negroes, we have two remarks to offer.

First. The legalizing of slavery was *positive*, the emancipation *negative.*

This distinction we hold to be of importance, as it helps to point out how far legislation is legitimate.

To emancipate a slave is merely to refrain from exercising that power which keeps him in bondage; and when the question of emancipation arises, the question

* To show how correct credence *progresses*, even where we least suspect it, we have only to turn to Fox's speech, April, 1791. After a noble appeal for the suppression of the *trade*, and a full declaration of the natural rights of man — after citing the doctrine of Christianity, that "high and low, rich and poor, are equal in the sight of God," and the fact that slavery has ever disappeared before the progress of Christ's religion — after bursts of noble and generous eloquence on behalf of the negro — he concludes by falling into the common snare, and stumbles at the evils that would follow the *emancipation*. The *trade* he would suppress; and so far his credence was correct; but he had not progressed so far in correct credence (although necessarily flowing from his own principles) as to advocate the suppression of slavery in the West India islands. Mr. Fox said, "that if it were asked whether they meant also to abolish slavery in the West Indies, he would candidly say he was sorry he could not go so far. It was possible for men to be slaves so long as to make it *dangerous* all at once to give them liberty," &c. — that is, dangerous to refrain from oppressing them by force; for the moment the positive and forcible oppression is withdrawn, the man becomes free. What Fox, however, could not see to be correct, the religious community of England saw more clearly; and for half a century a great combination of knowledge, reason, and religion maintained a contest that finally resulted in the purchase of the emancipation at the expense of £20,000,000.

is not one of performing a positive act, but of *refraining* from performing a series of positive acts, by which another is deprived of his natural liberty.

Every moment that a negro is kept a slave, he was so kept by the positive power of the British law, backed by the British arms; for had the negro said, (as he had an undoubted right to say,) "You wish to oppress me, therefore I stand on my defence," the strong arm of the law would immediately have appeared against him, and reduced him again to slavery.

The law was a positive enactment armed with power, and the moment the law ceased to exist, the negro was emancipated, not by the law, but by nature. The law may make a slave; but it is beyond the power of the law to make a freeman. These laws were of course made by human legislators, and the question arises, "Has any human legislator, or body of legislators a right to reduce any individual whatever to slavery?" "Clearly not," is the answer now given by Britons; and if so, then could there never be *justly* a question of *gradual* abolition, for gradual abolition only means, "Shall we continue positively to exercise our power for so many years to come for the purpose of keeping men in slavery?" The only question that can ever be legitimately taken into consideration, with regard to slavery, is *immediate* and *total* abolition, and so of all similar cases where injustice is established or systematically perpetuated by law.

Second. The people of Great Britain were taxed by force for the purpose of paying the planters for their slaves. Theoretically, the Commons imposed the taxation on themselves; but nine tenths of the population have nothing to do with the election of members of Parliament, and, so far as they were concerned, the taxation was *ab extra* — forced on them by a government which they had no voice in electing. We maintain that this act was one of downright injustice and oppression, whatever may be said of its magnanimity.

The planters knew perfectly well that they never had a *moral* right to the slaves, and consequently they could have no moral claim to compensation. Now, the slave laws were not enacted by this generation, and it is admitted that those who enacted them had no possible right to do so. The payment of the twenty millions, therefore, resolves itself into this, "The law of Britain will not cease to lend its aid and its arm to perpetuate slavery, unless the people of Britain pay an immense sum to the planters." The only course that was really legitimate was for the government of Britain to declare that it had no possible right to make or keep men slaves, and at once to expunge the statutes, letting the planters take their chance, at the same time protecting the negroes, as British subjects, born on British ground. A few years ago, the French law authorized gambling houses. Now, will it be maintained that the keepers of those "*hells*" had any just claim for compensation against the laboring population of France? (Or the keepers of those other houses which the law still sanctions?) It was a just, and, as the world goes, a glorious thing for Britain to abolish slavery as it did; but most certainly the laboring man of England, who pays five per cent. on his tea, sugar, and tobacco, to pay the planters, is as surely oppressed and defrauded as was the negro, although not to the same extent. No man in the world, and no association in the world, could ever have an equitable right to tax a laborer for the purpose of remunerating a man-robber; and, although the measure is now passed and done with, we very much question whether some analogous cases will not be cleared up by the mass of the nation ere many years pass over the heads of Englishmen. When the question of landed property comes to a definite discussion, there may be little thought of compensation.

The other instance of a great and successful combination, in which knowledge and reason triumphed over the law, the government, and the privileged classes of the country, was recently exhibited in the repeal of the corn laws.

The case of the corn laws appears to have been this. The seller of the raw material being the official governor of the country, enacted a statute to enhance the price of the manufactured product, thereby obtaining for himself, in his private capacity, a higher price from the manufacturer for his raw material.*

The seller of the raw material was the land owner, and the raw material sold (or rented for a longer or shorter period) was the productive power of the land.

The manufacturer and retail merchant was the farmer, the article manufactured and sold was corn, and the consumer was the mass of the population.

The farmer, in taking a farm, has three great sub-

* See note A, Appendix.

jects to consider: 1st. The quantity of produce. 2d. The probable price of produce. 3d. Amount of rent.*

The first question which the would-be farmer has to answer is, "Can he make a profit by taking land from the land owner, and selling corn to the consumer?" This question he has to answer by a comparison of the whole expense with the whole value of produce. And first, in current agriculture, (that is, agriculture divested of the extraneous expense of draining, building, &c., which come under the head of improvement of the farm, and not mere cultivation,) a given farm is estimated to produce a certain average *quantity* of grain. This quantity is the first item to be considered, as it is the basis of all future calculation. A certain portion of this quantity is requisite for consumption, and the remainder is *marketable.* The marketable portion, being the real merchandise which the farmer buys and retails again, must always be assumed at a certain value *in the terms of the price paid* for it. Whatever price the farmer pays for his marketable corn, he must expect, on the first principle of commerce, to receive a *larger* price (in the same terms) from the consumer. This larger price is the whole ultimate

* The expense of producing (exclusive of rent) we do not take into consideration, as that on any given farm is not subject to such fluctuation as either to "make or break" the farmer. Experimental farmers may, of course, ruin themselves by a bad investment in labor, &c.; but the expense of *improvement* should be distinguished from the expense of current cultivation; and we believe that the latter expense may, in the matter of the corn laws, be assumed as a fixed quantity, although, in reality, varying with the value of money where money wages are paid, and with the value of produce where the laborers are fed.

object of the farmer, and, provided it is sufficient, he is satisfied. To him it makes no possible difference what the *real* price paid or obtained is, provided the proportion between them be such as to leave a sufficient balance in his favor. What he wants is *profit*, and, provided he makes a sufficient profit, it matters little to him how that profit comes.

Our object in making these remarks is to show that the absolute amount of rent paid by the farmer is really a matter of indifference to him. If all the rents in the country were suddenly to be doubled, or increased tenfold, it would not injure the *farmer*, provided the price of his marketable grain were to increase in such a proportion as to leave him the same real profit. His condition would be exactly the same as at present; he would be neither richer nor poorer, nor would he know the difference, except in the nominal value of his rent and produce.

The fluctuating quantities on which the farmer depends are price of grain and rent. Assuming that he has calculated or estimated the average marketable quantity of corn for the currency of his lease, he then depends on the relation between his rent and the price of grain. If the price of grain be high, his rent may be high; if low, his rent must be low, to leave him a sufficient profit, which is all he has to contend for.

This, then, appears to have been the essence of the corn laws. At the price at which corn would be sold in the English market, provided that market were open to all the world, the farmer could only pay a certain rent for land; but, provided all foreign competition was excluded up to a given point, the farmer could afford to pay a much higher rent for land, and yet derive the same real profit.

To a country, however, that produces quite sufficient corn for the consumption of its inhabitants, a tax on foreign corn is of little moment; and it is only when the home produce is insufficient, or barely sufficient for the demand, that the influence of the tax is felt, and then its operation is neither more nor less than starving the inhabitants into paying a higher price than Nature would have supplied them at.

When, however, we turn to the class by whom the corn tax was imposed, and find that, so far from being disinterested legislators, they were in reality the land owners — the wholesale merchants of the raw material — the tax assumes another form, and becomes, in fact, a tax to produce more rent through the pressure of starvation. Not that people would in reality starve, but that they would escape the pressure of starvation by giving *more* for food, which more would pass through the pocket of the farmer into that of the land owner.

The ostensible reason advanced (and perhaps sincerely by some) for the imposition of the corn laws, was the encouragement of agriculture; that is, the putting money into the pockets of agriculturists. But the laws were found at last to be eminently detrimental to the farmer, (on account of the fluctuations of price,) as well as ruinous to another class of which we have not spoken; namely, the manufacturers and manufacturing artisans of the country, who now form the largest portion of the population. The farmer was deluded into the idea of obtaining a high price for corn, and naturally gave, or stipulated to give, a high price for land. The evil was unseen in its real malignity, until it pleased God, in the bounty of his providence, to send such abundant harvests, (1835, 1836,) that the corn tax was defeated. The farmers were then reduced to sell at a natural price, while they had to pay a taxation rent, and of course they felt the weight of that system of legislation which attempted to amend the order of Providence, and on which, with all its nice adjustments, the landed legislators had descanted so wisely.

The low price of corn at that period let the manufacturers into a secret; they obtained great sums of money, and with the money obtained what was of more value to the country — they obtained *knowledge*. They were taught that their commercial prosperity depended, in a great measure, on the low price of corn in Britain; and a very cursory consideration may explain how this happens. Let us suppose that there are five millions of the laboring population, who have a gross income of from 10s. or 12s. to 30s. or 40s. per week. The laborer, out of his income, has to provide the three great requisites — food, shelter, and raiment; and, even at the best and most prosperous of times, his earnings are not much more than sufficient to procure these in decent abundance. Now, let any supposition whatever be made with regard to the rise or fall of wages, and the rise or fall of the price of corn, it is evident that the manufacturers of Great Britain must be injured by a *high* price of corn. For, first, let it be granted that wages rise with the price of corn, (which is certainly *not* the case,) then the expense of manufacturing increases on account of the increase of wages, and the foreign market is supplied with *dear* goods — that is, (for in commerce it is much the same thing,) the foreign sales must decrease on account of the rise in price. The difference of a few pence may stop the sale of a certain description of goods; and stopping the sale stops the manufacture, the manufacturer's profit, and the employment of the artisans. But, second, let us ask how the home market is affected by a great rise or fall in the price of corn, while wages remain nearly the same, as in reality they do, with the majority of the laboring population. Let us suppose that wheat is at 40s. per quarter, and that a laborer's family consumes 4s. worth of bread per week. He then has the remainder of his week's income to dispose of in the purchase of his other requisites. But let wheat rise to 80s. per quarter, and he must then expend 8s. per week for the same quantity of bread that he previously purchased for 4s. We have here a difference of 4s. per week; and the question is, What does the laborer do with those 4s. when bread is cheap? The answer is very simple — *he spends it with the manufacturer.* He wants a coat, and a hat, and shoes, and hose, and shirts; and his wife wants a gown and a bonnet; and the children want frocks and pinafores; and the bed would be the better for an extra blanket or two, and some sheets. Nor is this all: the little furniture of his home wants replenishing; the knives and forks are too few, and the children exceed the spoons. The plates and dishes which were broken in the dear times could not then be replaced; but now, when corn is cheap, visions of a new set flit before the imagination of the thrifty housewife. Perhaps even a clock is purchased, and it is most likely that some addition will be made to the little stock of books. The laborer is at ease in his circumstances, because he has this little revenue of 4s. a week to come and go on. It is true, he must lay it out carefully; but then how different to have it to think about, instead of having it screwed out of him by a crying pressure for food! When he has it, he feels himself a free man; he has a new social and domestic existence; he is a buyer from choice, not from necessity; and the family deliberations as to *how* it shall be spent, give a new interest to the hours he spends at home. All goes on merrily, and old England is worth all the countries under the sun.

Let us take even a moderate estimate of this 4s. a week, and we shall see how vast a sum it amounts to in the course of a year. Suppose that five millions have it to spend, and that those five millions spend £10 with the manufacturers. Fifty millions sterling arising from the difference in the price of corn! Had the corn laws operated according to the intentions of land proprietors, and kept wheat at 80s. in the year 1836, there can be no doubt whatever that they would have deprived the laboring population of fifty millions' worth of goods, and the manufacturers of fifty millions' worth of sales, as directly as if those fifty millions had been wrested by violence from the laborer; but this is one of the facts which the indirect system of taxation is employed to conceal.*

* Since writing the above, we have seen the following notice of

The repeal of the corn laws was effected by a great combination of knowledge and reason — such, perhaps, as we might look for in vain in the history of any other European country. Certain individuals found that their lawful interests were seriously injured by the interference of the enactments, and they resolved to make an effort for the abolition of those enactments. Of themselves they were utterly powerless, and all their individual exertions would have been ineffectual to achieve their end. They had, however, knowledge and reason on their side; that is, they were in possession of certain facts, which led by necessary inference to the conclusion, that the corn laws were eminently prejudicial in their operation, and that, therefore, the corn laws should no longer be allowed to exist. Con-

the "prosperous state of the kingdom," A. D. 1836, in Wade's excellent "British History, chronologically arranged:" —

"At the close of the past, and commencement of the present year, the United Kingdom exhibited unusual signs of internal contentment and general prosperity. With the exception of partial depression of agriculture, all the great branches of national industry were unusually prosperous. In the great clothing districts of Yorkshire and Lancashire, the times were never known to be more favorable. In spite of the great development of the cotton trade, it still continued to expand, and its utmost bounds seemed illimitable. It was the same with the woollen manufacturers of Leeds and Huddersfield, the stuff manufacture of Bradford and Halifax, the linen manufacture of Barnsley and Knaresborough, the blanket and flannel manufactures of Dewsbury and Rochdale; they were all thriving. Even in the silk trade of Macclesfield, Coventry, and Spitalfield there were no complaints, no more than in the lace trades of Nottingham, Derby, and Leicester. The potteries of Staffordshire continued prosperous, and the iron trade in all its branches was unusually flourishing."

scious that they had truth on their side, they came fearlessly before the nation, and staked their cause on the power of truth to convince the mass of the population. They lectured, and published, and spoke, and argued, all for one specific end; namely, to communicate knowledge to the nation, and thereby to make the nation change its credence on the subject of the corn laws. The truth gradually prevailed; that is, was generally disseminated; that is, the same knowledge was received by a larger number of individuals, who naturally drew the same necessary inference. A great combination was formed, such as must ever remain one of the historic glories of Britain and of Britons. It was essentially a combination of knowledge and reason; and well-grounded argument was the only weapon with which it maintained the contest. Far more was involved than a mere change in the economical laws of the kingdom; it was a contest between the two great classes of British society — the unprivileged laborers and the privileged land owners. The privileged classes, almost to a man, were against the change; and they also, on their side, endeavored to establish a combination — a combination of class interest, in which the only available argument was *the pecuniary interest of the order.* The exertions made by the anti-corn-law party to convince the judgment of the nation were prodigious; and never had any political agitation so much the appearance of *instructing*, and so little the appearance of exciting the passions. Instead of the vague harangues of noisy and designing demagogues, there was the sober communication of information which would have been interesting and instructive, even had it been altogether unconnected with the great practical consequence. The nation was convinced at last; and notwithstanding all the influence of the aristocracy, and all the unwillingness of the government, the laws were repealed, and as there is every reason to suppose, abolished forever.

In these two cases (the abolition of negro slavery and the repeal of the corn laws) we have an illustration of some of the great principles which are called into operation, whenever the social condition of the community is ameliorated and rendered more consistent with the dictates of reason and religion.

1st. The only action that is a political crime, is a forcible, fraudulent, or licentious *interference* of one man with another. Such actions, and such actions alone, is it competent for any legislature to prohibit, unless with the free consent of all who are to be affected by the law. Where there is no *interference* there is no political crime, and consequently nothing which the legislature can *justly* prohibit.

2d. Both the slave laws and the corn laws were *à priori* enactments, to prevent men from doing actions which were in nowise criminal. They were positive enactments to restrain and diminish the natural liberty of men who had infringed no law of equity, and who had in no respect injured their fellow-men by force, fraud, or licentiousness.

3d. The legislators of the country were, in their private capacity, extensively interested in the maintenance of the unjust laws; and thus, in opposing their repeal, were using their official influence for their own personal advantage, to the eminent detriment of their fellow-subjects. Those, therefore, who were interested, either as slave owners or landed proprietors, were (according to the principle that a man ought not to be judge in his own cause) incompetent to sit in deliberation on their repeal.

4th. The institutes of nature, as established by God's providence in the world, teach us that a man should labor for the advantage of himself and of his family; but all slave laws are attempts to controvert this principle, and blasphemously to overrule the order of nature, as established by the divine Being. All slave laws *make freedom criminal*, and thus establish an artificial rule of morality, which gives entrance to every kind of political error, and consequently to every kind of political licentiousness.

5th. To transfer corn from one part of the world to another, according to the necessities of the inhabitants, so far from being an act which requires restriction or prohibition, is an act which every man has a natural right to perform for his own commercial advantage, and which no legislature is *competent* to restrict or prohibit, unless it be admitted that the legislature stands in the place of the divine Being, and that all the ordinary acts of life are to be performed only on its supreme permission.

6th. Both the slave and corn laws were enactments to restrict or prohibit men from performing actions which were naturally proper, profitable, and legitimate; that is, to prevent the negro from laboring for his own advantage, and the trader from engaging in legitimate commerce; the repeal of those laws, therefore, did not consist of any positive enactment, but of the removal of legislative interference from actions which in themselves were naturally legitimate. The abolition of those laws, therefore, *was only to allow things to remain as they were established by nature ;* and when the world discovers that God has constituted nature aright, men will have arrived at the first and greatest principle of social science.

7th. The abolition of the slave and corn laws was only attained after a long and arduous struggle; and though horrible iniquities were committed under the sanction of the former, and great national detriment was produced by the latter; and though the nation was long convinced of the propriety of repealing the unjust and injurious enactments, the country was for years compelled to bear the sin of the injustice, and to suffer the national detriment, because the legislators refused to remove restrictions whose nature was infamous, and whose fruits were evil continually.

8th. The legislature of Great Britain, so far from taking the initiative in the repeal of the slave and corn laws, offered every possible opposition to the wishes of the nation; and it was only when the pressure from without became so imperative that further resistance might have been dangerous, that the deliberative assembly of the freest state in the world declared that it was not a crime for a man with a dark skin to enjoy natural freedom, or for a trader to import corn without being subject to a tax so enormous, that it usually operated as a prohibition.

9th. The slave and corn laws were at last repealed, by a process which, we doubt not, will ultimately achieve the repeal of every law which restricts or prohibits actions not naturally criminal — *the wiser and better part of the nation combined against the legislature;* on the one hand were knowledge, reason, and religion; on the other, prescriptive privilege and the will of the legislator.

10th. The two cases which we have adduced represent two great classes of cases, against each of which a particular argument is employed. The abolition of slavery was a question of *justice*, (equity;) the abolition of the corn laws a question of *benefit*, (economy.)

The argument of justice, however it may be extended and illustrated, may always be summed up in this, "Refrain from interfering by fraud or force with another;" and, although no precept can be more in harmony with the dictates of natural reason and with the injunctions of divine revelation, it must be confessed that this argument is among the least powerful to influence men, or to induce them to form their conduct aright. History teaches us, that it is not sufficient for men to know that an action or an enactment is unjust to induce them to abandon the action, or to abolish the enactment; for this they seldom do until the evidence of the evil fruits of the injustice are so superabundant, that no mere sophism can be longer held as an excuse. The argument of justice, instead of being the most practically influential, as it is the most morally valid, is seldom of avail until backed by a knowledge of the economical evils that never in any one case fail to accompany injustice; and though the voice of God and the voice of universal reason may ever be heard proclaiming,

"Do not unto others as ye would not that others should do unto you," it is not until some summation of evil consequences has convinced men of their error, that they abandon their course of lawless selfishness, and allow the constitution of society to remain on the natural footing established by the Creator. And in this we may see the reason why the political progress of mankind has been so slow, and why an extensive knowledge of facts must accompany an admission of principles, before society awakes to the necessity of remodelling their constitution, and returning from the systems established in barbarous ages, to the more simple and equitable system which the eye of reason may read in the constitution of harmonious nature. It is ever immutably and irrevocably *wrong*, that any man, or any body of men whatever, should constrain another man, not a criminal, to labor for the advantage of any save himself and his kindred; yet half a century of agitation was necessary before England withdrew her oppressing arm from the negro; and then the negro was only emancipated by wresting his price from the population of Britain.

The argument of justice may thus be pure or mixed; pure, when it confines itself to the dogma, "Refrain from interference," — mixed, when it collects and exhibits the evil *consequences* of interference. For the operation of the pure argument, all that is necessary is, to ascertain, on good evidence, that there is interference (constraint, restraint, compulsion, or evasion) by force or fraud, and the dogma is in itself, taken alone, a good and valid reason for the cessation of the injustice; for no man, and no majority of men, can possibly, under any circumstances whatever, have a right to interfere by force or fraud with another. But though the pure argument is morally valid, it is seldom or never effectual; knowledge as well as reason must be brought to bear on society, and the practical consequences of injustice must be made apparent, before the mass of men are stimulated to clamor for change. Thus, though the reduction of man to slavery, next to judicial murder, be the highest political crime, the population of Britain — perhaps the most religious, the most humane, and the most just population ever assembled together — could not be brought to emancipate the negro, until the horrors of West Indian iniquity had been portrayed in all their blackness, and until the detestable nature of the system had been so exhibited that men's feelings of humanity revolted, and the abolition became a matter of moral necessity to the nation. The argument of benefit is of another kind. The argument of justice proceeds upon the principle that certain actions may not be done, whatever be their consequences. Grant that slavery was beneficial, in a commercial sense, to Great Britain; that the negroes were better fed and better clothed, &c., in their state of slavery than in their state of freedom, (if such a state be entitled to that name;) grant that all the *physical* advantages were in favor of slavery; yet can slavery never be otherwise than contrary to the law of God, a system of injustice detestable to all good men. Let the consequences be what they may, no man can justly make or keep another man a slave;

neither would any consequences whatever justify the deprivation of that natural liberty with which the Creator endows all men alike. The argument of benefit, however, assumes that the action itself is indifferent; that is, that it has not in itself any such moral character as will enable us to pronounce at once whether it ought or ought not to be done. Let us grant that a tax upon the importation of corn were *beneficial* to Great Britain, and that all the inhabitants freely consented to the imposition of the tax, there is nothing in the tax itself to prevent such imposition, (morally,) but it must stand or fall entirely and exclusively according to the *consequences* that are found to follow in its train.

The main argument advanced against slavery was, that it was unjust; and this argument was impressed on the population by a relation of the many abominations that accompanied the system. The main argument against the corn laws was, that they were prejudicial to the country. They had been established ostensibly for the benefit of the agriculturists; and it was proven, by a superabundance of facts, that they were in no wise beneficial to the cultivators of the soil, while they were notoriously prejudicial to all the rest of the population, except the thirty or forty thousand individuals who hold the nation's land. As a measure of national economy, they had wrought only mischief; they had embarrassed trade, impeded manufacture, repressed industry, and made the laborer pay dear for his food, while they operated at the same time to diminish his employment. In every respect they were bad; and because the nation was convinced they were bad, the legislators, who are ever the last to promote beneficial changes, were ultimately obliged to abolish them, and to leave the supply of the national food to that natural course which is ever found the most beneficial in the end.

Such were two modern instances of the combination of knowledge and reason — spirit-stirring exhibitions of the energies of a noble people warring for the abolition of injustice, and for the emancipation of legitimate industry. Nor, however invidious may be deemed the comparison, can we refrain from asking, what form these agitations would have assumed in any other European country? What country in Europe could have presented the spectacle of a calm and resolute combination of a large portion of the inhabitants against the laws of the land? What country in Europe could have carried on so much agitation without a breach of the public peace, or without riot and confusion? In France, there might have been a revolution; in Italy, a secret combination, bound with oaths on death's-heads and cross-bones; in Russia, an assassination of the autocrat; in Spain, an insurrection only more wicked than contemptible; but in no country, except Great Britain, could such great changes in the law be procured, by the mass of the population first ascertaining what was correct, and then patiently waiting till the power of truth had convinced the legislators that the desired change was good, and for the benefit of mankind. France, notwithstanding all her revolutions, has yet to learn the practical operation of a *moral power;* and until she masters this most essential element of peaceable progression, the sword must be the umpire between the rulers and the ruled.

Notwithstanding the length of our argument concerning the combination of knowledge and reason, we shall not consider it too lengthened, if it in any wise contributes to elucidate those means that must be put in operation for advancing the political progress of mankind. It is the greatest possible absurdity to suppose that all the changes that take place in the political condition of societies are only portions of a routine which, when fulfilled, is to commence again, and again to present the same phases, and the same or analogous phenomena. No; the political progress of mankind is a passage to one definite end, to an ultimatum, to a condition that requires no further change, to a stable system of law that does not demand perpetual deliberation, but only perpetual administration; and the great question for the political world is, "What is that end? What is that system? What is that ultimatum?" What, in fact, is the political condition of society that controverts no principle of reason, and sins against no precept of religion? for this, we may rest assured, is the ultimate end towards which all civilized societies must progress.

No man for a moment can hesitate to pronounce, or to prophesy with unlimited assurance, that the negroes in the slave states of America will ultimately obtain their freedom, and that the serfs of Russia will ultimately be emancipated. The future history of Russia may be read in the present history of France and England; and this, not on account of the propagation of

French or English ideas, but because the substantive element — *man* — is the same in both cases, and his progress in every country in the world must be characterized by the same abstract phenomena, whatever may be the concrete or real occurrences under which the abstract principles happen to be developed.

The progress of the European nations is a progress from serfdom and lordship towards freedom; that is, a progress from inequality towards equality. And although some of the newer states appear to overleap many of the intermediate steps through which the older societies have passed, it must not be forgotten that the newer states have merely borrowed from the older, and adopted such improvements as the new foundation of a state rendered possible under the given circumstances. Thus the North Americans did not, by their declaration of independence, advance themselves from a condition of semi-barbarism to a highly equitable system of political rule; but having to found a new state, they adopted the best principles which had been gradually, and during the course of many centuries, developing in Europe; at the same time making such further progress towards equality as the occasion of commencing a state naturally afforded opportunity for.

The real history of political progress commences only at that period where the maximum of disparity between the various orders or classes begins to be systematically diminished. From this point (which is chronologically different in the various countries) there is a natural course of progress, different in the outward circumstances of its manifestation, but essentially the same in its abstract characters, in every country that achieves civilization. The essence of this progress is the gradual emancipation of the rights of the serf or unprivileged laborer, and the corresponding diminution of the privileges of the lord. Now it may be observed, that the great revolutions which take place in the earlier portions of this progress are physical force revolutions; — changes brought about by the sword, because there are no other means sufficiently powerful to effect them. Nor is it difficult to see why this must be the case. In the earlier stages of society, force and privilege rule — not reason and equity; and as those who have the privileges will not abandon them, those who suffer the oppression must resort to the only influence whose authority is acknowledged. Were the privileged classes to admit reason as the umpire, there would be no necessity for force revolutions; but as the changes come to be necessary, they must be achieved by such means as will affect them, however undesirable it may be that such means should be necessary. We can have little hesitation in asserting, that the changes brought about in the political condition of the people of France by the first French revolution, were imperatively necessary; that is, that the condition of France was such that those changes must take place, independently of the mere will of any individual, because such changes were the necessary consequences of such a condition. The means, to a certain extent, might be within the control of the actors; but the end — the change in the political condition of the people — must have followed from the operation of those general laws that regulate the political progress of mankind.*

When, however, a nation has made some political progress, and its despotism has become relaxed; or, in other words, when some degree of liberty has been attained by the mass of the population — a revolution by physical force (which is always attended with lamentable evils) may be obviated or rendered unnecessary. Where liberty has made a real progress, *knowledge* must have made a real progress; and where knowledge has progressed, reason becomes as powerful an agent as force, and one which ought ever to be chosen, if the alternative be in our choice.

To conclude our argument with regard to the combination of knowledge and reason, we lay down the following propositions: —

1st. On the sure word of divine prophecy, we anticipate a reign of *justice* on the earth.

2d. That a reign of justice necessarily implies that every man in the world shall, at some future time, be put in possession of all his rights.

3d. That the history of civilized communities shows us, that the progression of mankind in a political aspect is, from *a diversity of privileges* towards *an equality of rights.*

4th. That one man can have a privilege only by depriving another man, or many other men, of a portion of their rights. Consequently, that a reign of justice will consist in the destruction of every privilege, and in the restitution of every right.

* See note B, Appendix.

5th. That, under the supreme direction of divine Providence, man is the agent employed in working out his own political well-being.

6th. That man cannot work out his political well-being unless he knows wherein that well-being consists.

Knowledge, therefore, is necessary to enable man to work out his political well-being.

7th. That men must *know* correctly before they can *act* correctly.

8th. That the political well-being of mankind involves two things — correct knowledge and correct action. Correct action is *knowledge carried into practical operation.*

9th. That the political regeneration of mankind is dependent on the acquisition and promulgation of political knowledge.

10th. That in the laws which should regulate man's political action, there is a truth and a falsehood, as much as there is a truth and a falsehood in matters of geometric or astronomic science.

11th. That the political condition of men can never be what it ought to be, until men have acquired the requisite knowledge; that is, until they have perfected political *science*, and reduced it to the same form and ordination as any of the other sciences.

12th. That, with the perfection of political science, there will necessarily follow an amended order of political action, and consequently an amended condition of society.

13th. That political knowledge is divided into two distinct branches. *First.* A sensational branch which furnishes us with the facts of man's condition, and the actual results of human action. *Second.* A rational branch, which furnishes us with the principles that ought to regulate human action.

The first is political economy; the second is politics, or the science of equity.

14th. That the actual political condition of no country in the world is the practical illustration of the propositions of political truth. Consequently, that the actual political condition of every country in the world requires to be revised and amended.

15th. That improvements in the political condition of a country are made exactly in proportion as the truths of political economy and political science are reduced to practice.

16th. That in every country there are privileged classes who have more power or more property than they are justly entitled to, and unprivileged classes who have less power or less property than they are justly entitled to. That the *difference* between these two classes has been undergoing a gradual but sure process of diminution. This *fact* we learn from history.

17th. That the further progress of the diminution in the difference between the privileged and unprivileged classes, may be surely anticipated as the continuation of a process that has already been going on for centuries.

18th. That the absolute equality of men in all political rights is the ultimate end of political progression. That so long as there is not absolute equality of political rights, there is the constant element of further change, and consequently good reason for anticipating further change.

19th. That while a single individual may or may not determine his actions according to his knowledge, (for man is erring,) the constitution of humanity *in the mass* necessarily determines, that wherever knowledge is obtained, systematically ordinated, and generally diffused, an amended order of action will invariably result.

20th. That the theory of political *progress* is, —

1. The present condition is felt to be grievous, and seen by the intellect to be partial and unjust.

2. The present *condition*, when translated into *language*, furnishes a proposition which will not bear the investigation of the reason, and which is consequently rejected as superstitious or erroneous.

3. With the condemnation of the proposition, of which the present condition of society (at any given period) is only a real exemplification, there necessarily follows the condemnation of that condition, and a desire for change is necessarily generated.

4. But, in course of time, a new proposition is discovered or suggested, and this proposition, if it will stand the investigation of the reason, is posited as *true*, that is, classed as a portion of *knowledge*.

5. The proposition which is *true*, is then translated into a practical rule of action, and from this practical rule of action there would necessarily result a certain *condition of society* different from that condition which had been condemned as erroneous.

6. The new condition of society is then posited as an end to be attained, as a thing to be striven for, in a free country by the power of well-grounded argument

and social combination, and under a despotism by the power of the sword and the convulsion of revolution.

7. But as the old condition necessarily involves the interests of *some* parties, (placemen, slave owners, land owners, for instance,) the transition from the old condition, which was erroneous, to the new and amended condition, is always the cause of a social struggle between the partisans of the old condition and the partisans of the new.

8. This social struggle may assume two forms, according to the nature of the question in dispute, and according to the character of the political institutions of the country where it takes place. (1.) If change be sought in a country where there are no legal and constitutional means whereby the masses of the population may obtain that change, the sword must necessarily be resorted to, and a physical force revolution, so far from being a *crime*, is one of the highest political *duties* of man.* (2.) If, on the contrary, the change

* We must distinctly reiterate that we speak only of *political duty*, whose *only* rule is the *law of justice*, as developed in the propositions of political science. Man's *religious* duty we do not profess to teach. Politics has this world, and this world alone, for its sphere of action; and the sword (that is, *compulsion*) is the instrument whereby all should be compelled to adhere to the strictest rules of equal and even-handed justice. Justice neither gives nor forgives, bears nor forbears. Religion, on the contrary, introduces a higher and a divine principle of action, which may enjoin a man to refrain from the forcible assertion of his rights, and rather to bear an ill than to redress it by the sword. Man, as man, is universally bound by the laws of justice, and may universally carry those laws into operation; but man, as a Christian, is bound by the laws of Scripture, and must regulate his conduct by the precepts of divine revelation.

be sought in a country that has attained to liberty of discussion, a free press, a tolerably extensive representation, &c., (that is, where *deliberative judgment* and not mere *will* rules,) the sword (always an evil, though sometimes necessary) may be superseded by the moral force of truth. Knowledge disseminated will *convince* the masses, and when the masses are convinced, they will *combine*, and when they combine, the change, sooner or later, will follow as a necessary consequence.

9. We have said, however, that the *nature of the question*, as well as the *character of the political institutions*, may determine the character of the social struggle. A country may be possessed of much freedom, and yet there may remain some questions which moral force is incapable of deciding. The interests involved may be of such magnitude, or the questions may entail such radical changes in the very constitution of the state, that no legal means whatever may exist for bringing about the change. When, therefore, the mass of the population have resolved that the change shall take place, and there exist no legal means for effecting it, or when those in official authority positively refuse to make the change, even when its necessity is apparent to the nation, the sword must be the umpire as between two parties who have severed all political connection, and are openly at war.

10. But even where a temporary appeal to the sword may be requisite, because there are no other means capable of removing the barriers that stand in the way of political *progress*, the sword is the mere *instrument* employed to effect a change which could not be effected without its aid. Where knowledge has ex

hibited the malignant character of the present condition, and reason has shown how that condition may be amended, the change *must* come as a necessary consequence of man's constitution. It is not in the power of man to prevent it; for he is as much bound by the laws which regulate his intellect and his actions as he is by the laws which regulate the condition of his bodily frame. Knowledge does *necessarily* produce change, as much as heat necessarily produces change; and where knowledge becomes more and more accurate, more and more extensive, and more and more generally diffused, change must necessarily take place in the same ratio, and entail with it a new order of society, and an amended condition of man upon the globe. Wherever, then, the unjust interests of the ruling classes are required to give way before the progress of knowledge, and those ruling classes peremptorily refuse to allow the condition of society to be amended, the sword is the instrument which knowledge and reason may be compelled to use; for it is not *possible*, it is not within the limits of man's choice, that the progress of society can be permanently arrested when the intellect of the masses has advanced in knowledge beyond those propositions, of which the present condition is only the realization.

21st. We posit, finally, that the acquisition, scientific ordination, and general diffusion of knowledge, will necessarily obliterate error and superstition, and continually amend the condition of man upon the globe, until his ultimate condition shall be the best the circumstances of the earth permit of. On this ground we take up (what might in other and abler hands be an argument of no small interest, namely) *the natural probability of a millennium*, based on the classification of the sciences, on the past progress of mankind, and on the computed evolution of man's future progress. The outline alone of this argument we shall indicate; and we have no hesitation in believing, that every one who sees it in its true light will at once see how the combination of knowledge and reason must regenerate the earth, and evolve a period of universal prosperity, which the divine Creator has graciously promised, and whose natural probability we maintain to be within the calculation of the human reason.

CHAPTER II.

ON THE THEORY OF MAN'S INTELLECTUAL PROGRESSION.

SECTION I.—THE ORDER OF THE SCIENCES.

1st. THE sum of all things which man can *know* is circumscribed in quality, although in each quality there may be combinations of indefinite extent. That is, there are only so many *possible sciences*, although each science, in its own department, may be pursued indefinitely.

2d. The sciences are capable of being *classed* on a system which is not arbitrary.

3d. The *discovery* of the sciences as an historical fact is correlative with the scheme of classification. The *classification* is a mere process of the intellect, whereby the sciences are arranged in a certain order, according to a principle. The *discovery* of the sciences is an historical fact, extending over many centuries. We assert that the order of discovery has been correlative with the order of classification.

4th. In the order of discovery, we are at a certain

point, or at a certain number in the series, according to the scheme of classification.

5th. There is, therefore, the strongest ground for believing that the future sciences will be discovered and reduced to ordination in the same order that they stand in the scheme of classification.

6th. Correlative with the *sciences* are the *arts*.

The sciences are *knowledge*, the arts are *action*.

7th. With the discovery of the sciences, there follows invariably a new and amended order of *action;* that is, the *arts*, or the products of human activity, continually improve with the progression of the sciences. [The word *art* we use not in its restricted and partial sense, as applying more particularly to the *fine* arts, but in its general sense, as signifying the systematic products of human activity. The fine arts are, to a great extent, the gift of the individual, and consequently are so far independent of science.]

8th. The sciences are classed *on their complexity*. To determine the position of a science in the scheme of classification, we have only to ask how many substantive concepts does it necessarily involve; that is, with how many *nouns-substantive* can it be made and expressed.

9th. The order of the sciences is as follows: —

1. The mathematical sciences.
2. The force sciences.
3. The inorganic physical sciences.
4. The sciences that treat of vegetable organization.
5. The sciences that treat of animal organization.
6. The sciences that treat of man and his functions.

Let it be remembered that *science* is not a *reality*,

but only a form of *thought*. Science exists in the mind, and in the mind alone; it is the mind's mode of viewing reality.

The realities are matter and mind.

Let any portion of matter be subjected to our investigation, and the mind, from the necessary laws of its constitution, *abstracts* the qualities of that portion of matter, the one from the other, and then investigates the laws of those abstractions.

The laws of those abstractions constitute the mathematical sciences.

These abstractions form the much-decried (and much less understood) *categories*, under which all scientific knowledge must range itself.

These categories are for the mathematical sciences—

1. Identity. What *is* A?
2. Equality. What *is* A *part* of?
3. Number. How *many* parts?
4. Quantity. How *much* is each part?
5. Space, (position, extent, direction.)
6. Force, (classed especially hereafter.)

And each of these *primary and undefinable* abstractions, or substantive concepts, furnish us with a distinct science.

The rational process of thought in every science is *subjective*, and does not require to be taken into consideration. The abstract sciences arise from the application of the rational process of thought (*subjective*) to the above concepts, which are the *objects* of the sciences.*

* Anterior to all reasoning whatever, there is the ontological necessity, or *necessary form of thought*, which precedes all science.

Every *object* in every department of human thought may and must be considered under three aspects.

1st. Existence. 2d. Relation. 3d. Function.

All that man can know of any thing whatever comes under one of these heads.

1st. The thing; 2d, its condition; 3d, its function; and to these three answer the three processes of the mind.

1st. Apprehension. 2d. Classification. 3d. Reasoning.

When, therefore, the *categorical concepts* are apprehended by abstraction, the *second* process is the *classification of the forms* of the concept, and the *third* process is *reasoning*. In every science, therefore, we have classification and reasoning; and we have only

The most universal *form* of science is logic, or *syllogistic*, in which we have the *blank* form into which the mathematical sciences place numbers, quantities, and spaces. Logic is the first form of *reasoning;* which reasoning in the mathematical sciences is called *calculating*. But anterior to reasoning, there is the mode of the substantive terms, and the mode of the propositions which are to enter into reasoning; and these modes are determined by ontology or metaphysic, which furnishes the *axioms* or self-evident truths. These axioms are taken as subjectively true in the sciences, but ontology considers them first as objective. Thus ontology pronounces nothing whatever on the *reality* of being, but on the *mode of being in thought.* Ontology, then, divides substantive thought into substance, attribute, cause, effect, necessary existence, contingent existence, power, function, &c.; and when the *mode* of these has been determined, these substantives are transformed from objective consideration into subjective use. Science exists in the *mind*, and thus when forces, for instance, function in the mind, they function through the laws of ontological classification: without ontology there could be no science whatever.

to ask *what* do we classify, and *with what* do we reason, to determine the name and the nature of the science. The most ultimate abstraction which the human intellect can form, is the noun-substantive in its generic character without attribute. It therefore is the primary and fundamental element of science, which, by the addition of attributes or *predicates*, shall become the substantive element of any science whatever. We assert, then, that the *first possible predicate* that we can attach to the noun-substantive, in its *generic* character, is *Identity;* the *second*, *Equality;* the *third*, *Number;* and so on.

Correlative with the course of nature and of thought (or knowledge) is the course of language; and here we have the same exhaustive triplicity, beyond which it is impossible for us to go.

Apprehension furnishes us with *the name*, classification with *the proposition*, and reasoning with *the syllogism.* The name, the proposition, and the syllogism include every thing that can be expressed as science.

We have, then,—

The course of nature.

1st. The thing. 2d. Its condition. 3d. Its function.

The course of knowledge.

1st. The concept. 2d. Its classification. 3d. Reasoning.

The course of language.

1st. The name. 2d. The proposition. 3d. The syllogism.

The concept is the thing (ens) apprehended by the intellect.

The name is the expression, in language, of the concept, and consequently of the thing.

Classification is the apprehension of the condition of the thing, in which are included all its *quiescent relations;* and the proposition is the expression, in language, of that classification.

Reasoning is subsequent to propositional knowledge, and is the process whereby a new proposition is made to evolve from two anterior propositions.

The syllogism is the complete expression, in language, of reasoning; and both are correlative with all the active functions of real nature.

Were man incapable of reasoning, he might apprehend all the realities of nature, and classify all on the most perfect system of ordination; but never, by any possibility, could he explain and *calculate the functions* of realities. Every function is *active*, and every action involves an agent, (or *cause;*) and were man not endowed with the intuitive principle of causation, all motions, combinations, functions, in a word, all *changes*, would immediately become inexplicable, and the universe would forever remain a vast enigma.

The actual constitution of the human intellect is as absolutely necessary to all *science*, as is the existence of the realities of which the sciences respectively treat.

Such, then, are the *general* characteristics of all the sciences, that is, of all the true sciences that involve functions and reasoning; for the so-called sciences that do not involve functions and reasoning (descriptive botany, zoölogy, &c.) are mere classification, and not sciences. The general form of scientific knowledge, then, is A, — the name, the concept, the thing.

A is B, — the proposition, the classification, condition, or relation of A.

B is C, — the classification, condition, or relation of B.

Ergo, A is C, — the consequent of the two anterior propositions. The whole forms the syllogism or reasoning, which is the expression of the *function* of realities.

Let us now turn to the formation and growth of the abstract sciences.

Let A, B, and C be called *terms;* and, as nomenclature is at first purely arbitrary, these terms may be made to stand for any thing we please.

The *first*, most simple, and most elementary form of reasoning, is reasoning in identity, or *with* terms of which identity (or its opposite, non-identity) is predicated.

A is B; B is C; *ergo*, A is C.

A is B; B is not C; *ergo*, A is not C;

where the terms are *singular*, is the very simplest form of all reasoning, and consequently the most general and least specific form of all science whatever.

The *second* form of reasoning is reasoning *in* equality, or *with* terms declared to be *equal* (or its opposite, *unequal*) to each other.

When we reasoned in identity, the terms were incapable of division; but when we reason in equality, the most general form of division is introduced, and our terms are now divided into *whole or parts.* We have therefore become more specific, and can say, *the whole of* A, *part of* A; the whole of B, part of B; *e.g.*, —

The whole of A is equal to part of B.

The whole of B is equal to part of C; *ergo*, the whole of A is equal to part of C.

The *third* form of reasoning is reasoning in *number*, or reasoning with terms, which are not merely divided generally into whole or parts, but into parts that have been specifically numbered. A is now divided, not merely into whole or parts, but into 1, 2, 3, 4, 5, 6, &c., parts.

Reasoning in identity and in equality is what is termed logic, although in logic there are *two* sciences; the one the science of identity, the other the science of equality. The science of number is called arithmetic, and is nothing more than logic with the terms divided into numbers.

The *fourth* form of reasoning is reasoning in quantity, or reasoning with terms which are not only numbered, but which have a *quantity* attached to each of their parts. In arithmetic, all the units are supposed to be absolutely equal to each other; in algebra, on the contrary, the units are capable of various magnitudes.*

Our terms are now divided into numbered parts, which have quantity attached to them; let us now add a new predicate to the quantities, and a new science arises.

The *fifth* form of reasoning is reasoning in *space*—

* Quantity and number are frequently confounded with each other, and algebra has been termed universal arithmetic. They are essentially distinct, inasmuch as arithmetic starts from the unit, which is indivisible, and the number continually increases with the repetition of the unit. Quantity, on the contrary, starts from infinity, which is divisible *ad infinitum*, the quantity diminishing continually as we increase the number of the parts. Number and quantity are in the inverse ratio of each other.

geometry. What were before only *quantities*, have now become quantities of space; and the laws of position, direction, and extent constitute the *fifth* science.

The *sixth* form of reasoning is reasoning in *force;* and our terms, becoming more and more specific with the addition of each new concept, have now become *forces.*

Such is the necessary order of the mathematical sciences.

1st. Logic; which really includes *two* sciences.

3d. Arithmetic; that is, logic applied to units or number.

4th. Algebra; that is, arithmetic applied to quantities.

5th. Geometry; that is, algebra applied to space.

6th. Statics; that is, geometry applied to force.

In this order, the mathematical sciences must necessarily be classed, and in this order the mathematical sciences must necessarily be discovered. Ten thousand men originating the mathematical sciences by a process of independent investigation, would necessarily discover them in this order; and were ten thousand worlds, peopled with human beings, to go through the process of making anew the mathematical sciences, every one of those human races would pass through the same intellectual course, and evolve the abstract sciences exactly in the same necessary order. The constitution of human reason forbids that it should be otherwise; one science being impossible until its antecedent is so well known as to be capable of subjective operation. Thus, unless the laws of identity are known, there can be no investigation of the laws of equality; and until the laws of equality are known, there can be no investigation of the laws of number; and until arithmetic is known, there can be no investigation of the laws of quantity; and until the laws of quantity are known, there can be no investigation into the relations of spaces; and until geometry is known, there can be no statics.

But the mathematical sciences are abstract, *à priori*, and deductive; their principles are not principles of observed truth, but of rational necessity; they emanate, in their scientific character, not from the operations of nature, but from the operations of mind; *sense*, at the *utmost*, furnishes only the subject matter from which the intellect derives the element, — the one noun-substantive, of the science; while all the propositions, and all the reasonings, and all the far-off conclusions, are furnished by man's rational mind, as exclusively as if matter had no existence. And these mathematical sciences form the abstract preparation of man for the acquisition of real or physical knowledge. Without the mathematical sciences, there can be no physical science — there may be classifications, facts, propositions innumerable; but science, which involves the syllogism, there never can be till the abstract sciences are so far advanced as to be capable of subjective application to the real facts of nature.

Let us now make an observation on the method by which one science grows out of another, by the introduction of only one single new concept or substantive idea.

For want of better names, (at present,) we shall

call the sciences of identity and equality simple and compound logic.

In simple logic the rational process of the intellect is *subjective*, and the terms (of which nothing is predicated except identity; for instance, A is B, B is C) are *objective*.

In compound logic the terms have a new predicate; they are no longer *identicals*, but *equivalents*, and simple logic is now subjective, (that is, *in operation*,) while the equivalents are objective, that is, *operated upon*.

Logic being the first, most general, and most abstract of all the sciences, is universally *applicable ;* it may be applied to every subject of human thought.

Logic is the universal *form* of all science; it is the general formula or expression of science. The mathematical sciences are only *logic*, with numbers, quantities, spaces, or forces for the *terms ;* and the physical sciences are only logic, with physical realities for the terms. The *form* remains universally the same; and the progression of the sciences, or the advance from one science to another, consists in adding predicate after predicate to the terms, and thereby rendering them continually more complex. The *form* remains exactly the same; but in the mathematical sciences we *commence* with the major and minor propositions, and thence *deduce the consequent.* In the physical sciences, we first commence with the consequent and minor proposition, and thence *infer the major.* When the major is inferred, we can then reason deductively, as in the mathematical sciences.

Let us therefore *apply* logic to numbers; that is, instead of our terms being merely *equivalents*, let us make them numbers, and every proposition that was true in logic is now true with regard to numbers; that is, we create arithmetic, which is nothing more than logic applied to numbers, and in which logic is subjective, and number objective. Having made arithmetic, let us *apply* it to quantities, and we have algebra where arithmetic is subjective, and quantities are objective; arithmetic being the process of operation, and quantities being the substantives operated upon. Let us now *apply* algebra to space, that is, to *positions, directions, extents,* and geometry is originated. In geometry, algebra is subjective, and *the forms of space* are objective.

Let us now *apply* geometry to force, and statics is originated where geometry is subjective, and forces are objective.

In the above sciences, not one single idea has been introduced that requires sensual observation, and all the *operations* have been operations of the mind.

Let us now apply the above sciences to the substantives and operations of real nature, and the physical sciences arise one after another in a similar order of complexity.

In statics, the whole question was, whether the forces did or did not neutralize each other at a given point; but nothing was said as to the consequences if they did not neutralize each other.

Let a new substantive concept be introduced, and let the consequence of force, which has not been neutralized, be *motion.*

Let us remember, that in every department of knowledge we have to consider, 1st. The thing. 2d. Its condition and relations. 3d. Its function.

The six sciences of which we have spoken, treat only of quiescent conditions and relations; and when applied to the realities of nature, they apply only to the quiescent conditions and relations of those realities. But the realities of nature have functions, and those functions form the groundwork of the physical sciences.

In the transition from the abstract sciences to the physical sciences, it is usually supposed that we overstep a broad line of demarcation, about which there can be no possible mistake. It is usually advanced, that in the one class of sciences we have nothing but *abstractions* and their necessary relations; while in the other class we have tangible or visible realities — good solid *matter*.

Such a mode of viewing the sciences is as clumsy as it is empirical, and calculated only to satisfy those who (however deeply versed in the specialities of any one particular science) have never turned their attention to the relations of the sciences among themselves.

The transition from the abstract sciences to the physical sciences is not the abrupt leap so commonly supposed; it is a gradual transition, that is, a transition *step by step*, in which the step that lands us on the real universe is neither greater nor less than any of the previous steps that had conducted us from one science to another; or if, indeed, it can be called greater, it is only greater in a gradual ratio of increase, which might be already observed to pervade the abstract sciences. The *difference* between the sciences may be viewed as gradually increasing; but we maintain that, if this view be taken, the increase of the *difference* is in a progressive ratio, and that there is no such thing as stepping out of one region (the region of the mathematical sciences) into another region, (the region of the physical sciences,) by a passage that brings us into a sphere altogether dissimilar. So long as mere *classifications* are called sciences, there can be no just views of science, and consequently no just views of the relations of the sciences to each other. Classification, wherever it may be found, and to whatever it may refer, is only one of the preliminaries of science; and it is only when we can *reason*, that is, deduce a new proposition from propositions already ascertained, that science has properly commenced.

Let us, then, inquire what is the step by which we pass from the mathematical sciences to the physical sciences. Our *terms* from equivalents become numbers, and from numbers become quantities, and from quantities become spaces, and from spaces become forces. Force *involves* space, quantity, number, equality, and identity; but it does not involve matter. As a real fact, we may have no force without matter; but in logical analysis force may be considered, and may be reasoned with quite independently of matter. In statics, then, our terms were forces, and the question was, Do the forces neutralize each other, or do they not?

Now, every portion of matter must be considered, like every thing else, under the three phases. 1st. Existence; 2d. Condition and relation; 3d. Function. And the physical sciences, properly so called, treat of the *functions* of matter.

What, then, is the simplest and most universal function of matter? for this is the criterion by which we recognize the first physical science.

The simplest and most universal function of matter is *motion;* the science of motion, therefore, is the first, the simplest, and the least specific of all the physical sciences.

Let us now examine the step that leads from *force* to *motion.*

It is evident that all the physical sciences must be based on the observation of the existence, condition, and function of the real matter with which man is acquainted; and that every real motion must be the motion of some one particular portion of matter. But every portion of matter has a certain number of *accidents* attached to it; that is, has a number of *predicates,* which are quite superfluous in treating of motion, and which, consequently, must be *abstracted.* Color, density, chemical composition, &c., &c., must all be reserved for future consideration, until the most general laws of motion are discovered.

In statics our *terms* were forces, and the question was, Did or did not the forces neutralize each other?

Let us consider the simplest form of motion; and as a physical body would involve a number of predicates, let us take only the essential one, namely, the one that is absolutely necessary to the formation of a new science. In statics we had no motion; and as every motion requires a something that shall move, let that something be (not a planet nor a portion of real matter, both of which are as yet much too complex) but *a point,* with no other physical predicate than that it is *movable.*

Our term has now become a *movable point*, and the *forces* which in the previous science were objective, now become subjective; that is, the laws of force which were to be *discovered* in the previous science, are now to be called into actual operation for the purpose of evolving a new science, which, in its turn, will again be called into subjective operation for the purpose of evolving another new science, and so on till the whole series of the real sciences is completed.

With forces acting on a movable point, all that we can treat of is the *direction* and *extent* of the motion, with the *position* of departure, the *positions* of transit, and the *position* of arrival; that is, the three substantives of geometry, *position*, *direction*, and *extent*, exhaust all that can be discovered until a new concept is introduced.

Hitherto the concept *time* has not been taken into consideration. As *space* is the necessary condition of the existence of matter, so is time the necessary condition of the functions of matter. *Space* is the necessary condition of *statical* science; *time* is the necessary condition of *dynamical* science.

Let us, therefore, add *time* to the motions whose directions and extent have been previously treated of, and we immediately add the laws of *velocity;* that is, the relation between time and space.

The science of motion (dynamics) brings us to the verge of the physical sciences.

We have said that the functions of realities constitute the bases of the physical sciences. Let us, then, ask, What is involved in *a function?*

We hold the principle to be absolutely universal,

that, "wherever man observes a change, there he infers a cause." A function, then, is necessarily composed of three items. 1st. A cause; 2d. An object; 3d. An operation, or phenomenon. The cause is the agent, the object is the thing operated upon, and the phenomenon is the change in the condition or relation of the object.

But we have stated that *reasoning* is correlative with *function*, and reasoning is expressed in language by the syllogism. In the syllogism, therefore, we must find a correlative triplicity answering to the component items of the function.

The function gives us the cause, the object, and the phenomenon; and, answering to these, the syllogism gives us,—

1st. The major premiss; 2d. The minor premiss; and, 3d. The conclusion, or consequent.

In the mathematical sciences we have, *given* the major and minor premises to find the conclusion; in the physical sciences (*while they are in process of discovery*) we have, *given* the minor premiss and conclusion to find the major premiss. But when a physical science *is* discovered, that is, when its facts have been generalized in such a mode as to cast aside dispute, we are then enabled to reason deductively, in the same manner as in the mathematical sciences; and so long as a science is incapable of this deductive reasoning, it is only undergoing the process of discovery.

In the physical sciences, all that we can *observe* is, 1st. The condition of the object; and, 2d. The phenomenon. The *cause* is forever hidden from sensual observation, and is only apprehended by the reason.

proposition, or a series of propositions, or even a syllogism; but the final result in every case is, that the whole are at last assembled into one syllogism, however extensive, and however complex may be the character of the premises.

Those who are familiar with logic, (and every one ought to be so,) will at once observe that B is the middle term of the syllogism; and consequently the problem of the physical sciences is to discover the nature of that middle term that will connect the condition of matter, or the *circumstances* of matter, with the phenomena manifested in those circumstances.

Now, it will be observed, that in nature we find no proportions, ratios, squares, roots, forces, &c., &c.; these are all mental abstractions; yet these are the great middle terms of the physical sciences that enable men to reason of the effects of new combinations. No man, for instance, ever *observes* "the inverse ratio of the square of the distance;" all that he can possibly observe is actual distance — so many inches, feet, miles; but the ratio he discovers by his reason, generalizing from particular facts to the general expression of those facts. And when he has discovered such a ratio as shall coincide with all his observed measurements, he is then enabled to reason deductively, having found the middle term of his syllogism. This middle term may be a generalized fact or general proposition, or it may be a force or cause; and the difference between these is, that the general fact or proposition produces the *logical* consequent, and the force is conceived as external to the mind, existing in real nature, and producing the *real* consequent, or effect, or *phenomenon.* In the physical sciences, therefore, two distinct classes of problems present themselves,—the problems of *inference*, and the problems of *deduction*, expressed logically as,—

1st. *Given* the minor premiss and consequent, to find the *major premiss.*

2d. Given the major and minor premises, to find the *consequent.*

In the process of *discovering* the physical sciences we have the first problem; namely, *given* the observed conditions of matter, and the observed phenomena, to *infer* the force, or forces, that in those conditions would produce those phenomena. And when such forces have been suggested as would, by acting regularly, produce the phenomena in the given conditions, the facts are said to be explained, and a vast power of future calculation (reasoning) is immediately acquired by man. For immediately the middle term has been discovered, we are enabled to reason deductively, that is, from the two premises to the consequent; and this middle term being a *constant*, we have only to ascertain any new *conditions* to enable us to *predict future phenomena.* If the real phenomena coincide with the predicted phenomena, (that is, if the effect in nature coincide with the consequent of the syllogism,) a verification is afforded that the inferred major premiss was correct; but if they do not coincide, we are immediately led to the conclusion, either that the inferred major was erroneous, or that in the minor some condition had been overlooked, which has tended to alter the character of the phenomena.

Between the syllogism, the intellectual reason of

mankind, and the operations of external nature, there is the most perfect parallelism; and this parallelism affords a most undoubted proof of the *objective veracity* of the *subjective convictions* of the human mind. Were the general convictions of the human reason (its axioms) not true *objectively*, as well as necessarily true *subjectively*, the prediction of physical phenomena would be absolutely impossible. And although the philosophic sceptic may by ingenious ambiguities involve that question in doubts and sophisms, surely we may rest satisfied that the same hand that made the heavens and the earth in so wonderful a harmony of order, has not made the human reason only a mockery and a delusion.

Having indicated the general process by which the sciences evolve one after the other, thereby giving a necessary order of classification, and a necessary order of chronological discovery, we shall not attempt the particular classification of the physical sciences, but confine ourselves to a few remarks bearing on the definite meaning of our argument.

In dynamics, as an abstract science, our *term* was a movable point. Let that point be endowed with *physical* characteristics one after another, and the physical sciences arise. From a point let it be transformed into a body possessing *weight*, or *resistance*, and we have general mechanics — a science partly physical, partly mathematical.

But here we must guard against being imposed on by a system, however simple that system may appear.

In the mathematical sciences we found that there was but *one* series, and that all were coördinated upon one single line. We must not thence infer that we shall find exactly the same simplicity in the physical sciences. Man has only one reason, but he has several senses; and those senses may furnish us with elements independent of each other, although in the order of the sciences depending both on the mathematical sciences, and both requisite before we can proceed to other and more complex sciences.

Such we presume *light*, *sound*, and *heat* to be. Now, although we can have no hesitation in affirming that optics is impossible until the mathematical sciences have been evolved and are capable of application, and although we must necessarily have optics *before* we can possibly have the physiology of the eye; yet there may be no such mutual dependence between optics and acoustics, and we may therefore be obliged to group these together as holding the same rank in the classification, and consequently as likely to be discovered about the same time.

And here another question is necessary, of considerable importance to the true understanding of the character of science. "How far are the real physical sciences (astronomy, for instance) to be considered as true *sciences?*"

All the phenomena of nature are operations — things *done*. Now, science consists of *knowledge*, and knowledge exists in the *mind*. How, then, are we to view the real operations of nature, considered as external to the mind?

The real operations of nature are to be viewed as *arts* — as divine arts — and their *comprehension* alone can be called *science*. The universe is God's great workshop, and man is the rational spectator, whose office it is to comprehend the processes that are there carried on. The motions of the planets do not *constitute* science; it is the rational apprehension of those motions in the human *mind* that constitutes science. But the principles of mechanics are far more general than all the facts of astronomy; they apply not only to the real sun and the real planets, but to all possible suns, and to all possible matter constituted in a manner similar to the matter with which we are acquainted.

Consequently astronomy, vast as it is, must be viewed only as a real illustration of the principles of mechanics, as an exemplification of dynamics; which exemplification in every real item might have been totally different, and yet have exhibited the very same principles. The heavenly bodies might have been twice as numerous or twice as few, and yet have exhibited exactly the same principles of construction; in which case the science of mechanics would have remained exactly as it is, while actual astronomy would have been totally dissimilar.

From the more simple motions of matter we turn naturally to those that are more complex; that is, from those that are more *general* to those that are more *specific*. When the mere motion of a body is considered, it is evident that this motion is subject to the same laws, whether the body be a stone, an apple, or an animal. But when matter is subdivided and classified, it is found that some motions and some phenomena are altogether distinct from the general motions of matter. The phenomena of magnetism, electricity, and chemistry, therefore, take their rank after mechanics, and these in their turn are the necessary preparations for a new order of sciences.

We have said that the classification of the sciences, and their chronological discovery, (or reduction to ordination,) must follow the order of their complexity. From the more simple we pass to the more complex; from the more general to the more specific.

Let us then ask, What is necessary to the *complete understanding* of a single portion of inorganic matter — a pint of water, for instance? (Speculations on things which *cannot* be known respecting matter, of course we altogether exclude.) This matter may present itself in three forms; vapor, liquid, and solid — the phenomena of *heat*, therefore, are involved. It may be decomposed; chemistry, therefore, is involved; Electricity may be generated in its passage from a liquid to a vapor; electricity, therefore, is involved; it may move as a solid, or as a liquid, or as a gas; the motions of solids, liquids, and gases, therefore, fall under separate consideration. It may sound — acoustics; may transmit or reflect light — optics; it may appear in the form of rain, hail, or snow; as a solid, its sides may be numbered, their angles and their area measured; and that measurement involves the theory of quantities; and finally, without logic, we could not reason about it at all. It will be found, on close examination, that the *complete* understanding of this pint of water involves *all* the physical and *all* the mathematical sciences. But this pint of water does not as yet involve *organization.* Let it, however, be presented as a constituent part of a plant, and a new series of phenomena immediately present themselves; and, for the understanding of these new phenomena, every one of the previous sciences is absolutely requisite. After the inorganic sciences, therefore, come the sciences of *organization*, of vegetable and animal physiology, showing a continual increase of complexity until we arrive at man, the most complex and most highly organized of all the earth's inhabitants.

To consider man, however, merely in his physiology, is to regard him only as an animal made up of certain organs, each of which has its function. Physiology teaches us *of what* the human body is composed, and *how* the mechanism of life is carried on. It teaches us what man *is* in his bodily frame, and it endeavors to give us a rational view of the functions and uses of his parts. It points out the relation of those parts to the whole, and it shows us how the living man — the active, thinking, and sentient agent — is a compound of wondrous and varied mechanisms. But still, though physiology be the highest and most complex of all the physical sciences, there is something beyond it, something that comes after it in the logical order of classification. Man himself has his functions; and when we have considered what man *is*, we may turn to what man *does*.

Man is by nature a social being, made to live in society, and his social acts have their laws, which, when understood, give us a new order of knowledge, altogether distinct from the knowledge contained in the previous sciences.

Men must buy and sell, cultivate and navigate, trade and manufacture; in a word, men must *act;* and, as there is no necessary power determining them

17

to act in any one particular direction, there is ever before them a right course and a wrong course; the one tending to a good and beneficial condition of society, the other to a bad and detrimental condition of society. And again, men may trespass on each other; may inflict pain on each other; may do evil to each other. Men, therefore, must *legislate.*

And here an evident distinction presents itself, which enables us to *classify* human action. We may ask, "What means will lead to a certain end?" and "What is the end that *ought* to be produced?"

We have here *two* social sciences, in each of which there is the same stable truth that prevails in all the other sciences, if man can only discover it and reduce it to scientific ordination. It *must* be within the reach of man, or else we must admit that all rules of social action are purely arbitrary; that is, in fact, that there are *no* rules. Such a supposition, however, is perfectly absurd, and can never be *consistently* maintained.

On the above distinction is grounded the division of social science into *non-moral* and *moral;* the one treating exclusively on the relation of means to an end, and the other exclusively on the end that *ought* to be the object of pursuit.

In these new sciences, *human action* is the element with which we have to reason; and the *conditions of men* are the phenomena that result directly from that action. We have, therefore, —

1st. An inductive science of human action, which presents itself in the following form: —

1. Given the actual *actions* of men in their social capacity. This is the minor proposition of the syllogism.

2. Given the actual *conditions* of men.

This is the consequent or conclusion of the syllogism, the conditions of men being *the effects* of their actions.*

And the problem is to find "the general expression of the relation between the actions of men and their social condition." When this general expression is found, it supplies the major proposition of the syllogism; and the criterion of this major being correct, is, that the observed phenomena contained in the consequent of the syllogism would follow logically from the major and minor premises. If such a major cannot be found as would logically produce all the observed phenomena from all the observed conditions, we must seek further until a satisfactory major is discovered.

2d. A deductive science of human action.†

It is evident that, anterior to all induction whatever, there are certain acts which ought *not* to be done. The first man who committed *murder* was as

* The *conditions* of men here spoken of must not be confounded with the *conditions* of the syllogism. The syllogistic conditions are the conditions of the subject with which we reason, and here we reason with human actions. Were we, however, to reason inversely from the conditions of men to the probable actions of men in those conditions or *circumstances*, (quite a legitimate and a most important syllogism,) then those conditions would really become the logical conditions, or minor proposition; whereas, here they are the consequent, or conclusion.

† This science is perfectly *distinct* from any deductions that might be made in the previous science when the major proposition was discovered. And yet there cannot be the slightest doubt that the two sciences, perfectly understood, would lead to the same identical conclusion.

guilty of committing *a crime* as the last man who shall raise the unhappy hand of violence against his brother. He could, however, have no *inductive* evidence of the effects of his action; and the same holds true of robbery, fraud, and every other crime. Consequently we may inquire, What was it that made the first murder a crime, and how could man know that such an act ought not to be performed?

The mind of man views actions not merely in their physical characteristics, but as being equitable or unequitable, just or unjust; and this *equity* gives an *à priori* boundary to action, and lays a moral restriction on man, which will prevent him from injuring his fellow, even where he has no inductive evidence whatever.

The principles of this equity are abstract and universal convictions of the reason, and the problem presents itself in the following manner: —

1st. Given the general axioms of equity. (This is the major proposition;) and, —

2d. Given the physical or non-moral characteristics of an action. (This is the minor proposition of the syllogism.)

To find the moral character of that action, namely, whether it be a *duty* or a *crime*. (This is the conclusion of the syllogism.)

The first of these sciences is political economy, which is purely inductive, and treats of the physical effects of human action so far as those effects are to be discovered in the condition of societies. The second is politics, the science of equity which is purely abstract, and treats of the universal principles that ought to regulate human action, so far as men can affect each other by their actions.

The fundamental noun-substantive of political economy is *utility*, of which *value* is the *measure*.* The fundamental noun-substantive of politics is equity, which, having its abstract laws in the very constitution of the human mind, gives us the moral measure of human action.

We now turn to the practical bearing of our argument, for which the rough sketch we have given of the classification of the sciences was only the requisite preliminary.

We maintain, then,—

First. That the sciences, classed on their complexity, must be classed in the following order:—

1st. The mathematical and force sciences.

2d. The inorganic physical sciences, beginning with the most general, and terminating with the most specific.

3d. The organic physical sciences, composed of vegetable and animal physiology.

4th. The sciences that relate exclusively to man, and that treat of human action. These are, (1) *non-moral*, political economy, which treats of the beneficial or prejudicial effects of human action; (2) *moral*, politics, which treats of the moral character of human action, whether that action be the action of a single individual towards another individual, or whether it

* And value (the abstraction) is itself measured by the outward fact of exchangeability, and exchangeability is again measured by the middle term *money*; in Britain, for instance, by *gold*. which is called the standard.

be the action of a whole society, or portion of a society, with all the formality of legislation, &c. Politics is, in fact, nothing more than the moral law which ought to regulate the actions of the individual, extended to the actions of men when associated as a political society, the same moral law being obligatory on multitudes that is obligatory on the individual.

Our argument then is, that "*there is a natural probability in favor of a millennium;*" and this natural probability is based, —

1st. On the division and classification of human knowledge.

2d. On the fact that the chronological order of the *discovery* of the sciences is the same as the order of classification.

3d. On the power of *correct credence* (knowledge) to produce *correct action.*

Let us, in the first place, endeavor to settle definitely what we mean by a *millennium.*

1st. We do not mean any particular portion of time.

2d. We do not mean a miraculous condition of society, produced by the power of Almighty God working supernatural changes in the *nature* of man. It may be *true* that God, in his infinite goodness, shall, ere the world's end, so enlighten mankind by the divine spirit of grace and wisdom, that it may almost be no metaphor to say that man has become a new creature. This may be *true;* but this is not what we refer to.

3d. We do not mean a personal reign of the Son of God, the Savior of the world. On this subject we can offer no possible opinion. That the Lord Jesus

Christ shall reign in *power*, and that his will shall be done on earth ere the earth's history closes, we believe with the most undoubted assurance. But that the Redeemer of mankind shall again appear in *person* before he cometh to judge the world, this is a question which we must leave unanswered.

4th. By a millennium we mean a period of universal peace and prosperity — a reign of knowledge, justice, and benevolence — a period when the condition of man upon the globe shall be the best the circumstances of the earth permit of — when the systematic arrangements of society shall be in perfect accordance with the dictates of man's reason — and when societies shall act correctly, and thereby evolve the maximum of happiness possible on earth.

A millennium, therefore, is for us a period when truth shall be discovered and carried into practical operation. This is the essence of human welfare, — *truth discovered and carried into practical operation.*

Let it be remembered that the progress of mankind, in the evolution of civilization, is a progress from superstition and error towards knowledge. Superstition and error present themselves under the form of *diversity* of credence; knowledge presents itself under the form of *unity* of credence. Wherever there is knowledge, that knowledge is the same in all parts of the earth, and the same in substance whatever language it may use as the instrument of expression. The progress of mankind, therefore, is a progress from diversity of credence towards unity of credence. There is but *one* truth, *one* scheme of knowledge; and consequently, wherever knowledge is really attained, diversity of credence is impossible. Where men differ in credence, they differ because one or all have *not* knowledge.

We have, then, to ask, "Into what branches is knowledge divided?" "What is the *logical* order of those branches in a scheme of classification?" "In what *chronological* order have the various branches been reduced to scientific ordination?" "At which branch are the most advanced nations *now* in the nineteenth century?" and, "What are the branches that yet remain to be reduced to scientific ordination, and in what *order* may we expect those future branches to be reduced to the form of *science*, which excludes diversity of credence?"

The natural probability of a future *reign of justice* is based on the answers to these questions. If there *be* a scheme of knowledge, and if the past history of science proves that the sciences have been evolved one after the other in accordance with that scheme, we assert that there is nothing unreasonable in anticipating that the future progress of discovery will continue to go on in the same direction. On the contrary, we maintain that such anticipation is a fair, legitimate, and impartial inference from the facts before us. We are well aware of the ridicule which practical politicians endeavor to throw on the anticipation of a political millennium, and too often with a levity which we cannot esteem other than unbecoming, when we know that the Creator of mankind has distinctly promised a period of peace and prosperity to our race. It may not be given to man to know the times and the seasons, but most certainly it is given to man to know *the fact;* and surely it would be as wise to speak of that fact with modest reverence, instead of associating it, or even a wrong anticipation of it, with the scoff, and the jeer, and the gibe of ridicule.

To the above questions, then, we give the following answers: —

1st. *Into what branches is knowledge divided?* Into the facts of sensational and psychological observation, rational science, and history. Savage nations may see the sun rise and set, and the moon wax and wane, and they may see for centuries these and the other phenomena of nature without advancing in intelligence. The son, like the father, may live and die a savage. It is not till man begins to *reason* — that is, to make rational science — that the foundation of natural civilization is laid, and the first step taken in that course which continually tends to distinguish man more and more from the animals, and to make the intellectual portion of his nature predominate over the instincts of his bodily frame.

History, again, is a branch of knowledge *common* to every reality with which we are acquainted. In it, therefore, we must not look for the great element of human progression. That element is found in rational science, and rational science is divided into the following branches: —

1. The mathematical and force sciences, beginning at logic, and ending with dynamics.

2. The inorganic physical sciences, beginning with the most general, and ending with the most specific.

These we have attempted to arrange *generally* in the table in the Appendix.* What are called the mixed sciences are only *general* physical sciences; and these, of course, would come first, while chemistry and galvanism probably would occupy the most advanced station in the series.

3. The organic physical sciences, including (1) vegetable physiology, and (2) animal physiology.

Anatomy is not a *science*, it is a mere classification forming a portion of physiology. Physiology is the *architecture*, (anatomy,) *dynamics*, and *chemistry* of organized bodies; that is, architecture, dynamics, and chemistry applied to the functions of *vitality*.

4. MAN SCIENCE.

The sciences of human action are, —

(1.) A sensational and inductive science, called political economy.

(2.) A moral and deductive science, which we call politics.

The order in which we have given the sciences answers the second question, namely, "What is the logical order of the branches of knowledge in a scheme of classification?"

The third question is, "In what *chronological* order have the various branches been reduced to scientific ordination?" The chronological order in which the sciences have been discovered, or reduced to ordination, is correlative with the logical scheme of classification. As a history of the actual evolution of the sciences would be out of place in the present volume, we must be content with stating the fact, that the mathematical sciences were first evolved, then the more simple of the physical sciences; and that the progress of discovery, since the time of Newton down to the present day, has been, as nearly as we could possibly expect, on the very same principle of complexity that forms the ground of classification. And it would not be difficult, we think, to prove not only that it *has* been so, but that it could not possibly have been otherwise. Without geometry, statics and dynamics are *impossible;* without statics and dynamics, hydrostatics and hydrodynamics are impossible; and without hydrostatics and hydrodynamics, that portion of physiology which treats of the phenomena of vegetable and animal circulation is also impossible. Here the one science must precede the other in chronological discovery, because it is requisite to render that other science discoverable. The one is the means whereby we attain to the other, just as, in a single science, one problem must be solved before we can, by any possibility, attain to the solution of another problem. And *the law* of this dependence of one science on another is, that the truths of the antecedent science, which *are the objects of research* when we study that science, become subjective — that is, *means of operation* — when we study the consequent science.

It is impossible, therefore, that the sciences should be discovered in any other than a certain order; that is, man must acquire knowledge on a scheme which has laws as fixed and definite as the very laws of the sciences themselves.

We may remark, however, in the evolution of the sciences, that it is not necessary that the whole (all that can be known) of an antecedent science should be evolved *before* the elementary portion of the consequent science is commenced. When geometry has made a certain progress, statics may be commenced; and thus the earlier portion of statics may be evolved coincidently with the more advanced portion of geometry. Again, when inorganic chemistry has made a certain progress, organic chemistry may be commenced; and its more elementary truths will be undergoing a process of evolution coincidently with the more advanced truths of inorganic chemistry.

Thus, although the sciences are necessarily antecedent and consequent to each other, they interweave or overlap each other in their chronological evolution; just as father and son may be alive at the same time, yet the father is necessarily older than the son. And in the evolution of the sciences we may have several generations on foot at a given period; we may have three, four, five, or six sciences all undergoing the process of evolution, but all at different stages of progress. The first may be tolerably complete; the second less so; the third still less so; the fourth may be but beginning to assume the form of a teachable branch of knowledge; the fifth only settling its nomenclature and classification; while the sixth only shows symptoms of commencement, attracting perhaps a large share of attention, but being replete with arbitrary opinion, superstitious credence, and general diversity of statement. When geometry was a science, astronomy was a superstition; and when mechanics and astronomy were sciences, chemistry was a superstition; and when chemistry had assumed the form of science, political economy was a superstition; and now that political economy begins to assume somewhat of scientific ordination, politics is little better than a superstition.

We may, therefore, have several sciences on foot at the same period, yet all at different stages of progress. And this brings us to the next question, —

"At which branch or branches of knowledge are the most advanced nations now in the nineteenth century?"

There are several tests which we may apply to a branch of knowledge to ascertain whether it is or is not a science; that is, whether it is as yet reduced to scientific ordination.

1st. It must have a definite province, so that we distinctly understand what we are reasoning about.*

* The great error of *philosophy* has been the want of a definition. Philosophers have forgotten to tell us what it really was that they were going to treat of. It is quite evident that *thought, and the laws of thought*, are perfectly distinct from *realities, and the laws of realities;* and no science under the same name can be allowed to treat of both. Philosophers have jumbled the two together in a most illegitimate manner; and the consequence was, that when they encountered something connected with *thought* which they could not explain, they astounded the world with inconceivable assertions with regard to *realities.* Some, by this rather curious process, discovered that there was no *matter;* others, that there was no *mind;* and some, though we almost hesitate to affirm it, dared to call in question the existence of our divine Maker, and to dethrone the Lord of heaven and earth.

If philosophy will treat of *thought*, let it confine itself to thought; and if it will treat of *realities*, let it confine itself to realities, and become theology, or any other branch of knowledge; but we maintain that it is quite illegitimate for philosophy to jump backwards and forwards, from thought to reality, and from reality to thought. Such a method necessarily produces *inextricable* confusion, and the very foundations of human credence become shaken in the minds of those whose intellectual constitution enables them to see only as far as the difficulty without seeing through it. Hume, perhaps,

2d. It must be *teachable* as a branch of knowledge. For this purpose, its propositions must be coördinated, so that we can know whether we are at the commencement, or how far we have progressed beyond the commencement. Philosophy, as yet, has scarcely a commencement, middle, or end; although symptoms are beginning to show themselves that, ere long, we may expect something very much more satisfactory.

3d. It must be capable of subjective application. This we consider to be the proper criterion of the state of a science. If it is incapable of application, it is only undergoing the process of discovery; if it is capable of application, it is so far complete. It is then the same for all men alike, (there is but *one* truth,) and it becomes a means of operation whereby things are done which could not otherwise have been done.

We ask, then, at what sciences are the most advanced nations now in the nineteenth century?

It is evident that the mathematical sciences, and the more general physical sciences, fulfil the above

only intended to *puzzle* people; and his amazing acuteness enabled him to baffle and to mystify many an honest head. But it was a fearful amusement: it might be a mere game, but it was a fiend's game; and although we cannot but admire the clearness and purity of Hume's intellect, we have often thought — and not without regret — how much greater and how much better a man he would have been, had he endeavored, in honest sincerity of heart, to *solve* the difficulties as well as to propound them. We have no doubt whatever that Hume knew that his sophisms *were* sophisms, and in his own mind saw much farther through them than he liked to acknowledge. Had Hume not been a sceptic, he might probably have been at the head of all modern writers on philosophy; for he undoubtedly possessed that exquisitely subtile intellect, without which a man — however great his other acquirements — can never be more than a second-rate philosopher.

conditions. The question, then, is with the advanced physical sciences, and with those that follow them in the scheme of classification.

Let us take chemistry as the most advanced inorganic physical science, and classify the sciences that follow chemistry in the natural scheme of classification. We have then

Chemistry.
Vegetable physiology.
Animal physiology.
Man science.

The new *term* acquired in the passage from the inorganic to the organic sciences, is *vitality* — *life*.

Vegetable physiology presents itself under two aspects, which give us two sciences; the one treating of the structure and functions of the *organs* of plants, the other of the structure and functions of the whole vegetable kingdom, considered as one of the great organs of the terrestrial economy.

A science, we have said, contains, —

1st. A nomenclature. 2d. A classification. 3d. Reasoning.

And the correlatives of these in *nature* are, —

1st. The objects. 2d. Their conditions. 3d. Their functions.

Vegetable physiology, then, has two forms; that which relates to the life, growth, and propagation of a single plant, composed of many *organs*, and that which relates to the vegetable kingdom, composed of many *species* of plants.

Let us designate these as *internal* and *external* physiology, and we shall then be able to classify the various branches of botany.

A SCIENCE IN GENERAL.

1. NOMENCLATURE.	2. CLASSIFICATION.	3. REASONING.
The objects described and named.	Statement of the conditions and relations of the objects.	Syllogistic scheme of the functions of the objects.

GENERAL FORMULA APPLIED TO,

1st. *Internal Physiology.*

Nomenclature of the various parts, or organs, of the single plants. Description of the organs.	Classification of those parts, including their mechanical and chemical adaptation.	Function of those parts in the phenomena of life, growth, and propagation.

2d. *External Physiology.*

Comparative nomenclature of the various plants that inhabit the globe. Comparative anatomy.	Classification of those plants, and their arrangement.	Function of plants in the terrestrial economy.

The support of the animal kingdom is the great practical function of the vegetable kingdom.

The same principles of classification apply to animal physiology, where we have, —

First.

Nomenclature and description of organs. Descriptive anatomy.	Classification; that is, the organs assembled into *apparatus* — *e. g.*, digestive apparatus, respiratory apparatus, &c.	Function of those parts in the phenomena of animal life.

Second.

Comparative nomenclature of the various animals that inhabit the globe. Comparative anatomy, and description.	Classification of those animals, and their arrangement into groups.	Function of the animal kingdom in the terrestrial economy.

The individual nomenclature of the various plants and animals is in the first place *arbitrary*, and subject to no rules; comparison, however, introduces the element of coördination, and a systematic nomenclature is adopted, constituting the scheme of species, genera, classes, &c.

It will be observed that chemistry, hydrodynamics, &c., are absolutely requisite before internal vegetable physiology can make a scientific progress. The functions of the organs of plants are explicable only in and through the perfection of the inorganic sciences, and the latter must necessarily be so far advanced as to be capable of subjective application before the former can by any possibility be explained.

But if the immediate use of plants in the physical economy of the earth be the maintenance of animal life, external vegetable physiology, which treats of the functions of the vegetable kingdom, is the necessary preparation for internal animal physiology; no theory of the *nutrition* of animals being possible without first of all arriving at a knowledge of the nutriment. Hence, also, the chemistry of inorganic matter, and the chemistry of vegetable substances and products, must be evolved before there can be a theory of vegetable nutrition.

The maintenance of animal life is the physical ultimatum of the earth — the last final function of matter. When we proceed beyond this, we arrive at a region where the functions are no longer purely physical; for although man in his political economy may partly be viewed as a higher kind of animal, yet his functions, even in that region, are essentially distinguished from those of animals by the introduction of *intellectual* computation. The physical world may, it is true, sustain mankind — may feed, clothe, and shelter man's animal frame; but in the *production* of food, and in its *distribution*, there is a function of intelligence which prevents the maintenance of man from being classed as a mere *physical* phenomenon.

When, therefore, we turn to the sustentation of men associated together in society, we have passed from the region of *mere* organization, and have entered the sphere of rational intelligence.

The science that treats of the production and distribution of food, and the other physical requirements of man, is termed political economy; and the ultimatum of that science is, "How may the greatest physical good be procured for the greatest number?" *

This ultimatum is not *arbitrary*, as some would almost have us suppose; it is the necessary end of the science, if that science have any existence. Just as we are necessarily led to view the surface of the earth in its function of sustaining vegetable life, and the vegetable kingdom in its function of sustaining animal life; so are we led by the very laws of our intelligence to posit the physical benefit of mankind as the

* It is usual in Britain to confine the province of political economy to the *production* of wealth; and this view is correct and convenient, if the name POLITICAL ECONOMY be reserved for the first and simplest embranchment of social science. But as the *distribution* must have its laws, as well as the *production*, those laws require investigation, and a special name must be accorded to this portion of social science, which is, in fact, of greater practical importance than the other.

ultimatum to which all economical arrangements should tend, if they do not depart from the very intention which is the ground and origin of their existence.

But political economy is a mere computation of antecedences and sequences: it tells *what* results follow certain conditions; and, generalizing its facts, it at last arrives at the laws which regulate the physical condition of man, so far as that condition is the consequence of human *action.* The utmost that it can tell is, "what means lead to a certain end;" but being based purely on *observation*, it can never lay on us a *duty*, nor deter us from a *crime.* Even in its ultimatum, it can only say that, if men do not pursue their advantage, they act *irrationally*, but never can it say that they act *criminally.* It computes the mechanism of human action, but never can determine the *end* of human action. *Duty* and *crime* are terms with which it has no concern, and to which it can attach no meaning. It is merely observational, and must confine itself as a science to the generalization of facts, while, when taken as a practical rule of action, its sphere extends no further than the physical well-being of mankind; and the "benefit of the greatest number" is fixed on, not from any idea of moral duty, but merely because that ultimatum exhibits the *greatest quantity.* In no sense is this science one iota more *moral* than astronomy, which furnishes the practical rule of navigation; or geometry, which furnishes the practical rule of mensuration. To confound it with *duty*, is essentially to destroy its character as an inductive science.

In answer to the question, then, "At what sciences are the most advanced nations now in the nineteenth century?" we reply,—

The marks by which we recognize the condition of a science, and its relative perfection, are, —

1st. It must have a definite province.

2d. It must be teachable as a system.

3d. It must be capable of subjective application. And a science consists of a nomenclature, classification, and reasoning. The genuine criterion of the perfection of a science is, that it is capable of subjective application, and only in so far as it is thus capable can it be considered perfect.

A slight attention to the recent labors of scientific men will convince us that chemistry fulfils the above conditions; that not only have its nomenclature and classification been tolerably well perfected, but that its reasoning is so far advanced as to render it capable of application to the regions that lie beyond it. Here it is only necessary to refer to the researches of Liebig and his fellow-laborers in the region of chemico-physiology.

Vegetable physiology is, and must ever be, *consequent* on chemistry and electricity; and, being logically consequent, must also be chronologically subsequent in the order of its discovery; that is, of its reduction to scientific ordination. If chemistry, therefore, have only been recently rendered capable of subjective application, we must naturally expect that vegetable physiology shall present a less degree of perfection; and that, at all events, some years must elapse before it shall be so completely developed as to change from an object of study to an instrument of operation.

But vegetable physiology, although necessarily posterior to chemistry, and in the present day only undergoing its process of evolution, is already further advanced than chemistry was one hundred years since. As the various sciences are necessarily antecedent and subsequent to each other, so are the various parts of the same science necessarily antecedent and subsequent; and when we analyze vegetable physiology into its various parts, we find that the earlier portions have already assumed the form of scientific ordination.

Vegetable physiology consists of mechanics, (including architecture, statics, dynamics,) chemistry, and electricity, applied to the objects endowed with vegetable life; and the ultimate object of research is, the explanation of the process by which the functions of life, growth, and propagation are carried on. In the architecture we have the enumeration, nomenclature, and description of the organs; in the mechanics we have their adaptation for the performance of certain functions; and in the chemistry and electricity we have a physical explanation of certain phenomena which take place under the influence of life, but by means of the laws which regulate the world of inorganic matter.

In determining, therefore, the position occupied by vegetable physiology at the present time, we must bear in mind that the portions of that science stand logically in the following order: —

Nomenclature of organs.
Description of organs.
Mechanical functions.
Chemical and Electrical functions.

Of these, the first three are so far advanced, that although *formal* improvements may be expected, yet the *knowledge* may, for the most part, be said to be obtained; and the question that remains is, rather how that knowledge should be reduced to the most simple and most convenient expression. The fourth is now occupying the attention of many eminent men, and the progress already made is sufficient to assure us, not only that the right track has been discovered, but that ere long the chemistry of vegetation will be so far advanced as to form the instrument of investigation into the chemistry of animal organization. In fact, very considerable progress has already been made in the latter direction.

External vegetable physiology consists of comparative nomenclature of all known plants.

Classification of plants.

Function of plants in the terrestrial economy.

The two former of these are achieved, although probably susceptible of formal improvement. The latter is undergoing a process of evolution.

As we have only proposed to ourselves to indicate the outline of an argument without insisting on its details, we need scarcely advert to the prodigious labor expended on a knowledge of the structure of animal bodies, or to the astonishing accuracy with which some men have made themselves acquainted with anatomy, both human and comparative. Anatomy, as we have already said, is not a *science;* it is merely the nomenclature and *classification* of the science of physiology; and as such it would probably have been considered, had it not received an accidental character from its connection with the medical art. Had anatomy been studied for purely scientific purposes, (and not, as now, for the purpose of alleviating human suffering, or preventing human dissolution,) its entire subserviency to what is termed physiology would probably have been acknowledged, and it would no more have been called a science than the description of the lines and figures of geometry. It is merely the description of the substantives whose *functions* form the subject of future investigation.

At what point, then, is the present generation in its knowledge of animal physiology?

The distinction we have drawn between internal and external physiology, will enable us to allocate the various portions of zoölogy. Internal physiology discourses of, —

1st. The constituent organs of animal bodies.

2d. The conditions of those organs.

3d. Their function.

And the science presents these under the form of, —

1st. Nomenclature and description of the organs.

2d. Classification of the organs.

3d. Reasoning. That is, the syllogistic statement of a scheme whereby the actually observed phenomena would, when stated in language, follow logically from the premises. One premiss being the expression of a cause, force, or generalized fact; and the other, the expression of the conditions of the organs functioning.

It might, perhaps, be too much to assert that the nomenclature, description, and classification of the organs of animal bodies had arrived at a state of perfection; but these branches have undoubtedly arrived at a state of ordination which is likely to remain permanent, unless, indeed, a general revolution of scientific nomenclature should at some future period be agreed upon. The *knowledge* is obtained; and when we consider the manner in which a nomenclature necessarily grows out of a mass of the most heterogeneous materials, derived, perhaps, from a multitude of languages, it may fairly be asserted that that knowledge is presented in as perfect a form as could reasonably have been expected.

When we turn to the *functions* of the organs of animal bodies, we find that the principle of *progressive complexity*, which we have assumed as the basis of our argument, still aids us in allocating the various portions of the same science, and enables us to understand how one portion of physiology happens to evolve chronologically before another. Thus geometry is necessarily anterior to optics, and optics necessarily anterior to the physiology of the eye, both logically and chronologically. Again, the general principles of mechanics must first be ascertained before an explanation can be given of the action of the muscles on the bones, and of the motions that result from that action.

But optics can explain only *a portion* of the functions of the eye. The eye contains solid and liquid parts, which not only refract light, but which have a chemical composition. And mechanics can explain only *a portion* of the phenomena of muscular action. And thus, although the *geometry* of vision may be tolerably perfect, and a satisfactory explanation is given of the *result* of muscular action, there is a course of inquiry that lies beyond both optics and mechanics, in which those sciences can afford no information. When the muscular force *is* generated, and acts in a particular direction, its results may be explicable on the same principles that apply to nonvital forces acting on non-organic portions of matter. But according to what laws is the muscular force itself generated? And, when generated, does it act in any such similar manner to voltaic electricity, as would enable us to conclude that the motion resulted from a galvanic power acting on nervous cords and muscular fibres, as they are shown to be disposed by the scalpel and the microscope?

As we do not pretend, in the slightest degree whatever, to discourse upon *science*, but only on the principles that must pervade the classification of the sciences, and the theory of the order in which they must chronologically evolve, we need only refer to the fact, that within these few years the dynamics of the blood and the chemistry of the blood have been made subjects of special research, and that they are now undergoing their process of evolution and reduction to scientific ordination.*

* Among other labors, we may refer to those of Magendie on the dynamics of the blood, and to those of Andral and Gavarret † on its chemistry. But, in addition to these, we have only to turn over the advertising pages of the medical journals to be convinced that physiology is, as it were, laboring to assume a more definite and more satisfactory form. As straws are said to indicate the direction of the current, so we may infer some notion of the direction in which physiological science is progressing, from the titles of the works that daily issue from the press. Works are now produced whose very titles would have been unintelligible half a century since. Such titles as "Electro-Biology" are at all events *indications;* they show us, however insignificant might be their real merits, that the human mind is directing its efforts towards a region altogether unknown to our ancestors.

† J. L. Gavarret, author of the "*General Principles of Medical Statistics.*"

The general principle which we conceive to pervade the evolution of the various portions of physiology is this: "In the same order that the non-organic sciences have themselves been reduced to ordination, will they be applied to the phenomena of animal life."

And in endeavoring to determine the present position of animal physiology, we shall, perhaps, not be far from the truth if we reckon the nomenclature of the organs and the description of the organs to be tolerably complete, the explanation of the mechanical functions to have made very considerable progress, and the chemical and electrical functions to be now attracting a large share of the attention of scientific men.

We now turn for a moment to what we have termed external animal physiology, which consists of

Comparative nomenclature of all known animals.

Comparative description and classification of animals.

Function of animals in the terrestrial economy.

And here, perhaps, it would be unsafe to assert that more has been achieved than the nomenclature; for, although there is no doubt a classification, that classification is open to such serious objections, that naturalists themselves are beginning to acknowledge the necessity of revising it, and constructing it on principles more sound, because more in accordance with the great analogies of nature.

To take one instance, which will suffice for our purpose.

If, among the birds, the first rank be accorded to the birds of prey, (the eagles, vultures, hawks, &c.,) and not to those birds in which the nervous system is most highly developed, and the manifestation of intelligence most apparent, (the parrots, &c.,) why, on the same principle of classification, is not the first rank among the mammifers accorded to the beasts of prey, (the lions, tigers, wolves, &c.,) which, among quadrupeds, are the undoubted representatives or correlatives of the eagles and vultures?

If the relative development of the nervous system determine the rank among the mammifers, no good reason can be alleged why it should not also do so among the birds; and there can be little doubt that the anomaly that now prevails must give way to a more consistent system, which shall take the analogies of nature as its basis, instead of any fanciful notions about the nobility of the eagle.

Were we to hazard an opinion on this head, which we can only do as looking at these subjects from a distance, we might express a conviction that the principles of classification proposed by that amiable and accomplished naturalist, Dr. Kaup of Darmstadt, are those which must ultimately prevail.

Human physiology is the last, the highest, and the most complex of all the physical sciences. It is the termination of man's intellectual labors, so far as regards the universe of matter. It is the ultimatum of material manifestation, the final type of complex arrangement, the summit beyond which we leave the material world, and enter into a new region of thought. Nor is it merely a metaphor to say, that "man is the epitome of the world." *Every* science that precedes human physiology is necessary to the complete understanding of the human frame. That frame has parts

— number is involved; those parts have quantity and extent — algebra and geometry are involved; the body may move or be at rest — dynamics and statics are involved; the motions of solids, liquids, and aeriform fluids are involved; optics, acoustics, chemistry, electricity, and galvanism all play their parts in elucidating the phenomena of the wondrous mechanism. But, granting that human physiology is the last and most complex of all the physical sciences, has man no further region into which he may push his inquiries, and extend the field of intellectual research?

Man has his *functions* — What are their laws?

SECTION II. — DETERMINATION OF THE CHARACTER, POSITION, AND BOUNDARIES OF POLITICAL SCIENCE.

§ I. *General Observations.* — The most simple functions of man, and those which naturally fall to be considered first, are those in which he acts on the external world.

First. Man may act on the physical world that surrounds him. These actions, when systematized, constitute the mechanical arts, chemical arts, &c. Under this head are assembled agriculture, navigation, manufactures, trade, commerce, systems of locomotion, fisheries, mines, &c.; in fact, all those occupations in which man is employed for the purpose of extracting from the earth the objects he requires, or of distributing or transforming them for his legitimate remuneration.

[Some of the French writers have most appositely termed this "l'exploitation de la terre par l'industrie," in opposition to "l'exploitation de l'homme par l'homme." When such expressions come to be placed in opposition to each other, it needs no prophet to tell us that the present social systems must soon undergo a radical revision.]

Second. Man may act on man.

This he may do either mediately or immediately. *Mediately*, when, at the same time that he is engaged in the above occupations, he reacts on his fellow-men through those occupations, either to their benefit or prejudice. *Immediately*, when he acts on his fellow-men by constraint, restraint, compulsion, violence, fraud, or defamation.

The principles involved in man's action on man are included under the term *social science* or *politics*, when those terms are taken in a general signification.

Social science is divided into two embranchments; namely, political economy, the object-noun of which is social utility; and politics proper, the object-noun of which is equity.

The problem of political economy is to discover the laws (generalized facts) which preside over human actions, where there is no direct interference between man and man.

The problem of politics is to discover the laws (principles of the reason) which ought to preside over human actions in the matter of interference.

In both sciences, human actions are the substantives with which we reason. In endeavoring to determine the present position of man in his knowledge of political economy and politics, we must premise that we here approach the region where *superstition*, and not science, prevails.

Knowledge is credence based on sufficient evidence, and superstition is credence without sufficient evidence.

No truth can be more satisfactorily established by history than that man is gradually emerging from superstition — gradually emancipating himself from those unfounded credences which have, in every department of science, enslaved his intellect and misdirected his actions. It is too much the practice, however, of this age to indulge in self-adulation, and to imagine fondly, that the light which has begun to dawn has dispelled all the darkness from the atmosphere of knowledge. Men seem to think that, because they can now look rationally at the phenomena of nature, they have read the whole riddle of the universe; that *they* are the wise men; that superstition no longer enfolds *them;* and that, from their high monument of wisdom, they can look back on their credulous fathers, and smile complacently in the vastness of their own superiority.

Great, no doubt, has been the emancipation of mind from religious and natural superstition; but we should, indeed, be sitting down in contented ignorance, were we to imagine that superstition does not now enslave us in the same manner that it enslaved our forefathers, except that her domain has been removed a little farther onward. Superstition has retired just as the sciences have been reduced to ordination — just as they have emerged from the chaos, and been moulded into form by the intellect of man. In the very same order, and to the very same extent, and at the same chronological period that the sciences have appeared, has superstition gradually retired, and taken her new stand in those fields of thought where the reason of mankind had not yet beheld the divine light of truth. When the mathematical sciences had made some good progress, the physical sciences were yet in the womb of futurity, and their place was occupied by a series of superstitions. These superstitions retired, but retired only gradually as science lit her peaceful lamp in the various chambers of nature. And *now* is it at all difficult to find superstition? to point out the region she still occupies? to show where vast systems of credence are as baseless as the credence of the alchemist, and vast systems of action are founded on the baseless credence?

The whole realm of political science is as yet little better than a superstition; and though humanity is perpetually making convulsive throes to escape from the evils entailed by the erroneous credence, we may rest surely convinced that those evils will never be obliterated until the human intellect has fairly mastered the theory of man's political relations, and reduced that theory to universal application.

Nor do we here refer to any theory which we ourselves may advance. Our views may be true, or they may be false. We, of course, believe them true; but, be they true or false, we lay down the proposition in the most general signification, that the evils that afflict the large masses of the population never *can* be obliterated until man's reason has mastered the theory of man's relation to man, and until he has reduced the principles of political science to practical realization in the constitution of society.

To observe the manner in which men legislate,—and legislators, be they who they may, are only men,—we should naturally be led to the conclusion, that there was *no truth* and *no falsehood* in political science. How otherwise can we explain the circumstance, that laws are perpetually undergoing a process of change? A law enacted only a few years since, is now found to be incorrect—so bad, in fact, that it must be abolished. In that law, perhaps, the interests of millions were involved; yet, notwithstanding, legislators are allowed to make these vast experiments with the property and the liberties of their fellow-men on no surer ground than *opinion*, which, in the great majority of cases, is mere presumptuous superstition.*

Truth, in fact, has almost as little to do with legislation as it had with alchemy or astrology; and this is the case, whatever may be the real matter of truth. According to law in England, the Episcopalian church is the true church; truth, according to law, is in the Thirty-nine Articles; the bishop is not only a churchman, but a legislator—a member of the supreme Parliament, and a ruler of the state. But in another part of Britain the church of England is not the true church, it is a scandalous hierarchy, because in the northern part of Britain the *Presbyterian* church is the true church; truth, according to law, is in the Confession of Faith; and the bishop, so far from even

* Since the beginning of the present century, there have been passed between *five and six thousand* public acts of Parliament.

being entitled to reverence, is a vile intruder on the equal rights of his brethren. He would not be allowed to address his fellow-Christians from the legal pulpits of the legal church; he is a "dumbe dogge," a small pope, a hireling shepherd; he is, in fact, that incarnation of Presbyterian abhorrence — *a prelate.*

In Ireland, again, (unfortunate Ireland!) Popery — which is, root and branch, totally false in England and Scotland — is partially legally true; and perhaps, by and by, it is going to be *more* true. Not that it can be true in England, because the law cannot allow *that;* but that it may be true in Ireland — or true enough, at all events, for Ireland — as any thing does for Ireland.*

Now, is it any thing else than mere superstition that allows any legislature whatever to establish systems of propositions which are legally true in one part of the kingdom, legally false in another? Whatever is true, it is quite evident that *truth* did not preside at the legislation — that truth was not the basis, the ground, the *reason* of the legislation. But if truth did not preside at the legislation, what did preside? Superstition.

Again: God gave the earth to the children of men. Now, is it *true* that the gift of a king (a *man*, with a different name) is a good title to as much land as would support a thousand families; that the legisla-

* "The quantity of specie coined in the reign of James I. was about £5,432,000; of which £3,666,000 was in gold, and £1,765,000 in silver. *It still continued the practice to issue some base money for the use of Ireland.*" — WADE, p 173. Yes, truly; and it has long continued the practice to issue base money for the use of Ireland.

ture (other *men*) should enact a law to secure that land in perpetuity to the descendants of the person who received the gift; that this person and his heirs should be called *proprietors* of that land, and should, by the law, be treated as such; that from *that* portion of the earth's surface all other persons are excluded by the law, save only those who have the permission of the proprietor; that this proprietor may be always absent from that land, and yet that he is to receive from the cultivators of the land *the rent* — that is, the profit that God has graciously been pleased to accord to human industry employed in the cultivation of the soil? Is this *true*, or is it only a mere groundless *superstition* that lies at the bottom of nine tenths of the evils of society? It cannot be *right*, unless there is a principle of *truth* on which the system is based; yet where, either in the study of external nature, or of man, or of revelation, can we find true propositions on which to base so iniquitous a system?

Again: Is it *true* that a deliberative assembly, chosen by a small part of the population, has *a right* — in morals, or religion, or any other *measure* of right and wrong — to determine that the legislators of the country shall be chosen by certain individuals, whose number, at the utmost, does not amount to more than one fourth of the adult male population of the country? Is it *true* that this deliberative assembly has an equitable right to *prevent* the other three fourths of the adult male population from having any voice in the election of those who are to tax their labor? Is it *true* that those three fourths of the adult male population are, in any way whatever, morally bound to obey a deliberative assembly chosen and elected in this manner? Is this *true*, or is it only a portion of that more general superstition which once pervaded all the physical sciences, but which has now been driven before the advance of knowledge, and obliged to take refuge in the regions of politics and religion?

Again: the present age is one in which we hear much of a "surplus population," a "redundant population," &c., while it seems to be forgotten that the man who can earn his daily bread can never be redundant, while the man who consumes vast revenues, without working for them, must necessarily be so. This redundant population, finding the difficulties and miseries of a residence in their native country more painful than even expatriation and removal to another hemisphere, begin to emigrate to Australia. A Solon of a political economist, theorizing on the terms *labor*, *capital*, *supply*, *demand*, &c., arrives at the conclusion that one square mile of the earth's surface is the exact quantity that should be sold to the emigrant, and that the best of all possible prices for that land is exactly one pound sterling per English statute acre. The governors of this country, convinced of their own ignorance, and happy to listen to a man who can discourse fluently on such mysterious matters as labor and capital, determine to apply the magic formula; and thenceforth no man who cannot purchase one square mile of land, at one pound per English statute acre, is allowed to settle down and earn his livelihood in one vast district of the southern hemisphere. Is it *true*, or is it *false*, that a few men in England have the right to impose such a restriction on the liberties of mankind? Is any other evidence required than that furnished by the *Wakefield system*, that political economy, in its practical application, is at present only a *superstition*—a mere tissue of the most arbitrary and groundless propositions, not one iota better than the propositions of judicial astrology?

Again: the legislators of Britain (who at that period represented a very small fragment of the population) enacted laws against the supply of food from foreign countries. Millions of pounds sterling were involved in the operation of the laws, and millions of persons were affected in the price of their daily food. Some years later, the population discovered the effect of the enactments, and the governors were obliged to abolish them, because the masses would no longer tolerate their existence. Now, is it *true*, or *false*, that any men, call them what you will, have the right to make these vast experiments? Are not these cases, and many others, exactly similar to the cases in which rulers have attempted to make a true or a false theology,—a true or a false system of astronomy,—or a true or a false system of nature, when they persecuted sorcerers, and devoted the victim to the fagot and the flames?

Again: What is the whole system of criminal legislation now carried into force in Great Britain? What is it but a great *superstition*, an arbitrary superstition, where there is no regulative principle for the intellect to rest upon? Why should one criminal be *fined*, another *imprisoned*, another *transported*, and another *hanged?* Is there any *connection*, either inductive or deductive, between the crimes and the punishments?

Is the allocation of the punishment based upon *any* principle that connects just such a kind, and such a quantity, with the offence? Is not the selection of the punishment *arbitrary;* that is, dependent not on any principle discoverable in nature, but dependent on vague and groundless opinion — that is, *superstition?*

Crimes are the maladies of society, and punishments are the medicines which laws administer for their correction. Now, are the recipes at present in use in politics one atom less arbitrary, less superstitious, or less absurd, than were the recipes of medicine two hundred years since? Could we see things present in the same light that we see things past, we should regard the affected wisdom of legislators and lawyers with the same ridicule and contempt so lavishly bestowed on the quacks, diviners, and necromancers of a former age. Where there is no *truth* to rest upon, there can only be error or superstition.

§ II. *The Province and Position of Political Economy.* — Entering our protest, therefore, that the regions of political economy and politics are at present pervaded by endless *superstitions,* we shall endeavor to point out the position of the present generation in its attempts to evolve those sciences.

First. The object-noun of political economy has been ascertained, and definitions have been attempted of the substantives of the science; that is, attempts have been made to describe and classify the objects with which men must reason when they reason in political economy.

Second. Large masses of facts have been collected

relating to a variety of subjects. These have been collected with more or less accuracy, and arranged with more or less judgment. In some cases, tabulated forms have been produced which leave little or nothing to be desired on the score of accuracy, purity,* and facility of manipulation. In other cases, immense records of facts have been accumulated, of so heterogeneous a character, or involving so many separate considerations, that conclusions altogether incompatible with each other are drawn from them to serve the purposes of the political reasoners.

Third. In some cases, the aid of mathematics has been called in to methodize the facts, and to determine the general value of the inferences that we are entitled to draw from them.

1st. Of the object-noun of political economy.

Every proper science has an object-noun, and the exclusive end and intention of the science is to discover and reduce to logical order the *relations* that exist between the substantives of the science *in* that object-noun. Thus, arithmetic treats of relations *in* number; geometry, of relations *in* space, (position, direction, and extent;) dynamics, of relations *in* force, &c.

Political economy then treats of relations *in* social utility, and we ask, "What are the relations of this, that, and the other action, or system of action, *in social utility?*" The answer to this question belongs exclusively to the science of political economy. [The

* By *purity*, we mean that the facts are strictly *comparable;* that improper facts have been left out.

same action may be judged *in social utility*, or *in equity;* in the former case we are engaged with a question of political economy; in the latter, with a question of politics. Endless ambiguities and discussions arise from confounding the one science with the other.]

2d. We now ask, "With what do we reason? What are the substantives of the science?"

Political economy is entirely and exclusively conversant with *human actions.*

We reason *with* human actions *in* social utility. Social utility is the *object*-noun of the science, and the forms of human action are the *subject*-nouns, which are to be *named, classed,* and *reasoned with.**

Wherever human action is not involved, there is no

* Thus, the cultivation of the earth is *a form* of human action; trading is *a form* of human action; restrictive laws and prohibitory laws, when carried into execution, are *forms* of human action. These *forms* have to be classified; and science is achieved when the classified forms are made to function in a rational scheme—that is, when the premises expressed in language will produce, logically, such consequents as are actually observed to take place in the real world.

In the external world we observe *antecedence, coincidence,* and *subsequence,* (or antecedent events, coincident events, and subsequent events;) but the mind alone furnishes the idea of *consequence,* (causation,) and, as the stream of time rolls on, with the whole functions of nature going on coincidently, we require to *observe* what antecedents are invariably followed (and in all circumstances) by certain subsequents, and thus to arrive at particular causes and particular effects. For this, the classification of events is requisite, and when they are arranged into species and genera, they become capable of functioning in a logical scheme, which scheme constitutes science.

political economy. Whatever results from the general action of the laws of the non-human universe, does not belong to political economy. The goodness or badness of a climate, the fertility or non-fertility of the soil, the existence of coal, iron, or other minerals—these in no respect whatever enter the science of political economy, except just in so far as they are affected by *human action.* The fertility of the soil *produced by human industry*, the *production* of iron, the *cultivation*, *manufacture*, and *commerce* of cotton, wheat, tea, sugar, sheep, cattle, wool, &c., &c.,—all these enter into political economy, because they represent certain *forms of human action*, which have an appreciable value in social utility.

The destruction of all the sheep, for instance, and all the people in a highland district, by a storm or by a dreadful convulsion of the elements, would in no respect enter into the science of political economy. But the abolition of the sheep, and the abolition of the population, by the so-called proprietor, under the sanction of British law, and the conversion of the district into a game desert, *does* enter into political economy; and when we ask the questions, "Is this act socially beneficial or prejudicial?" and, "Are the laws that grant a legal power to perform such acts by force socially beneficial or prejudicial?" we reason in political economy.

These same acts and laws may also be judged of *in equity;* but in that case we have passed from political economy to true politics.

Political economy, then, is the science that treats of human *function.* Where human function is not involved, we are not engaged with political economy. But then there is a limitation on the other hand. Political economy is a *non-moral* science, and in no case can be allowed to pronounce a moral judgment. All that it can ever tell us is, whether certain actions or systems of action are *beneficial*, *indifferent*, or *prejudicial;* and when the terms *right* and *wrong*, (adjectives,) *ought*, &c., are employed, they are used to indicate *correctness* or incorrectness *in social utility*.

Acts of *interference*, whether by law, or merely by the individual, belong properly to the science of politics, but they may also be legitimately judged of through the medium of political economy. In the one mode, however, we reason synthetically, as in geometry; in the other mode we reason empirically, as if we were to infer the general properties of figures from an induction of the actual properties presented by an indefinite multitude of individual figures. The practical difference is this. By treating a question of interference by the rules of equity, we arrive at once at a conclusion; whereas, when it is treated by the rules of utility, it may require many years, many observations, and many disputations as to facts, before a conclusion can be drawn. The *equity* of the slave trade is a question so simple, that few intelligent men could fail to settle it satisfactorily in a few minutes; but the *economy* of the trade would require, and did require, many years to settle it; and even now there are not wanting hundreds who, on *economical* principles, would defend both the trade and the condition of slavery. Although *perfect* knowledge in both sciences would, no doubt, lead to exactly the same practical conclu-

20 *

sion, the argument of economy is sometimes set up against the argument of equity. The concise reply to such a mode of proceeding is this, "If equity have any existence at all, its rules are necessarily *imperative*." Deny the *imperative* nature of equity, and you obliterate all morals.*

Now, where there is no *interference* between man and man, no judgment in equity can possibly be pronounced. Where there is no *interference*, (and nothing that enters religion,) economy gives the canon; she holds the balance, and pronounces judgment, because the question belongs to the jurisdiction of her court. But where there is *interference*, we can have a judgment *in equity;* and where we can have a judgment in equity, no economical considerations whatever (even if it were *not* true that the just coincides with the beneficial) can ever relieve man from the imperative obligation. The moment it was admitted that economical considerations should outweigh the judgment in equity, that moment is man's moral nature obliterated, and he becomes an animal a little superior to the orang-outang.

We now turn to the mode in which political economy is usually presented. *Utility* is, no doubt, the object of investigation; but what is its *measure*, what is its criterion, what are the marks by which we know an action to be beneficial or prejudicial?

* It is true, however, that the argument of economy has a far more powerful influence on the world than the argument of equity. Men are not satisfied with the logical determination of right and wrong; they must have a picture as well as a specification; they must have the evils portrayed in all their malignity before they resolutely determine to amend them.

According to some writers, we should imagine that utility was measured according *to the wealth produced*. *Value*, *labor*, *capital*, *wages*, *profit*, *rent*, &c., are the substantives of their science; and the *production of wealth* appears to be the end, the sum and substance, the object of their desires.

We deny, from beginning to end, this view of political economy. It has some truth in it — the beginnings of truth; but such, in the general, is no more the end of political economy, than the determination of the chances in gambling was the end of the calculation of probabilities.

We assert — and we have no doubt whatever that this view will ultimately obtain the suffrages of all — that the welfare of *man* is the end of political economy.

To this it may be replied, that the production of wealth is the *means;* and that all economists intend to include the welfare of man as a matter of course.

We deny the whole theory from beginning to end.

We assert that *the production of man*, and man in a continually higher condition, is the object, the end, the ultimatum of the science.

Let us suppose that one thousand families were employed in the cultivation of one hundred thousand acres of land; that they lived, maintained themselves in decent plenty, reared their families in health, industry, honesty, and those manly qualities which, among the agricultural population of Great Britain, have assumed a higher character than in any other portion of the earth's inhabitants. Suppose that this population produce only as much as suffices for the plentiful support of all the individuals. Good. There is not, on the average of twenty years, any superabundance that can be called accumulated profit.

This population, according to some political economists, would be a most unproductive, most useless portion of society.*

* "In 1709, an application was made to Parliament for an act to divide and enclose the common fields and wastes belonging to the parish of Ropley. This served as an encouragement and example; and applications of the same kind became annually more frequent. It appears that, since that period, very nearly four thousand bills of enclosure have been passed; and it is also well known that, in numerous instances, the same end has been reached without legislative interference, by private agreement among the parties interested. In a word, we have scarcely a doubt that about five thousand parishes (a moiety of the whole territory of England) have been subjected to the operation of these measures in the space of about one hundred and twenty years; and as little (however beneficial the division and consequent improvement of this vast territory may have proved to the owners, and to some other classes) that the change has been a woful one for our peasantry. We believe that the final extinction of the class of small occupiers and crofters has, in almost every instance, followed the division of common-field parishes. Several small farms have been consolidated into one; and the little farmer has been either metamorphosed into a cotton spinner, or, continuing perhaps to occupy his old farm-house without any land attached to it, lingers as a day laborer on the soil which he once rented. Similar in character has been the effect of this change upon the condition of the cottager. Before the division and enclosure of the district, every cottager possessed a common right of some extent — a right, for instance, to turn out a cow, a pig, a few sheep and geese, upon the wastes of the parish: most of them were in possession of small crofts, which supplied the cow with winter fodder; where this did not happen to be the case, the cottager either purchased hay for her keep, or paid for her run in the straw yard of some neighboring farmer. Hence it is clear that, under the above system, not only the little farmer, but also the

We deny the fact. This population has reared and produced *men*.

Suppose, again, the great body of this population should be set to spin cotton, smelt iron, grind cutlery, and weave stockings; that at these occupations, by incessant toil, they should *produce* not only as much as support them, but one half more; according to political economists, these occupations would be incomparably more *profitable* than the agricultural occupations, and consequently much better for society.

We deny the fact, and scout the inference. The production of *man*, and of man in his best condition, is the physical ultimatum of the earth; and any system whatever that sacrifices the workman to the work — the man who produces the wealth to the wealth produced — is a monstrous system of misdirected intention, based on a blasphemy against man's spiritual nature.

The whole system of modern manufacture, with its factory slavery; its gaunt and sallow faces; its

humblest cottager, drew a very considerable portion of his subsistence directly from the land. His cow furnished him with what is invaluable to a laborer — a store of milk in the summer months; his pig, fattened upon the common and with the refuse vegetables of his garden, supplied him with bacon for his winter consumption; and there were poultry besides. It has been very much the fashion to decry the advantages which accrued from the enjoyment of common rights; but to him who has, and who fortunately wants, but little, a trifle is of importance. This *trifle* amounted, probably to half the subsistence of the man's family.

'And buirdly chields and clever hizzies
Were bred in sic a way as this is.' "

Quart. Rev. July, 1829.

half-clad hunger; its female degradation; its abortions and rickety children; its dens of pestilence and abomination; its ignorance, brutality, and drunkenness; its vice, in all the hideous forms of infidelity, hopeless poverty, and mad despair, — these, and, if it were possible, worse than these, are the sure fruits of making man the workman of mammon, instead of making wealth the servant of humanity for the relief of man's estate.

The day is not far distant when the *labor* of England will hold her court of justice; let those who may await the sentence of the tribunal.

That system of political economy which makes *wealth*, and not *man*, the ultimatum, is based on a monstrous fallacy — on a fallacy so slavish and so detestable, that the wonder is, how accomplished and personally amiable men can be found as its abettors.

The fallacy is, in taking *the rents of the landlords*, and *the profits of the capitalists*, as the measures of good and evil, instead of taking the *condition of the cultivators, and the condition of the laborers*, (the many,) as the sure index of the character of a system.

Whatever tends to *debase man*, to make him physically, intellectually, or morally a lower being, is *bad*, however much or however little the wealth produced may be.* The wealth is not the stable element; it

* The *distribution* of wealth is a question of incomparably more importance than even its *production*. This appears a paradox. It is not so, however. Place man on the earth, and it is his *nature* to produce wealth. Hunger and want will impel him; and as his intellect becomes more and more enlightened, and his ingenuity

is an accidental, and by no means the most important, adjunct. *Man* is the stable element. *His* condition is the standard; *his* improvement is a good; *his* deterioration is an evil. And this, independently of all other considerations. All other considerations are secondary, dependent, subsidiary to the great intention. Man is not useful as he produces wealth, but wealth is useful as it sustains man, ameliorates his condition, improves his capacities, gives opportunities for his further cultivation, and aids his progress in the great scheme of human regeneration.

Such views, then, of political economy as make wealth the ultimatum, (and this wealth, be it always remembered, is the wealth of the land owner, the mill owner, the iron master, &c., and not the wealth of the

becomes greater under the influence of the enlightened intellect, his arrangements will be more complex, more far-sighted, more independent of any sudden shocks or derangements that might accrue from accident. Great advantage, of course, attends the study of the best *mode* of producing wealth. In the *distribution*, however, another circumstance has to be taken into consideration. All history proves man to be a *fallen* creature. No theory of human nature can stand for a moment, that does not admit man's fallen condition. Such theories invariably lead to endless contradictions, because they cannot explain the facts and phases of human manifestation. Now man as a *fallen creature*, though necessarily impelled to produce wealth, more or less, is also *tempted to commit injustice*. The strong individual appropriates more than his equitable share at the expense of the weak individual; and all privileged classes are merely classes of individuals who have obtained more land, or more power, or more license than *equitably* could have been assigned to them. The laws of *distribution* are of incomparably more practical importance than the laws of production, and the public mind will not allow many years to elapse without bringing them to vehement discussion.

multitude of human laborers,) are merely *the beginnings* of the science of political economy. This science, like every other, must pass through its stages; it must have its errors, its superstitions, its partial truths, its truths misunderstood, before it comes forth as a system over which man has no power of control, but which he must contemplate as a system of truth designed by the Creator of the world for the instruction of his intellect, and the improvement of his condition.

Political economy is now struggling to assume a position among the sciences. It is daily growing, daily assuming a more definite form, and daily shaking off those questions that do not belong to it, although so intimately allied with it that they are sure to occur, over and over again, to its cultivators.

That it is a science in the same sense in which chemistry is a science, no person can for a moment maintain. But so much has already been done, that any day might see it transformed by the hand of some master, and presented to the world in the aspect of a teachable branch of knowledge, capable of application to the great problems of legislation.

At the same time we must remark, that the *natural* science of political economy has labored under the immense disadvantage of collecting facts which were not the result of nature's operations, but which were, in a great measure, the result of human legislation, which varied from time to time, and from country to country. The statistics of the corn trade, for instance, and consequently the statistics of the price of corn throughout Britain, were encumbered with sliding scales, fixed duties, and all the other concomitants which the aristocratic rulers of the country have invented for the purpose of taxing labor instead of land. Now, nature has no sliding scales to-day, and fixed duties to-morrow. She acts harmoniously; and the study of her facts is not disturbed by the consideration of causes which may vary indefinitely. Had matter gravitated towards matter according to a sliding scale at one period, and according to a fixed scale at another, and according to no scale at all at a third, it is at all events questionable whether even Newton would have been able to unravel the intricacy of her laws. Consequently we must regard the labors of political economists with lenity, nor must we demand from them the same unity of credence which we expect from the chemist, the anatomist, or the physiologist, because a disturbing force of *variable* character has interfered with the objects of their investigation. At a future period, there can be no doubt that political economy will assume exactly the same form and ordination as the other sciences, and that the economist will, to a great extent, drive from the field both the demagogue and the legislator who makes laws on *opinion.*

Before leaving the subject of political economy, however, we have one remark to offer. God has given to man, and to the world, a certain constitution. By the laws which God has established for the government of the world, certain consequences follow certain antecedents. All human laws whatever are attempts to alter the *natural* arrangement, and to substitute some other consequent, which, according to the ordinary course of nature, would not have followed. It is therefore evident that man, in making laws, must have the most clear and perfectly justifying *reason* for so doing; or otherwise he is attempting to controvert the arrangements of the Almighty, and to substitute *human* arrangements for those that are *divine*. Many of the evils of society are mainly to be traced to the disturbing influence which human laws have exercised on the natural arrangements of Providence.

On the conveyance of the productions of one country to another, for instance, God has placed certain restrictions. Distance must be overcome, storms must be encountered, and risks of various kinds must be incurred. Suppose that the whole of the *natural* risks amount to one fifth of the cost price of the articles. [God, in giving man ingenuity, has given him a power, not of diminishing distance or abolishing storms, but of continually improving the means of transport, and thereby diminishing the natural risk. But let us suppose that, at a given period, the risk did amount to a fifth of the cost price of the article.]

Now, what has man done? Has he accepted the conditions under which God allowed him to exercise his ingenuity? Has he thankfully taken the good, and endeavored to diminish its cost as much as the circumstances of the earth allow? Or has he, on the contrary, taken the conditions such as they were presented in nature, and vastly increased that part of the liability which it was man's constant interest to diminish? According to the laws of nature, (or of God, the author of nature,) the condition annexed to the supply of the foreign goods was the payment of one fifth of the cost; but man, by restrictive laws, customs, duties, &c., increases the cost of supply to two fifths, or a half, or a whole, or perhaps double, the cost price of the articles.*

We are fully aware that, to many, this mode of viewing restrictive laws will appear, at all events, irrelevant; at the same time, there can be little doubt that, so long as restrictive laws of this character are allowed to exist, man must *suffer*. We do not say that the persons who make the laws will suffer, that *they* will be poorer, or that they will reap the inconvenience of the arrangements. *Their* pecuniary interests are often diametrically opposed to the welfare of the great body of the population. But so long as any legislators whatever are allowed to originate restrictions, and thereby vastly to increase the cost of those natural productions which the population requires, the great body of the inhabitants of a country must be *in a*

* The mode in which the taxation of articles of consumption operates, is thus set forth by the Liverpool Financial Reform Association: —

	s.	d.
Cost of tea, per pound, - - - -	1	0
Add profit, 25 per cent., - - - -	0	3
Duty, per pound, - - - - -	2	2¼
Add profit on the duty, - - - -	0	6¾
Price to consumer, instead of 1s. 3d., - -	4	0

Those who are interested in the *facts* of politics (and who is not?) will find the best account of the present political condition of Britain in Wade's "Unreformed Abuses in Church and State." London: E. Wilson. Price 2s. 6d. This is, perhaps, the best exposition of the fruits of aristocratic government that has issued from the press.

worse condition than Providence intended, in a worse condition than they would have been had there been no such laws, and in a worse condition than they would have been had the arrangements of nature been left to themselves, and not interfered with by the enactments of the legislators.

There is the greatest possible difference between taking advantage of the laws of nature, and *originating* laws. It is not man's office to originate laws. God has made the laws, and given man an intellect to *discover* and *apply* them. As well may man make laws in the physical sciences, or in theology, as in political economy. It is true he may make laws and enforce them; but what he never *can* do is, to make the operation of those laws beneficial to the world. This is beyond his power; and, though the laws may be for the pecuniary advantage of the privileged classes of a country, they are necessarily followed by a concomitant series of evils, which bear on the masses of the population.

The great truth which political economy will ultimately teach is this: "That God has constituted nature aright; that it is man's interest to take advantage of the arrangements of nature according to the laws which God has established in the world; that all human laws originating in man are prejudicial arrangements, which interfere with the course of nature; that all such laws ought universally to be abolished, so that man may have free scope to extract the maximum of benefit from the earth." Social arrangements for the benefit of all are not laws — they are adaptations of the laws of nature. These are requisite for society;

and to these arrangements, legislation, in its economical aspect, ought to be exclusively confined. When men persecute each other on account of their religious tenets, (either by positive infliction or by exclusion from civil rights,) they *make* laws — they *originate* laws; when they make it a *crime* to kill a wild animal, they originate laws; when they tax the population for the support of a national creed and national ceremonial, they originate laws; when they allow the king to grant fifty or a hundred thousand acres of the nation's land to an individual, they originate laws. There are no such laws as these in nature; no such laws in reason; no such laws in Scripture. They are mere human inventions, having no truth to rest upon; they are the productions of man during the era of superstition.

But, on the contrary, when men make light-houses for the protection of maritime commerce — public harbors for the safety of ships, seamen, and cargoes — when they make a police to watch — when they pave, light, and clean towns — when they make roads and arrangements for communication — when they support such national defences as are judged requisite at any given time — when they support judges and other officers to administer the laws of justice — when they do these, and many other similar acts, at the common expense, and *enforce* the payment, they do not make *laws*. They make only such arrangements, based on the laws of nature or equity, as are deemed fitting at a given period; they take advantage of the world, such as they find it, and endeavor to evolve from it a greater amount of good than they could do individually, were there no such social arrangements. Men may make laws, if they will; but what they cannot do is, to make good to follow them.

§ III. *The Province and Position of Politics Proper.* — From political economy we turn to politics. Here we approach the argument that a millennium, or reign of justice on the earth, is a *natural* event; that it belongs to the course of human evolution; that it is *computable* on the very same principles that men employ to compute other events; that it may be *inferred* from the past history of human progression, which gives us the actual line of progress, and from the logical ordination of the sciences, which gives us the abstract line of progress.

First, then, we have to determine the *position* of politics in the scheme of classification. Before doing so, however, we must remark that *no* science of politics, whatever be its form, or whatever be its matter, can hope to meet with impartial investigation. Whatever may be the real system of truth, (and a truth there must be somewhere,) that system cannot fail to controvert the opinions of multitudes, and to be favorable or unfavorable to the pecuniary interests of multitudes. A few there may be who are able to look calmly; but the minds of the vast majority are occupied by habitual prepossessions, which, in spite of every effort of the will, prevent the intellect from shaking off its fetters. What they have been accustomed to, or one short step beyond what they have been accustomed to, is the extent of their intellectual horizon. All beyond is a fabulous region of mysterious portent —

an *Ultima Thule*, whose thick waters are unnavigable — a land of darkness, which perhaps some of our far-off descendants may possibly visit, but which *we* can never hope to explore.

Admit the fact of human progression, however, (nor can it reasonably be denied,*) and all the objections, and all the difficulties connected with the habitual credence of a present generation, vanish into air. Let political truth be what it may, it cannot receive general adoption at *any* period. It must grow; it must be suggested, misunderstood, denied, discussed, adopted in part, rejected in part, re-discussed, further adopted, and so on. Were any generation of men (constituted as men now are, and manifesting similar tendencies to what may every where be observed) to continue to live on instead of being replaced by successive generations, it appears highly probable that the progression of man would be for the most part arrested, or, at all events, it would be much less rapid than at present. In general, men form their opinions young, and adhere to them for the remainder of their lives. *New* intellect must be brought forward, with its elasticity, its inquisitive scepticism, and its ardent desire to form a system

* It may be necessary distinctly to reiterate, that by *human progression* we do not mean the progression of man's *nature*, but the progression of man's *knowledge*, and the progression of his systematic arrangements. We are well aware that there is a doctrine which teaches the progressive improvement of human nature. And even this latter doctrine appears to be *so far* correct, that the higher sentiments of human nature come more and more into general action the more men depart from barbarism. But that any amount of natural improvement will make man other than a fallen creature, is out of the question.

satisfactory to itself. It also, in time, fixes its credence, and a new generation is required to continue the onward progress, and to pioneer the way into new regions of thought. Truths, which the last generation regarded as wild romances, or as destructive instigations of the devil, are by the next adopted in sober earnest, and beheld as links in the vast chain of natural revelation,* which, century after century, goes on unfolding itself.

Doubts, disputes, denials, and diversity of opinion, therefore, are of little importance. They are natural; they must come. They are the modes in which man

* We use the term *natural revelation* intentionally, not for the purpose of putting science on an equality with Scripture revelation, but for the purpose of redeeming it from sensational degradation. The grand question of philosophy is, whether the material world furnishes only a summation of sensual impressions, or whether it is really and truly a revelation. That is, can we, or can we not, see through material phenomena into a region which is not appreciable by sense? If we say *no*, we are sceptics; if *yes*, we are idealists, or (a much better name) *intellectualists*. To put the question in a clear light, we ask, "Is the material world a final object, which conveys only sensual impression?" or, "Is the material world *a book*, that affords sensual impression, (the letters, figures, pages, &c.,) and which, *over and above the sensual impression*, conveys an *intellectual meaning intended by the Author?*" A dog, looking at a book, *sees* the same that a man sees; but he understands not the *intellectual meaning* intended to be conveyed to the reader by the aid of the symbols. Now, is the universe an object *final*, or *a book?* This is the great question of philosophy. If we admit it to be a book, as St. Paul does, (Rom. i. 20,) we thereby admit science to be truly *a revelation*. Even if the question were doubtful, which we do not believe, we esteem St. Paul's declaration a settlement of it, as here St. Paul has pronounced divine judgment on a question of philosophy.

expresses his ignorance, and frequently the means he uses to acquire knowledge and determine truth. Where there is diversity of opinion, there must be ignorance on one side or on both; and bold would be the man who, in politics, should assert that he had so completely mastered all truth, that all other men ought to come over to his side. And yet there must be a truth somewhere; and, as knowledge does not admit of diversity of opinion, if ever man can have a system of politics other than empirical, other than superstitious, diversity of opinion must disappear from politics, just as it has disappeared from the sciences which man has already mastered.

First, of the position of politics as a science.

1st. Man may act on the external world of matter, and we may consider the laws of such actions without taking into consideration the reflex effect on man.

2d. We take into consideration the reflex effects on man, and in them we find the laws of political economy.*

3d. Man may act on man *directly*, by interference. The laws which prohibit, limit, or regulate these actions of interference, constitute the science of politics.

* Political economy may have a restricted or an extended signification. It may mean an exposition of the laws according to which man creates or produces wealth. In this sense it is the science of *value*. Or it may mean an exposition of the laws which regulate social welfare, including the *distribution* of wealth, the public health, the public education, &c. In this sense it is the science of *social utility*, of which the production of wealth is only

We here proceed according to a regular progression, beginning at the most simple forms of human action, and passing to those which are more and more complex.

Politics has to do exclusively with the relations between men, and to determine the principles that should regulate their actions towards each other. Where *interference* is not concerned, there is no question in politics. This, then, is the anterior limitation of the science — that where there is no interference between man and man, there is no question of politics.

We have, then, to determine the posterior boundary — that which separates it from any science that might lie beyond it.

This posterior limit is likely, from the prevalence of socialist and communist doctrines, to become the great desideratum of political theory. Those doctrines, whatever may be the contempt heaped on them in England, are far more generally diffused than most Englishmen are aware of. They are now revolutionizing Europe; and no one can predict the extent of the changes that must follow them, if once they gain the complete mastery of the public mind. Instead of railing at them, however, it is much more profitable to endeavor to understand them, and to seize the fallacy on which they are based. Those doctrines contain a profound truth; and more than this, they are the convulsive cries of man's spiritual

the first and simplest embranchment. The economists of England have strenuously adhered to the first meaning; but their place must soon be taken by men of a different stamp, who take a wider range of investigation.

nature, seeking after a better and a holier world than is found in the present condition of society. It is *true* that men are brethren — the children of one Father; it is *true* that universal benevolence is a virtue; it is *true* that man ought not to seek his own advantage at the expense of his fellow; it is *true* that in the present system of society there are stupendous abuses which cannot be justified; and it is also true that socialism and communism are based on fallacies, although the above truths are ostensibly at the bottom of those systems.

There is a true communism and a false communism. Christianity itself teaches us that men are brethren; and no dogmas that have ever been uttered are more communist than some precepts of the New Testament. It is a fact, also, be it *explained* as it may, that the early Christians were *de facto* communists, — that they held all things in common, and that no man called any thing his own. These very doctrines have revived in our day, and they are now playing havoc with the institutions of Europe. They are revived *in the world of politics*, however, and not in the world of religion; and, as a phenomenon in the history of man, this circumstance is well worthy of attention.

All that we have here to do with communism is to point out the fallacy on which it rests, when advanced, as it is, into the region of politics.* This fallacy will

* Of course, we speak here only of that communism that would obliterate private property altogether. The abolition of private property *in land*, and the restitution of the soil to the state, is an

be found the moment we can determine the posterior limitation of the science of politics. And if that posterior limitation cannot be determined, if it cannot be settled satisfactorily by the fairest principles of reason, then no man is entitled to say that communism may not, after all, be the correct theory of politics; and though he may asseverate as he will, or rail, or abuse, he has no right to do so till he can point out the line of demarcation that separates political questions from those that lie altogether beyond the sphere of politics. Nor would any thing that could be said be of much avail to stem the torrent of credence that has set in. Stem it we cannot; but it may be possible to give it a right direction.

Political relations are *not* relations of fraternity. Love, charity, benevolence, and generosity have nothing whatever to do with politics. These substantives, and the principles of action to which they give rise, lie *beyond* the region of politics. This they do *necessarily*—just as necessarily as light and sound, optics and acoustics, lie necessarily *beyond* the region of geometry. Unless this truth is fairly apprehended, and unless the line of demarcation between politics and the regions that lie beyond it is logically determined and clearly perceived, there is a continual danger of sliding imperceptibly into socialism. Whatever may be true, or whatever may be false, in socialism, (using that term in the *most unobjectionable* sense—

entirely different question. Every political state is a communist association; and its common property, the taxation, must be taken either from *land* or *labor*. In Britain, the common property, *the revenue*, already exceeds the rental of the soil.

Christian socialism, for instance,) the principles of *equity* must *first* be taken into consideration before we can, by any possibility, proceed to the consideration of those higher principles of action which may come into play, when once the principles of justice are acknowledged and carried into general operation.

This question is, perhaps practically, the most important in modern politics. Insurged millions let loose on the world, with vague ideas of fraternity in their heads, with the courage of enthusiasm in their hearts, and with bayonets in their hands, are, at all events, formidable expositors of doctrine. Their *energy* is exactly what the continent of Europe has so long required; but their *ignorance* may transform what would otherwise have been a most useful reformation into a terrible hurricane of vengeance, and a blind exercise of destructive power. Now that the theorist and the orator can raise armed millions, the game of politics has assumed a new character. Theories are no longer barren speculations, nor is oratory mere declamation. It is, therefore, of the *first* importance that the most careful, impartial, and honest endeavor should be made to perfect the theory of politics — to base first on the immutable foundations of justice — to satisfy the *reason* before setting the passions in a flame — to evolve principles which can be calmly and soberly maintained by the *intellect*, before they are given as rules of action to enthusiastic populations, ready to march in any direction that is plausibly pointed out as the right one.

We have no intention, however, to attempt the correction of wrong theories. Wrong theories may be supplanted, but it is questionable whether they are ever corrected. The development of the *right* theory is the great object. It will do the work if once it can be finally cleared of logical objection. Men want political truth, and they are making desperate efforts to obtain it; and obtain it they will, ultimately, there can be no possible doubt.

Political relations, so far from being relations of fraternity, or of love, or of any of those sentiments that teach us to bear or to *for*bear, or to give or to *for*give, are relations of equity. They are relations of *justice*, which *gives* nothing, and *forgives* nothing. They are *jural* relations, and political society is a *jural* society.*

The moment this truth is forgotten, the door is opened for the wildest and most impracticable schemes. We have, in fact, broken down the barriers of *reason*, and admitted a flood of wild imagination. While, on the other hand, we repudiate every thing that assumes the form of *authority*, (as dispensing with reason;) so, on the other hand, must we as carefully deny admission to any propositions whatever

* This truth has been clearly apprehended, and very distinctly announced, by Francis Lieber, in his able "Manual of Political Ethics." [London: William Smith, Fleet Street.] That work is well worthy the perusal of those who take an interest in political science. It is far from being a formal treatise, but a most admirable preparation for the gradual introduction of scientific form. "The state, I said, is founded on the relations of right; it is a *jural* society, as a church is a religious society, or an assurance company a financial association. The idea of the just, and the action founded on this idea, called *justice*, is the broad foundation and great object of the state." — P. 160.

which cannot show a *rational* foundation, because they pretend to derive from the higher and more expansive sentiments of the heart. Nothing can be more delusive, nothing more certainly dangerous. Justice is stable, permanent, and strictly regulative. Its rules must determine the form of society, a form which may at all times be *enforced.* And if, as is the case in all known countries, that form shall have been departed from, then *force* may be legitimately used for its restoration.

The moment, however, that we attempt to substitute the relations of benevolence for those of justice, both the scales and the sword fall from the hands of the image. Benevolence can regulate nothing, and enforce nothing. First let me know what is *mine*, and then inculcate the duties and the pleasures of benevolence. But if *nothing* is mine, then is there not only no *justice*, but *no possibility of benevolence;* and those who advocate the absolute abolition of property, would do well to consider that the moment property is abolished, that moment is the practice of benevolence (such, at all events, as involves the objects of property) abolished also. The foundation, therefore, of political society on benevolence is suicidal; the only possibility of benevolence being the admission that something is mine (service or property) which I may lawfully give, lawfully withhold, but which I may choose to give if I please, when actuated by benevolence.*

* The question, whether there ought to be any property at all, is essentially distinguished from the question, *What* ought to be property, and *whose* property ought it to be? The abolition of

Love, benevolence, charity, fraternity, therefore, cannot enter a system of politics. No human society could be founded on them that attempts to regulate the distribution of natural property, and the allocation of that increased value which is created by the labor of individuals. Love may, to a certain extent, reign in a family; but in a state composed of a multitude of independent (although social) individuals, each producing according to his skill, energy, perseverance, and accidental opportunities, *justice* must be the regulative principle, without which the society falls either under the hand of tyranny, or falls into the equally destructive condition of anarchy and confusion.

slavery is a question of the destruction of property. Destroy the *property*, and the slave is a freeman. This circumstance shows that there is nothing so very alarming in the terrible phrase, "destruction of property." It is one question, whether there ought to be property in the abstract; and another and a very different question, whether the present distribution, enforced by law, is the correct one. For instance, Does the county of Sutherland belong to one man, and can he exclude all the rest of the inhabitants, except from the sea-beach and the king's highway? The law says so. Now, suppose the nation were to revise these laws, and to affirm that the *cultivators*, from time immemorial, had quite as good a right to cultivate, by prescription, as the landlord to receive rent for which he does not, and never did, labor. Suppose the nation were to go further in their revision, and to say, The king's grants of former times, or any arrangements of former times, do not deprive us of *our* right to our native soil. Suppose questions of this kind to occur. These are all questions of the "destruction of property!" but yet they are essentially different from the *abolition* of property. The *abolition* of property is a chimera; but the revision, and, to a very large extent, the destruction — that is, the transference — is a tolerable certainty. [Some, perhaps, might prefer the term intolerable.]

We posit, therefore, that political society is a society whose essence, end, and intention is to exhibit, in realization, the principles of equity or justice. And that benevolence has nothing whatever to do with political society, *as such*, may be proven by the following consideration: —

We can conceive that *intellect* should exist, separated from sentiment or passion. Let us suppose a nation of *intellectual* beings, of pure intelligences. It is evident that these might *contemplate* and *reason*, and that they might attain to *truth*, but that *action* is impossible for them, further than the mere action of the intellect. Let us now endow them with the power of action, with *will*, passions, and with the sentiment of *justice*, but without the sentiment of love or benevolence. It is evident that they would be able to perceive, and to carry into practice, the rules of equity for the regulation of their conduct. They would be able to determine that one member had infringed the rights of another; they would be able to enforce restitution where an injustice had been committed; but they would be unable even to comprehend what benevolence was, and the *giving* of property would be absolutely unknown and unintelligible. This society, nevertheless, would be a *political* society, fully and completely. Without even the thought of benevolence, they could carry justice into universal operation, and weigh acts with the utmost impartiality; and also they could carry out the laws of justice with the most scrupulous exactness, neither abating an atom nor superadding an atom. Political society, therefore, could exist, and be regulated by the most strict rules of justice, even where there was not the idea or the sentiment of benevolence; and consequently benevolence is not the basis of political society, and ought not to be taken into consideration when we profess to reason in politics. It lies *beyond* politics, and falls to be considered when the laws of justice have been fully and completely determined.

Although, however, benevolence has nothing to do with *politics*, it has much to do with *man*. And as it *does* lie beyond politics, its laws, whatever they are, or wherever they may be derived from, will fall to be considered at some period or other. Towards them the world is progressing, and *after* a reign of justice there will fall, in necessary order, a reign of benevolence. This is logically necessary. *When* such a happy period may come, or whether it may come in this world, is another question. But that it follows as logically as animal physiology follows vegetable physiology, we believe to be perfectly clear. In former ages, when love and war were esteemed the highest pursuits of man by the ignorant and semi-barbarous, an age of political economy, like the present, would have been looked upon with the most unmeasured contempt as to its character, and the most unmeasured scepticism as to the probability of its occurrence. From a reign of political economy, however, to a reign of justice, there is incomparably less distance than from a reign of barbarous power to a reign of political economy. May we not learn from this fact to expand our minds, and to anticipate, with bright hope, that the phases of human evolution, passing upwards through the *sentiments of man*, and exhibiting those sentiments one after another as they are of a higher and a higher character, shall at last present man as realizing the *highest* principles of his nature, and exhibiting in the outward figure of society the manifestation of those inward principles which make man a denizen of a spiritual world, and link him with the unseen region of light, and love, and immortality?

But if politics be the science of justice, and justice does not admit the idea of benevolence, that idea being necessarily posterior to justice, what is the radical distinction between justice and benevolence, and where is the line of demarcation that separates them?

That line of demarcation is found in the distinction between the *negative* and the *positive*. All the rules of justice are radically negative or restrictive, and present themselves in the form, "Thou shalt *not* do." All the rules of benevolence are positive or expansive, and present themselves under the form, "Thou shalt do, or thou oughtest to do."

Certain difficulties *of language* here present themselves, as they do wherever the theory of positive and negative is involved. A negative proposition may present itself with the same valid signification under the *form* of a positive proposition, and a positive proposition may present itself under the form of a negative proposition. This is universal. It applies no more to politics than it does to logic or mathematics; and though in those sciences it may cause little practical difficulty, in politics it may be made the basis of much unnecessary misunderstanding.

A very simple consideration, however, will place in a clear enough light the difference between the negative character of justice, and the positive character of benevolence.

If all men were socially passive, and did not in any wise interfere with each other, there would be the perfection of justice, while there might be the total absence of benevolence.

No rule of justice can ever *originate* an interference. All interference based on justice is *consequential;* that is, the consequence of a prior act of interference, which requires to be corrected. All primary interference, contrary to the will of the person interfered with, (he being of sound mind, sober, &c.,) is an injustice; and though injustice is usually made to imply also some matter of detriment, pain, or loss, yet this detriment is not its *essential* character. The essential character of injustice consists in the forcible interference of one man with another; nor is any man justified in constraining another to receive even a benefit (or what nine hundred and ninety men out of a thousand would pronounce a benefit) *against his will.* The essential character of injustice is, the overbearing of one man's will by another man's force or fraud. And no rule or principle of equity can ever *originate* such an interference.

The whole scheme of justice, therefore, is essentially and radically restrictive, and all its *positive* rules, or rules which justify or command interference, will be found to consist of those *which justify the restoration of things to that condition in which they would have been, had there been no interference.* That is, whenever the negative state of non-interference has been departed from, and the equilibrium of equity destroyed, justice furnishes rules for *positive* interference, whereby the negative state may be restored, and the equilibrium of equity reëstablished. But this in no wise affects the assertion, that the principles of justice, and the scheme of the science, are entirely *restrictive;* because, let all society be in the negative state of non-interference, and it would remain so forever, were the rules of justice attended to.

Benevolence, on the contrary, supposes that men shall be socially *active;* not that they shall interfere with each other without consent, but that they shall take a constant interest in each other's welfare, and be ready to offer the helping hand of sympathy when sorrows fall upon their brethren. Benevolence cannot *infringe* justice; it only superadds more than justice could require.

Such a condition of society, then, as would be compatible with the perfection of justice, might exclude benevolence altogether. Consequently, justice and benevolence are radically distinguished from each other; and politics, which is the science of justice, is independent of benevolence.

Here, then, we learn the posterior limit of the science of politics.

Where there is no question of interference between man and man, there is no question of politics. This is the anterior limit — that which separates it from all that comes before it; from political economy, the physical sciences, and the mathematical sciences.

And the posterior limit is found in the fact, that the science is confined exclusively to the exhibition of the laws relating to such interference as is consequent on a departure from the state of non-interference, and to the exhibition of the laws (intuitions of the reason) which prohibit all primary interference. [The latter, of course, come logically first in the exposition of the science.]

Having, then, determined the limits of the science of politics, we affirm (from the preceding data) that its position is immediately after the science of political economy, and that it is followed by the laws of benevolence, wherever these may be derived from.

CHAPTER III.

ON THE THEORY OF MAN'S PRACTICAL PROGRESSION.

SECTION I. — OUTLINE OF THE ARGUMENT, THAT THERE IS A NATURAL PROBABILITY IN FAVOR OF THE REIGN OF JUSTICE.

[THIS argument, the outline of which is given in the present section, is continued to the end of the volume. It is based upon, —

1. The analysis of the forms of scientific truth, and the order of the evolution of the sciences.
2. On the abstract forms of man's historic manifestations.
3. On the general arrangement of the component faculties of man, and the order in which these come into exercise.]

We have now to make good our argument, that there is a natural probability in favor of a millennium, or reign of justice. We assume from Scripture the fact that there *shall* be a millennium; and all we have to do is to point out the natural probability of its occurrence, and the probable *mechanism* by which that condition is to be brought about. We treat, therefore, not of a theological millennium, which may involve spiritual elements only to be known by the light of holy Scripture, but of the second causes which, operating in the world, shall at last bring man into the state most favorable for the operation of Scripture truth. A scriptural millennium is much *more* than a mere reign of justice, although that is a main element; but here we touch only on that part of the scriptural millennium which involves the improvement of the human race in those qualities and conditions with which we are naturally cognizant.

And we affirm that, beyond a doubt, a reign of justice is to be anticipated on the fairest principles of computation; and that the argument by which it is established will bear the closest scrutiny of the impartial reason. Setting aside Scripture altogether, (if the expression may be allowed,) we maintain that man has, within the range of his natural knowledge, sufficient means for determining, that if the course of human history continue ordinated on the same principles that may be inferred from a consideration of the past and present, then in the future there must come a time when *justice* shall be the regulative principle of the earth, and man shall carry it into systematic and universal operation.

And though we advance this argument for political purposes alone, we esteem it no mean thing that the good times of prosperity, graciously revealed in Scripture, are actually borne out to the natural reason of mankind. After all that has been said of the millennium, we cannot help thinking that there is a peculiar satisfaction in finding that nature, history, and reason contribute to authenticate the promise. That the more closely the intellect shall search, and the more widely it shall extend its views, it shall yet learn more and more to bow in simple faith before the divine Word, which, with all its mysteries, does continue to justify itself in each new view we gain of nature, and to unfold perpetual witness of its own divinity. Amid the wreck of empires, the turmoils of society, and the dark labyrinths of deceiving doctrines, it is pleasant to lay hold on a clew of hope which leads to better and happier times, and ends at last in a kingdom of righteousness, where they "shall sit under their own vine and their own fig-tree, none making them afraid."

Let us now endeavor to condense the argument, and to place it fairly before the understanding. We believe it valid, and do not fear to present it in its most naked form.

1st. The progression of humanity is in proportion to the acquisition of rational knowledge, and the reduction of that knowledge to practical operation.

2d. Rational knowledge is divided into the various sciences.

3d. A science is composed of nomenclature, (the name,) description and classification, (the proposition,) and reasoning, (the syllogism.)

4th. The sciences have among themselves a necessary coördination.

5th. The measure of this coördination is the relative

simplicity or complexity of the objects involved in the science.

6th. In classifying the sciences, the most simple sciences are necessarily placed first, then those that are more complex, and so forth.

7th. The sciences have a necessary order of chronological discovery.

8th. The order of chronological discovery is coincident with the order of logical classification.

9th. Consequently, if the logical classification be satisfactorily achieved, and the whole of the sciences are not yet evolved, we can predict what the future order of discovery will be.

10th. The general groundwork of the classification of the sciences is as follows: —

I. The abstract sciences, which give the universal forms of rational necessity. These are called the mathematical sciences, and they occur necessarily in the following order: —

1. Logic.* The universal *form* of all science whatever.

* Logic and statics may or may not be considered as *mathematical* sciences, according to the signification given to that term. But this is a mere question of the use of a *name*. Logic is purely abstract, and being the most general form of science, is necessarily anterior to arithmetic; so that, if the term *mathematic* be applied to all the sciences involved in the rational investigation of numbers, quantities, and spaces, logic (or *syllogistic*) is a mathematical science. Again, statics superadds to *space* the concept *force*, and there are *à priori* propositions with regard to force, of a character exactly similar to the axioms of mathematics; e. g., *two equal forces acting*

2. Arithmetic. Logic *applied* to numbers.
3. Algebra. Arithmetic applied to quantities.
4. Geometry. Algebra applied to the forms of space.
5. Statics. Geometry applied to forces.

Intermediate Science.

Dynamics. *Subject*, force. *Product*, motion.

II. The inorganic physical sciences.

Mechanics. *Phenomena*, equilibrium, motion.

The phenomena of solids.
" " " liquids.
" " " gaseous fluids.
" " " imponderable fluids.

Magnetism, chemistry, and electricity. *Phenomena*, motion, polarization, formation, combination, and decomposition, &c.

III. The organic sciences.

1st. Botany. } *Phenomena*, life, growth, propagation, &c.
2d. Zoölogy.* }

in the same straight line, but in opposite directions, will neutralize each other. Thus, statics may be considered as that portion of the general doctrine of force which has an intimate connection with the sciences of space and quantity; while dynamics may be considered as more nearly related to the matter sciences. Or a genus may be made for statics and dynamics, as in the table in the Appendix. To this genus there can be no objection, when we remember that science reads nature *backwards*, and takes the fundamental categories in an inverted order, so that force may be abstracted *in thought* from matter.

* These we have previously termed vegetable and animal physiology, for the purpose of insisting on the fact, that descriptive botany, descriptive zoölogy, anatomy, &c., are not sciences. They are mere *classifications* and *descriptions* of objects whose *functions* must be studied before we have science, properly so called.

IV. Man science.

Functions. Action on the external world.
" Action on man, without interference.
" Action on man by interference.
" Actions towards the divine Being.

The principles of *correct* action, for the first class of these functions, are derived from the sciences that precede man science.

The second class of functions gives rise to political economy, which furnishes the rule of correct action.

The third class to politics.

The fourth class to religion, the scientific groundwork of which is theology.

We posit, then, that human progression is from logic and the mathematical sciences, through the physical sciences, and up to man science.

In estimating human progression as a *fact*, we can only study it as it has manifested itself since the schoolmen, by the adoption of a rational organon, began to lay anew the foundation principles of human credence, and to develop the general doctrine of *method*. The schoolmen (notwithstanding the contempt so superfluously heaped on their memory) are undoubtedly the genuine founders of modern science; and Aristotle is the grand master of that association, whose object is to achieve a scheme of rational truth which shall be the same for all human intellect, wherever that intellect can comprehend it. Ontology and logic are necessarily anterior to the sciences of number, quantity, and space; and though the schoolmen attempted to carry their method into regions where it was not applicable, they went no farther astray in so doing than the sensationalists, who apply the method of matter to the phenomena of mind, and thereby attempt to obliterate all morals.

We ask, then, in what way knowledge tends to improve the condition of man upon the globe?

Correct *knowledge* is the only means whereby correct *action* can be performed. In advancing, therefore, the probability of a millennium in politics, we must, of course, imply that a millennium in other departments has actually taken place, or is now taking place. And this we do. The definition of a millennium is, for us, not any period of time, but a period of truth discovered and reduced to practice. And consequently, when we speak of a *political millennium*, we speak of a period when political truth shall be discovered and be reduced to practice; and such a period we maintain to be within the bounds of rational anticipation.

Let us reflect that the constitution of man, and the earth on which he is placed, permits of *possible* conditions. Some conditions are bad, some better, and some are the best that can exist with such an earth and such inhabitants. No person can, for a moment, maintain that man has achieved the *best* conditions of which the terrestrial economy (including the inhabitants of the globe) is capable. No country, no tribe, no nation, can lay claim to the honor of having placed itself in the best conditions which Providence had allowed it to enjoy. Now, in speaking of a millennium, we pronounce nothing whatever on the absolute amount of evil that is or is not inseparable from man. All we contend for is, that man is continually progressing towards the best conditions that the terrestrial economy renders possible, and that the day will come when his *political* condition shall be perfected, on the same principles that he perfects his other conditions.

Knowledge is the only means given to man to evolve correct *action*, and correct action is the only means whereby the best *condition* can be attained. And this principle is common to every branch of knowledge.

Let a political millennium then mean, the best political condition to which man can attain. A political millennium cannot mean *more* than this.

A political millennium, then, will take place whenever political truth is discovered and reduced to practice. We do not say what *is* political truth, or what is not political truth; but merely determine the general conditions of what we mean by a political millennium.

And we affirm that, according to the past progression of mankind in other departments of knowledge and of action, there are good grounds for believing that political truth *shall* be discovered and reduced to practice. In so doing, we treat political science, not as a mystery which refuses to be reduced to system, and which would thereby justify those who appeal to *necessity*, (whatever course they take,*) but as one of the

* When an action is so utterly defenceless that no reason can be alleged in its favor, its abettors usually fall back on *necessity*. "It is true the thing might not be quite right; but, after all, you must allow it to have been *necessary*." Such is a concise summary of the political reasonings of a class. As if any thing could be necessary whereby we interfered with others, unless it were based on the most clear and indisputable rational truth. As an instance, we give the following paragraph:—

sciences which it behoves man to study, exactly in the same manner that he would study dynamics, or any other branch of knowledge.

Whatever may be the *matter* of political truth, and whatever may be the condition of society that expresses that truth in outward manifestation, we have only to consider the sphere of political truth to determine that it is as much within man's reach as truth in any other department.

What, in fact, is the problem of politics? To discover the laws which should regulate men in the matter of interference. When those laws are discovered, political truth is discovered. Now, notwithstanding the perpetual misconception of the nature of political science, arising from the fact that it is almost invariably confounded with *government*, the right to *govern*, the king's *majesty*, the *authority* of the sovereign, and the other superstitious devices by

"*The Solas Removals.*—It was previously stated that Lord Macdonald had desired the removal of his smaller tenantry from the Solas district. We have since learned that the people are to remain over the winter, on condition of emigrating in the spring of next year. They have given up their stock, and Lord Macdonald allows them to remain in their houses, retaining also their grain and potato crops, a cow to supply milk, and a garron or horse to convey their winter peats. The destitute are to be supplied with meal and clothes, and all arrears of rent are abandoned. We have no wish in any way to encourage wholesale clearances, and sincerely regret that Lord Macdonald should find it *necessary* to remove large bodies of an attached tenantry; but where the means of emigration are provided for a depressed, poverty-stricken, and almost starving community, the true philanthropist will not be in haste to censure. This is the case in Solas."—*Inverness Courier.*

which men impose on themselves from the force of habit, what reason can possibly be alleged for asserting that the laws which should regulate men in the matter of interference, are not as much within the reach of the human intellect as the laws which should regulate the merchant in carrying on his commercial transactions?

But while we anticipate that the day will come when political truth shall be discovered, and be as generally acknowledged as truth in any other science, it is important to apprehend the reason why political truth has not yet assumed a systematic form.

If man progress in knowledge from the more simple to the more complex, — and there can be no doubt that he does progress according to this law, — it is plainly evident that *man*, being the most complex of all the objects that inhabit the earth, must be the *last* whose phenomena are subjected to analysis. Let the sciences be classed as they may, *man, and man's functions*, must always be placed at the extreme end of the scale of natural knowedge; and, consequently, it is no wonder that man science is not completed, when men are only approaching the completion of matter science.

Man first evolves logic and the mathematical sciences, then the inorganic physical sciences, then the organic physical sciences, and, last of all, he makes *man* his intellectual object, and endeavors to discover the laws of his functions. No matter how long or how short a time may be employed in the evolution, this is the necessary order in which the discovery of science must take place. And it would be quite as absurd for us now to affirm that politics cannot assume exactly the same form and certainty as the other sciences, as it would have been for men to affirm that chemistry could not reach its present perfection when their attention was devoted to mechanics, and the region of chemistry was occupied by groundless superstition.

But while we affirm that political science cannot fail to be reduced to such an unobjectionable system as shall command the assent of the unprejudiced intellect, we have yet to look back on the operation of scientific truth, and to observe how the mere dogma becomes transformed into an external reality — how the mere proposition, which the intellect apprehends, becomes the means of vast achievement, and of vast benefit to the race of man.

It has been well said that "error is the cause of human misery;" and as surely may it be said that knowledge is the antidote of error, and the means of man's redemption from misery. And though it is true that religion is the cause of individual regeneration, and the true and main cause of man's progression towards good, we must not, on that account, neglect the study of the *mechanism* of progression, or fail to note the route by which man must pass in his upward and onward progress. It is true that the Christian religion is what *makes* men progress; it gives the impulse, but it does not describe the various steps of the course which the human race must take in its passage to an equitable condition of society.

The steps of that course, so far as the *race* is concerned, must be looked for in the evolution of the sciences one after another. And each new science is not only a revelation to the intellect, but a new power for performing things which could not otherwise have been done; in fact, a new sceptre for man to rule the world, and to bend its elements in obedience to his will.*

* "It is never expected, and indeed it is not possible, that the mass of mankind should be acquainted with the process by which any kind of investigation whatever is carried on. The search after truth — even the truths of the phenomenal world — is a process to them completely enveloped in darkness; all they have to do is to reap the practical fruits of any discovery when it is made, without casting one single thought upon the steps by which others have arrived at it. If we look for a moment at the law by which thought is propagated, we find that it always descends from the highest order of thinkers to those who are one degree below them. From these, again, it descends another degree, losing, at each step of the descent, something more of the scientific form, until it reaches the mass in the shape of some admitted fact, of which they feel there is not a shadow of doubt; — a fact which rests on the authority of what all the world above them says, and which, therefore, they receive, totally regardless of the method of its elucidation. Take, for example, any great fact, or law of nature, ascertained by means of physical science. Such a fact is, first of all, perchance, wrung from the most close and laborious mathematical analysis. A few, perhaps, may take the trouble to follow every step of this process; but the mass, even of natural philosophers themselves, are content to see what is the method of investigation, to copy the formulas in which it results, and then put it down as so much further accession to their physical science. The mass of intelligent, educated minds, again, with a general idea only of mathematical analysis, accept the fact or law we are now supposing, as one of the many beautiful results of investigations which they acknowledge to be far beyond the reach of their own powers; and from them, lastly, it descends to the rest of the community as a *bare fact*, which they appropriate to their own use, simply as being a universally acknowledged truth." — MORELL'S *Hist. Mod. Philosophy — Introduction.*

Let us again repeat, that *knowledge* is the only means given to man to evolve correct *action;* and that correct *action* is the only means whereby man can evolve a correct, and consequently beneficial, *condition*. Let us also note well, that *knowledge* does not admit of diversity of opinion; that where knowledge is really attained and properly substantiated, uniformity of credence is its constant and necessary result; and, consequently, wherever we find diversity of opinion, we have a region where knowledge is not yet attained, or where it has not yet met with general acceptance.

Let us now ask, What is the essence of that ultimate condition of man, expressed for brevity's sake by the word millennium? *A period when truth is discovered, acknowledged, and carried into practical operation.* In so far as the millennium is a *religious* millennium, it is a period when *religious* truth shall be discovered, acknowledged, and carried into practical operation. And in so far as it is a *political* millennium, it is a period when *political* truth shall be discovered, acknowledged, and carried into practical operation. *And so forth for every other branch of knowledge that is capable of being reduced to practice.*

The Sacred Scriptures, it is well known, do not teach man science, nor do they even advert to some of the very greatest earthly consequences that flow from their acceptance. The Scriptures, in a most remarkable manner, confine themselves to *religion*. Their tendency is *moral*, not *intellectual*. As much as is required to convey the *moral* teaching is explicitly declared; but the most remarkable silence is preserved on many questions of the most intense interest, apparently for the very purpose of never allowing man's attention to be diverted, even for a moment, from the mighty purpose for which they were sent. Their province is *eternity;* and the things of time are apparently referred to only as they stand connected with man's eternal welfare. Let us take two circumstances alone to illustrate our position. In every region of the earth where Christianity has *not* prevailed, woman has more or less been looked upon as inferior to man, and in some regions has been reduced to absolute degradation. Christianity has every where restored woman to her moral equality with man; and it is questionable whether man has not been even the greatest gainer by the change. Again: *slavery* — or the subjugation of man to man, and the transformation of man from a *being* into a *thing* — has been almost universal. Wherever Christianity has prevailed, slavery has gradually disappeared; and there cannot be the slightest doubt that the prevalence of *Bible* religion will ultimately obliterate every remnant of slavery from the face of the earth. Enough has been already done to assure us of this unmistakable tendency of Bible religion; and though a corrupted Christianity may yet tolerate the abomination, there need be no hesitation in regarding the freedom of man and the emancipation of the slave as the necessary attendants which, sooner or later, will every where follow the acceptance of the gospel.*

* For a character of slaveholding religion, see "The Life of Frederick Douglass," written by himself.

And if we calmly consider the magnitude of these two social changes, can we estimate their importance, or match them by any other two changes which have taken place in the condition of mankind? Take the first alone—the emancipation of woman, and her restoration to that place which the divine Being designed her to occupy as the companion and helpmeet for man. And all this man owes to Christianity. It was not *man's* doing. It was God's Word that wrought the change. And yet, where in the whole record of revelation can we point to a single passage that affirms that such a change would follow the acceptance of the gospel? It is, in fact, the greatest change that has ever taken place in man's domestic condition. If it were possible to allow *man* to remain as he is, and to return woman to her inferiority and degradation, how long could society remain? Virtue would forsake mankind, and Heaven would hide its face and its favor from the injustice. The good elements of society would at once disappear, and the corrupted mass, putrefying, would return to its base and earthly elements. And yet, if we search Scripture, we shall find only the principles of the great change, and not one single prediction of its occurrence. And so with slavery. So little does the letter of Scripture pronounce judgment on the iniquity, that churches have not been wanting which dared to advance *Scripture* arguments for its justification.* And yet who can doubt that the spirit of Christ's holy religion is certain, wherever it prevails, to emancipate

* See "Chambers's Tract on Slavery." Edinburgh.

the slave, and to reinstate him in all those natural rights which, as a moral, intellectual, and *religious* being, are his birthrights, necessary to be preserved to enable him to fulfil the destiny of responsibility?

And so with the millennium. Scripture holds out the promise of a *religious* millennium; but can we suppose that the period of blessedness will not involve much more than is apparent on the page of Holy Writ? Is it at all illegitimate to infer, that *natural* truth shall have received a vast expansion; that there shall be a millennium of the *intellect*—a completion of the process of continual discovery; and, instead, only a process of continual adaptation? Is the field of intellectual research a field where continual warfare must be waged, where conquest after conquest leaves yet as much to conquer? Or is the march of human knowledge not rather the journey from the land of darkness? Is not this the time of the exodus? and may we not surely look forward to the period when the intellect, entering into the promised land of truth, shall journey no longer forward, but rest in the rich enjoyment of her sanctuary?

Such we maintain to be the case (not from Scripture, for Scripture is silent on these points, but) from the past progress of mankind, and from the present elements at work in a direction that cannot be mistaken. Scripture posits a religious millennium as a fact, and in Scripture that period appears isolated, if we may so speak. It appears separated from the anterior periods of history. It does not seem to follow as a natural consequence from the times which precede it. Its preparation is, at best, but slightly alluded to; and, though we are told that knowledge shall be increased, we are by no means explicitly informed what kind of knowledge that is, or what are to be its effects. And why, we may ask, does Scripture confine itself to such narrow bounds? Can we not see the very same principle pervading this portion of Scripture that pervades so many others; namely, that Scripture confines its declarations to the *religious* part of the predicted period, leaving it to *man* to discover for himself all the other concomitants, all the natural accessories, which are within the range of reason, and which man may estimate with some good degree of probability?

On this ground we maintain, that although the millennium in one sense may be an isolated period, essentially different from all we know of the earth's past history; yet, in another sense, it is a period for which preparations are continually going on; and if we conceive it to include the discovery and reduction to practice of *natural* knowledge, *as well as of religious knowledge*, then the natural portion of the millennium has already commenced, and we may expect it to grow more and more apparent at every future period of the earth's history. In fact, the religious millennium would in that case be only the completion of a series, the perfection of an evolution that had been going on for centuries, the final addition of the spiritual element over and above all that man could achieve for himself by the exercise of his unaided powers.* And when

* Of course we speak here, not of the *nature* of the religious millennium, not of its *internal* qualities, but of its external characteristic; that it is a period of the reign of religion, following the

we reflect that Scripture confines itself to that spiritual element alone, we need not be surprised that the millennium, as there presented, should appear much more isolated than it could possibly be in reality from all those improvements in man's terrestrial condition, which could not fail to accompany the universal prevalence of Christian piety.

A millennium, then, is a condition of society in which man shall evolve the maximum of good by acting *correctly*. And man can *act* correctly only where he has acquired *knowledge*. If, then, we have a scheme, according to which knowledge must be acquired, we have the means of estimating the order in which the natural portions of the millennium must be successively unfolded.

"Knowledge is power," power to turn the earth to better and better account; and thereby continually to improve the condition of man upon the globe. The

development of natural truth. In its internal details, it may be a period when man shall act on religious motive to an extent altogether inconceivable in the present day. But in its character, as a fact, it appears to be the last final termination of the progress that man can make on earth. It is, in fact, the completion of human evolution. And the completion of human evolution takes place logically, whenever the human race acts systematically under the influence of the highest sentiments of human nature. Whenever the *highest* sentiments of human nature are systematically the springs of human action, man has completed his possible progress, he has fulfilled his destiny, (we do not say his *duty*,) he can rise no higher, he can do no more, until the Creator, renewing man's spiritual nature, and abolishing the evil character of the desires, shall emancipate the soul from sin, and restore the freedom that was lost by man's transgression, and repurchased by the merits of the divine Redeemer.

moment, then, we ascertain the *order* in which knowledge must be acquired, we learn the scheme of human improvement, and ascertain the general outline of his course, in his passage from ignorance, poverty, and depravity, towards knowledge, prosperity, and virtuous action.

All that we have professed to do, was to point out the probability of a *political* millennium; that is, we have endeavored to show, that if man progress in future, according to the scheme that has regulated his past progress, there will come a time when political truth shall be discovered, acknowledged, and reduced to practical operation.

But to confine ourselves to this view alone, would be to take a very limited survey of the course and mechanism of human improvement.

A political millennium will come, but it will come only because it forms a portion of the still greater scheme of human improvement — of the more general millennium, that involves *all* human knowledge and all human operation.

The natural millennium, whose probability we maintain to be within the reach of human computation, although more especially to be desired in the region of politics, extends equally to *all* the sciences, and to every department of man's systematic action. Nor could a political millennium take place without being preceded by certain knowledge and certain conditions, independent, it is true, of political science, but necessarily anterior and preparatory to the complete evolution of a reign of justice.

When we reflect that the essence of a millennium

is, "truth discovered and carried into practical operation," we have generalized a term applied in Scripture to a period when *religious* truth should be discovered, acknowledged, and reduced to practical operation.

Consequently, wherever we have *truth discovered and carried into practical operation*, we have a millennium *in that department of knowledge.*

Therefore, the past history of human progress must supply us with *the beginnings of the natural millennium;* and these beginnings we must look for *in the sciences that have been already discovered and reduced to practice.*

Let it never be forgotten that there is but *one truth*, and all truth is the expression of the divine wisdom, and the revelation of the divine character and will. All truth is in fact *divine.* There is not one Deity of Scripture, and another Deity of Nature. Nor can we for a moment coincide with that kind of separation, which some appear anxious to establish, between the revelation in words and the revelation in realities. *Both* are expressions of the divine intentions, *both* are revelations of our Creator, *both* are intended for our guidance and instruction, and *both* are capable of enlightening man, although not in the same department, nor to the same extent. Admitting all that scriptural theology can teach, there is still a revelation through nature, which we may neglect, it is true, but which we can only neglect to our own detriment, as it is the expression of divine wisdom manifesting itself through actual works, and displaying before our eyes the *real* exemplification of the abstract *principles* which, by the same hand, had been impressed upon our *reason.*

All science, therefore, is *divine*, and divine, not in the sense of pantheism, but in the sense of its being the correlative object created in harmony with the human reason. Science is the object of reason, and reality is the object of science; and both reason and reality are the productions of the divine Creator.

Error and superstition are human; they belong to *fallen* humanity; they are not divine; they form no part of the original constitution of the earth; they are darkness, not light. But true knowledge is God's intention; for that purpose the intellect of man was made. Reason, on the one hand, and reality on the other, are the correlatives of creation, and science is the middle term that unites them; reality giving the *matter* of science, and reason giving the form. Knowledge, therefore, is the divine intention; and all the sciences may be viewed, not as human acquisitions, but as fulfilments of the divine purpose in creating an intellect to comprehend, and an object to be comprehended. Religion in the individual may exist without a particle of science; but can it be maintained, for a moment, that the *race of man* can reach its highest condition, and achieve its highest destiny, without becoming acquainted with those natural truths in which practical consequences of the most important kind are necessarily implicated?

Let us, then, conclude that all scientific truth is divine, (or, if that term appear too strong, let us say that all scientific truth is the natural intention of the Creator of our system,) that it is the intellect of the creature apprehending correctly the divine arrangements of the created. Natural science is the apprehension of the divine wisdom and power, as St. Paul himself teaches us, — "For the invisible things of him from the creation of the world are clearly seen, being understood by the things that are made, even his eternal power and Godhead; so that they are without excuse: because that, when they knew God, they glorified him not as God, neither were thankful; but became vain in their imaginations, and their foolish heart was darkened." — *Epistle to Romans, 1st chapter.*

Immediately, then, that we admit science to be not merely human, science acquires a new character. It becomes the exponent of humanity, and points out the order of human progression. We have here a sure basis of operation, a foundation on which the reason may at last rest in constructing its philosophy of man. Science is stable. It shifts not with opinion, and changes not with lapse of ages. Were all knowledge obliterated, and man to begin to-morrow a new course of research, he could come only to the same truths and to the same sciences; and those sciences would evolve in a similar order, were the experiment to take place a hundred or a thousand times.

SECTION II. — THE INFLUENCE OF SCIENCE ON MAN'S TERRESTRIAL CONDITION.

ADMITTING, then, the divinity of science, in so far as science has been really ascertained, we revert to its connection with man's practical function, and inquire how the dogma of knowledge is efficient to produce an amended condition of man upon the globe.

Every science has a millennium; that is, a period when its truths are discovered, acknowledged, and carried into practical operation.

First come the mathematical sciences. These, as mere exercises of the intellect, are by no means of a high character. They are little more, in fact, than mechanical reasonings, mere methods of computation performed by the aid of signs. The *discovery* of the methods has, no doubt, called forth some of the highest exercises of human genius; but genius looks beyond the mere computation of numbers, quantities, and spaces.

When we turn, however, to *the application* of the mathematical sciences, their influence in enlightening mankind is of the very highest order. Identity, equality, number, quantity, space, and force, mere abstractions of the reason, become fundamental elements of knowledge, by which the observed realities of nature are made to function in man's intelligent apprehension. Sensational observation furnishes only the very smallest part even of physical science. Strictly speaking, observation furnishes only a momentary image or impression, or a succession of momentary images or impressions. No man ever *observed* motion. He observes successively in time *material substantives* in successive positions in space; but the *motion* he never did observe, and never can observe. Let materialists or sensationalists reason as they may, they cannot tell what physical properties motion has. It has no color, no taste, no smell, no sound; it cannot be felt or appreciated by the senses, and to the sensationalist it has no existence. It is a word he has no right to use; but use it he must, and in so doing he *borrows* it from the intellectualist.* And so with *force*. Force is inappreciable by sense. Sense never saw force, never felt it, and never can assign one single sensational property to it. It is posited by the *reason;* and the moment we become sensationalists, we should drop the word and the concept as chimeras of human invention. And, in so doing, we must drop the science of dynamics. No greater absurdity was ever imposed on man, nothing was ever more frantically credulous, nothing that the wildest superstition ever raved in its most intense moments of insane imagination, was more utterly contrary to man's universal experience, and man's universal reason, than the attribution of all man's knowledge to *sense*. Nor can we approve of those arguments which drag the question into the region of theology. That is not its region. The battle cannot be fought there till won in another field. It must be fought as a question of philosophy *in the region of dynamics;* for if once we substantiate power, and can show *a science of force*, and perform with that science of force rational operations whose conclusions are *verified* in nature, and predict by its aid

* It is one of the *changes* which the reason includes in the general law, (necessary form of thought,) "Every *change* must have a *cause*." This is the condition under which man thinks. He may deny the proposition, or mystify it, from his inability to appreciate mental phenomena; but it is as much a condition of his thought *while engaged in the denial*, as it is while engaged in its admission. In mechanics, the *change* is motion, the *cause* is force.

far-off truths only to occur in reality years after the rational calculation has been made, we have grounded the validity of the reason, and proven beyond dispute its undoubted right to substantiate things hidden from sense, and forever beyond the reach of sensational apprehension.*

But if sense furnish so little in a science, *mind* must furnish all that is not mere momentary impression; and the rational operations of mind, applied to the material realities of nature, are expressed in the mathematical sciences when they are brought to bear on physical nature, and to lend the aid of their computing power to systematize the impressions of the senses. Number, quantity, space, and force, (essentially non-physical concepts,) are absolutely necessary for the formation of physical science; and all the *observations* that man could make would be forever dog's views of nature, were it not for the introduction of those rational elements which tear the veil from the world of matter, and lay bare the mysteries of its divine arrangement.

When man has evolved the mathematical sciences and dynamics, he has acquired a vast power over the world of matter; not merely a power of intellectual apprehension, but, over and above, a power of *action* — a power to perform things which react intensely on his own social condition, and place him on an entirely different footing as regards his relations to the

* "The most certain method that can guide us in the research of truth consists in rising, by induction, from phenomena to laws, and from laws *to forces*." — LAPLACE, *Essai Philosophique sur les Probabilités.*

material universe. His *observations*, without the mathematical sciences, go for little or nothing. He can neither number, nor measure, nor compute; and without *measurement*, his observations are mere sensations.

We shall remark only one or two of the effects of the mathematical sciences. The first great achievement, and one whose importance to the world is beyond all human calculation, is "the determination of the physical character of man's home or residence in space." *Astronomy* and *general geography* are the results. Now, passing over all that could be called mere knowledge, let us look to two *practical* effects, which forever place the *practical* influence of the mathematical sciences on man's condition, altogether beyond the power of question—*navigation* and the *measurement of time*. Navigation is possible without astronomical observation, or at least with the very rudest elements of observation. The Northmen were no doubt in the habit of sailing to America (Vinland) five hundred years before Columbus; and that they navigated all the European seas, from Iceland to Italy, is proven by abundant evidence. But what comparison can be established between such navigation, and that which now is one of the most powerful of all agents for the civilization of the earth? Such navigation was an adventure, not an occupation. And the wonder is, how even the boldest, hardiest, and most daring of all races should have undertaken such enterprises. No one can for a moment believe that such navigation as now takes place could possibly have arisen without a knowledge of astronomy and geography, or could possibly be continued were the astronomical elements to be dropped. The navigation of the Northmen was an adventure, and it ceased because it was an adventure. It had no systematic knowledge at the bottom of it, showing how the thing that had been done once could be done again. It passed away, and even the discovery of the western continent, with which they had traded, was all but forgotten. But can any one suppose, that so long as the present *knowledge* remains, navigation could again cease, or be confined to coasting expeditions? Were all the ships in the world destroyed, a few years only could elapse before the ensign of England would wave in the breeze of every navigable latitude; and the speedy reparation of the great catastrophe would only show the power that man has acquired from knowledge. Between the navigation of former times and the navigation of the present day, there is much the same difference that there is between Alexander's expedition to India and the unromantic overland journey, reduced to a monthly question of pounds, shillings, and pence.

Closely connected with navigation, and extending its influence throughout all civilized society, is the *measurement of time.* The measurement of time is in fact the measurement of the motions of the heavenly bodies. The firmament in one sense is a great *clock*, with a very singular dial, and a very curious method of notation. Let it *stop*, and all means of measuring time accurately, and of being sure that our measurements are correct, fade away forever. And who can estimate the practical influence on the world of the measurement of time?

Geography, astronomy, the measurement of time,

and systematic navigation, laid the foundation for the general civilization of the world. And one circumstance we may remark connected with ocean locomotion — *the most advanced nations in the world will always be those who navigate the most;* and, consequently, advancement, improvement, civilization, knowledge, and art, will always be disseminated through navigation. No instance can be adduced of barbarous nations navigating to a great extent, while at the same time more advanced nations did not navigate. Those who have navigated, in all ages, have been those who were full of life, energy, resolution, and progress. The advanced nations are the goers, the less advanced nations are the stayers at home. Sloth and barbarism are essentially stationary; energy and civilization are essentially expansive, cosmopolitan, and progressive. One circumstance alone shows us that navigation is essential to the regeneration of the earth. *The one true religion never could be propagated throughout the world, as there is no doubt it will be at some future period, without navigation.*

But to what does man owe geography, astronomy, the measurement of time, and systematic navigation? *To the application of the mathematical sciences to the observed conditions of material nature.*

Now, although the term may be new, and by some may be considered objectionable, we do not hesitate to speak of a *mathematical millennium.* A mathematical millennium takes place when mathematical truth is discovered, and reduced to practical operation. Mathematical science is the foundation of man's intellectual and practical progress, and the region of mathematics is the *first* region in which a natural millennium takes place. Without mathematics we have no astronomy, no geography, no measurement of time, and no systematic navigation, worthy of the name. That is, we have in those departments ignorance or superstition, instead of knowledge.

Next to a mathematical millennium is a *mechanical* millennium. And here we leave the *knowledge*, and turn only to the *action*, and to the consequent *condition* of man. The mathematical sciences are absolutely essential to the evolution of mechanics, and mechanical knowledge is absolutely necessary to enable man to turn the earth to the best account. One of the first great spheres of mechanical operation is "locomotion." The mathematical sciences teach men how to navigate, in what direction to go, how to make maps and charts, how to determine the locality of towns, capes, reefs, ships, &c., &c. But the mathematical sciences do not teach how to make ships. They help, but they do not complete. The properties of matter are involved, and these must be ascertained by observation.

The improvement of locomotion is one of the first essentials in the progression of mankind, and we might almost measure the relative advancement of nations by the condition of their means of locomotion. Advantages of the highest importance to man's intellectual and moral welfare are involved in facilitating locomotion; and every obstacle placed by governments in the way of perfectly free locomotion, is a barrier erected to defer the advance of civilization. It is a clog placed by ignorant despotism on the emancipation of mankind, not merely from political thraldom, but also from natural ignorance and natural degradation. It is a crime, not merely against the individual, but against *humanity itself.* And whoever has the power, has the most undoubted right to break down every such barrier as a duty to his race. Political freedom, in this respect, however, is not the only essential; we must also have the mechanical facility.*

Let us consider that the earth, as constituted, permits only of locomotion under certain conditions. It is possible for man to have *a maximum* of locomotive facility. A certain speed will be found beyond which we lose in safety, and below which we lose in celerity

* While mentioning *locomotion*, it is, perhaps, impossible to refrain from remembering the late Mr. Waghorn, (with whose name the title of *lieutenant* appears like that of *exciseman* in connection with the name of one Robert Burns,) as brave a heart and as true a genius as England has seen for many a long day. Mr. Waghorn was the Napoleon of communication; and when those who did *not* reward him have been long forgotten, his name will appear as one of those heroes to whom the world owes its progress. It is sickening to think that Waghorn should have died as he did, overborne by the material cares of this life; but when prime ministers, and first lords of the admiralty, and chartered East India companies, shall be mere matters of history, the name of Waghorn will appear with those of Eric the Red, and Marco Paolo, and Christopher Columbus, and Richard Chancellor, and La Salle, and Brindley, and Watt, and Telford, and those other heroes who have bequeathed the world's good, by stamping the impress of their genius on the destinies of humanity. To think that the wealth of England should have bowed before a Hudson, and brought rich offerings to the shrine of pampered sycophancy, and yet should have seen a brave man end as did Waghorn, when a few thousands might have gladdened the last days of the intrepid Englishman! But enough — he will not be forgotten.

without gaining in safety. And this applies to all *systems* of locomotion. The problem, then, is to discover the best *system;* that which combines the maximum of celerity with the minimum of danger. And when we have made as near an approach to this as the circumstances of the earth permit of, we have a locomotive millennium.*

All engineering is nothing more than the application of mathematics and mechanics to the world of matter. Roads, bridges, canals, ships, harbors, docks, railroads, tunnels, steam engines, steam vessels, steam locomotives, &c. &c., are the products of mathematics and mechanics. Man, with these, is man armed with the powers of nature. He has vanquished his opponent, and enlisted her forces in his service. Matter is no longer the object that opposes him, but the arsenal from which he draws his weapons and his stores. Coal and water become concentrated forces, whose powers he may develop and control for the extension of his dominion over nature, and for the improvement of his terrestrial condition. One single steam engine constructed by mankind is of more real importance than all the powers of Rome, and one single printing press than all the arts of Greece. They are *powers*, prodigious powers, placed at man's disposal. They are products of the reason; and just as reason learns to see farther and farther into the processes of nature,

* Letters, newspapers, &c., are entirely dependent on the means of locomotion; and who can possibly estimate the influence of postal communications on the civilization and advancement of mankind? But even the prodigies of steam have been eclipsed by the electric telegraph.

so does man acquire new power for extracting welfare from the earth.

Again: man makes a few observations on the phenomena of light; these he geometrizes. He makes a few observations on the power of various substances to modify the phenomena; and what is the result? He produces the telescope, which extends his vision to a distance altogether inconceivable; and the microscope, which reveals the minute operations of organic nature.*

And if we turn to chemistry, shall we find the practical effects of science one atom less important, or one atom less remarkable? What are the *metals*, and where do they come from? What is gas? that great moralizer of modern cities, more powerful than all police could be. Mechanics and chemistry furnish us with an endless variety of substances, and an endless variety of productions, all tending to give man more power, more leisure, more comfort; to make him in fact more free, and to elevate his position on the

* "In order to enumerate only a few of the instruments whose invention characterizes great epochs in the history of civilization, I would name the telescope, and its too long-delayed connection with instruments of measurement; the compound microscope, which furnishes us with the means of tracing the conditions of the process of development of organs, which Aristotle gracefully designates as 'the formative activity of the source of being;' the compass, and the different contrivances invented for measuring terrestrial magnetism; the use of the pendulum as a measure of time; the barometer; the thermometer; hygrometric and electrometric apparatuses; and the polariscope, in its application to the phenomena of colored polarization in the light of the stars, or in luminous regions of the atmosphere." — HUMBOLDT'S *Cosmos*, p. 473.

globe. Instead of being the slave of physical nature, science will make man its master, as the Creator intended him to be when he gave him an earthly dominion.

Electricity, again, has already achieved its wonders; and though we may expect many more practical effects, we have enough to prove that this science, which some years since was a plaything, is a mighty agent that endows man with power which, even a century since, would have been regarded as indubitably magical. The very circumstance that man can now communicate with man almost instantaneously, although separated by the breadth of a kingdom, ought to teach us that time and space, the former tyrants of mankind, may be overcome by means whose simplicity is, at least, as extraordinary as their power.

Nor, if we turn to vegetable physiology, are the practical effects that the advance of knowledge entails for man's benefit one hair's breadth less extraordinary. A few observations are made on the growth of plants, on the disposition of the soils, on the effect of moisture, and on the relation of surface water to the productions of the agriculturist. Certain reasonings are made, and certain experiments, to prove whether the reasonings are correct. The practical result, at last, is a general system of drainage, which transforms wretched pastures into fertile cornfields, and in many cases doubles, trebles, and quadruples the value of the produce. To countries like England, Scotland, and Ireland, the practical importance of this draining system is immense. These countries have, within themselves, an almost indefinite power of creating agricultural wealth; and, so far from being in danger of a superabundant population, they could, in ten years, with a tenth part of the annual expenditure of the kingdom *on unnecessary armaments*, so outrun the increase of the population, that it would be unnecessary to import one single grain of corn. Far more than this is within the limit of possibility, and it is only necessary to ascertain the progress made by Scotland within the memory of the present generation of agriculturists, to be convinced that the natural capabilities of the soil of Britain are abundantly sufficient for all its inhabitants; and that the true reason why the population increases more rapidly than the food is to be found, not in the laws of God, but in the political laws which have made such a disposition of the soil as absolutely prevents it from being turned to account. Under the present system of land occupancy, combined with labor taxation, want and starvation are the natural consequences. They may excite compassion, but they need excite no wonder. And until the present system is broken up, root and branch, and buried in oblivion, the laboring population of Britain and Ireland must reap the fruits of a system that first allocates all the soil to thirty or forty thousand proprietors, and then places the heaviest taxation in the world on the mass of the inhabitants. Let any man inquire of the Scottish agriculturists — the greatest landlord worshippers in Europe — what is the reason that the improvement of the soil does not go on more rapidly and more generally. The answer, we have invariably found, attributes the evil to the political tenure of land. The agriculturists *could* produce more corn.* Every one of them, except in a few small districts where the land is up to its pitch of production, will attest to this fact. They *could* make more food — more wheat, more oats, more turnips, heavier sheep, more and better wool, &c., &c. And they *would* do so, — both for their own profit, and from a spirit of emulation generated by the rapid improvements already achieved, — but they *cannot* do so; and the country, which allowed the crown to alienate the soil, must be content to see it half cultivated, and to depend for supplies on distant lands. They *cannot* improve, because, although the improvements would pay, and pay abundantly, in the first place they have not the capital to execute the improvements at the commencement of their lease; and, in the second, it is absurd for them to make permanent improvements during the currency of a lease, the only effect of which would be, — and, as a fact, often is, — that, at the end of the lease, the legal landlord would let the land, *with its improvements*, by auction. *Their* improvements would be put up to auction, the only difference being that the biddings are written instead of spoken; and, unless they will give more rent for their own improvements than any other person will give, they are turned out of the land, and, in many instances, carry their skill and capital to far distant countries. The difficulties are neither with the soil, nor the climate, nor the price of produce; they all hinge on the political arrangement that the law has made with regard to the soil and its tenure; and until this arrangement is

* See Mr. Caird's Pamphlet on "High Farming."

destroyed, the soil never *can* produce its maximum. The evil is immensely aggravated, it is true, by the system of entail; but the radical evil, the grand masterpiece of mischief, that requires to be corrected, is the alienation of the soil from the nation, and the taxation of the labor of the country.

With regard to draining the soil, however, a new scheme has recently been carried into execution. The government taxes the population, and lends the money to the landlords to drain the soil. The landlords are to pay a certain interest and quit capital, which discharges the debt in twenty-two years. This per centage the farmer finds to be *less* than the profit likely to accrue from the improvement of the land, and he agrees to pay it to the landlord. The consequence is, that the country has been taxed for the purpose of presenting the landlords with the clear amount of improvement at the end of twenty-two years.* Such is the wisdom and equity of British (landlord) legislation.

Notwithstanding the political arrangements, however, the advantages of draining are of the highest character. The soil improves, the climate improves,†

* Since the drainage money was advanced by the government, advertisements have appeared in the "North British Advertiser," in which the landlord offers to drain the lands on the payment of *ten* per cent. per annum by the tenant.

† "Comment en serait-il autrement quand les belles recherches publiés par M. Arago dans *l'annuaire*, ont demontré que les defrichements et les grands travaux agricoles suffisaient pour diminuer les chaleurs de l'été et les rigueurs de l'hiver, et peut être même influer sur la temperature moyenne de tout un royaume."—GAVARRET, *Principes Generaux de Statistique Medicale*, p. 182.

the character and condition of the agriculturists improve, and the amount of food is vastly increased. And to what do we owe draining, with all its sterling advantages? To nothing more than the application of hydrodynamics to vegetable physiology. This is its scientific character — its character as a product of human ingenuity, exercising itself on the physical world.*

It will scarcely be necessary to remark the power of man to modify the animal kingdom, and thereby to produce those animals that serve him better, and make his position more advantageous. The horses,

* Were the governors of England open to any scheme that would permanently improve the country, without being made a job, a very simple means is at their disposal. Take one million a year from the army and navy. This might be done without impairing the real security of the country. Let this money be expended on drainage and permanent improvements. Let it be lent to no person in the first place. But, wherever tenants in occupancy were willing to pay *the interest* of the money, let them be judges under inspection what drains are requisite, and *whether they are properly executed.* No person is so competent as the tenant to see that the work is well done, where his interest is so much involved. When the drains are specified, let their execution be done *by contract.* The tenant and inspector giving their certificate that the land is properly drained according to bargain, the contractor receives his money. The difference between the common interest of money, say three and a half per cent., and the quit per centage, say six and a half per cent., *to be paid by the landlord,* who receives the permanent benefit. The land itself to be accountable for all the liabilities. This scheme would prodigiously increase the produce of the country; and, as the land is so little taxed, the landlords would have no right to complain. With a landlord legislature, however, we fear there is but little chance for schemes of this nature.

cattle, sheep, &c., of Britain, are even now almost artificial races. The difference between those animals as they are, and animals of the same species as they would have been in a state of nature, is the product of human ingenuity. The Durham ox, or the Leicester sheep, is, in one sense, *a machine* — a machine for the manufacture of beef, mutton, fat, and wool, out of grass, turnips, and oil cakes. The improvement of the breed is exactly a similar occupation to the improvement of a cotton mill, or the improvement of the soil. If man wants more corn than will grow naturally on the soil, he must improve the soil, drain it, manure it, lime it, irrigate it, &c. It is no longer the same soil; it is the same species, but a different variety from what it was originally. Even let it alone, and it will bear a different series of plants. The original plants die out, and their place is taken by others more useful to man. And when man sows seed of a certain requisite character, he reaps a much better and more abundant crop. And so it is with a sheep, or a bullock, or a fowl. Naturally he grows wild, rough, hardy, and takes far too much exercise to fatten. He is developed in those parts that man esteems the least, — that do not *pay*. He is unmanageable, has his own way, runs, jumps, tears, flies, and does many things that no doubt amuse himself, but that do not recommend him as an investment. The improved animal, on the contrary, is quiet, solemn, fattens well, appears to understand the end of his existence, and takes to it kindly; bears beef and fat, or mutton and wool, to the very best of his power, and seems pleased with his prosperity. He even learns to look down on his less cultivated companions, and seems thoroughly imbued with a quiet sense of his own superiority. He does as he is bid, and in all respects is a man server. He does his work, and receives his wages.

The improvements that have hitherto taken place in agriculture, in horticulture, and in the races of horses, cattle, sheep, and the other domestic animals, are the direct results of *empirical* physiology, which observes and records the *resulting* fact, without inquiring into the various steps of the process by which the fact is eventually produced. The empirical physiologist inquires, "*Does* the earth become more productive by the application of certain substances, (called, generically, manures,) and if so, What are the relative advantages of these substances, compared among themselves?" The scientific physiologist, on the contrary, inquires, "In what *manner* does the earth become more productive by the application of these substances?" The one fixes his attention on the improvement of his *art;* the other, on the improvement of his *knowledge.* The one endeavors to read aright the laws of the practical world, and to apply them to his use; the other endeavors to read aright the construction of the material world, and the laws by which nature carries on her operations. The empiric is satisfied when he has learned the mode by which he can make his bullocks fatten in the shortest time and at the least expense; the scientific physiologist, on the contrary, is never satisfied till he has traced the particles of food from their primary prehension, through the process of their assimilation, to their ultimate deposition in the tissues. The one manipulates a mass, and endeavors to induce certain final consequences; the other attempts to seize a primary atom, and to determine the laws which regulate its evolution.

Empirical physiology and scientific physiology represent two great methods, whose tendency is to approach nearer and nearer to each other, and finally to unite in their results. The former commences with perhaps a great rude fact, plain and obvious, and as far as possible removed from any thing that would be called science. This fact, perhaps, might be merely the division of the year into its two great seasons — summer and winter; and the observation that domestic cattle thrive better if housed in winter, than if left exposed to the inclemency of the season. This, in many cases, is the first great practical step, or first great division, which is gradually to undergo innumerable subdivisions; and these subdivisions affecting many kinds of food, and many breeds of animals, at last evolve a complete art, whose principles are tolerably well ascertained. Scientific physiology, on the contrary, commences with a fact as far distant on the *opposite* side from its ultimate application. It begins with the analysis of the atmosphere, with the mysteries of oxygen and carbon, with theories of combustion, with what the air does in the fire, and what becomes of the smoke. And while engaged in these investigations, it knows no more of the process by which bullocks are fattened than the bullocks know of phlogiston. In course of time, however, it improves both its knowledge and its method; it attacks the fat itself, and begins to discourse of stearine, oleine, &c.;

and also begins a series of investigations on the process of respiration, on the possible modes by which animal tissues may be consumed, and on the *conditions* that accelerate or retard the consumption. This is the first fibre of communication shot across the interval which separates empirical from scientific physiology; and though only a fibre, it is like the ice shooting from opposite sides of the stream, the first frail forerunner of a solid communication. Step by step the two processes go on, the one descending into details more and more artistically minute; the other departing more and more from its elementary compounds, until it succeeds at last in constructing a scheme of knowledge which shall not only explain the results, but serve as a guide for the evolution of a correct systematic practice.*

* The difference between the empirical and the scientific method is expressed with logical accuracy, as follows: —

1. The empirical method manipulates those substantives (in any particular course of inquiry) which present the greatest *comprehension.*

2. The scientific method manipulates those substances which present the greatest *extension.*

Thus an animal frame *comprehends* the processes of combination, decomposition, respiration, the development of heat, &c., &c.; while the natural history of oxygen or carbon *extends* to all the objects in which oxygen and carbon are comprehended, although that natural history in reality comprehends nothing but its own series of phenomena.

The antagonism usually set forth as existing between the *inductive* and the *deductive* process of reasoning, is not only based on a misunderstanding of the methods of pure syllogistic, but absolutely opposed to the methods which *are* pursued in matters of induction. There is really only *one* process of reasoning, although this may be read in different manners. What is called the induc-

And when once the two methods have come to an *identity* of result, (as they have in some of the mechanical arts, and as they may soon in some branches of physiology, (a system of truth is developed for the world, for the human race, for humanity; not merely for the discoverers and improvers, but for man as man, for the human being tenanting the world, and gradually learning to read aright the universe, or cosmos, in which he finds himself placed. *Man* has made a new acquisition, and this new acquisition remains a permanent, stable, and lasting addition to the wealth of humanity.

But empirical physiology does not apply merely to

tive process of *reasoning* is only the inductive process of *observing*; and when the observations are made, the reasonings are all made by the same process.

Let the logician apply to any man in the practical departments of life, and he will find him reasoning from *a major premiss*; which will be found to consist of *two* propositions, and not, as the Baconians affirm, of *one*, which has been inferred from many observations.

For instance: —

Major. — In every case that I have given this food to my cattle, they have thriven well.

Minor. — This is a new case, in which I give the same food to my cattle.

Consequent. — Therefore they will thrive well, (the probability being greater or less according to circumstances.)

The Baconians divide the major premiss and call it a *reasoning*, whereas it is no more than an *observation*.

The essential difference, however, between the empirical and the scientific methods is this — the one classifies *events*, the other classifies *substances*. The empiric endeavors to find the law of *the events*; the man of science, the law of *the substances*; and in this light both pursue exactly the same *method*.

the organized or animated objects that man finds surrounding him. It applies to himself, and to the material conditions of his bodily frame. Of all animals, man is the most subject to disease, the most liable to be cut off from existence before his body has passed through its natural transformations, and at last sinks exhausted from the influence of age. History, however, proves that an immense amelioration has taken place even in this respect — that man has extended the limits of his life — that he has intelligently constructed circumstances less fatal to his organism — that he has diminished, and vastly diminished, his liability to dissolution — in fact, that he has to a certain extent beaten the evils of the physiological world, exactly as he has vanquished the difficulties of the mechanical world.*

* M. Moreau de Jonnés, in a notice on the mortality of Europe, has given the following table, which tends equally to prove the influence of civilization on the number of deaths: —

Countries.	Years.	One death out of	Years.	One death out of
Sweden,	1754 to 1768	34	1821 to 1825	45
Denmark,	1751 to 1754	32	1819	45
Germany,	1788	32	1825	45
Prussia,	1717	30	1821 to 1824	39
Austria,	1822	40	1825 to 1830	43
Holland,	1800	26	1824	40
England,	1690	33	1821	58
Great Britain,	1785 to 1789	43	1800 to 1804	47
France,	1776	25·5	1825 to 1827	39·5
Roman States,	1767	21·5	1829	28
Scotland,	1801	44	1821	50

— QUETELET'S *Calculation of Probabilities.* Notes by Mr. Beamish. See the whole note, (v.) p. 114.

This improvement man owes to empirical physiology, partly intentional and partly unintentional — partly to the exercise of a direct effort, and partly to the general amelioration of circumstances produced by the advance of civilization. Better clothing and better food — better dwellings and a better system of drainage — cleanliness, ventilation, and a more abundant supply of water — prompt treatment under acute disease, inoculation and vaccination — the improvement of jails, workhouses, and all other prisons and similar abominations — a more simple and natural mode of rearing children — in fact, a better and more rational system of treating the human frame both individual and collective, and placing it in circumstances more conducive to its healthy function, has at last evolved a longer life, and secured to the general man a longer tenancy of terrestrial existence.

SECTION III. — APPLICATION OF THE THEORY OF PROGRESSION TO MAN'S POLITICAL CONDITION.

We have said enough, however, to show the direct bearing of science on the improvement of man's condition on the globe. Knowledge is obtained, an improved system of action is consequently generated, and from that improved system of action an improved *condition* arises as the necessary result.

But, then, how comes it that, notwithstanding man's vast achievements, his wonderful efforts of mechanical ingenuity, and the amazing productions of his skill, his own condition in a social capacity should not have improved in the same ratio as the improvement of his condition with regard to the material world? In Britain, man has to a great extent *beaten* the material world. He has vanquished it, overpowered it; he can make it serve him; he can use not merely his muscles, but the very powers of nature, to affect his purposes; his *reason* has triumphed over matter; and matter's tendencies and powers are to a great extent subject to his will. And, notwithstanding this, a large portion of the population is reduced to *pauperism*, to that fearful state of dependence in which man finds himself a blot on the universe of God — a wretch thrown up by the waves of time, without a use and without an end, homeless in the presence of the firmament, and helpless in the face of the creation. Was it for this that the Almighty made man in his own image, and gave him the earth for an inheritance? Was it for this that he sent his Son into the world to proclaim the divine benevolence, to preach the doctrine of human brotherhood, and to lay the foundation of a kingdom that should endure forever and ever? We do not believe it; neither do we believe that pauperism comes from God. It is *man's* doing, and man's doing alone. God has abundantly supplied man with all the requisite means of support; and where he cannot find support, we must look, not to the arrangements of the Almighty, but to the arrangements of men, and to the mode in which they have portioned out the earth. To charge the poverty of man on God, is to blaspheme the Creator instead of bowing in reverent thankfulness for the profusion of his goodness. *He* has given enough, abundance, more than sufficient; and if man has not enough, we must look to the mode in which God's gifts have been distributed. There *is* enough, enough for all, abundantly enough; and all that is requisite is freedom to labor on the soil, and to extract from it the produce that God intended for man's support.

But what is the *cause* of British pauperism? Why are there periodical starvations in Ireland and the Highlands? Why is there a crisis every few years in England, when able-bodied men, willing to work, can find no employment? Why are Britons obliged to be shipped off to other countries? Is it because the natural capabilities of the soil have been wrought up to the highest pitch, and yet there remains a surplus population that the soil will neither employ nor feed? Is it because manufacturing has been carried to its utmost extent, and there really is no further room for the employment of a larger population? Is it, in fact, because man has done his best with Britain, made the most of it, got out of it all the food and all the wealth that it is capable of producing, and yet it will not keep its own inhabitants, either by the food it produces, or by articles of exchange that it might give to other countries for food? Is it a matter of *necessity* that there shall be *paupers* (that vile word) in the richest country in the world? Is it *true* that England can no longer support Englishmen; nor Ireland, Irishmen; nor Scotland, Scotchmen? Have we, in fact, arrived at the last term of population, and must all, over and above, expatriate or starve? Is this true, or is it *false?* It is *false* — false from beginning to end.

And what is *the cause* of human pauperism and human degradation? for the two go hand in hand. It is because the social arrangements of men have been made *by superstition*, and not *by knowledge*. The sciences, we have shown, lead to an amended order of *action*, and an amended order of action leads to an amended and improved *condition*. But we must have knowledge in the department in which we require the condition to be amended. That is, mechanical knowledge improves man's mechanical condition, as regards his power over external nature; agricultural knowledge, his agricultural condition; chemical knowledge, his chemical condition, and so forth. But *social* knowledge — that is, social *science* — is absolutely requisite before we can labor intelligently to improve man's *social condition*. These are the conditions under which man tenants the globe. Every department of nature, and of man's phenomenology, has its laws; and if those laws are infringed, evil is the immediate, invariable, and necessary result. And if man's social condition is evil; if we find at one end of society a few thousands of individuals with enormous wealth, for which they work *not*, and never have worked, and at the other end of society millions belonging to the same country, and born on the same soil, with barely the necessaries of life, and too often in abject destitution — there is no other conclusion possible than that this poverty arises from man's social arrangements, and that *poor* the mass of the population must remain until those arrangements are rectified by knowledge.

Does any man suppose that the nation will much longer believe "that Britain cannot support its inhabitants?" Does any man believe that the men who can make steam engines, and cotton mills, and railroads, and ships, and the largest commerce in the world, and spinning jennies, and steam printing machines, and Skerryvore light-houses, and electric telegraphs, and a thousand other wonders, could not make such a distribution of Britain as should enable every man in it, and many more, to earn an abundant livelihood by their labor? Does any man believe this? And if he does not believe it, does he suppose that any superstitious notions about the king's right to grant the soil to individuals will long stand in the way of *their doing it?* If Englishmen discover that pauperism and wretchedness are *unnecessary;* that the divine Being never intended such things; that the degradation of the laboring population, their *moral* degradation consequent on poverty, is the curse of *the laws* and not of nature, — does any man suppose that Englishmen would not be justified in abolishing such laws, or that they will not abolish them? Can we believe for a moment, that if any arrangement would enable the population to find plenty, that such an arrangement will not be made? If any man believe this, he is at all events willing to be credulous. For ourselves, we believe it not.

There are hundreds of thousands of persons in this country who cannot earn above from 7s. to 10s. per week, even when they have constant employment. The wages of the Scottish agricultural laborer — certainly as respectable a man as is found in the whole world in a similar situation, although unfortunately undergoing the same process of degradation that is undermining society in the towns — do not average £26 per annum. This, in fact, is a high estimate; but, to place the question altogether beyond the reach of minute wrangling, let it even be called £30 per annum, and here we are quite sure that we exceed the highest remuneration that the best, steadiest, most sober and most skilful laborer — the man who works a pair of horses — can obtain from the ordinary farmer. With this sum he brings up a family and educates his children. His life is a life of stern economy, and he faces it like a man. He respects himself, and feels that he has a right to be respected. He does manage to live like a moral being, and sometimes escapes the degradation of the poor roll in his old age.* This is the best position of the laborer, the maximum that the present condition of Scotland can afford to the highest class of her laboring children — milk, porridge, and potatoes, and with these he goes through his life of honest independence.

* "The class, perhaps, which suffers most in agricultural districts is that of single women; whose wages, when employed as out-workers in the vigor of life, are not more than sufficient to furnish them, in the scantiest measure and humblest style, with the necessaries of life; and who thus, in the absence of any of those resources, such as spinning and knitting, to which in old age females had recourse in former times, have no prospect before them, if they remain unmarried, *but that of living in their latter days supported by parochial aid.*" — *Report on Increase of Pauperism.* Edinburgh: A. & C. Black.

Such is the prospect which Britain holds out to her laboring children — a life of semi-starvation, and an old age of pauperism. The American republic is, at all events, clear of this evil.

But what is *the minimum*, what is the condition of the shoals of Irish peasantry who invade the west coast, and the tribes of Highlanders who have little or nothing to do? What can *they* earn? What food do they habitually use, and what is their moral existence? Let any one visit the Western Islands, and inquire into the social condition of the inhabitants, and the arrangements that *men* have made for the destruction of the population. See scores of men, women, and children gathering shellfish on the shore as almost their only food, while the rent of the island is all abstracted, and spent in London or elsewhere; and then say if it be *possible* that, with such arrangement, any soil, or any climate, or any profusion of natural advantages, would have compensated for the evil arrangements that men have made.* Does any one suppose that those same Highlanders, who find a wretched sustenance on the shore, could not, and would not, extract an abundant existence out of the soil of their native island? The law forbids them; that is, men have made such arrangements with regard to God's earth, that the stable population must be

* In some of the Western Islands the people are little or no better than bondsmen or serfs. In one island (and perhaps the practice is common, but on this we cannot speak) it is said that the tenants are not allowed to sell their grain except to the landlord. What is this but serfdom? It was, of course, proper to introduce *law* into the Highlands; but no principle, either of natural right, or religion, or social economy, could ever justify the law *in giving the property of the clan* to the head of the house, to be used by him as *private* property. This is the origin of all the Highland distress. No economical improvements are worth a farthing until this radical evil is corrected.

reduced to destitution, for the purpose of having one man endowed with a wealth which he, perhaps, knows not how to use, nor even to retain.*

But what, after all, is the practical conclusion to which we come? What system is it that would obliterate pauperism? On this we do not intend to enter in the present volume. We must *first* show the probability (a probability which, taken altogether, amounts to a reasonable expectation) that man, placed as he is on the globe, is not necessarily condemned to pauperism and degradation; but that a period will come, ere long, when the natural laws which govern society shall be discovered, and, being discovered, shall lead to a condition of prosperity altogether inconceivable at the present time. Two systems are open to us: —

Either pauperism and degradation are the work of the Creator of our system, the ALL-POWERFUL, who has placed present man in circumstances where the natural capabilities of the earth are insufficient for his support; —

Or, pauperism and degradation are the work of fallen man, who through ignorance has based

* A fact. The greater part of an island, the rental of which part was about £20,000 a year, has recently been found insufficient to support a family. The capital was spent, and the estate is for sale. On that same island we have seen the native population in numbers gathering their daily food on the shore. This island, in miniature, is a very exact representation of the social condition of Great Britain. It may take a little time for the mass of the population to see exactly how things really do stand; but they will discover the truth at last.

his arrangements of the earth on superstitious propositions, and thereby necessarily has rendered it impossible that the amount of good intended by the Creator *can* be extracted from the earth.

Of these two schemes we may take our choice. We may blasphemously rush to the conclusion, that the earth is for man a terrible prison, with necessary horrors, from which, do what we will, we cannot escape. Or we may believe, with humble reverence, that, notwithstanding man's transgression, the Almighty God has yet, in the abundance of his compassion, plentifully provided him with the means of terrestrial existence. That *man's doings* are the cause of man's distress; that man's ignorance, and man's error, and man's injustice, and man's *wrong* arrangement of the world, is the true and only cause why man is afflicted with poverty, and thereby placed in circumstances almost incompatible with his proper existence as a moral agent and an accountable creature. And if we admit that moral degradation does, for the most part, accompany physical degradation, then must we admit, that if any new arrangement of the natural world, which man did *not* create, would have the effect of obliterating poverty, and, consequently, of obliterating the necessary evils of poverty, that new arrangement is right, just, and good, and ought to be carried into execution, whatever the present arrangements, inherited from past generations, may actually be.

And we affirm, without the slightest hesitation, that the very same kind of improvements that have followed the mathematical and physical sciences, will follow *social* science, and achieve in the world of man far greater wonders than have yet been achieved in the world of matter. It is not trade Britain wants, nor more railroads, nor larger orders for cotton, nor new schemes for alimenting the poor, nor loans to landlords, nor any other mercantile or economical change. It is *social* change. New *social* arrangements, made on the principles of *natural equity.* No economical measure whatever is capable of reaching the depths of the social evils. Ameliorations may, no doubt, be made for a time; but the radical evil remains, still generating the poison that corrupts society.

The evil is expressed in a few words; and, sooner or later, the nation will appreciate it and rectify it. It is "the alienation of the soil from the state, and the consequent taxation of the industry of the country." Britain may go on producing with wonderful energy, and may accomplish far more than she has yet accomplished. She may struggle as Britain only can struggle. She may present to the world peace at home, when the nations of Europe are filled with insurrection. She may lead foremost in the march of civilization, and be first among the kingdoms of the earth. All this she may do, and more. But as certainly as Britain continues her present social arrangements, so certainly will there come a time when — the other questions being cleared on this side and on that side, and the main question brought into the arena — the *labor* of Britain will emancipate itself from thraldom. Gradually and surely has the separation been taking place between the privileged land owner and the unprivileged laborer. And the time will come at last that there shall be but two parties looking each other in the face, and knowing that the destruction of one is an event of necessary occurrence. That event *must* come. Nor is it in man to stay it or to produce it. It will come as the result of the laws that govern nature and that govern man. As in the island we have spoken of, the population must be destroyed or the land must be open to their cultivation, and not accorded to the landlord. Of the two parties, one must give way. One must sink to rise no more; one must disappear from the earth. Their continued existence is incompatible. Nature cannot support both. Nature cannot afford to support the population in plenty, and over and above to pay, on a small island, £20,000 a year to the proprietor. Such things cannot be. We may as well attempt mechanical impossibilities as political impossibilities; and, notwithstanding the almost universal prevalence of the current superstition about the rights of landed property, we have no hesitation in affirming that a very few years will show that superstition destroyed, and the main question of England's welfare brought to a serious and definite discussion.*

* The theory of Highland pauperization is one of the simplest things imaginable. Nature has only so many sources of wealth; and if these are taken away, by the laws, from the inhabitants of a district, it stands to reason that the inhabitants must be poor. Were the wealth *produced* in the Highlands *to remain* in the Highlands, the inhabitants would be rich; but the annual profits, for the most part, go away and never return. There is a perpetual drain outwards — an export without a corresponding import, either of money or goods. If the money produced by the sheep, cattle,

In politics, there are only two main questions — first, personal liberty; second, natural property. England has been at work for centuries in the endeavor to settle the first, and when that is definitively settled, she will give her undivided attention to the second.

grouse, and salmon, actually returned in *any* form to the districts producing them, the inhabitants would receive the remuneration intended by nature. As it is, pauperism is the natural and necessary result.

"Since the period that the Highlands were brought under the dominion of the law, the inhabitants have been found by all who have visited them from other quarters of the country to be a people annually on the brink of starvation, and annually, to a greater or less degree, feeding on shellfish or seaware. Their indolence and their dirtiness have also been observed by all observers during this whole period. Their ignorance of the arts of bettering their condition, and of the comforts enjoyed in other quarters of the kingdom, have also been uniformly taken notice of. Their destitution was an annual thing; but the usual and ordinary distress was every now and then aggravated by a recurrence of a bad season for the crops on which they principally lived. They were cheerful in the years when they could get any thing like a fair supply of the coarsest and meanest food, but they never labored for any thing more; and hence an unfavorable season, when it came, found them with nothing, and reduced them to starvation. When the season was what might be called good, they never taxed their industry to devise measures for warding off the fatal effects of the bad season which might be close at hand. Such a season was that of 1836, in which, if the potatoes were not a total failure, there was a more general failure of crops in the country. It was followed by the destitution of 1836-7, which called forth the bounty of the other parts of the kingdom, and directed much attention to the state of the Highlands. When I ask the people here, whether the present destitution of 1847 or that of 1837 was the worst, they all declare that the present is far the worst; but when I inquire how those people lived in 1837, I find good reason to believe that it was about as bad as 1847." — *Scotsman, February* 17, 1847.

Before the discussion of the question of property, (*natural* property, the *object*,) there is, however, a main and principal question of liberty. Englishmen have achieved their liberty in *one* sense; that is, they are equal in the eye of the criminal law, (nearly so,) have a right to be tried by their peers according to law, and cannot on any occasion be subjected to punishment by the rulers, as such. So far the progress of England has been satisfactory; and, above every country in the world, she has been distinguished for her race of independent judges, whose conduct for many years past has been one of the greatest moral wonders of the world. In the whole history of the administration of justice, there is nothing to compare with the quiet grandeur with which the judges of England have unostentatiously performed their duties. Apart from religion, this has been England's truest greatness, her most solid claim to the admiration of all mankind. The deeds of her greatest commanders are as dust in the balance, compared with the deeds of her judges. These have been truly great; and England owes to them *that moral supremacy of the law*, which is the surest basis of civil society, and the grandest natural phenomenon that comes within the limits of man's cognizance. Long may Heaven continue to favor England with upright judges, and long may Englishmen continue to regard them with the highest honor.

But, in another sense, Englishmen have *not* achieved their liberty, and a main question remains to be decided. Its *ultimate* decision is by no means a matter of doubt, but it may be years before it comes to definite issue. This question is, "the right of the deliberative assembly to make laws for, and impose taxation on, that portion of the population *who have no voice in the election of the representatives;*" in other words, the question of universal suffrage. It is plainly evident, that those who have no power to elect *are not citizens of the state.* They are an inferior class, *ruled by force;* and the emancipation of this class, and their equalization in the eye of the law, is the first *great* question that will agitate the kingdom. *Economical* questions as to whether there shall be three soldiers or half a dozen, or whether a certain duty shall be ten per cent. or twenty, or whether the government should give more or less aid to emigration, all these are quite unimportant compared with the main question, of whether two or three millions of men are morally bound to obey and acknowledge a government *that excludes them from representation.* Let this question be treated as it may, of one thing we are quite convinced; namely, that the non-electing population will either obtain the right by the consent of the present rulers, or ultimately *they will take it by force.* The change *must* come as it lies in the order of human progression; but what the means of effecting the change shall be, remains to be determined. In all probability, when once the question is thoroughly a national one, the present rulers will admit the necessity of the change, and place the whole population on an equality as regards their political functions. And when once this last great question of *liberty* has been disposed of, the country cannot fail to commence another evolution, and to enter on a line of progress that shall ultimately place men on the same equality with regard *to natural property* that will then prevail with regard to political liberty.*

But let the *mechanism* of the changes be what they may, let our views be right or wrong with regard to the *process* of improvement, we yet maintain that our major proposition is fully borne out. We allege, as the most general proposition, that the improvement of social science will improve man's social action, and that the improvement of man's social action will improve man's social condition; in fact, that the acquisition of social science will ultimately produce a social millennium. There *is* a science of man, and of man's action, if we can only discover it; and the discovery of that science will produce effects analogous to the effects produced by any other science. Let us, then,

* We hope, at some future time, to be able to lay before the public some remarks on the equalization of actual property. An absolute equality of actual property is neither possible, nor desirable, nor *just*. We do not believe that there is an insuperable difficulty in showing how a system, perfectly just in theory, can be carried into practice, and yet preserve to every man the absolute control of the fruits of his personal skill, labor, and industry. The great question of modern times is, "What is the theory of a perfect political *state?*" Admitting man's fallen nature, and all the elements that might be supposed to interfere with the *realization* of a perfect state, what is its *theory?* There *must* be a theory, be what it may. That theory is the great desideratum of modern times. It settles definitely and forever what must be *the end* of man's political progress. For ourselves, we believe assuredly that God has made man's logical reason to harmonize with man's condition; and thus, whatever the reason can ascertain to be *true*, must, when reduced to practice, produce *good*, and not evil. The more men advance, the more will they perceive that *truth*, the intellectual proposition, is the foundation of *good*, the outward condition.

endeavor to estimate, for a moment, some of the effects that may reasonably be anticipated from the discovery, acknowledgment, and reduction to ordination, of social science.*

But, in the first place, let us observe that the *natural history* of a science always begins at the wrong end. We do not mean that it *ought not* to do so; on the contrary, it ought to do so, and must do so, because it cannot do otherwise. Nature furnishes us with *wholes*, and these must first be manipulated as whole individuals. These are named, described, and classed after a fashion. Neither the nomenclature, however, nor the classification, are destined to remain. They serve a temporary purpose; and are of use to facilitate communication. Thus chemistry cannot commence with

* The term *discovery* is perhaps liable to be misunderstood, or perhaps rather to be objected to. We do not mean that any object called a science is to be discovered like a fossil or a new planet. Science exists *in the mind*, not in external nature; and the discovery of science is the discovery of *the truths* of a science, and of the process by which those truths are substantiated. Thus, Aristotle discovered logic when he laid bare the process of reasoning, and exhibited the necessary *forms* under which man's intellect works. Aristotle did not discover that man could reason; neither did he discover a new object; but he discovered *a science*, *a mode of knowledge*. Newton did not discover the sun, nor the moon, nor the earth; but he discovered the *mode* of their operations. The sun, the moon, and the earth remained unaffected by the discovery; they performed their functions as usual, without the slightest attention to the great philosopher. The *change* was *in the credence of mankind*. And so it is with all science. The change *is in the credence of mankind*. Now, intellect (taken as intellect, without regarding the moral influences that may bias its judgments) is of that nature that it is convinced by evidence. All human intellect is

oxygen, hydrogen, calcium, and potassium, &c. These are the *logical* primaries, or simples, of chemistry; but they are by no means the *chronological* primaries. Neither does anatomy begin with fibrine, albumen, nor globules, but with a whole animal, and with a head, a thorax, an abdomen, thoracic members, and abdominal members. Neither does zoölogy begin with organic substance, its arrangement into the organs of nutrition, locomotion, sensation, reproduction, &c.; but with a great number of different animals, presenting different outward appearances. This principle is universal in science, that the chronological commencement is with *a whole*, a complex mass; while the logical commencement of the science, properly so called, is with a sim-

radically the same, only variable in quantity. And scientific discovery is the discovery of that mode of presenting propositions which necessarily leads intellect, or any number of unbiased intellects, to the same identical conclusions. There is but one truth, and consequently there is but one scheme of *knowledge;* and the great final result of scientific discovery, is the restoration of the *unity* of human credence. Men may differ in *taste*, in likings, and in dislikings; but their intellect cannot differ in judgment, except through superstition or error. The discovery of science, therefore, is the discovery of the knowledge itself, and of that mode of presenting it that shall convince intellect as intellect. On this account it has been said, that "he discovers who proves." As science advances, diversity of opinion dies away, and unity of knowledge takes its place. To produce this unity of knowledge for the whole race of man, is the magnificent destiny of science; and the humblest cultivator of natural knowledge is, like the coral insect, helping to rear an edifice, which, emerging from the vexed ocean of conflicting credence, shall be first stable and secure, and, at last, shall cover itself with verdure, flowers, and fruits, and bloom beautiful in the face of heaven.

ple primary, from which we start to build up the complex mass.*

To express this in logical formula, let us say that the chronological commencement is with an individual presenting the greatest *comprehension* and the least *extension*, and that the logical commencement is with an individual presenting the greatest *extension* and the least *comprehension*.†

The process of science, therefore, is in the first place analytic, and when the analysis has been carried down to the last elements, the process is reversed, and it then becomes synthetic. And this is true of the mathematical sciences as well as of the physical sciences, although the mathematical sciences are invariably presented in the synthetic form. In them we have the first and most simple appearance of analysis, and the greatest preponderance of synthesis. In the ad-

* "All, or almost all, the substances found on the globe of the earth have been subjected to chemical investigation. The result has been, that all the animal and vegetable substances, without exception, and by far the greatest number of mineral bodies, *are compounds*."

† To Sir William Hamilton, of the University of Edinburgh, the logical world is indebted for an exposition of the theory of comprehension and extension.

Among the individual objects of natural science, *man* is the one that presents the greatest comprehension; but the name, man, extends only to himself. The name *animal*, on the contrary, *extends* to an immense variety of organized beings, but *comprehends* only a sensitive organized individual. A blood globule, as a matter of real science, has a great extension, but comprehends only a very simple form of organization. The word *being* (noun substantive) is

vanced physical sciences, on the contrary, we have the greatest amount of analysis; so great, in fact, that the analytic portion of the science has frequently been mistaken for the whole science. The whole science, however, is not completed until both the analytic portion and the synthetic portion are achieved. Geometry has its preparatory analysis, exactly as chemistry has its analysis; and though no mention is made of this in geometrical treatises, the fact cannot be overlooked when we take a survey of the philosophy of science. Nature does not furnish us with points having no extent, with straight lines having no breadth, with perfect circles, squares, and triangles, &c. On the contrary, nature furnishes us with *forms* very imperfect for the most part, and very complex for the most part, and these we analyze into the elementary forms of position, (the point,) and direction and ex-

that which presents the *greatest possible* extension and *least possible* comprehension. What is called the *universe*, on the contrary, presents the greatest possible comprehension, and the least possible extension. There *can* only be one universe; but there may be an infinity of beings, or rather an *indefinity*. Extension appears to represent *number*, where we begin with unity, and repeat indefinitely; and comprehension appears to represent *quantity*, where we begin with infinity, and subdivide indefinitely. The difference between number and quantity has been far too much overlooked, apparently from the circumstance that unity is (absurdly) allowed to be divisible. That is, we divide *one* unit into *two* units. Now, the fact is, we have *doubled* the *number* and *halved* the *quantity*. Unity in pure arithmetic is absolutely indivisible until we assign it a value, or quantity, and then it may represent any number; but in pure arithmetic, unity is the *one simple*.

tent, (the line,) and with these we proceed to construct extent in two directions, (the superficies,) and extent in three directions, (the solid.*)

In politics, therefore, as in every other science, the natural history comes first, and then the science. The most obvious divisions of things as they are, are the first clumsy attempts at analysis; and laws begin, not by constructing the state as it ought to be *constructed*, but by attempting to remedy the most obvious evils. This is the case even where laws have been made in a good intention. We do not refer to those bad, and unjust, and despotic laws which have prevailed in all European states, but to the best portion of the laws viewed in their best light; and these we maintain to have begun at the latter end of the question, and not at its beginning.

* *Space*, as an unlimited solid, we take to be, not simple, as usually represented, but as compound. The concept space is composite, and may be analyzed into position, direction, and extent. These three concepts are simple, cannot be defined, and form the elementary substantives of geometry. *Direction* and *extent* give rise to two different methods. For instance, by measuring the distances (extent) between all the points of a country, (suppose by chain,) we may construct a map, and the map shall have a scale; but we shall not be able to tell, in the least, how to place the map — that is, we know nothing about the *direction*. And if we measure only the direction (suppose by compass) of the various points, we shall also have a map, and this map we shall place correctly, but it will not have a scale — that is, we know nothing about *the extent*. To have both the direction and the extent, we must combine both methods; and on this account a survey by triangulation requires a measured base line, the only use of which, however, is to give *the scale*, the *form* being determined by the direction of the points.

The first and most obvious requirement in a country is some degree of security for life, liberty, and property. This gives birth to criminal law, the great end of which is ostensibly to prevent crimes. Now here we have the whole evidence of history that law began at the wrong end. Law ought to emanate from ethics, and the very first and most important question to determine is, "What is a crime, and what is not a crime?" Instead of *ascertaining* what was a crime, men *assumed* the crime, and then proceeded to enact laws for its punishment. They made a synthesis before making an analysis, and made that synthesis the basis of political enactment, and committed murder and robbery, and every other crime, under the shelter of their legislation. So far as the *science* of politics was concerned, they were in much the same position as those who made astronomy *without* observation; that is, they were wholly and totally basing on arbitrary assumption. But wrong proceedings in politics are far more serious than wrong proceedings in other departments, inasmuch as man and man's welfare are concerned; and the laws of former times, and to a large extent of the present time, being based on superstition, necessarily produced, and continue to produce, effects the most detrimental to society. Even admitting the major proposition of the law, that "crime ought to be punished," the minor, "this act and that act are crimes," was purely *arbitrary;* it was determined on no principle of stability, was variable, contradictory, often absurd, and very generally unjust. Thus, at one period it was a crime for a man to be *free,* (as it still is in Russia and the southern states of America;) at another period it was a crime to have a slave. At one period it was a crime to go to church; at another, to refrain from going to church. At one period it was a crime to shoot a deer; at another, no crime. At one period it was a crime to be a witch; at another period it was admitted that there were no witches. Now all this diversity is exactly similar to the diversity that prevailed in the physical sciences before Bacon's time. The major principles of investigation were not in dispute; but Bacon, with a grasp of magnificent genius, laid hold of the minors of the sciences, and told men that they must first ascertain *them* before they could arrive at knowledge.

And so it is in *law*, the exponent of men's views of political science. The minor proposition, "What is a crime?" requires to be determined on exactly the same principles as we determine "What is a square?" or, "What is the orbit of the earth?" Without this determination, made on principles which are not arbitrary but scientific, law is despotism; and no man in the world is morally bound to obey it, except as Scripture may enjoin him to obey even unjust laws. If legislatures will make arbitrary crimes,—that is, make actions legally criminal which are not naturally criminal,—no population is bound to obey them. On the contrary, it becomes one of the highest duties of man to resist such laws—to use every effort to procure their abolition; and, if he cannot do so by reason, then to do so *by force*. The welfare of humanity demands this at the hand of every man; and the base and slavish doctrine of non-resistance is fit, not for men who study truth in God's universe, but for hireling sycophants, who care not what man may suffer so that their vile carcasses are clothed and fed. The liberties we have in England are mainly owing to the fact, that England would not tolerate the determination of crime by the executive rulers, but reserved this for the deliberative assembly; and, in so doing, England has undoubtedly made a declaration — not so explicit as it would be now — that she reserves the right to try the issue by force of arms with any government that should make artificial crimes, or punish the population for actions which were neither contrary to the laws of God, of reason, or of nature. The power of the ruler to determine "what is a crime," is the origin and sole basis of the political degradation of the continent of Europe. Abstract this determination from the power of the rulers, — let it be made on a principle of *independent* investigation, and let the rulers be the executors of the laws, — and we have the first great practical reform that envelops the germ of all others, and that cannot fail ultimately to entail the best blessings of liberty and security. All the revolutions of the continent, from the day of the *Jeu de Paume* down to the year 1849, have originated in nothing else than the *false* determination of crime by the law, and the power of the ruler not merely to *execute* laws, but to make, alter, and originate them.

But intimately connected with the theory of *crime* (much more so than is usually imagined) is the theory of natural *property*. The law assumed crime *arbitrarily*, and proceeded to punish it; it assumed property *arbitrarily*, and proceeded to protect it. The king, who had the power to make or unmake crimes, had the power to dispose of the land that belonged to the state.* He sold or gifted it, and thus in the long run the whole of the lands of England, with some trifling exceptions, have been alienated from the nation, and the burden of taxation has been placed upon the people.† Superstition — that is, unfounded cre-

* James I. considered that, "as it is atheism and blasphemy in a creature to dispute what the Deity may do, so it is presumption and sedition in a subject to dispute what the king may do in the height of his power. Good Christians will be content with God's will revealed in his Word; and good subjects will rest in *the king's will*, revealed in his law." — (*Works*, 557–531.) This profane comparison was familiar to the servile lawyers of the day. (*See* Finch, *Law*. 81. 3.) — Euc. Met.

† As an instance of the manner in which the lands of England have been disposed of, and consequently the taxation placed on the industrious classes, we give the following from the *Biographia Britannica*: —

"In the year 1695, King William made this nobleman [Lord Portland] a grant of the lordships of Denbigh, Bromfield, Yale, and other lands, containing many thousand acres, in the principality of Wales; which, being part of the demesne thereof, the grant was opposed, and the House of Commons addressed the king to put a stop to the passing it, which his majesty accordingly complied with, and recalled the grant, promising, however, to find some other way of showing his favor to Lord Portland, who, he said, had deserved it by long and faithful services; and this promise the king after made good. . . . . . It was not long after King William recalled these grants, before his majesty found means to make Lord Portland others in recompense for the revenues of the principality of Wales, namely, a grant of certain buildings in Whitehall, for forty-five years, at the rent of six shillings and eight pence; a grant of the manor of Grantham, in the county of Lincoln; Honor of Penrith, in the county of Cumberland; manor of Dracklaw and

dence — was at the bottom of the king's right in both cases; and the present inhabitants of the British islands are bound to observe the laws made in former times, concerning crimes and property, *just in so far as those laws are now equitable, or would now be re-enacted were there no laws on those subjects.* The present possessor of a portion of land derives not one iota of present right from the former gift of a defunct monarch; and his right, to be *now* valid, must be such, that, were all his titles destroyed, the nation would proceed to place him in possession of the lands, because he, as an individual man, had an *equitable* claim to them. Just as, if all the laws and statutes of England were destroyed, the nation would proceed as usual to the arrest and punishment of the murderer or robber — those persons being punished, not because there are laws for their punishment, but because it is *just* that they should be punished, and *just* that there should be laws to punish. The justice of the punishment does in no case derive from the law, but the

Rudneth, in Cheshire; manor of Torrington, in Norfolk; manors of Partington, Bristol, Garth, Hornsey, Thwing, Burnisley, and Leven, in the county of York — all parcel of the ancient revenue of the crown of England; the manor of Pevensey, in the county of Sussex, parcel of the duchy of Lancaster; and all the lands and tenements, &c., thereunto belonging, to hold to his lordship and his heirs; and also his majesty's manor of East Greenwich, in the county of Kent, under the rent of £4 13s. 4d. a year."

The *present* effect of these grants is exactly equivalent to the addition of the *present* annual value of these lands to the present taxation of the community of Britain. Had the lands of England not been alienated from the state, there need not have been one penny of taxation on the industrious classes.

whole force and validity of the law derives from the justice of the punishment; and where the punishment is not just, that punishment is a crime, whatever the law may be, or whatever it may declare.

One striking fact is apparent in considering the past history of laws with regard to crimes and property. The laws with regard to crimes have been considered *alterable;* the laws with regard to property have been considered *unalterable.* One generation of legislators and rulers made an action a legal crime; but the next generation did not, on that account, consider itself bound forever so to esteem it. On the contrary, every generation of legislators has considered itself at full liberty to alter, revise, amend, and abolish such laws, according to its own judgment. But with regard to the king's gift of lands it has been quite otherwise. The deeds of past rulers have been supposed to extend to all future generations; and the doctrine now prevalent is, that the lands, once alienated by the king's gift, could not be reassumed by the nation without a breach of equity — without, in fact, committing that crime abhorrent in the eyes of aristocracy — "attacking the rights of property." This discrepancy is at once explained, when we reflect that the legislators of Britain have been for the most part the landlords themselves, or those so immediately connected with their interests, that the government was, to all intents and purposes, a landlordocracy. But the question still occurs, and must occur again and again, "If the acts of past rulers were not morally permanent with regard to crime, how can they possibly be so with regard to property? and if they are morally permanent with regard to property, how can they be otherwise with regard to crime?"

We have now to show that crime and property are not distinct; in fact, that, so far as regards legislation, they are *identical;* and that the laws (or king's grants, which are, in fact, nothing else than laws, although this fact is overlooked) regarding landed *property* are neither more nor less than laws regarding *crime. Property* is usually regarded as an object — as something essentially distinguished from *action.* Yet we shall undertake to show that *action* alone is concerned, and that all laws regarding property are merely laws regarding action. And if we succeed in doing this, we have unhinged the superstition that prevails on the subject of landed property — we have loosened the fabric of aristocracy, and laid open a question that for many years to come will occupy the attention of Great Britain. There is already in the public mind a very extensive *suspicion* that the present distribution of the land is the true and main cause of England's distress and Ireland's wretchedness; but the supposed difficulty of presenting a scheme which should be perfectly just in theory, and practicable and beneficial if carried into effect, appears to have deterred many from openly attacking the question, and from subjecting it to the same kind of calm and rational investigation so lavishly accorded to other questions of incomparably less importance. The apparent hopelessness, also, of affecting any radical change in the present system, and the fear of advocating "wild" doctrines, have both exerted an influence in repressing investigation. This apathy, however, cannot continue long.

Whatever may be the *result*, the investigation cannot fail to be made; and even if it only terminated in substantiating the validity of the "rights" of the landlords, it would be satisfactory to the country to know that there was truth and not superstition at the bottom of the arrangements. But that such *would* be the result is, at all events, doubtful; and when the country is thoroughly convinced of the futility of the economical schemes that appear one after another, — and it is fast approaching that conviction, — it will allow the administrators of the government to pursue their course unheeded, while it fixes its own attention on prospective changes far more extensive than ever could emanate from a government constituted like that of Britain.

We now undertake to show that the gift of land by the king is nothing more than a law affecting *action;* and, consequently, is of the same character as a law relating to *crime.* And if so, it must follow the general course of the laws relating to crime; and if those laws are not morally permanent, neither is the king's gift of land morally permanent, but may be revised, amended, or *abolished*, exactly in the same manner as a law affecting crime. And over and above, we maintain, that neither the one nor the other is one atom more valid, or more binding, on account of legislation, but that they are right now, or wrong now, wholly and solely according to their own merits; that the law cannot *make* a crime, although the law may call an action by this name, and treat it as such; and that the law cannot make a portion of land property, although it may call it property. Both crime and property are anterior to law, and superior to it; and it was not to *make* either the one or the other, but to prevent the one and protect the other, that legislative law was called into existence. Law is not the moral measure of right and wrong; but the rule of practice for the policeman, constable, jailer, judge, sheriff, and hangman; and until law is absolutely *perfect*, there is a canon higher than the canon of law, one more valid and more stable — the *canon of reason* — to which law itself must be subject.

A law against crime is a public declaration that certain acts ought not to be performed; and that he who performs them shall be visited with certain specified penalties. This, we maintain, is exactly the essence of the king's grant of landed property. Because, —

1st. The king's grant of land is an authorization *to use* the land in favor of the grantee. And, —

2d. The king's grant is *a prohibition to all other persons to use the land.* And, —

3d. The law declares that if any persons use the land without permission of the grantee, they shall *be punished.*

Now the essential part of this political arrangement is this: "All persons in the nation are forbidden, under pains and penalties, to use a certain portion of land, with the exception of the grantee, or by his permission." This, then, is essentially a law against *action* — a law declaring that to use a certain portion of land is a crime for the vast majority of the population.

Now, if we turn to the effects of this arrangement,

we find that the grantee is in no respect bound to make the land *produce.* He may utterly neglect it; nay, he may, as has actually been done recently in the Highlands of Scotland (and as the king himself did ages ago at the New Forest) — he may drive off the population, drive off the sheep, (the food of man,) and convert the district into a game desert for his own amusement — he having plenty of wealth, derived perhaps from *other* lands, wherewith to support these costly pleasures — *at the expense of the nation.**

Such, on the side of the grantee, is the limit of liberty. Let us now ask, what the limit is on the part of the nation. No matter what may be the state of the land — even if it is lying waste, and producing nothing for man's support, as is actually the case in many parts of the kingdom — no man in Britain may put into it a spade or a potato, to save his family from starvation, without incurring the penalties of the law. He would be a *criminal,* (the law would call him so,) and he would be treated as such.

This state of affairs represents the *extremes;* and

* "The Marquis of Breadalbane's forest of Corrichebach, or the Black Mount, in Glenorchy, was restored at great cost (having been previously converted into sheep walks) in 1820; it covers 35,000 acres." — *Quarterly Review.*

That is, if we understand the passage aright, these 35,000 acres were formerly wild, and without sheep. Afterwards, sheep were introduced, and consequently so much more food was produced. And in 1820 the sheep were driven off, and the land *again* made a game desert for the amusement of a single individual. Rights of property!

all that is better than the extremes is due, not to the law, but to the laws of nature. Now, the law has done this grievous injury; it has deprived the poor of the natural remedy whereby they would have corrected so enormous an abuse. Let us suppose that there was *no* law, and that one man claimed thirty thousand acres (*see last note*) for *his amusement.* Other persons require the land for *their support.* They begin to occupy it, and he endeavors to repel them. Now, what would be the natural consequence? What ought the cultivators to do? Should they retire and starve? or expatriate themselves? They would resist the aggression by force, and in so doing they would only do their *duty.** But the law will not allow them to resist. The law has first deprived them of the land, and then enlisted a standing army to prevent them from using the *natural* means of recovering it.†

But independently of the specific character of the actual laws and arrangements prevalent in Britain, we take the question up on the most general ground,

* This principle, however startling in words, is universally acknowledged and acted on by civilized communities. When they form colonies in lands inhabited by tribes which do not cultivate the soil, but occupy it as a hunting-ground, the cultivating colonists always repel the aggression of the hunters.

† Exactly as the laws of Britain *did*, and the laws of the southern States *do*, first deprive a man of his natural liberty, and then use the power of the state to prevent his recovering it by force. One of the most curious superstitions in the world is the belief that we may lawfully go to war with foreign men for a very slight cause; and that we must not go to war with what people call our own countrymen, even when they wrong us ten times more than the foreigners.

and we affirm, as a universal proposition, that where there is not a question of *action*, there is no question of *morals*. And, consequently, if any object be treated of independently of human action, it does not come within the limits of morals, and can give rise neither to crime nor to duty. And, consequently, if the land be separated from the question of *human action*, it is no longer *property*, but a mere physical object that enters the physical sciences. And, consequently, the moment we endeavor to establish a distinction between laws relating to property and laws relating to action, we have obliterated property, and left only land in its physical character, and not in its moral character. It is the theory of human action alone that can make land, or any thing else, *property*. The very moment we have used the word *property* in its moral sense, as giving rise to duties and crimes, (or, rather, becoming the *object* of duties and crimes,) that moment have we involved it in the theory of human action, from which it can never be separated until we return it to its *physical* signification. And, when so returned, it can neither be the object of a duty nor of a crime. In its physical sense, land can give rise to no crimes, nor can it ever be *property* until we consider it as involved in the doctrine of human action.

And this being the case, the laws and arrangements of past rulers relating to *property* are in no possible respect more binding than their laws and arrangements relating to crime, *property* being only a concise expression of a proposition that prohibits actions of a certain character. *Drop the prohibition of the action*, and the *property* has altogether disappeared. And, consequently, all past arrangements with regard to land are as open to be revised, amended, or abolished, as past arrangements with regard to actions called crimes, and, consequently, there is no such thing as "the rights of landed property" separated from the mere dictum of the law, which the nation has an undoubted right to alter or abolish whenever it shall see fit to do so. And if the nation were to resolve to resume and take back all lands which had been granted by the crown, (with considerations affecting those individuals who had *purchased*,) the nation would not be guilty of any crime, or wrong, or impropriety, but would be exactly in the same position as it is when it abolishes laws against witchcraft, or laws in favor of the slave trade, or laws which make it a legal crime to be a Jew or a Catholic.

Superstition, on this point, may endure for a few years longer; but no truth can be more certain than that God gave the land for the benefit of all; and if any arrangement interfere with or diminish that benefit, then has man, as man, as the recipient of God's bounty, an undoubted right to alter or abolish that arrangement, exactly as he alters his arrangements in agriculture, in medicine, in mechanics, or in navigation. No more crime, and no more wrong, attaches to his alterations in the one case than in the other.

We have now, therefore, opened up the way for a consideration of some of the effects that may reasonably be expected to follow the discovery of political science.

1st. The major proposition, "Crime ought to be prevented; and there ought to be laws, and an executive administration of those laws, for the prevention of *crime*." This major proposition is not in dispute; and the progression of man in his political aspect does not consist in any alteration to be made in the *major* proposition.

2d. The minor proposition, "What is a crime? This and that action are crimes." In this minor lies the whole essence of political progression and political amelioration. Political improvement takes place exactly as men discover and definitely determine the true nature of crime; and exactly as they confine their laws to the prohibition of those actions which *are* crimes, and to the *non-prohibition* of those actions which are *not* crimes. The laws of man cannot *make* a crime, neither can they *unmake* a crime. Crime is logically anterior to human legislation; and the very end and intent of legislation, in its first and most essential capacity, is to *prevent* crime.

All nations with which we are acquainted have punished, *as crimes*, actions which were not crimes; and the gradual improvement of the laws of man in this respect is one of the great phenomena that we learn from history. On the gradual alteration of the laws (of Britain, for instance) may be based a most conclusive argument, that political science is undergoing a gradual *process of discovery*, those laws being altered invariably in accordance with a *change of credence*, gradually gaining ground with the population.

But while we have a *positive* major proposition, we have also a *negative* major proposition, which is,—

"No action that is not a crime ought to be prevented by the law."

Now, as legislators and rulers are only *men*, (there is no divine wisdom nor divine sacredness* about them,) *they* may be the criminals as well as any of the population; and if they assume powers and enforce laws which emanate from their *will*, (and not from an impartial judgment,) they are exactly in the case of an individual who commits crime by resorting to *violence*.

It is quite easy for the generality of writers on these subjects to treat of crime as committed by the population. They see *so far*, and sometimes their views are valuable and correct. But they have first perched the government on a great height, which they do not intend to survey, and then confine their observations to the subject population. To include both at one view appears a stretch beyond their power, and hence their admirable dissertations are *unsatisfactory;* and by unsatisfactory, we do not mean that they are not distinguished by talent of the highest order, and by upright sincerity; but that they treat

* "James I. was so accustomed to regard himself, and to be addressed by his flatterers as 'the Lord's anointed,' 'the vicegerent of God upon earth,' in fact, a kind of deputed deity, that he was constantly tempted to accuse his subjects of blasphemy and irreligion when they presumed to oppose his will, or to call in question his lawless assumptions of authority; at the same time, there was no form of impiety, from the light and irreverent mention of the sacred name in familiar speech, to profane cursing and swearing, and to the blasphemous and audacious assumption of a kind of parity with the Supreme Being, by which the lips and mind of the prince himself were undefiled...... James was the first of England to whom the unappropriate title of *sacred majesty* was applied." — Miss Aikin's *Mem. Court, James I.*

only one portion of the phenomenon, and omit its correlative. Exactly as if one were to write an able dissertation on the earth's motion, furnishing us with a perfect diagram and specification of the orbit, and an exact determination of the velocity, *and yet should altogether omit to mention the sun.* Such a dissertation, let its details be as perfect as they may, would be altogether *unsatisfactory;* because the correlative, the sun, has not been exhibited in its relations to the earth.

And so it is with *crime.* He who studies crime as a portion of man. science, (and not merely as accidentally treated of in this system of law that happens to be in force in Britain, or that system of law that happens to be in force in another country,) must include in his view the *whole phenomenon,* and must inquire what does man do, as man. And when we turn to Britain with this principle, we must regard the whole population, king, lords, commons, soldiers, judges, laborers, paupers, in fact, the whole mass of society, as merely *men.* And when we define *crime,* and find that actions coinciding with that definition are performed by any of these parties, by whatever name they may be called, or under whatever pretences they may appear, we must not hesitate to call the action by the name of *crime,* and to say, This is a crime committed by *men.* Reverence for *law,* as law, as a human rule of action *de facto* enacted by legislators, is mere debasing superstition; nor, however venerable law may be in some men's estimation, do we consider either their law or their worship of it at all entitled to respect.* Men venerate *law* and care nothing for *justice*, just as they venerate the priest and forget the Deity. And if any legislature, or any king, commit an act, which act would not be equitable between two individuals, we no more hesitate to call it *a crime* in the one case as well as in the other. And when legislators, taking advantage of the superstitious veneration which men still have for power and human authority, proceed to prohibit actions

* As an instance of the manner in which lawyers regard the social institutions of men, we may give the following quotation from Crabb's "History of English Law," p. 7: —

"It is worthy of observation, that all the Saxon lawgivers *showed great wisdom in the business of legislation*, by admitting no laws into their selections but what were adapted to the temper and manners of their subjects, being for the most part taken from people that were nearly allied to themselves."

On the very next page, we have an illustration of the *great wisdom* of the Saxon lawgivers. "*The Saxon people were divided into freemen and slaves.*"

Slavery, servitude, villenage, and every one of its modifications, is a *political* institution, though this fact is apt to be overlooked when the slave comes to be viewed as the *property* of another man. But what is politics? The system of rules which ought to prevail *between man and man;* and *law* ought to consist of those rules reduced to human enactment. Individual injustice may make a man a slave, and the action is *a crime;* but the criminality does not in the slightest degree diminish when the action is authorized by human laws. Now, in a country that has assumed the form of *a state*, slavery could not exist unless it were authorized by *the law:* and the evil influence of human law has been, that *it sanctioned* this, and many other abominations, using the armed force of the state for their continuance, and transmitting them to posterity as institutions under which men were born, and which, to a certain degree, were to them natural, or, rather, *habitual.*

which are not crimes, and to burden the population with unequal taxation, and to exclude large portions of the population from equal rights in the eye of the law and in the scheme of the state, we do not hesitate to affirm that such legislation should be regarded exactly in the same light that individual violence or restraint would be regarded. *Men* are the agents, the actors, in the one case as well as in the other; and the action which is wrong for individuals without titles, is equally wrong for individuals called by any names that the imagination could devise. Man, as man, is bound by the moral laws of justice, and no arrangements which the human race could make can ever emancipate any portion of that race from the same rules and requirements that are binding on individuals. The whole idea of *a ruler*, of a man, or body of men, who may interfere with others on principles *different* from those that regulate individual or private interference, is a mere idolatrous superstition, debasing in its influence, and disastrous in its effects. The almighty Maker and Ruler of mankind will have men subject to *justice*, and not to *men;* and the very moment the rules of justice, which vary not, nor can vary, are departed from, that moment is man relieved from his allegiance to the ruler; and if the population have the power, they may arrest the rulers, and bring them to the same judicial trial that would be reserved for the individual.*

* This principle, although frequently represented as seditious, is not only clearly acknowledged, but reduced to specific law in Magna Charta. The *principle* is acknowledged, although the application of it is restricted to twenty-five barons, chosen by the whole

And hence the necessity for a "science of justice," that men — definitely ascertaining, on principles which are not arbitrary, the real actions which are criminal — may appoint a first magistrate to carry into execution the laws of justice. And this first magistrate — king, president, or any thing else, — is not to govern men, but to regulate them according to the laws of equity; and, in performing this function, he occupies the highest position to which man may attain, and, performing his duties with impartial sincerity, he merits the constant respect, aid, and support of every person in the land. This portion of the British constitution, the first magistrate king, the independent judges, and the jury from the locality, is unsurpassed, if not unequalled, by any thing in the whole history of man. In England, we have in *this* portion of our political mechanism the most profound reason for thankfulness to God. And we do not hesitate to make a curious assertion — *that if our political rulers (those who tax and restrict us) were brought into the courts of law as individuals performing certain specified acts towards other individuals, the ordinary process of criminal trial*

of the barons; and a reservation is made in favor of the persons of the king, queen, and royal children. Chapter xxxviii. specifies the manner in which four barons, chosen out of the twenty-five, shall notify any grievance, and petition to have it redressed without delay: "And if it is not redressed by us, (the king,) or if we should chance to be out of the realm, if it is not redressed by our justiciary within forty days, &c., the four barons aforesaid shall lay the cause before the rest of the twenty-five barons, and the said twenty-five barons, *together with the community of the whole kingdom*, shall distrain and distress us all the ways possible; namely, by seizing our castles, lands, possessions," &c.

by jury, and judge, and law, would at once rectify nearly every political evil in the country. Had the slave owner been tried, he could not have been convicted because of the law; *but had the legislature been tried for making laws to allow slavery, and for using the British arms to support it*, there can be no question that, if the ordinary decisions were adhered to, the jury would have found the legislature guilty, and England may proudly say that her judges would not have hesitated to pronounce the condemnation.

Only let the taxer, and the taxee, who is excluded from a voice in the representation, be viewed as two *men*, or two bodies of *men;* let them enter the present courts of law, and let the case be tried irrespective of political considerations, and there can be no doubt that the taxee would establish his right to dispose of his property without the interference of the taxer. They are only *men*, neighbors; and what is not just between two men, never can be just, however great the number of individuals, or however euphonious the names that may be applied to them.

This principle of allowing no man whatever, and no body of men whatever, to emancipate themselves from the strict requirements of justice, but in all their corporate actions to be subject to the same principles of equity that are binding on the individual — this principle is the great end of political amelioration. In advocating it, we teach doctrines, it is true, which are little less than revolutionary; and revolutions, either moral or physical, there *must* be until the ultimate term of man's political progression is evolved, and the course of transition from the rule of power to the rule of reason is complete. We advocate, not a breach of justice, but its *universal extension;* its extension to all the acts of *man, as man,* whether he appear under the form of an isolated individual, or under the more imposing aspect of a deliberative assembly and executive government, ruling the millions of a state. All we ask is, that the same principles that regulate the laws as they affect individuals, should be extended to the political actions of the rulers; and if once this principle were realized, all partiality, class legislation, privilege, commercial restriction, customs laws, game laws, &c., would immediately disappear. These things have no foundation except in the will of the rulers; and man, as man, is neither bound to obey or acknowledge as a dispenser of justice that government that persists in imposing on the population its own superstitious and destructive devices, instead of the impartial laws of equity, made equally for all men and equally administered.

Under these circumstances, it may be affirmed that the first great effect that will follow the discovery of political science, is the definite and non-arbitrary determination of the great minor, "What is a crime?" And this being determined according to a scientific method which shall command the assent of the human intellect, the practical consequence will be, that every restriction will be removed from every action that is *not* a crime. And consequently there will be perfect freedom for every man to exercise his talents and his industry without state interference, or restriction, or taxation of any kind whatever, so long as he shall continue to refrain from those actions which, according to the science of equity, are demonstrated to be *crimes*. Progression — that is, *change* — must be anticipated as natural and necessary, until the political aspect of mankind shall present a realization of this condition. Definitely to determine what is a crime, and what is not a crime, is one of the first great problems of political science. We define crime to be, "a breach of equity;" * and consequently we maintain that whatever is not a breach of equity is not a crime, and under no circumstances whatever ought to be prohibited or restricted by the laws. Absolute freedom, then, to perform every action that is not a breach of equity, constitutes the great final termination of man's political progress, so far as *liberty* is concerned.

But what is man's final termination with regard to the other great substantive of politics, *property?*

Here we approach a subject that, in the course of a few years, (in all probability,) will be the great element of strife and contention. Here is the rock on which England's famous constitution of king, lords, and commons will suffer its final shipwreck. Such an assertion is, of course, at present a mere opinion; but if the scheme we have advanced be in the main

* It may, perhaps, be necessary to add, "or of decency." The repression of offences against decency forms, however, a very small portion of man's political action. With the exception of these, and the observance of the Sabbath, we believe our definition to be general. It is the true *political* definition; but the political definition does not exactly include *every thing* that men in society have to take into consideration. Political science is *abstract;* but the real substantive, *man*, is concrete; and his *conditions* must be considered in applying the science to his circumstances.

correct, then we do not hesitate to affirm, that if we continue that scheme into the future, we may see that the question of landed property will be the cause of a stupendous struggle between the aristocracy and the laborocracy of Britain, and that its final settlement will entail the destruction of the constitution. And the question lies in narrow bounds, all that is required being an answer to a question virtually the following: "Is the population to be starved, pauperized, and expatriated, or is the aristocracy to be destroyed?"* For ourselves, we have not the slightest hesitation in predicting the final result; but what may be the mechanism of the changes requires altogether a different course of investigation. On the mode of change we pronounce no opinion; but on the matter of change we no more hesitate to prognosticate than we do to predict that, ere a few years longer, the millions of Russian serfs will have gained their emancipation; and surely serfdom is as ancient and venerable an institution as aristocracy.

Serfdom and aristocracy are, in fact, the correlatives of each other. Wherever there are serfs, *there* there are aristocrats; and wherever there are aristocrats, *there* there are serfs; and though the laborers of England are not serfs in one sense, inasmuch as they may emigrate if they can find the means, they are, to all intents and purposes, serfs so long as they remain in

* By the destruction of the *aristocracy*, we do not mean the destruction of the aristocrats, any more than by the destruction of pauperism, we should mean the destruction of the persons of the paupers. It is to the *system* that we refer exclusively, and only as either system has been created by the arrangements of men.

England. It is a mere fallacy to suppose that serfdom has been abolished in England. It has not been *abolished*, it has only been *generalized*. And here we must have recourse to an illustration to show that serfdom, or even slavery, may be abolished in appearance, and yet retained in reality, *the means of compulsion being changed* with the advance of society, which would no longer tolerate the open employment of individual force.

Let us suppose an island divided into thirty estates. These estates belong to thirty proprietors, and are cultivated by *slaves*, by genuine out-and-out salable negroes. These slaves are the *property* (!) of the white proprietors, each of whom has a stock of one hundred. There are then thirty proprietors, and three thousand laboring slaves, supported by the island — the slaves having sustenance and the *labor*, the proprietors having indolence and *the luxury*. As the slaves belong to the proprietors, they are *individual* slaves, confined to the cultivation of their respective estates. Let us now suppose that the proprietors made a new arrangement of their affairs; that, instead of possessing each a hundred slaves, they thought it would be more convenient to establish a system by which those proprietors who wanted the labor of *more* at any particular time should be able to have it, and those who at any particular time had not work for a hundred, should relieve themselves of the expense of their keep. To effect this, and to throw *the trouble* of the new system on the slaves, they abandon the system of individual slavery, and *generalize* it. Each proprietor gives up his right to his negroes; but the negroes are still to do the *work* of the island, and the proprietors are still to have the profit. Nor is it difficult to effect this arrangement without compulsion — all that is necessary being to establish the rule, that the negroes shall be fed by those for whom they work, and that their wages shall be their *sustenance*. All the land being in the hands of the proprietors, the negroes can obtain support only by laboring *for* the proprietors. But it is found that the new arrangement has still its inconveniences. At certain seasons of the year there is not work for the whole three thousand laborers; and as they can only obtain support from the proprietors, the latter establish a general or corporate fund for the sustenance of those who happen to be out of employ. This is a poor-law.

But still the system is capable of improvement; that is, more of the trouble may be allotted to the negroes, without the profits of the proprietors being interfered with. The proprietors under the present system are obliged to provide the aliments of the laborers, and this of course is not only troublesome, but the regulation of the quantity is attended with inconveniences. The proprietors, therefore, knowing that they have all the land, and that the laborers cannot find support except by laboring for them, establish an intermediate class, (of shopkeepers,) who receive the provisions from the proprietors and dispense them to the laborers. The shopkeepers are only transformed laborers, employed in a particular department of the economy of the island.

This new system, however, requires a *means of exchange* to enable the proprietors to be certain that none of the laborers obtain food without doing the necessary work, and labor must therefore have a representative, which shall enable the laborer to obtain his day's food when he has done his day's work. This representative is *money*. The laborer does a day's work, and receives a coin, a shell, a token, or a piece of paper, the essential character of which is — that it is "*an order for a day's food.*"

But the shopkeeper being a laborer, must receive *his own food*, and this he does by receiving for the tokens which represent labor a larger quantity from the proprietors than the quantity he gives to the laborers.

The figure might be extended, and the system of modern society might be made to grow out of the two primary elements, the proprietor and the slave.

But what we ask is this, Are the laborers, when their slavery has been generalized, and money has been introduced, are they not still *the serfs of the proprietors?* True, the proprietors have no longer *individual* slaves, and cannot inflict individual punishments; but the whole body of the laborers still belong to the whole body of the proprietors, inasmuch as the land belongs to the latter, and the laborers cannot obtain their sustenance without laboring *for them.*

Now, suppose the accumulated profits of the proprietors were sufficient to enable them to live for a certain number of years without the cultivation of their lands, and they should by any mad freak resolve to do so, and not to employ the laborers; the latter would, of course, be reduced to destitution and starvation; so that, although the individual life of a laborer is not in the hands of an individual proprietor, the lives of the whole class of laborers would be in the hands of the class of the proprietors. And if a large proportion of the latter were to absent themselves from the island, and not to cause the lands to be cultivated, of course a large portion of the laborers would be reduced to want, or perhaps to hunger-fever and death. And this is what takes place in Ireland.*

Now, are not the laborers *serfs* under these circumstances? We maintain that they are, and that the laborers † of England, Ireland, and Scotland are *serfs;* though the name is a disagreeable one, and the fact of their serfdom is *concealed* by the economical arrangements by which the internal business of the country is carried on. The laborers are the *serfs*, and the proprietors are the *aristocracy;* and it makes little or no difference whether we have an imaginary island with thirty proprietors and three thousand laboring serfs, or

* General statement in acres of the cultivated, uncultivated, and unprofitable land of the United Kingdom. — (*From the Third Report of the Emigration Committee.*)

	Cultivated.	Uncultivated wastes capable of improvement.	Unprofitable.	Total.
England. . . .	25,632,000	3,454,000	3,256,400	32,342,400
Wales.	3,117,000	530,000	1,105,000	4,752,000
Scotland. . . .	5,265,000	5,950,000	8,523,930	19,738,930
Ireland.	12,125,280	4,900,000	2,416,664	19,441,944
British Islands.	383,690	166,000	569,469	1,119,159
	46,522,970	15,000,000	15,871,463	77,394,433

† By laborers, of course, we mean all who labor for their bread, whether merchants, manufacturers, professional men, artisans farmers, agricultural laborers, operatives, &c.

a real island with thirty thousand proprietors and five or six millions of laboring serfs. Let the political arrangements be what they may, let there be universal or any other suffrage, so long as the aristocracy have all the land, and derive the *rent* of it, the laborer is only a serf, and a serf he will remain until he has uprooted the rights of private landed property. *The land is for the nation, and not for the aristocracy.*

We affirm, then, that serfdom has not been abolished, but only *generalized*, in England, Ireland, and Scotland; and this generalization appears to be the step of transition through which society must pass, in its progress from the condition of individual lord and individual serf, to the condition of equitable equality, in which there shall be no lord and no serf, but only freemen without privileges and without oppressions.*

But it is necessary to understand what we mean by a lord and a serf.

A serf is a man who, by the arrangements of

* "These villeins, belonging principally to lords of manors, were either villeins *regardant*, — that is, annexed to the manor or land, — or else they were *in gross*, or at large; that is, annexed to the person of the lord, and transferable by deed from one owner to another. They could not leave their lord without his permission, but, if they ran away or were purloined from him, might be claimed and recovered by action, *like beasts or other chattels.* They held, indeed, small portions of land, by way of sustaining themselves and families, but it was at the mere will of the lord, who might dispossess them whenever he pleased; and it was upon villein services, that is, to carry out dung, to hedge and ditch the lord's demesnes, and any other the meanest offices; and their services were not only base, but uncertain, both as to their time and quantity. A villein, in short, was in much the same state

mankind, is deprived of the object on which he might expend his labor, or of the *natural profit* that results from his labor, and, consequently, is under the necessity of supporting himself and his family by his labor *alone*. And a lord, or an aristocrat, is a man who, by the arrangements of mankind, is made to possess *the object*, and who, consequently, can support himself and his family *without labor*, on the *profits* created by the labor of others. This is the essential distinction between the lord and the serf; and we maintain that the constitution of the world forbids that any arrangement of this kind should result in any other than an evil condition of society, which must necessarily condemn a large part of the population to physical degradation; and if to physical degradation, to *moral* degradation. No instance can be adduced of a population reduced to extreme poverty — as must ever be the case where the land, the great source of wealth, is allotted to a few who labor *not* — where that popula-

with us as Lord Molesworth describes to be that of the boors in Denmark, and which Stiernhoak attributes also to the *traals* or slaves in Sweden, which confirms the probability of their being, in some degree, monuments of the Danish tyranny. A villein could acquire no property either in lands or goods; but, if he purchased either, the lord might enter upon them, oust the villein, and seize them to his own use, unless he contrived to dispose of them again before the lord had seized them, for the lord had then lost his opportunity.

"In many places, also, a fine was payable to the lord if the villein presumed to marry his daughter to any one without leave from the lord; and, by the common law, the lord might also bring an action against the husband for damages in thus purloining *his property*." — BLACKSTONE'S *Commentaries*, book ii. chap. 6.

tion has not been *also and in consequence* reduced to moral and intellectual degradation, and where the spirit of man has not been depraved and borne down by the circumstances in which man, and not God, has placed him.*

In endeavoring to estimate what must be the ultimate condition of mankind with regard to natural property, we have two methods of determination: first, that of political science; second, that of analogy, based on the actual history of the past evolution of mankind with regard to natural liberty. We have already stated that the too great substantives of politics are *liberty* and *property*. Each of these gives rise

* Poverty and want are evils, inasmuch as they produce human suffering; but they are far greater evils, as they tend to produce the *deterioration of man*. And when this deterioration is produced by the political arrangements of a country, with regard to the land and the other natural sources of wealth, the alteration of those arrangements becomes a *moral duty* of the very highest character. As an illustration of this *deterioration of man*, we quote the following passage from the *Edinburgh Review*, October, 1848, where the writer is treating of man *scientifically*, and without reference to politics. Let the reader contrast this passage with a *political* article in the same number of the *Edinburgh Review*, where the writer appears to assert, that "of a hundred honest, industrious, and upright men, the vast majority are certain to do well." According to the laws of *nature* they would do well, but according to the laws of Ireland no personal qualifications would relieve the masses from hopeless poverty so long as the present politcal arrangements are allowed to remain. In Ireland, the *object* of labor (the land) has been taken from the inhabitants, and vast districts are lying unimproved and uncultivated in the face of a population willing to work for the lowest wages. On the one hand is the land lying idle, and on the other is the labor lying idle; and the landlordocracy is the obstacle that prevents the two from being brought into contact, and

to a course of evolution, and the two courses of evolution are analogous; that is, the *process* is similar, while the substantives involved in the process are diverse. Thus the lord and the serf present the farthest possible remove from equity, both as regards liberty and as regards property; and the process by which the serf gradually emancipates his personal actions from the power of the lord, may be taken as an indication of the process by which he will ultimately succeed in depriving the lord of his exclusive possession of the earth, and thereby emancipating his own labor from the burdens that oppress it, and from the depreciation of value which it must necessarily

thereby securing an abundant provision for the population. So long as the land is unimproved and uncultivated, it is nonsense to assert that Ireland is over-populous, or that she could not support a much larger population. It is the law, and not nature, that reduces Ireland to starvation.

"Races which have advanced the farthest in civilization, and attained the greatest perfection of physical form, produce also examples of physical inferiority in individuals or families. Among other consequences of long-continued want and ignorance, the conformation of the cranium appears to have been affected. The Sanatory Commission would arrive at this conclusion, we believe, were it to examine the worst part of the population of our great towns; the most convincing proof, however, is unfortunately furnished by the lowest classes of the Irish population." There are certain districts in Leitrim, Sligo, and Mayo, (as pointed out by an intelligent writer in the *Dublin University Magazine*, No. 48,) chiefly inhabited by the descendants of the native Irish, driven by the British from Armagh and the south of Down, about two centuries ago. These people, whose ancestors were well grown, able bodied, and comely, are now reduced to an average stature of five feet, two inches, are pot-bellied, bow legged, and abortively featured, and are especially remarkable for "open, projecting

experience, so long as the great body of the population are merely laborers for the lords. And laborers for the lords the great body of the population must be, so long as the soil, the mines, the fisheries, &c., are accorded to a small number of individual proprietors.

As regards personal liberty, the lord and the serf present the greatest possible diversity. They are the antipodes, the positive and negative poles, of man's possible condition. The antagonism cannot be greater; it is absolute, ultimate, final. Man cannot make the disparity more perfect; it is the absolute dominion of strength, and the absolute subjection of weakness. The lord is the possessor, the serf is the

mouths, with prominent teeth and exposed gums, their advancing cheek bones and depressed noses bearing barbarism on their very front." In other words, within so short a period they seem to have acquired a prognathous type of skull, ["the third type of configuration of the skull has been very happily named by Dr. Prichard *prognathous*, to express its most distinctive character, namely, the forward prominence of the jaws,"] like the savages of Australia, "thus giving an example of deterioration from known causes, as almost compensates by its value to future ages for the suffering and debasement which past generations have endured in perfecting its appalling lesson." "The hordes of wretched Irish, whom famine has driven to seek subsistence in the seaports and manufacturing towns of Great Britain, must have enabled many of our readers to make this observation for themselves: every gradation being perceptible, from the really noble type of countenance and figure seen in some of them, to that utterly debased aspect which can be looked at only with disgust. . . . . . . In both cases (the Irish and the Australians) the same cause — a long-continued deficiency of food and social degradation (where a sufficient elevation to resist these depressing agencies had not been previously attained) — has terminated in the same results."—*Edinburgh Review*, October, 1848, p. 443.

possessed; the one is a being who commands, the other a thing who obeys. The one has the profit without the labor, the other the labor without the profit.

Such a condition — contrary as it is to every principle of reason, of equity, and of religion — is not only established by licentious *power*, but authorized and perpetuated by *human law*. And thus the iniquity was made to receive a sanction, which, although based on the darkest superstition, yet lent a kind of moral authorization to the system, and enabled the lords to speak of their *rights;* while the serfs, on the other hand, were impressed with a kind of fear that they might be doing wrong when they resorted to force to rid themselves of the oppression.

And the history of the acquisition of liberty (in Britain, for instance) is only the history of the gradual destruction of the privileges of the lord, and of the *legal* title which the serf has from time to time succeeded in establishing to those natural rights of which he had been deprived. The vast transformations that have taken place in the social conditions of Englishmen may be concisely expressed in the proposition, that "they have gradually, and through the course of many centuries, been progressing from the extreme of antagonism and disparity towards absolute equality in the eye of the law, so far as the matter of *liberty* is concerned." * It is true that this process is not

* "The rest of their slaves have not, like ours, particular employments allotted to them. Each is the master of a habitation and household of his own. The lord requires from him a certain quantity of grain, cattle, or cloth, as from a tenant; and so far only

yet complete, and that considerable changes must yet take place before the government of the country becomes the impartial administrator of equal law, made the same for every inhabitant of the country, without the slightest distinction of individuals or of classes, except in so far as individuals may be made to fill offices; which offices may have peculiar duties, peculiar responsibilities, and peculiar remunerations attached to them. But this question of *official* disparity is a mere question of executive administration, similar to the appointment of directors or managers in a corporate concern, where some are appointed to act for all; without, however, establishing any disparity of *rights*, but only such a disparity of *functions* as the common judgment of the society may find advisable for the success of its operations.

If, then, the progress of modern society has been a gradual but sure progress from the extreme of disparity towards absolute parity in the eye of the law, so far as *personal liberty* is concerned, we have only to identify the laws of property with the laws of lib-

the subjection of the slave extends. His domestic offices are performed by his own wife and children. It is unusual to scourge a slave, or punish him with chains or hard labor. They are sometimes killed by their masters; not through severity of chastisement, but in the heat of passion, like an enemy, with this difference, that it is done with impunity. Freedmen (manumitted slaves) are little superior to slaves, seldom filling any important office in the family; never in the state, except in those tribes which are under regal government. There they rise above the freeborn, and even the nobles; in the rest, the subordinate condition of the freedmen is a proof of freedom."—TACITUS, *Manners of the Germans*, XXV (Aiken's Translation.)

erty to arrive at a firm conviction, that the progress will continue in the same direction until parity in the eye of the law shall be evolved, so far as *natural property* is concerned. If we were to view the laws relating to natural property (the earth) as *distinct* from the laws relating to personal liberty, then we should base an argument on analogy, and we should maintain that the evolution that has taken place in the matter of liberty would also take place in the matter of natural property. And this argument would be valid, and would afford a high probability that the equalization of natural property was to be anticipated as the conclusion of human evolution in that department.

But if *property* be considered as one of the substantives of moral dynamics, and if we reason the question on the scheme of *human action* — inquiring not into the laws that have reference to the object, but into the laws that have reference to man and man's actions — we thereby *identify* the laws of liberty and the laws of property, and come to view both as the laws that should preside over human function; because, to allocate a certain portion of the earth to one individual, is only to prohibit all other individuals from using that portion, and the question, viewed in this light, can only be argued as a branch of the more general question, "How can one man justly lay restrictions on another man?" And when the question is viewed in this light, it is plainly evident that there is no such thing as a law of property, distinct and separate from a law of liberty, but that the theory of liberty must *include* the theory of property; and if the time should come when the law shall be impartial with regard to human action, then of necessity must the law be impartial with regard to natural property; in fact, with regard to every thing *that is not created by the skill and labor of the individual.*

Let us consider that the very essence of just law is, that it is "no respecter of persons," and that *à priori* it acknowledges no difference and no distinction between the individuals who are to be regulated by its enactments. Law, to be just, must be *the same* for all the individuals who are to be subject to it; and if law be made in such a manner that it imposes on one man a restriction which it does not impose on another, then is that law not just, nor is man morally bound to acknowledge it or obey it. The validity of law depends exclusively on its equity and impartiality; and wherever the law starts by acknowledging or establishing diversities of privileges, there is the law unjust, partial, and wicked; and it is the duty of man, as man, to destroy that law, and to reëstablish the equilibrium of equity, which ought never to have been disturbed. The very end and intention of impartial law is the prevention of the disturbance of the equilibrium of equity; and where the law, instead of preventing this disturbance, originates, defends, and perpetuates it, that law has altogether departed from the true intention of law, and its abolition is absolutely necessary before man can attain to the best condition possible for him on earth.

We are fully aware that there exists in the minds of many persons a vague apprehension, that if the present laws relating to landed property were to be disturbed, evils of the most malignant character would invade the society of Britain. Nothing can be more absurd, more puerile, more dastardly. The very same fears have prevailed with regard to every other change that has taken place; and, down to the last change that man shall make in his political arrangements, we may rest satisfied that the craven, the placeman, and the aristocrat will not fail to vent loud lamentations on the evils which, in their estimation, are sure to follow. The oft-repeated quotation from the great bard, "'Tis better to bear the ills we have, than fly to others that we know not of," is dragged in to give the sanction of that proud name to fears which he would have regarded with scorn, and to interested representations which he would have rejected with detestation. True, in Shakspeare's sense, it *is* better to bear the ills of human life than to rush with the red hand into the presence of the almighty Giver of life. True, this is true. And even in our own lot it may be better to bear one worldly evil than to make a change which might entail other worldly evils which we know not of. This also is true. But surely none can be so besotted as not to perceive that the question comes in another form, and that a new reading must be adopted before we can have an applicable sentiment. The question, *wherever there is injustice*, is not, whether it is better to bear the ills we have; but, whether it is better to make others bear the ills we inflict upon them; and, whether it is better for them to bear the ills which *men* inflict, than fly to changes which deliver the oppressed from the *pain*, and the oppressor from the *sin*, of the injustice.

But while we maintain that the continual progress of mankind is towards *equality in the eye of the law*, and that as men were once at the utmost extreme of inequality, and have been gradually and surely decreasing that inequality; and consequently that we have the evidence of past history to give us the line of progress, and the evidence of reason that, if that line continue, it must terminate in the total abolition of privilege and the establishment of absolute equality; we have also the dogma of political science, which proves equality to be *right*, and evidence from the other sciences to prove that what is right ultimately comes to be adopted in practice.

This portion of the argument presents itself in the following aspect:—

1st. There is no possibility of establishing a diversity of rights between the various individuals of which the human race is composed, in so far as those individuals enter into relation with each other for the formation of a state or community, acting for the common advantage.

In saying that there is no possibility of establishing such a diversity of rights, we mean, that there is no natural source of knowledge whatever from which such a diversity could possibly flow. There may be a diversity of strength, or of intellect, or of skill, or of cunning; but the very moment we admit an abstract or general moral law, we absolutely obliterate the possibility of a diversity of rights. Men find themselves on the surface of the globe, and find themselves also possessed of a reason which furnishes *general* propositions applicable to the race; and there exists no natural means whatever of determining what individual men should possess more rights than their fellows, or what individual men should possess fewer rights than their fellows. The only *possible* means by which such a diversity *could* be established, would be a revelation from the Creator of mankind; and except in the one case, of the Hebrew nation, we have no evidence that the Creator has ever pointed out any individuals, or any families, who were to enjoy *specified* rights, in contradistinction to the *general* rights which men derive from the intuitions of the reason.

2d. Men having fallen from the first estate in which they were created, have in their moral actions and political arrangements followed, not the dictates of their impartial reason, but the dictates of their selfish passions; and thus those in power have not only acted wrongfully, but have enacted wrong, bad, and wicked *laws*, thereby perpetuating the injustice under the formal sanction of legislation.

3d. On this account, human laws and human arrangements, instead of being impartial and for the benefit of human society at large, have originated and perpetuated systems of partiality, whereby power and privilege were accorded to certain individuals, families, classes, castes, &c., at the expense of the other members of the race; who, of necessity, were restricted in their rights in the same ratio that the privileged classes were endowed with privileges.

4th. Human society, therefore, instead of presenting an ethically homogeneous aspect, resulting from the universal prevalence of impartial law, (which laid on all exactly the same moral restrictions, and which accorded to all exactly the same liberty for the development of individual labor, skill, industry, and enterprise,) has exhibited the human race as divided into classes endowed with *diverse* privileges; and has figured forth the antagonism of the oppressor and the oppressed, instead of the harmony of equal freemen, each developing his own fortunes within those moral restrictions which are immutable.

5th. But the arrangements of mankind have not only established diversities of rights affecting mere action, (in Britain, for instance, we have a *franchised* class and an *unfranchised* class; that is, a *freed* class, or class of *freed serfs*, and an *unfreed* class, or class of laboring serfs *not yet freed*,) but they have established diversities of rights affecting the possession of the earth, which the Creator intended for the race; and thus one man was endowed with vast extents of territory, while, on the other hand, multitudes were thereby necessarily deprived of every thing except their labor. So singular a system could only originate in the *reign of power*, and could only be perpetuated through the ignorance of the masses of the population. But the arrangements of mankind with regard to the earth did not stop here. One generation was not content with making arrangements which were to be in force for that generation alone; but laws were enacted, and customs were acknowledged, whereby the arrangements of one generation were to descend to future generations, and to be imposed on men not yet born, who were to be born into a world already portioned out, and, consequently, to which they had no title. Those, therefore, who were born into the world in a country where the land had been accorded to individual proprietors, could obtain their livelihood only by laboring for other men; and as those to whom the land had been accorded could not cultivate it themselves, and as the land was required for the support of the population, the *laborers* were under the necessity of paying *a rent* to those who thus procured a vast revenue without labor. This system of diversity of rights to the natural earth, which God intended for the race, being perpetuated from generation to generation, entails with it, as its necessary attendant, that baneful condition of society, in which we have a few aristocrats endowed with vast wealth without labor, and a multitude of laborers reduced to poverty,* destitution, and sometimes to actual starvation.†

* "La condition des paysans est des plus malheureuses. Les fortunes sont tellement disproportionnées, qu'on ne voit que des riches et des pauvres, les petits proprietaires sont fort rares. Il en resulte un manque d'emulation et de courage pour fonder des établissements d'industrie et pour ameliorer l'agriculture." — *Dict. Geog. Univ., Art. Calabre.*

† One would scarcely imagine that in London, the wealthiest city in the world, people could be starved to death. We mention an incident that came within our own experience. Some years ago we were present at a dispensary, one of those admirable and unostentatious institutions established to afford medical relief to the poor in London, and supported principally by the efforts of the *medical* officers. A widow appeared as a patient. She stated that she had six children to support, and that her whole earnings amounted to 7s. a week. We saw the medical officer shake his head, doubting that the case was beyond the reach of medicine. The surgeon was a humane man, and he did what he could for her. Some months after, we saw him again, and inquired for the widow. She had died. We asked the nature of her disease; and the reply was,

6th. The whole idea of a diversity of rights and privileges originates in the corrupted heart of mankind, and in the darkened intellect that has allowed superstition to dictate its credence, instead of basing its propositions on the axioms of the reason.

"*She died of starvation!*" With the hand of death upon her, she had labored for her children, and at last she died for want of food. Such is London.

Does the reader suppose such things do not occur? Let us take a sketch by the great depictor of modern manners, Mr. Charles Dickens:—

"'Ah!' said the man, bursting into tears, and sinking on his knees at the feet of the dead woman, 'Kneel down, kneel down—kneel round her every one of you, and mark my words. I say she starved to death. I never knew how bad she was till the fever came upon her, and then her bones were starting through the skin. There was neither fire nor candle; she died in the dark—in the dark! She couldn't even see her children's faces, though we heard her gasping out their names. I begged for her in the streets, and they sent me to prison. When I came back, she was dying; and all the blood in my heart was dried up, for they starved her to death. I swear it before the God that saw it—they starved her!' He twined his hands in his hair, and with a loud scream rolled grovelling upon the floor, his eyes fixed, and the foam gushing from his lips."—*Oliver Twist.*

Fain would we express a hope that Mr. Dickens, to whom God has given so admirable a genius, might one day turn his attention to the condition of the laboring classes in the manufacturing towns of England. He might then become indeed a benefactor to his country; and, as no pen can command a more powerful interest than his own, he might reap the noble satisfaction of alleviating those dreadful evils that prey on the population. The warning voice might, it is true, be heard in vain; but so certainly as those evils are not removed by better social conditions, accompanied by moral and intellectual education, so certainly will they one day produce their natural fruits of frantic revolt.

However long men may be in coming to the conclusion, they must ultimately accord that there are no natural means known by which a diversity of rights could possibly be established. A diversity of rights implies, that some *individuals* are to be endowed with certain privileges not common to the race. And these individuals would require to be *recognizable.* Now, no natural means whatever, no methods of appreciation known to man, ever did, or ever could, enable the human race to say, *à priori*, "This individual is entitled to more rights than that individual." Nothing but a revelation from the Creator could ever establish such a distinction; and consequently all diversities in the human race must be diversities *of office*, and *diversities of condition, produced by the more or less successful result of individual labor, enterprise, or skill.* Every other diversity is contrary to reason; and when established by human law, such law is bad, wrong, and wicked, and ought to be abolished.

7th. The whole history of man informs us that the human race is gradually emerging from superstition, gradually acquiring knowledge, and gradually applying that knowledge to rectify the arrangements which were made in times of superstition. And history also informs us, that wherever truth is substantiated, it does, sooner or later, receive the assent of the human intellect; and though the progress has been partial, both as regards the quantity of truth received, and the extent to which it has been received by the nations of the earth, the advances already made leave no possible doubt as to the system, process, or scheme, according to which man abandons superstition, and adheres at last to those propositions which are properly substantiated. In every department of human action, we may in the present day observe the gradual substitution of *scientific method* for *empirical method*, or for *the fictions of superstition;* and as no doubt can possibly be entertained that men are now approaching man science, we may rest satisfied that the political relations of man will, ere long, be treated according to a scientific method — that fictions will be abandoned, and that arrangements will be made in accordance with the dictates of the reason, instead of emanating from the right of the strongest, confirmed by legislation.

8th. The great theoretic change that must take place in Britain, is the abolition of the belief that one generation of men can be bound by the arrangements of past generations; and, instead of that belief, the substitution of a belief that men in every age must be governed by *reason;* that, whatever the arrangements or laws of past generations may have been, those arrangements or laws are binding *now* only in so far as they are now *right*, quite independently of any sanction they may have received from legislation. The acts of past men are no more binding on present men in matters of politics than they are in matters of astronomy or theology; and when we find the soil of Britain disposed of, not according to any scheme that pretends to be now right, but according to the arrangements of men long since dead, who enacted *the perpetuity* of their arrangements, we may rest satisfied that the nation must ere long turn its attention to the revision of those arrangements, and inquire, "*What ought to be the present disposition of the soil, supposing no arrangements whatever had been inherited from past generations.*"

No political truth requires to be more strenuously impressed upon the world, than that the men of every succeeding generation have *the same right* to make their own arrangements, unburdened with any responsibilities, restrictions, diversities of rights and privileges, other than those restrictions imposed by the general laws of equity, or those diversities *of office* which they may agree to make for their general advantage. Nothing can be more absurd than to suppose that a past generation can make arrangements to deprive the present generation (at any given time) of its full right to dispose of the earth in the mode that is best *for the present generation;* and though the laws of Britain are utterly contrary to reason, in this respect, inasmuch as lands are entailed in particular families, to whom other Britons must pay a rent for the use of the soil, we need not hesitate to affirm, that the moment a scientific method (whether inductive and economical, or deductive and moral) comes to be applied to the question, "Whose is the soil, and how should it be distributed?" that moment will the fabric of English aristocracy be undermined, and the social laws of Britain will undergo a thorough regeneration. Superstition on this point may endure for a few years longer; but so certainly as men achieve equality in the eye of the law with regard to natural liberty, so certainly must they ultimately achieve equality with regard to natural property. And so certainly as men reduce to practice the propositions of knowledge in the other sciences, so certainly will they ultimately reduce to practice the propositions of political science; and instead of being the slaves of superstition, held in awe by the bugbears of *hereditary rights, the authority of (wrong) laws, and the impositions of legal fictions*, they will make *reason* the ruler, moral science the expositor of reason, and subject themselves to the laws of *justice*, and no longer to the laws of men.

If, then, we admit that every generation of men has the same free right to make its own arrangements, and to carry into effect the principles it knows or believes to be true, quite independently of the arrangements that have been made by any anterior generations, we must also of necessity admit, that the earth and all it contains belong, for the time being, to every *existing generation*, and that the *disposition* of the earth (as the great storehouse from which man must derive his support and sustenance) is not to be determined by the laws, customs, arrangements, king's gifts, or prescriptive rights of any past generation of men, but by the judgment and reason of the existing generation, ordering all arrangements according to the rules of equity, which are always valid and always binding, and which at every given moment of time are the rules which ought to determine human action. Consequently the question at *every* period is, "What is the equitable disposition of the earth?" Is it equitable that any arrangements of past generations should cause one man now to be born heir to a county, or half a county, or quarter of a county, while the other inhabitants of that county are thereby deprived of all right to the soil, and must consequently *pay a rent* to the one individual who naturally has not one particle of right to the earth more than they have themselves? And if such an arrangement be not now equitable, most undoubtedly it ought not to be allowed to continue; and if any government (instead of *administrating* the laws of equity) use the armed power of the nation for the purpose of *enforcing* such arrangements, such government has departed from its proper intention, and is not entitled to obedience.

If, then, we admit that every generation of men has exactly the same free right to the earth, unencumbered by any arrangements of past ages, the great problem is to discover "*such a system as shall secure to every man his exact share of the natural advantages which the Creator has provided for the race; while, at the same time, he has full opportunity, without let or hinderance, to exercise his labor, industry, and skill, for his own advantage.*" Until this problem is solved, both in theory and in practice, political change must continually go on.

The great practical termination, therefore, towards which modern societies are continually progressing, is *equalization in the eye of the law*, both with regard to natural liberty and natural property. And if we view *property* (*natural* property — that is, *that which is not created by human labor, industry, or skill*) as entering the theory of morals — and we must view it in this light when we view it by the aid of a scientific method — we *include natural property in the theory of human function*, and posit finally that the progression of mankind is towards that political condition in which the law shall be exactly one and the same for all men, without diversities of rights or privileges, and without diversities of condition other than diversities *of office*, and diversities of condition produced by the more or less successful result of individual labor, skill, or enterprise. And the ground on which we *identify** the laws of property and the laws of liberty is this: *When human laws accord to one man a portion of the earth as property, the essential character of such an arrangement is, that all other men are prohibited or restricted from using that portion of the earth; and consequently this law is merely a law restricting action, inasmuch as the prohibition is specific, whereas there is no injunction on the proprietor to cultivate the land, or make it produce its maximum for the increase of human welfare.*

Absolute equalization in the eye of the law with regard to natural rights, is the final termination of man's political progress, the last term in that grand series of changes that commenced with the two opposite elements — the lord and the serf; and which will terminate with the one element — the *freeman* without privileges and without oppressions.

There cannot be the slightest question that the progression of modern states *is towards universal suffrage;* that is, towards absolute equalization of the political function of the individuals of whom the state is composed. The necessary attendant of universal suffrage must be, "the equal eligibility of every member of the state to fill any office in the state."

When a state arrives at this ultimatum with regard

* *Identify* — to make *one;* or to establish an identity between two things that appear under different names or different aspects.

to the political function of each individual, the question of natural property must fall to be discussed; and as no possible reason can be alleged why one individual should, *à priori*, be endowed with more of the earth (which God, the Creator and Father of mankind, has given to the human race) than any other individual; and as every generation of existing men must have exactly the same title to a *free* earth, unencumbered with any arrangements of past generations, we may rest satisfied that, through whatever transformations men may pass, the ultimate point at which they must necessarily arrive *is absolute equality with regard to natural property.* And if so, the intention of Providence will then be realized, that the industrious man shall be rich, and the man who labors not shall be poor. Such is the intention of nature, and such is the intention of the almighty Maker of mankind.

The great social problem, then, that cannot fail ere long to appear in the arena of European discussion is, "*to discover such a system as shall secure to every man his exact share of the natural advantages which the Creator has provided for the race; while, at the same time, he has full opportunity, without let or hinderance, to exercise his skill, industry, and perseverance for his own advantage.*"

Of this problem, we maintain that there can be but one general solution possible; and the whole analogy of scientific discovery assures us that, sooner or later, the problem will be solved, that the solution will be acknowledged, and that it will be transformed from an intellectual dogma into a practical rule of action, thereby presenting a realization, in outward condition, of those propositions which the reason has seen to be correct.

The solution we propound (and which we hope to defend more at large at some future period) is the following, although, of course, there is no supposition that any general solution can be immediately applicable to the circumstances of this or any other country.

[For convenience' sake, we neglect all speculations as to what may or may not be the *geographical* arrangements of states at a future period. We shall speak of England alone, and consider the state of England as composed of an indefinite number of members, all equal in the eye of the law, all on a parity with regard to primary political function, and all equally eligible to fill any office to which they may be elected by the suffrages of the majority. All authority of *man* is of course excluded, and the CANON OF RIGHT is the SCIENCE OF EQUITY; that is, the rules of divine and immutable justice, as capable of being apprehended by the human reason.]

1st. Reason can acknowledge no difference of original rights between the individuals of which the human race is composed.

2d. Equality of rights cannot be sacrificed by any arrangements which one generation of men make for succeeding generations; but equality of rights is perpetual, inasmuch as that equality derives from the human reason, which varies not from age to age.

Even if it were true that there ought to be an inequality of rights among the individuals of the human race, it would be absolutely impossible to determine which individuals of the race should be born to more rights, and which individuals to fewer rights, than their fellows.* An inequality of rights can only be based *on superstition*, and the very moment reason is substituted for superstition in political science, (as it has been in the physical sciences,) that moment must men admit that no possible means are known by which an inequality of rights could possibly be substantiated. Even if it were true, for instance, that there should be an aristocracy and a serfdom, *there are no possible means of determining which individuals should be the aristocrats, and which individuals the serfs.*

3d. The state of England, then, would present a soil (including the soil proper, the mines, forests,

* "Whilst we maintain the unity of the human species, we at the same time repel the depressing assumption of superior and inferior races of men." ['The very cheerless, and, in recent times, too often discussed doctrine of the unequal rights of men to freedom, and of slavery as an institution in conformity with nature, is unhappily found most systematically developed in Aristotle's *Politica*, i. 3, 56.'] "There are nations more susceptible of cultivation, more highly civilized, more ennobled by mental cultivation, than others, but none in themselves nobler than others. All are in like degree designed for freedom — a freedom which, in the ruder conditions of society, belongs only to the individual, but which, in social states, enjoying political institutions, appertains as a right to the whole body of the community." If we would indicate an idea which, throughout the whole course of history, has ever more and more widely extended its empire, or which, more than any other, testifies to the much contested, and still more decidedly misunderstood perfectibility of the whole human race, it is that of establishing our common humanity — of striving to remove the barriers which prejudice and limited views of every kind have erected amongst men — and to teach all mankind, without reference to religion, nation, or color, as one fraternity, one great community, fitted for the attainment of one object, the unrestrained develop-

fisheries, &c., in fact, *that portion of the natural earth called England*) which was *permanent*, and a population that was not permanent, but *renewed by successive generations.*

4th. The question, then, is, "What system will secure to every individual of these successive generations his portion of the natural advantages of England?" Of this problem, we maintain that there is but one solution possible.

5th. No truth can be more absolutely certain, as an intuitive proposition of the reason, than that "an object is the *property* of its creator;" and we maintain that *creation** is the *only* means by which an

ment of the psychical powers. This is the ultimate and highest aim of society, identical with the direction implanted by nature in the mind of man towards the indefinite extension of his existence. He regards the earth in all its limits, and the heavens as far as his eye can scan their bright and starry depths, as inwardly his own, given to him as the objects of his contemplation, and as a field for the development of his energies. Even the child longs to pass the hills, or the seas, which enclose his manor house; yet, when his eager steps have borne him beyond those limits, he pines like the plant for his native soil; and it is by this touching and beautiful attribute of man, this longing for that which is unknown, and this fond remembrance of that which is lost, that he is spared from an exclusive attachment to the present. Thus deeply rooted in the innermost nature of man, and even enjoined upon him by his highest tendencies, the recognition of the bond of humanity becomes one of the noblest leading principles in the history of mankind." — HUMBOLDT'S *Cosmos*, vol. i. p. 368; *Bohn's edition.*

* In the *arts* man creates *form;* in political economy he creates *value;* and in politics he creates *property*. And as the evolution is in this order — 1st, the Arts; 2d, Political Economy; 3d, Politics; the laws of political economy must be discovered *before* there can be a *system of property* rational in its theory and scientific in its form.

individual right to property can be generated. Consequently, as no individual and no generation is the creator of the substantive, earth, it belongs *equally* to all the existing inhabitants; that is, no *individual* has a special claim to more than another.

6th. But while on the one hand we take into consideration *the object*,—that is, the earth,—we must also take into consideration *the subject;* that is, man, and man's labor.

7th. The object is the *common property* of all, no individual being able to exhibit a title to any particular portion of it. And individual or *private property* is, *the increased value produced by individual labor.* Again: in the earth must be distinguished the permanent earth and its temporary or perishable productions. The former,—that is, the permanent earth,—we maintain, never can be private property; and every system that treats it as such must necessarily be unjust. No *rational* basis has ever been exhibited to the world on which private right to any particular portion of the earth could possibly be founded.

8th. But though the permanent earth never can be private property,—although the laws may call it so, and may treat it as such,—it must be *possessed* by individuals for the purpose of cultivation, and for the purpose of extracting from it all those natural objects which man requires.

9th. The question, then, is, Upon what terms, or according to what system, must the earth be possessed by the successive generations that succeed each other on the surface of the globe? The conditions given are—*First.* That the earth is the common property of the race; *Second*. That whatever an individual produces by his own labor — whether it be a new object, made out of many materials, or a *new value* given by labor to an object whose form, locality, &c., may be changed — is the private property of that individual, and he may dispose of it as he pleases, provided he does not interfere with his fellows; *Third*. The earth is the *perpetual* common property of the race, and each succeeding generation has a full title to a *free* earth. One generation cannot encumber a succeeding generation.

And the condition required is, such a system as shall secure to the successive individuals of the race their share of the common property, and the opportunity, without interference, of making as much private property as their skill, industry, and enterprise would enable them to make.

The scheme that appears to present itself most naturally is, the general division of the soil, portioning it out to the inhabitants according to their number. Such appears to be the only system that suggests itself to most minds, if we may judge from the *objections* brought forward against an equalization of property. All these objections are against the actual division of the soil; and certainly such a division is theoretically erroneous, especially when the fractional parts are made the *property* of the possessors. But independently of this, the profits arising from trade, &c., would induce many individuals to forsake agriculture, and to abandon their portion to those who preferred the cultivation of the soil to any other pursuit. A purely agricultural population is almost impossible at any period; but when men have made considerable advances in the arts, &c., a general return to agricultural pursuits is a mere chimera, a phantom. Men must go forward, never backward. To speak of *a division of lands* in England is absurd. Such a division would be as useless as it is improbable. But it is more than useless; it is unjust: and unjust, not to the present so called proprietors, but to the human beings who are continually being born into the world, and who have exactly the same natural right to a portion that their predecessors have. For instance, let us suppose a hundred thousand acres divided into a thousand portions, and accorded as *property* to a thousand persons. This *appears*, at first sight, to be an equitable arrangement; and if the persons were immortal, and begot no children, the arrangement might be unobjectionable. But if the soil were made *property*, it would be *alienable*, and one of the thousand persons might alienate his hundred acres to another proprietor, who would then come to have two hundred acres. This might be perfectly equitable between the two parties themselves; but there are *others* interested in the transaction, and *their* rights must not be overlooked. Let us suppose that, in a few years, the adult population had increased to one thousand and fifty. The *fifty new men* have exactly the same right to a fractional share that the original one thousand had — mere priority of time making no possible difference in the right of men to the natural globe. What, then, would require to be done? It would be necessary, either, 1st, to preserve the original proprietors in their so called properties, thereby depriving the fifty new men of all share of the globe; or, 2d, to make a new division of the whole lands, dividing them into one thousand and fifty portions. This, of course, would destroy the proprietorship of the first occupants, and, in the practical division of the lands, would involve the recasting of the whole thousand farms or holdings. Every one would require to shift its boundaries every time that an increase of the population rendered a new division requisite. Such a system would be destructive to the cultivation of the soil; and though perhaps *possible*, it would be attended with inconveniences which render its reduction to practice out of the question.

The *actual* division of the soil need never be anticipated, nor would such a division *be just*, if the divided portions were made the property (legally, for they could never be so morally) of individuals.

If, then, successive generations of men cannot have their fractional share of the actual soil, (including mines, &c.,) how can the division of the advantages of the natural earth be effected?

By the division of its annual value or rent; that is, by making the rent of the soil the *common property* of the nation. That is, (as the *taxation* is the common property of the state,) by taking the whole of the taxes out of the rents of the soil, and thereby abolishing all other kinds of taxation whatever. And thus all *industry* would be absolutely emancipated from every burden, and every man would reap such natural reward as his skill, industry, or enterprise rendered legitimately his, according to the natural law of free competition.* This we maintain to be the only theory that will satisfy the requirements of the problem of natural property. And the question now is, How can the division of the rent be effected? An *actual* division of the rent — that is, the payment of so much money to each individual — would be attended with, perhaps, insuperable inconveniences; neither is such an actual division requisite, every requirement being capable of fulfilment without it.

We now apply this solution to England. England forms a state; that is, a community acting through public servants for the administration of justice, &c. In the *actual* condition of England, many things are at present unjust; and the right of the government to tax and make laws for those who are excluded from representation is, at all events, questionable. However, we shall make a few remarks on England as she is, and on England as she ought to be; that is, as she would be, were the rules of equity reduced to practical operation.

1st. The state has alienated the lands to private individuals called proprietors, and the vast majority of Englishmen are born to their labor *minus their share of the taxation.*

2d. This taxation of labor has introduced vast systems of restriction on trades and industry. Instead

* We have no hesitation whatever in predicting, that all civilized communities must ultimately abolish all revenue restrictions on industry, and draw the whole taxation from the rents of the soil. And this because (as we shall endeavor to show in a future portion of the subject) the rents of the soil are the common produce of the whole labor of a community.

of a perfectly free trade with all the world, England has adopted a revenue system that most materially diminishes both the amount of trade and its profit. And, instead of a perfectly free internal industry, England has adopted an excise that is as vexatious in its operation as can well be conceived. Both the customs and excise laws, and every other tax on industry, have arisen *from the alienation of the soil from the state;* and had the soil not been alienated, no tax whatever would have been requisite; and were the soil resumed, (as it undoubtedly ought to be,) every tax of every kind and character, save the common rent of the soil, might at once be abolished, with the whole army of collectors, revenue officers, cruisers, coast guards, excisemen, &c., &c.

3d. Taxation can only be on land or labor. [By land we mean the natural earth, not merely the agricultural soil.] These are the two radical elements that can be subjected to taxation, *capital* being originally derived from one or the other. *Capital* is only hoarded labor or hoarded rent; and as all capital must be derived from the one source or the other, all taxation of capital is only taxation of land or of labor. Consequently all taxation of whatever kind is, 1st, taxation of labor, that is, a deduction from the natural remuneration which God intended the laborer to derive from his exertions; or, 2d, taxation of land; that is, the appropriation of the current value of the natural earth to the expenses of the state.

Now, *labor* is essentially private property, and *land* is not essentially private property, but on the contrary is the common inheritance of every generation of mankind. Where the land is taxed, no *man* is taxed, nor does the taxation of land interfere in any way whatever with the progress of human industry. On the contrary, the taxation of land, rightly directed, might be made to advance the condition of the country to a high degree of prosperity.

4th. For the expenses of a state there must be a revenue, and this revenue must be derived from the taxation of labor, or from the rent of the lands. There is no other alternative; either the rents of the soil must be devoted to the common expenses of the state, or the labor of individuals must be interfered with; and restrictions, supervisions, prohibitions, &c., must be called into existence, to facilitate the collection of the revenue.

5th. In England, exactly the same injustice was practised with regard to natural property that was practised with regard to natural liberty; and though the laws and customs that took away the natural liberty of the laboring serf have been for the most part abolished, the laws and customs that make the land the exclusive property of the aristocracy remain almost intact, and have yet to undergo their progress of abolition. Let us first look at the circumstances of the case. And here we shall make a few quotations from the impartial Blackstone.*

* Every Englishman should diligently peruse the first few chapters of the second book of Blackstone's Commentaries, "Of the Rights of Things," and, in addition to these, an article in the *Quarterly Review* for July, 1829, on the condition of the English peasantry. From these, and a history of the resumption and subsequent alienation of the church lands, he will gather a tolerable idea of

"The constitution of feuds had its original from the military policy of the northern, or Celtic nations — the Goths, the Huns, the Franks, &c. . . . . . It was brought by them from their own countries, and continued in their respective colonies as the most likely means to secure their new acquisitions; and to that end large districts, or parcels of land, were allotted by the conquering general to the superior officers of the army, and by them dealt out again in smaller parcels or allotments to the inferior officers and most deserving soldiers. These allotments were called *feoda*, feud, fiefs, or fees; which last appellation, in the northern languages, signifies a conditional stipend or reward. Rewards, or stipends, they evidently were; and the condition annexed to them was, that the possessor should do service faithfully, both at home and in the wars, to him by whom they were given; for which purpose he took the *juramentum fidelitatis*, or oath of fealty; and in case of the breach of this condition and

the circumstances that have led to the present condition of England. The lands of England have been disposed of according to two laws — *the law of the strongest* and *the law of the most cunning*; hence England's pauperism and England's moral degradation. There yet remains another law, and its reduction to practice will, one day or other, regenerate the social condition of the population — *the law of equity*.

The article on the "condition of the English peasantry" is well worthy of republication in a separate form. Its appearance in that periodical prevents all suspicion of its having been written for the purpose of exciting discontent; and yet we do not hesitate to affirm, that if once the laboring classes were seriously to take up the questions on which it treats, they would resolve never to rest satisfied till they had abolished the landed aristocracy of England, and emancipated their own labor from the burdens that have been imposed upon them from the allocation of the land to the aristocracy, and of the taxation to the laborers of the country.

oath, by not performing the stipulated service, or by deserting the lord in battle, the lands were again to revert to him who granted them."

This explains the mechanism by which the lands were *allocated;* but *the right to allocate* was the right of the sword, or right of the strongest; and consequently any future person who should prove strong enough to overcome the occupiers, would have exactly *the same right* to allocate them to other individuals. The whole of the feudal system was based on the right of the strongest; and if the unfortunate Irish were *strong enough* to reconquer the lands of Ireland, they would have exactly *the same right* that was reduced to practice by the feudal laws.

"But this feudal polity, which was thus by degrees established over all the continent of Europe, seems not to have been received in this part of our island—at least not universally, and as a part of the national constitution, till the reign of William the Norman. . . . . From the prodigious slaughter of the English nobility at the battle of Hastings, and the fruitless insurrections of those who survived, such numerous forfeitures had accrued, that he was able to reward his Norman followers with very large and extensive possessions. . . . . The king held a great council to inquire into the state of the nation; the immediate consequence of which was the compiling of the great survey called Domesday-book, which was finished in the next year; and in the latter end of that very year, the king was attended by all his nobility at Sarum, where all the principal landholders submitted their lands to the yoke of military tenure, became the king's vassals, and did honor and fealty to his person.* This may possibly have been the era of formally introducing the feudal tenures by law; and perhaps the very law thus made at the Council of Sarum is that which is still extant. . . . . This new polity, therefore, seems not to have been *imposed* by the Conqueror, but nationally and freely adopted by the general assembly of the whole realm, in the same manner as other nations of Europe had before adopted it, upon the same principle of self-security. And, in particular, they had the recent example of the French nation before their eyes, which had gradually surrendered up all its allodial or free lands into the king's hands, who restored them to the owners as a *beneficium* or feud, to be held by them and such of their heirs as they previously nominated to the king; and thus by degrees all the allodial estates in France were converted into feuds, and the freemen became the vassals of the crown. The only difference between this change of tenures in France and that in England was, that the former was effected gradually by the consent of private persons; the latter was done at once all over England by the common consent of the nation. . . . . . The grand and fundamental maxim of all feudal tenure is this: That all lands were originally granted out by the sovereign, and are therefore holden either mediately or immediately of the

* This, in fact, was the *formation* of the state of England, after its conquest by the Normans. But it was the construction of the state on *false* principles. This formation, so far as the landlords were concerned, was legally dissolved in the reign of Charles II., when the lands became the property (in law) of the aristocracy. The state is now beginning to be *re-formed* on true principles; and it appears probable that its *ultimate* form will be that of a republic with universal suffrage, with all the lands rented from the state, and consequently without any other taxation of any kind or character whatever

crown. The grantor was called the proprietor or *lord*, being he who retained the dominion or ultimate property of the feud or fee; and the grantee, who had only the use and possession, according to the terms of the grant was styled the feudatory or *vassal*, which was only another name for the tenant or holder of the lands. . . . . . Besides an oath of fealty, the vassal did usually *homage* to his lord; professing that he became his *man* from that day forth, of life, and limb, and earthly honor. When the tenant had thus professed himself to be the man of his superior or lord, the next consideration was concerning the *service* which, as such, he was bound to render in recompense for the land that he held. This, in pure, proper, and original feuds, was only twofold — to follow or do *suit* to the lord in his courts in time of peace, *and in his armies or warlike retinue when necessity called him to the field.* The military branch of service consisted in attending the lord to the wars, if called upon, with such a retinue, and for such a number of days, as were stipulated at the first; donation in proportion to the quantity of the land. . . . . . At the first introduction of feuds, as they were gratuitous so also they were precarious, and held at the *will* of the lord, who was then the sole judge whether his vassal performed his services faithfully. Then they became certain for one or more *years*. . . . . . In process of time, feuds came by degrees to be universally extended beyond the life of the first vassal to his *sons*, or perhaps to such one of them as the lord should name; and, in this case, the form of the donation was strictly observed; for if a feud was given to a man and his *sons*, all his sons succeeded him in equal portions; and, as they died off, their shares reverted to the lord, and did not descend to their children, or even to their surviving brothers, as not being specified in the donation. But when such a feud was given to a man and his *heirs* in general terms, then a more extended rule of succession took place; and, when the feudatory died, his male descendants *in infinitum* were admitted to the succession.

"These were the principal and very simple qualities of the genuine or original feuds, which were all of a military nature, and in the hands of military persons; though the feudatories, being under frequent incapacities of cultivating and manuring their own lands, soon found it necessary to commit part of them to inferior tenants, obliging them to such returns in service, corn, cattle, or money, as might enable the chief feudatories to attend their military duties without distraction; which returns, or *reditus*, were the original of rents.

"In this chapter (chap. vi.) we shall take a short view of the ancient tenures of our English estates, or the manner in which lands, tenements, and hereditaments might have been holden, as the same stood in force till the middle of the last century; in which we shall easily perceive that all the particularities, all the seeming and real hardships, that attended those tenures, were to be accounted for upon feudal principles, and no other; being fruits of, and deduced from, the feudal policy.

"Almost all the real property of this kingdom is, by the policy of our laws, supposed to be granted by, dependent upon, and *holden* of, some superior lord, by and in consideration of certain services to be rendered to the lord by the tenant or possessor of this property. The thing holden is therefore styled a *tenement*, the possessors thereof *tenants*, and the manner of their possession a *tenure*. Thus all the land in the kingdom is supposed to be holden, mediately or immediately, of the king, who is styled lord *paramount*, or above all. Such tenants as held under the king immediately, when they granted out portions of their lands to inferior persons, became also lords with respect to those inferior persons, as they were still tenants with respect to the king; and thus, partaking of a middle nature, were called *mesne*, or middle lords. So that if the king granted a manor to A, and he granted a portion of the land to B, now B was said to hold of A, and A of the king; or, in other words, B held his lands immediately of A, but mediately of the king. The king, therefore, was styled lord paramount; A was both tenant and lord, or was a mesne lord; and B was called tenant *paravail*, or the lowest tenant, being he who was supposed to make a vail, or profit, of the land. In this manner are all the lands of the kingdom holden which are in the hands of subjects; for, according to Sir Edward Coke, in the law of England we have not properly *allodium;* which, we have seen, is the name by which the feudists abroad distinguish such estates of the subject as are not holden of any superior. So that at the first glance we may observe, that our lands are either plainly feuds, or partake very strongly of the feudal nature.

"All tenures being thus derived, or supposed to be derived, from the king, those that held immediately under him in right of his crown and dignity were called tenants *in capite*, or in chief, which was the most honorable species of tenure; but, at the same time, subjected the tenants to greater and more burdensome services than inferior tenures did. This distinction ran through all the different sorts of tenure, of which I now proceed to give an account.

"There seem to have subsisted among our ancestors four principal species of lay tenures, to which all others may be reduced; the grand criteria of which were the natures of the several services, or renders, that were due to the lords from their tenants. The services, in respect of their quality, were either free or base services; in respect of their quantity, and the time of exacting them, were either *certain* or *uncer-*

tain. Free services were such as were not unbecoming the character of a soldier or a freeman to perform; as to serve under his lord in the wars, to pay a sum of money, and the like. *Base* services were such as were fit only for peasants, or persons of a servile rank; as to plough the lord's land, to make his hedges, to carry out his dung, or other mean employments. . . . .

"The first, most universal, and esteemed the most honorable species of tenure, was that by knight-service, called in Latin *servitium militare*, and in law French *chivalry*, or *service de chivaler*, answering to the *fief d'haubert* of the Normans. This differed in very few points from a pure and proper feud, being entirely military, and the general effect of the feudal establishment in England. To make a tenure by knight-service, a determinate quantity of land was necessary, which was called a knight's fee, *feodum militare;* the measure of which in 3 Edward I. was estimated at twelve ploughlands, and its value (though it varied with the times) in the reigns of Edward I. and Edward II. was stated at £20 per annum. And he who held this proportion of land (or a whole fee) by knight-service, *was bound to attend his lord to the wars for forty days in every year if called upon;* which attendance was his *reditus*, or return, his rent or service for the land he claimed to hold. If he held only half a knight's fee, he was only bound to attend twenty days, and so in proportion. . . . . .

"The personal attendance in knight-service growing troublesome and inconvenient in many respects, the tenants found means of compounding for it, by first sending others in their stead, and in process of time making a pecuniary satisfaction to the lords in lieu of it. This pecuniary satisfaction at last came to be levied by assessments at so much for every knight's fee; and therefore this kind of tenure was called *scutagium* in Latin, or *servitium scuti* — *scutum* being then a well-known denomination for money; and in like manner it was called in our Norman-French *escuage*, being indeed a pecuniary instead of a military service. The first time this appears to have been taken was in the 5 Henry II., on account of his expedition to Toulouse; but it soon came to be so universal that personal attendance fell quite into disuse. Hence we find in our ancient histories, that from this period, when our kings went to war, they levied scutages on their tenants, that is, on all the land holders of the kingdom, to defray their expenses and to hire troops; and these assessments in the time of Henry II. seem to have been made arbitrarily, and at the king's pleasure; which prerogative being greatly abused by his successors, it became matter of national clamor, and King John was obliged to consent by his *Magna Charta*,* that no scu-

* *Villeins* were not protected by *Magna Charta; nullus liber homo capiatur vel imprisonetur*, &c., was cautiously expressed to exclude the poor villein; for, as Lord Coke tells us, "the lord may beat his villein, and if it be without cause he cannot have any remedy." — *Note in Christian's Blackstone.*

"He that holds in *pure villenage* shall do whatsoever is commanded him, and always be bound to an uncertain service."

The villein was originally a serf or slave, whose political condition gradually underwent improvement with the progress of society. The villeins of England have attained to *personal liberty;* that is, the present laborers who do the work of England — who create its wealth —are no longer subject to the *personal tyranny* of either lord or king. But from the *generalization* of serfdom they are compelled by natural causes, starvation, hunger, &c., to do the work *for a bare subsistence,* in contradistinction to the law of nature and the law of God, that he who does the work shall reap the *profit* which the Almighty has annexed to labor expended on the natural earth. Aristocracy, like serfdom, has also been *generalized;* that is, instead of *individual* aristocrats ruling individual serfs, a general court or assembly of aristocrats now rules the whole mass of labor-

tage should be imposed without consent of Parliament. But this clause was omitted in his son Henry III.'s charter, where we only find that scutages or escuage should be taken as they were used to be taken in the time of Henry II.; that is, in a reasonable and moderate manner. Yet afterwards, by statute 25 Edw. I. c. 5 and 6, and many subsequent statutes, it was again provided that the king should take no aids or tasks by his common assent of the realm: hence it was held in our old books that escuage or scutage could not be levied but by consent of Parliament; such scutages being indeed the groundwork of all succeeding subsidies, and the land tax of later times.

"Since, therefore, escuage differed from knight-

ers, and taxes their labor to an extent equal to the whole rental of the country.

"Under the Saxon government there were, as Sir William Temple speaks, a sort of people in a condition of downright servitude, used and employed in the most servile works, and belonging, both they, their children, and effects, to the lord of the soil, like the rest of the cattle or stock upon it. These seem to have been those who held the folk-land, from which they were removable at the lord's pleasure. On the arrival of the Normans here, it seems not improbable that they, who were strangers to any other than a feudal state, might give some sparks of enfranchisement to such wretched persons as fell to their share, by admitting them, as well as others, to the oath of fealty; which conferred a right of protection, and raised the tenant to a kind of estate superior to downright slavery, but inferior to every other condition. This they called villenage, and the tenants villeins, either from the word *viles*, or else, as Edward Coke tells us, *a villa;* because they lived chiefly in villages, and were employed in rustic works of the most sordid kind, resembling the Spartan *helots*, to whom alone the culture of the lands was consigned, their rugged masters, like our northern ancestors, esteeming war the only honorable employment of manhood." — *Blackstone*, book ii. chap. 6.

service in nothing but as a compensation differs from actual service, knight-service is frequently confounded with it. And thus Littleton must be understood when he tells us that tenant by homage, fealty, and escuage, was tenant by knight-service; that is, that this tenure (being subservient to the military policy of the nation) was respected as a tenure in chivalry. But as the actual service was uncertain, and depended upon emergencies, so it was necessary that this peculiar compensation should be equally uncertain, and depend on the assessments of the legislature, suited to these emergencies. For had the escuage been a settled invariable sum, payable at certain times, it had been neither more nor less than a mere pecuniary rent; and the tenure, instead of knight-service, would have then been of another kind, called socage; of which we shall speak in the next chapter.

"For the present I have only to observe, that by the degenerating of knight-service, or personal military duty, into escuage or pecuniary assessments, all the advantages (either promised or real) of the feudal constitution were destroyed, and nothing but the hardships remained. Instead of forming a national militia, composed of barons, knights, and gentlemen, bound by their interest, their honor, and their oaths, to defend their king and country, the whole of this system of tenure now tended to nothing else but a wretched means of raising money to pay an army of occasional mercenaries. In the mean time the families of all our nobility and gentry groaned under the intolerable burdens which (in consequence of the fiction adopted after the Conquest) were introduced and laid upon them by the subtlety and finesse of the Norman lawyers. For, besides the scutages, to which they were liable in defect of personal attendance — which, however, were assessed by themselves in Parliament — they might be called upon by the king or lord paramount for *aids*, whenever his eldest son was to be knighted, or his eldest daughter married, not to forget the ransom of his own person. The heir, on the death of his ancestor, if of full age, was plundered of the first emoluments arising from his inheritance, by way of relief and *primer seisin;* and if under age, of the whole of his estate during infancy. And then, as Sir Thomas Smith very feelingly complains, 'When he came to his own after he was out of *wardship*, his woods decayed, houses fallen down, stock wasted and gone, lands let forth and ploughed to be barren;' to reduce him still further, he was yet to pay half a year's profits as a fine for suing out his *livery*, and also the price or value of his *marriage*, if he refused such wife as his lord and guardian had bartered for and imposed upon him; or twice that value if he married another woman. Add to this the untimely and expensive honor of *knighthood*, to make his poverty more completely splendid. And when, by these deductions, his fortune was so shattered and ruined that perhaps he was obliged to sell his patrimony, he had not even that poor privilege allowed him without paying an exorbitant fine for a *license of alienation.*

"A slavery so complicated and so extensive as this called aloud for a remedy, in a nation that boasted of its freedom. Palliatives were, from time to time, applied by successive acts of Parliament, which assuaged some temporary grievances, till at length the humanity of King James I. consented, in consideration of a proper equivalent, to abolish them all, though the plan proceeded not to effect: in like manner as he had formed a scheme, and began to put it in execution, for removing the feudal grievance of heritable jurisdictions in Scotland, which has since been pursued and effected by the statute 20 Geo. II. c. 43. King James's plan for exchanging our military tenures seems to have been nearly the same as that which has since been pursued, only with this difference, that, by way of compensation for the loss which the crown and other lords would sustain, an annual fee-farm rent was to have been settled, and inseparably annexed to the crown, and assured to the inferior lords, payable out of every knight's fee within their respective seigniories — an expedient seemingly much better than *the hereditary excise*, which was afterwards made the principal equivalent of these concessions. For at length the military tenures, with all their heavy appendages, (having during the usurpation been discontinued,) were destroyed at one blow by the statute 12 Car. II. c. 24, which enacts 'that the court of wards and liveries, and all wardships, liveries, primer seizins, and ousterlemains, values and forfeitures of marriages, by reason of any tenure of the king or others, be totally taken away; and that all fines for alienations, tenures by homage, knight's service, and escuage, and also aids for marrying the daughter or knighting the son, and all tenures of the king *in capite*, be likewise taken away; and that all sorts of tenures, held of the king or others, be turned into free and common socage, save only tenures in frankalmoign, copyholds, and the honorary services (without the slavish part) of grand serjeantry;' — a statute which was a greater acquisition to the civil property of this kingdom than even *Magna Charta* itself; since that only pruned the luxuriances that had grown out of the military tenures, and thereby preserved them in vigor, but the statute of King Charles extirpated the whole, and demolished both root and branches." — *Blackstone*, book ii. chap. 4.

"The abolition of military tenures, which was effected by statute, was one of the most acceptable measures that have been adopted. . . . . . The principal and original purpose of these tenures was *to secure an efficient military force for the protection of the realm*. . . . . .

"To supply the deficiency in the king's revenue, which the subtraction of the feudal profits and the successive grants of the crown had occasioned, was of course the next subject of consideration for the legislature. King James conceived the plan of securing an equivalent for the feudal profits by an annual fee-farm rent, which was to have been settled and inseparably annexed to the crown, and assured to the inferior lords, payable out of every knight's fee within their respective seigniories. This plan appears to have been pursued in regard to inferior lords; but in respect to the king, the principal equivalent for these concessions was *the excise.*

"The excise was a novel mode of taxing commodities, either immediately on their consumption, or more frequently on their retail sale. It is said to have been first devised in the reign of Charles I., and was given to the crown by act of Parliament as an equivalent for the profits of the feudal tenures; and although a very unpopular tax, *it has been imposed on fresh commodities in every subsequent reign.* . . . . . In consequence of the abolition of the feudal tenures, a permanent kind of military force was now raised, *called a standing army*, of which it appears that this king, Charles II., had not more than the number of 5000."—*Crabb's Hist. English Law.*

"The origin of a permanently embodied military force may be dated from the commencement of this reign. . . . . These formed at first a force of about 5000 men; but in the latter part of the next reign this force was augmented to 30,000. Parliament, however, never sanctioned the enrolment of this large army, nor did it vote the money required for their maintenance. They were embodied by the authority of the crown only, and were paid for either out of the civil list, or by diverting money voted for other purposes. It was on this unconstitutional force that

James II. mistakenly depended for the success of his anti-Protestant and arbitrary schemes."—*Wade's British Chronology.*

Such is the most concise history that we could lay before the reader, *in quotations*, of the *politics* of English landed property. We shall show, presently, what a momentous change is recorded in this little history; but, before proceeding to any remarks of our own, we must advert to another change in the disposition of a large portion of the soil of England.

"In the course of the fourteenth century, the demand for wool to supply not only the markets of the Netherlands, but also the infant manufacturers of our own country, rapidly increased. This circumstance brought about an important change in the distribution of the population. The owners of land, finding sheep-feeding more profitable than husbandry, commenced the same system which we have all witnessed in full operation in the Highlands of Scotland. The peasantry, previously employed in tillage, were turned adrift upon the world; the allotments of arable land, which had afforded them and their families the means of subsistence, were enclosed, consolidated, and converted into sheep-walks; and the policy of Henry VII. greatly accelerated a social revolution which had commenced before his accession. The misery and suffering which this change of system inflicted upon the ejected peasantry, have been depicted in beautiful and glowing language by Sir Thomas More, in his *Utopia.*

"'Your sheep,' says he, 'which were wont to be so meek and tame, and so small eaters, now become so great devourers, and so wild, that they eat up and swallow down the very men themselves. They consume, destroy, and devour whole fields, houses, and cities; for, look in what part of the realm doth grow the finest, and therefore dearest wool; there, noblemen and gentlemen — yea, and *certain abbots, holy men, God wot!* — not contenting themselves with the yearly revenues and profits that were wont to grow to their forefathers and predecessors of their lands, nor being content that they live in rest and pleasure, nothing profiting, yea, much annoying, the weal public, leave no ground for tillage. They enclose all into pastures, they throw down houses, they pluck down towns, and leave nothing standing but only the church, to be made a sheep-house. And, as though you lost no small quantity of ground by forests, chases, lands, and parks, those good, holy men, turn all dwelling-places and all glebe lands into desolation and wilderness.

" 'Therefore, that one covetous, and unsatiable cormorant and very plague of his native country may compass about and enclose many thousand acres of ground together within one pale or hedge, the husbandmen be thrust out of their own, or else, either by cozen and fraud, or by violent oppression, they be put beside it, or by wrongs and injuries they be so wearied that they be compelled to sell all. By one means, therefore, or other, — either by hook or by crook, — they must needs depart away, poor, silly, wretched souls! — men, women, husbands, wives, fatherless children, widows, woful mothers with their young babes and their whole household, small in substance and much in number, as husbandry requireth many hands; for one shepherd or herdsman is enough to eat up that ground with cattle, to the occupying whereof about husbandry many hands were requisite. After that so much ground was enclosed for pasture, an infinite multitude of sheep died of the rot; such vengeance God took of their inordinate, unsatiable covetousness — sending among the sheep that pestiferous murrain, which much more justly should have fallen on the chief masters' own heads. . . . . .

" A very considerable portion of the discarded occupiers were thus absorbed; but the remainder, amounting, as it appears from all the records of the period, to no inconsiderable number, either unable to find a small spot of land to rent and occupy, or unwilling to submit to the confinement of towns and manufactories, became wandering beggars, infesting the roads and villages of the country. *Hence the English poor-laws.* During this memorable period in the history of our peasantry, various laws were enacted for the suppression of vagrancy, and these were finally amended and consolidated in the celebrated act of 43 Elizabeth. . . . . . But another revolution was now approaching, and one which has affected their (the peasantry,) welfare more extensively, as well as more intensely, than even the momentous change wrought under the dominion of the Tudors. The numerous small farms which had escaped consolidation, and consequently supplied an asylum for the peasantry discarded from the larger estates, were now doomed to undergo a similar revolution. Through the operation of too obvious causes, several of the smaller farms in each parish had come to be the property of one landlord. It was then discovered *that the division and enclosure of the common fields and wastes* of the parish would render this property more profitable, by facilitating the introduction of an improved system of tillage. In 1709, an application was made to Parliament for an act to divide and enclose the common fields and wastes belonging to the parish of Ropley. This served as an encouragement and example, and applications of the same kind became annually more frequent. It appears that, since that period, very nearly 4000 bills of enclosure have been passed; and it is also well known that, in numerous instances, the same end has been reached without legislative interference, by private agreement among the parties interested. In a word, we have scarcely a doubt that about 5000 parishes (a moiety of the whole territory of England) have been subjected to the operation of these measures in the space of about one hundred and twenty years; and as little (however beneficial the division and consequent improvement of this vast territory may have proved to the owners, and to some other classes) that the change has been a woful one for our peasantry. We believe that the final extinction of the class of small occupiers and crofters has, in almost every instance, followed the division of common field parishes."—*Quarterly Review*, July, 1829.

The political history of landed property in England, therefore, appears to have been as follows:—

1st. The lands were accorded by the king to persons who were to undertake the military service of the kingdom.

2d. The performance of this military service was the condition on which individuals held the national land.

3d. The lands were at first held *for life*, and afterwards were made *hereditary*.

4th. The military service was abolished *by the law*, and a *standing army* introduced.

5th. This standing army was paid by the king.

6th. The king, having abolished the military services of the individuals who held the national land, resorted to the taxation of articles of consumption for the payment of the army.

The lands of England, therefore, instead of being held on condition of performing the military service of the kingdom, became the *property* of the individuals who held them, and thus the *state* of England lost the *lands* of England. And the military service of the kingdom, instead of being performed by those individuals who held the national land, was henceforth (after the reign of Charles II.) to be paid for by the general taxation of the inhabitants of the country.

Therefore the present system of taxation, and the *national debt*, the interest of which is procured by the forcible taxation of the general inhabitants of England, are both due *to the alienation of the lands from the state*, inasmuch as the national debt (incurred for war expenses) would have been a debt upon *the lands*, and not a debt upon *the people* of England.* If,

* *Total Expense of the Army, Navy, and Ordnance, from* 1790 *to* 1815, *inclusive, in millions sterling, (round numbers.)*

Years.	Millions.	Years.	Millions.	Years.	Millions.
1791	4	1800	29	1808	39
1792	8	1801	26	1809	42
1793	13	1802	23	1810	43
1794	20	1803	21	1811	47
1795	28	1804	30	1812	49
1796	30	1805	36	1813	54
1797	27	1806	37	1814	60
1798	25	1807	36	1815	43
1799	27				

To this it may be added, that the war charges of the kingdom, from the year 1815 to 1848, amounted to 484 millions sterling; and the advantage to the country of an aristocratic House of Commons, having an unlimited power to tax the labors of the community, may be inferred from the fact, that from 1835 to 1847, (inclusive,) the expenses of the war establishments increased rather more than a

therefore, the legislature had a right to abolish the military services of those who held the national land, and thereby to impose on the general community all the liabilities of the military service of the kingdom, the legislature has the same right to abolish the general taxation of the community, and to allocate to those who hold the land all the expenses that have been incurred, and are still incurred, for the war charges of the kingdom.

The alienation of the land from the state, and its conversion into private property, was the first grand step that laid the foundation of the modern system of society in England — a system that presents enormous wealth in the hands of a few aristocrats, who neither labor, nor even pay taxes in proportion to those who do labor, (land pays no legacy duty on being transmitted;) and a vast population laboring for a bare subsistence, or reduced sometimes by millions to the condition of pauperism.

So long as this system is allowed to continue, it appears (from the constitution of the earth, and of man's power to extract from it a maintenance) an absolute impossibility that *pauperism* should be obliterated; inasmuch as the burden of taxation necessarily falls on *labor*, and more especially as the *value of labor*

million every two years. Nothing less that miracles could save the country from pauperization under such a system of government.

No reformation of the public expenditure, however, can possibly be anticipated until men of an entirely different class form the majority of the House of Commons; and this change can only be secured by a total revision of the whole system of representation.

is necessarily diminished wherever there is a soil allocated to an aristocracy.*

The abolition of the military tenures, however, did not complete the great evolution by which the lands of England have been transformed into the *property* of a few thousand aristocrats. That evolution consisted of three great facts, —

1st. The allocation of the church lands to individual proprietors.

2d. The abolition of military tenure, and the substitution of the taxation of articles of consumption; in other words, of *the taxation of labor.*

3d. The enclosure of the *common lands*, whereby vast numbers of the peasantry were ruined, deprived of their legal rights, which were quite as valid as the entails of the aristocracy, and, being separated from the land, were sent to propagate pauperism in the

* Political economists have insisted much on the *small* matters that affect the value of labor. By far the most important is, *the mode in which the land is distributed.* Wherever there is a free soil, *labor maintains its value.* Wherever the soil is in the hands of a few proprietors, or tied up by entails, labor necessarily undergoes depreciation. In fact, it is the disposition of *the land* that determines the value of labor. If men could get the land to labor on, they would manufacture only for a remuneration that afforded *more profit* than God has attached to the cultivation of the earth. Where they cannot get the land to labor on, they are starved into working for a bare subsistence. There is only one reason why the *labor* of England, Ireland, and Scotland is of so little marketable value, and that reason is, *the present disposition of the soil.* Were the soil disposed of according to the laws of *equity*, there cannot be the least doubt that the labor of the laboring classes would at once rise to at least double its present value.

towns and villages. Such were the great political events that terminated in the separation of the people of England from the soil of England, and such was the price paid for that *personal freedom* and *personal independence* which has been gradually evolving from the time of the Norman formation of the state of England, and which will come to a natural termination the moment men are equalized in their political functions. The moment the law becomes impartial, and recognizes no *à priori* difference between the *individuals* of whom the state is composed, that moment has the grand *evolution of liberty* come to a conclusion, and the *evolution of natural property* will then enter on its course.

On the three events which have at last left the lands of England in the hands of a small number of aristocrats, we shall make only one or two observations.

Every one of these events has a *right* side as well as a wrong side; and unless we learn to estimate impartially the value of the changes, we are in danger of taking a distorted view of the morals as well as of the matter of the changes.

1st. It was right to abolish the monasteries.

2d. It was right to abolish the military tenures.

3d. It was right to enclose the common lands.

And it was wrong, —

1st. To allocate the church lands to individuals.

2d. To allow the lands to remain as the *property* of those who neither cultivated them, nor were liable for the performance of the military service of the kingdom.

3d. To make such a disposition of the common

lands as disinherited the peasantry, and at last left the common lands in the hands of the aristocracy as *property*.

So soon as the Roman religion was supplanted in England, there can be no question that it was right to abolish the monasteries; and though many hardships were no doubt inflicted on some excellent men and women, (for the church in England contained both,) the *system* had grown old. It had outlived its time, and the day of its departure had arrived. Man was to take a new expansion; to enter on a course of *thought;* to begin to exercise his reason, and no longer to believe on mere authority. And the removal of the Papal church of England was the first great requirement for the commencement of a course that must terminate at last in absolute liberty of thought, and absolute non-interference of the legislature with the credence of any individual. But the iniquity of the mode in which the monasteries were suppressed was in the fact, that the *lands* were transformed into the *property* of the aristocracy. If the king resumed them in his official character of *head of the state of England*, he could not justly transform them into his own private property, nor could he justly transform them into the private property of any individual members of the state. Such a transaction is utterly beyond the intention of civil government, and its toleration could not take place in a community governed by reason. And when we take into consideration that there are but two objects of taxation, namely, individual labor or the natural earth, the allocation of these lands as private property was only tantamount to the prospective abstraction of the *value* of the lands from the future laborers of the country. Were there no such thing as *taxation*, the gift of lands would be *comparatively* a matter of indifference, (provided there was no restriction whatever on its sale and purchase;) but so long as taxation on labor exists, the gift of lands is exactly equivalent to the *present abstraction* of the present annual value of those lands from the *present* laborers of England. And herein lies the injustice and evil of the king's gift of the abbey lands.

Again: the abolition of military tenures was right, because that system had also grown old. It was inefficient; useless for the military service of the kingdom; it did not work; its evil remained without its good. But the transformation of the lands into *the property of the aristocracy*, and the establishment of a system of taxation that has entailed the heaviest debt and the heaviest taxation in the world on the laborers of England — these were the evils that entailed England's pauperism. Had the *lands* of England been liable (as most justly they should have been liable) for their own defence, there can be little or no doubt that the national debt (at all events, the 600 millions incurred in attempting to arrest the progress of Europe) would not have been incurred at all. Had the *land* been liable, the aristocracy, who held the land, would never have plunged into a war, the principal effects of which appear to have been the deferring of the requisite changes on the continent of Europe, and the infliction of a debt on England which will ultimately effect the destruction of the aristocracy. The king never could justly, as the head of the state, abolish the liability of the land to defray the war charges of the state, by attaching those liabilities to the individual laborers, while the land holders were allowed to carry off a free land. This, in fact, is the greatest political change that has taken place in England—of infinitely more importance to the present generation than the revolution that expelled the Stuarts. The prerogatives of the crown could not have failed to undergo changes in the natural order of evolution. As knowledge progressed, the king, from a ruler, *must* have become an administrator. But the legal establishment of labor taxation, and the accordance of the land as the *property* of the aristocracy, fixed upon the country a system that had the appearance of right, and that brought with it the impress of imperial legislation; while it originated in the darkest ignorance or the most licentious overstretch of power, and could not fail to produce ultimately the most pernicious results. The tax-payers of England can never be sufficiently reminded, that there need have been no taxes had it not been for the alienation of the land from the state.

The enclosure of the common lands, again, was a proper measure, inasmuch as the lands were *producing* little; and every measure that caused the lands to produce *more* for the consumption of the country was *so far* beneficial. It would have been quite absurd to leave the common lands in pasture, while their enclosure would produce for the service of the country a much larger quantity of food. And the same argument that took away the lands of the peasantry, would now take away the lands of those proprietors who allow their lands to lie uncultivated.

On the effects of the enclosure of the common lands, we quote another passage from the same article in the *Quarterly Review*, July, 1829 : —

"Here, no doubt, it will be observed, that in every instance an allotment of land was, on the division of the waste, assigned to the owners of common rights," (*incumbents*, rather than *owners* ;) "and that an allotment in severalty, if properly attended to and cultivated, must have proved much more valuable to the cottager than what he had lost. If such had been the case, we readily admit that the division could not have proved detrimental to him ; but, unfortunately, this very rarely happened. These allotments were assigned, under enclosure acts, not to the occupier, but *the owner* of the cottage. Few cottages were in the occupation of their owners ; they generally, indeed, we may say universally, belonged to the proprietors of the neighboring farms ; and the allotments granted in lieu of the extinguished common rights were generally added to the large farms, and seldom attached to the cottages. The cottages which were occupied by their owners had, of course, allotments attached to them ; but these have by degrees passed by sale into the hands of some large proprietor in the neighborhood. *De facto*, in ninety-nine cases out of the hundred, the allotment has been detached from the cottage, and thrown into the occupation of some adjoining farmer.

"That such a change should have been attended with most important consequences, can excite no surprise in any reflecting mind. So far as it goes, *a complete severance has been effected between the English peasantry and the English soil.* The little farmers and cottiers of the country have been converted into day laborers, depending entirely upon daily earnings, which may, and frequently in point of fact do, fail them. They have now no land, upon the produce of which they can fall as a reserve whenever the demand for labor happens to be slack. This revolution is unquestionably the true cause of the heavy and increasing burdens now pressing upon parishes in the form of poor-rates. Independently of all reasoning founded upon general principles, this is a truth capable of being substantiated by a mass of evidence, so clear and so well authenticated as to leave no room for doubt. In almost every instance the increase of poor-rates has kept pace visibly with the progress of enclosures."

The passage we have underlined—"a complete severance has been effected between the English peasantry and the English soil"—points out the great economical cause of England's periodical distress; a distress which, were it not for the poor-laws, would occasionally manifest itself (as it did in 1830–31) in tumultuous assemblages and breaches of the law. And assuredly that *severance* between the subjective labor and the objective soil will yet rectify itself. No class of society can be visited with long-continued evils, without entailing evil on the other classes. And though the manufactures of England, taking an expansion altogether unprecedented in the history of the world, were able to *consume* the redundant population, the time must come when the rate of increase will diminish, when the population shall find no maintenance either in the towns or in the country, and social changes, attended with a more equitable distribution of the sources of wealth, will result in spite of all that men can do to prevent them.

While the increase of the poor rates in England reached to such an extent, that in not a few cases the half of the rental, and in the case of the parish of Cholesbury the whole of the rental, was absorbed; and while new legislative enactments were *absolutely necessary* to prevent the ruin of the land holders — it is singular to observe how little inquiry was made into the radical *cause* of England's pauperism. *Rates* and *paupers* are correlatives, and the rates increase because the paupers have increased. No remedial measure that attempts only to supply the wants of those who *are* paupers will ever reach the depths of pauperism; and while there is of course an imperative necessity to relieve a famished population, there is quite as great a necessity to inquire, "*Why* does it happen, that in the richest country in the world a large portion of the population should be reduced to pauperism?" Until the *causes* of pauperism are satisfactorily ascertained, and until the remedy is applied *to the cause*, no remedial measure can do more than alleviate the evil. Apply the remedy to the cause, and the evil is eradicated. The cause, or at least one of the great causes, is that expressed in the words of the reviewer, "the severance between the English peasantry and the English soil;" and until the peasantry recover that soil, the inhabitants of England may rest satisfied that the curse of pauperism will pursue them; and if the remedy be not applied in time, that the vengeance of Heaven will be manifested against a nation — with so many privileges — that allows her children to be condemned to want, and ignorance, and moral degradation.

Although we have presented the reader with this sketch of the historical politics of landed property, we attach little or no importance to it. *No historical argument is ever capable of deciding a present question of equity.* Men must go *forward*, never backward. History may enlighten, may instruct, may teach us what has been, and may afford us the groundwork of an argument for anticipating what shall be in future; but history will not supply the motive for action, nor can it ever furnish the rule of action. For these we must look to the present times: the motive must be a living one, not a dead one; and the rule must be a rule that depends, not on one age rather than another, but a rule that always was valid had man been able to see it, that is valid now, and that will be valid when we shall have passed away, and our places are supplied by the generations that come after us. In the past we see the concrete manifestations of man's phenomena, we see the phases through which he *has* passed, and we may learn to extract or evolve the law of the direction in which he is progressing. In man's actual history, all variable as it is, like the outward appearances of nature, we behold a stupendous series of real phenomena, in which men and nations are the actors. The rulers and the ruled, the monarch, the aristocrat, and the serf, the priest, the artist, the merchant, and the soldier, all play their respective parts in man's political drama. Events roll on, and history records the scenes.

But beneath the outward variety of man's historic *representations*, can we not plunge below the surface and seize some *stable* element, some scheme, some law, some generalized fact, some plan or principle on which the drama has been constructed, some permanent truth that evolves amid all the apparent diversity of images? Can we not transform the real elements as they appear into some abstract form that enables us to state them in a rational equation? Can we not apprehend the *essential* character of the changes, as well as their empirical character, and derive instruction for the reason, as well as materials for the memory and the understanding?

No truth appears to be more satisfactorily and more generally borne out by the history of modern Europe, than that the progression of men in the matter of liberty "is from a diversity of privileges towards an equality of rights;" that is, that the past progress has been all in this direction since the maximum of diversity prevailed in the aspect of individual lord and individual serf. And if this be the case, it cannot be an unreasonable conclusion, that if sufficient time be allowed for the evolution, the progress of change will continue to go on till some *ultimate condition* is evolved. And that ultimate condition *can* only be at the point where diversity of privilege disappears, and every individual in the state is legally entitled to identically the same political functions. Diversities of office there may be, and there must be, but diversity of rights there cannot be without injustice.

Such, then, is the *theoretic* ultimatum that satisfies the reason with regard to its equity, and such is the historic ultimatum that the reason infers from the past history of mankind. Such, then, is the point towards which societies are progressing; and when that point is reached, the ultimatum of equity is achieved, and the present course of historical evolution is complete.

But while on the one hand we cast our eyes on the ultimate object to be obtained — on that which is *theoretically right* — it should never be forgotten that two other questions nearer at hand claim as urgent an attention — the questions, "Where are we at present in the line of progress?" and "What are the *next steps* that require to be taken to lead society towards its final destination?" These are questions for the practical statesman and for the present generation, who require to deliver themselves from the evils that have grown to a height, and whose real character has been apprehended by the nation. On these questions we shall only make a passing remark.

Diversity of opinion may arise between two men who are both apparently in the right, if the attention of the one be directed to what is theoretically right, and the attention of the other to what is practically expedient as the next step which the present balance of powers in the state renders possible. At every period there are some men in advance of their age, some suited to the practical requirements of their age, and others behind their age — the *gepidæ* or loiterers, who remain in the rear. The latter class, for the most part, are composed of those whose interests are implicated in the present disposition of affairs, and who dread change of every description, perhaps from a vague apprehension that they may lose their present powers, while the increase of those powers is an event not to be anticipated. This class is gradually losing its influence, gradually receding from the direction of the state, and submitting to a current that it can no longer control, but which it may to a certain extent impede. The other two classes are the real laborers; with them lies the motive of progression, and the judgment to determine in what particular direction change ought to be effected. For the loiterers, *every* change is bad; and the whole of their practical function is to retard, to contrive obstacles, to find impediments, and if possible to prevent investigation. But for the other two classes, not only is the impulse necessary, but on them lies the burden of devising new conditions, which shall be more beneficial than the present conditions, of exploring, pioneering, preparing the way, and finally of dragging onward the cumbrous car of state, held back as it is by those who inherit from darker ages the power of retardation. Between the first two classes, however, there must ever be diversity of opinion, so long as the one class is bent on *what is theoretically right*, and the other on what it deems to be *practically expedient*. The first regards the measures of the second as unsatisfactory, as half measures, as mere sops to allay the Cerberus of popular discontent. The second, on the contrary, regard the measures of the first as impracticable schemes, as *theoretic* measures, good enough perhaps in the abstract, (that is, measures that satisfy *the reason*,) but which, from some peculiarity in present circumstances, are quite incapable of application. The one professedly takes *reason* for his criterion, and rejects every measure that falls short of its requirements; the other extends his view no farther than to the single point that enables him to take one step in advance. The one takes the unchangeable and imperishable element of man, the objective reason,* crowns it with imperial authority, and demands that all should at once acknowledge its supremacy. The other takes the variable element of man — his subjective condition — and, rejecting every dogma that claims to be absolute, discourses only on the proximate possibility of improving that condition. The one sees the transparent image of truth divested of the garb of humanity; the other sees the outward raiment in its frailty and imperfection, and heeds not to draw aside the drapery that conceals the divinity of reason.

Between these two parties, therefore, there is not so much a perpetual warfare as a perpetual misunderstanding. Their point of view is different. They stand on different elevations, and have quite a different range of horizon. Granting that some of both parties (and who can doubt it?) have the honest and sincere desire to advance society in the right direction, there is between them an incompatibility both of conviction and of *feeling*, which forbids that they should coöperate as laborers in the same field, and for the same ultimate object. The one views society as in *a*

* Axiomatic truth is *subjective* when in spontaneous operation, but it is *objective* when reduced to language, and expressed in propositions. This fact is altogether overlooked by those who descant on the subjectivity of axiomatic truth. On the very same principle, heat, color, sound, &c., &c., matter, mind, and every thing else, are subjective according to these philosophers, so that there really *is* nothing — in fact, it is quite a mistake to suppose that there *can* be any thing — the universe being only a great delusion. If the *simplicity* of a philosophical system be the criterion of its perfection, this system can scarcely be excelled.

state of transition, and presses forward towards an ultimatum. The other views society as engaged in its ordinary labor, believes in no ultimatum, but acknowledges that certain changes are rendered necessary by a change of circumstances. The one views the revival of learning as the passage out of Egypt, and the present time as the journeying through the wilderness towards the promised land of rest. The other believes in no Egypt and no promised land, but feels that the daily labor must be done in the world of politics as well as in the world of matter. The one stands on the top of Pisgah, and beholds afar off the Canaan of his hopes, the land of long expectation, and the land for which the past journeyings of the race have been but the necessary preparations. The other, like Lot, beholds the plain of Jordan that it is well watered every where, and journeys eastward that he may find sustenance for his flock. The one is an intellectualist, who believes in the supremacy of reason, and attributes the systematic errors of society to erroneous propositions. The other is an empiric, who admits no absolute criterion, but admits that the conditions of mankind may be gradually improved. The one fixes his eye on *truth*, and forgets the intermediate distance that separates man from its realization. The other fixes his eye on *man* as he appears at present, forgetting alike the history of his transformation and the probable goal that must form his destination.

To a certain extent, both are necessary; both are workers in the great field of human improvement and of man's amelioration. Incomprehensible as they must ever be to each other, (till the last final item of change shall bring both to an identity of purpose,) they are fellow-laborers in the scheme of human evolution. The one devises afar off the general scheme of progress; the other carries the proximate measures of that scheme into practical operation. The one is the hydrographer who constructs the chart; the other, the mariner who navigates the ship, ignorant, perhaps, what may be its final destination.

Between the man of theory and the man of practice, therefore, there is (at present) a perpetual though fluctuating difference. Seldom is it given to man in this world to understand aright his own position; and though he may labor, and labor well, it is rare that he can appreciate correctly the true *position* of his labors. And thus in the field of politics, the theorist and the man of practice appear to misunderstand the bearings of their respective occupations. The theorist, too often trusting to his individual perceptions, forgets that propositions which appear to him of absolute certitude can never be accepted by the world until they have received a far wider authentication than any one man could possibly bestow upon them. And though perchance he might evolve some propositions which should ultimately be able to stand their ground, experience will prove that the diffusion of truth is no less necessary than its discovery. Truth, like leaven, must pervade the mass before the requisite transformation is effected. On the other hand, the man of practice moves, for the most part, as he is impelled by the convictions of the multitude, and his object is not to theorize but to design the requisite changes, and to carry them into execution. The theories of to-day he regards with indifference or aversion; they are of no practical avail; he is pressed with the necessity of action, and act he must, or his place must be ceded to another. But he also forgets. He forgets that the very measures which he now reduces to practical operation were the *theories* of the past generation, and that he is only carrying into execution the schemes which the practical men of other times regarded in the same light as he regards the theories of to-day; and the very theories (some of them at all events) which he regards with aversion, are destined to become the measures of some future man of practice, who bestows on the theories of *his* day the same characteristic abhorrence. He forgets that he moves in *action* because the multitude have moved in *mind;* and that the multitude moved in mind because they had imbibed the theories of former speculators, and changed their credence under the influence of conviction. He forgets that change of action comes from change of credence, and that change of credence comes from theoretic speculation. He forgets that if there were no theories there would be no change, and if no change, no necessity for him to execute it.

In assigning, then, a *theoretic ultimatum* to man's political progress, we posit, —

1st. That this ultimatum is the only one that satisfies the reason.

2d. That its probability is borne out by the history of the past changes that have taken place in the relative conditions of the various political classes of which society has hitherto been composed.

3d. That if society continue to progress on the same scheme or plan that may be inferred from an observation of its past progress, and if sufficient time be allowed for the completion of the evolution, there must come a period when the equilibrium of equity shall be restored, and every individual in the state shall be exactly equal in his primary political function.

4th. That all diversities of rights and privileges, being contrary to the theoretic reason of mankind, shall altogether disappear; and the law, which is (in its proper sense) the expression of the theoretic reason, shall acknowledge no political difference whatever between the individuals who form the state, except such diversities of office as may be found advisable for conducting the business of the body politic. And this diversity of office to be determined exclusively by the free election of the whole associated individuals who form the state.

5th. That law derives from the general or abstract reason of the human race, and therefore it can never acknowledge a political difference between the individuals of the race without being guilty of partiality and injustice.

6th. Absolute equality in the eye of the law, without the slightest distinction of individuals or classes, is, therefore, the ultimatum of political progression; and this ultimatum is the only condition that satisfies the requirements of the reason, and the only condition that presents a rational termination to those changes which, according to history, have been gradually taking place for centuries.

CHAPTER IV.

BRIEF OUTLINE OF AN HISTORICAL SKETCH, BEING AN ATTEMPT TO APPREHEND THE *SENTIMENTS* OF THE HUMAN MIND WHICH HAVE RULED SOCIETY, AND TO APPRECIATE THE *PSYCHOLOGICAL* DEVELOPMENT OF MAN THROUGH HIS HISTORIC MANIFESTATIONS.

BUT, while an equality of political rights may be posited as a logical ultimatum that satisfies the reason, and therefore as an ultimatum that may surely be expected to evolve in one nation after another, as knowledge progresses and the arrangements of superstition are broken down before the advance of truth, it must be remembered that *the organization of society* is the end to be achieved; and the practical ultimatum is the organization of society on *true* principles instead of on *false* principles.

To suppose that theoretic principles are incapable of being reduced to practice *because* they are theoretic, is not only an assumption that God has created man's reason in opposition to the requirements of his terrestrial condition, but it is also a palpable inconsistency utterly untenable. *All* arrangements are necessarily based on theoretic principles of some kind or other; nor can man, by any possibility, make any construction of society which is not *de facto* the actual realization of *a theory.* It is exactly the same with philosophy. Every man might reject, in words, the claims of philosophic theories; yet no sooner does he proceed to *act* than he immediately gives his unconditional assent to *some* philosophical theory, and declares, in the most explicit and intelligible of all modes, his unreserved belief in philosophic propositions which involve the highest abstractions of the reason. Let the whole phenomenon of his action be translated into language, and at the bottom will necessarily be found a philosophic theory. Incapable as he may be of reflection, or of reducing his credence to its ultimate form, he has by the very fact of *action* pronounced judgment on the great questions of philosophy. No intelligent act can be performed without also involving, as an absolute necessity, *a theory;* and therefore the question lies, not between the acceptance or the rejection of theories, but between the acceptance of a *true* or a *false* theory, for one must necessarily be chosen.

Every form of society, every form of government, every system of association, every actually existing form of civil polity, is the realization of speculative propositions. Every government necessarily has its theory, of which that government is only the practical realization. Every system established by man, either in church or state, has been only the outward expression of an inward credence, which credence involved a theory; and this theory is *true* or *false.*

In the past arrangements of society, therefore, it is possible to detect the theories on which those arrangements have been based, to inquire whether they were true or false, and to trace them in their evolution as they changed from one to the other, under the influence of new circumstances and newly developed truth.

In Britain, the constitution of civil society, like that of ecclesiastical society, has only once been subjected to systematic arrangement; once only has the state been formed in such a manner that each individual has had his civil position allocated to him by law, while, at the same time, he was directly connected with the other individuals, forming together one political association.

The church, as one association, presented itself under the form of the papacy; the state, as one association, presented itself under the form of the feudal system. The papacy was the complete organization of the church on *false* principles; the feudal system was the complete organization of the state on false principles; and the history of modern society is the history of the gradual destruction of those two great systems — of the de-organization of the papal church — of the de-organization of the feudal state — of the reduction of both to unassociated elements; and of the gradual growth of those new principles, which shall ultimately rearrange those elements into a new form, and present once more a united church, constructed upon two principles; and an organized state, or real political *association*, completely organized on those principles of political truth which took their birth in the reformation of religion, and since that period have been undergoing development, becoming more powerful, more generally received, and more and more extensively applied.

The political construction of society, under the feudal system, was essentially based on the assumption of a diversity of orders, or classes, or castes. In its origin, the feudal system had been a genuine and true expression of man's requirements. Superiority of position was acquired by superiority of skill, courage, or enterprise; and so long as it was a war system, and the lands were accorded to the warriors, the feudal system was correct in principle, and efficient in its operation. But when the system had grown, and had become not an accidental form produced by circumstances, but an intentional form confirmed by parchment laws, — when the settled warrior became a hereditary noble, and society presented no longer a genuine war construction, but a civil construction, which was the parchment representation of the genuine feudalism, — the superiority of *merit* disappeared, and its place was taken by a superiority of *rank*. The war feudalism was a spontaneous allocation of offices to individuals according to their capacities; but the parchment feudalism was the construction of civil society on the principle of hereditary rank, hereditary jurisdiction, hereditary legislation, and hereditary landed property. This system was the construction of civil society on *false* principles; and modern society is gradually growing out of this form of construction to assume another form of organization, based on the principle of *equality*.

Let us, then, ask, What was the essential form of society in its feudal construction?

A, B, C, D, and E will represent individuals, to whom the feudal system allocated the following positions: —

A is a king by right.

B is a great landlord by right, vassal of A and lord of C.

C is a vassal, holding land from B by military service.

D is a sub-feudatory, holding land from C for services not immediately military.

E is a serf belonging to A, B, C, or D, without political rights. He is *property*, not a *person*.

Such would be the *feudal* constitution of society. Of course the word *right* is employed, in its customary false sense, to indicate what is received by law, or custom, not in its *moral* sense.

According to the feudal theory, A was supposed to derive his rights from God, and to be subject to God alone; and this doctrine was asserted in France down to a short period before the revolution. In England, it was considered to be abolished by the revolution of 1688.

B was *subject* to A, and derived his rights from A, whose *vassal* he was. These rights, however, became *hereditary*, and, when sanctioned by custom, B maintained them as *inherent*. B's son was *born* a lord.

C was subject to B, and subject also to A; so that B was subject to A, and lord of C.

D was subject to C, and was *proprietor* of E.

E was property of D. He was master of nobody, not even of himself. All that he had belonged to his owner.

In this scheme of political society, A legislates for B, tries B in his great court, and punishes him on occasion. B, however, has a jurisdiction of his own, and tries C in his little or baronial court, and punishes *him* on occasion. C has a minor jurisdiction over D. And D, being proprietor of E, legislates for him, and punishes him as he thinks proper.

Such was the feudal arrangement of society with regard to political rights. And this was the system effectually uprooted and destroyed by the French revolution — the system that has been, and still is, gradually undergoing a process of destruction in Britain. Feudalism has not been *destroyed* in Britain; it has only been *generalized* and modified. Vast changes have yet to take place before it finally disappears.

Let us now turn to the aspect of this society, when the doctrine of equality has been applied to it so far as *liberty* is concerned.

A is no longer a king, but a freeman.

B is no longer a lord, but a freeman.

C is no longer a military vassal, but a freeman.

D is no longer a socman, but a freeman.

E is no longer a serf, but a freeman.

And these freemen, being equal in rights, proceed to form a state, and *elect a government* for the regulation of the whole.

In the former case we have the rule of superstition and prescription; in the latter, the rule of reason and equal justice to all. In the former case we have privileges accorded to a few, at the expense of the rights (the *moral* rights) of the many; in the latter case we have no *privileges*, no hereditary distinctions, and no diversity of conditions, except those *of office*, or those produced by the more or less successful result of industry, skill, or enterprise. In the former case we have a system that contains within itself the *de*struction of justice; in the latter a system that contains within itself the *con*struction of a jural society. In the former case we have a system that contains necessarily, —

1. A cause of war of B against A, (the barons bridle the king.)

2. A cause of war of C against B.

3. A cause of war of D against C.

4. A cause of war of E against A B C and D, because A B C and D had deprived him of his rights as a man — as a moral being accountable to God.

In the latter case we have the obliteration of all just cause of war. Where none has a legal right which is not accorded to another in the scheme of the state, the cause of internal strife is obliterated; and though governments go to war on very insufficient pretexts, populations seldom or never do so without a just cause. The obliteration of the cause, therefore, may fairly be expected to obliterate the fact.

The feudal system, with all its modifications past and present, however mild or constitutional, is nothing more than systematized slavery. At the *bottom* of society there must always be found the great masses in a worse condition than nature intended. And wherever the feudal system exists, or any remnant of it, that system, or its remnant, creates a *cause of war* among the classes of society; which cause of war creates perpetual uneasiness, frequent agitations, and occasional revolutions.

It must be observed that the feudal system had no

place for the *trader*. The trader is a non-feudal element in society, and belongs to a different system of organization. *His* day is fast approaching, and he will ultimately push out hereditary feudalism from the direction of the state. He began without a place, without a rank, and almost without ordinary protection. As a Jew he was persecuted and cruelly wronged, barbarously treated because he had no brute force to repel aggression.* As a foreigner he was taxed and

* "Another considerable article of the crown revenue was the profits arising from the Jews. Our histories are every where full of the great and extraordinary taxes and impositions laid on them; they were a constant fund for a necessitous court. Mr. Maddox has produced a multitude of the exchequer records to evince this truth; but as he has not given any reason for the exercise of this arbitrary power, but only taken notice of the fact that they were so taxed; and as this conduct of our ancient kings seems to have perplexed Lord Coke in some parts of his works, — we shall beg leave to inquire into the grounds and reason of this behavior; because such arbitrary and extraordinary methods are contrary to the analogy of our constitution in other respects.

"Some think our kings had a right to use the Jews in what manner they pleased, and that their fortunes and estate were absolutely at the king's disposal, and this by a grant from the legislature. For it appears by the twenty-ninth law of the Confessor, that the Jews were the absolute property of the king. The words are, *Judæi et omnia sua sunt regis; quod si quispiam detinuerit eos, vel pecuniam eorum, perquirat rex si vult, tanquam suum proprium:* and the reader may see this law enforced among the ordinances of Henry II. and Richard I., concerning the Jews. He may likewise find a very memorable record in the first volume of Rymer's Collections, where Henry III. mortgages for £5000 to his brother, the Earl of Cornwall, *omnis Judæos regni Angliæ*, with a power of distraining the bodies of all or any of them, if the money was not paid at the times prefixed." — *History of Taxes from William the Conqueror to A. D.* 1761.

tolerated, and as a native he was a base trader engaged in ignoble pursuits.

The feudal system was organization on false principles, but it *was* organization; and so long as the organization was genuine and spontaneous, the feudal system was the true and living expression of man's necessities. The leader *was* a leader, a lion heart who could dare and do. He led because he *could* lead, and was followed from instinct, which knows its leader and follows him. But when the feudal system was transplanted from the field to the court, — when the pen of the lawyer supplanted the sword of the knight, and the banner of parchment was more powerful than the pennon, — the life of feudalism was gone, and a clattering skeleton remained with its dead formalities. War feudalism was a good, and genuine, and true man; but parchment feudalism was a mock man, — the one was the organization of force, — the other the law copy of that organization, and the attempts to fix in perpetuity the form without the elements. In the one, power was the essential, and form the accidental; in the other, form was the essential, and power was the accidental. The one had a leader who did govern; the other, a king who was supposed to govern. The one had an aristocracy of talent; the other an aristocracy of sheepskin. The one gave lands because he first conquered them; the other gave lands because they fell into his hands. The one gave lands to men of the sword who could defend them; the other to fools and favorites. The one was a real lion who showed himself; the other was a stuffed lion with a fox for a showman.

Every human system grows, expands, arrives at maturity, decays, and dies. The *system* dies, but man does not die. Man goes on to new systems, which grow, expand, and die also; and again to new systems, which also die. But beneath the surface of the human systems there is a reality which does not die — a reality which *evolves.* One system teaches one truth, and another system another truth, and the truth remains when the system has disappeared. All attempts to fix systems in perpetuity are unnatural. The vital element is fled, and the body must perish, or if preserved is a mummy. And all systems preserved by law beyond their natural existence are *mummy* systems. And it would be no less absurd to allocate a maintenance to a mummy than to a system. If the man is alive, he must support himself; if dead, he needs no maintenance. And if the system is alive, it will make its maintenance because men require it; and if men require it not, it is a mummy system, and should have no maintenance.

All human systems, intentionally established, or reduced to legal institutions, originate in the credences of man; and so long as the credences last, the systems are natural, and do not decay. But when the credence advances, the system is no longer the expression of man's requirements; and the system if preserved can do evil, and only evil. With the advance of credence the system ought to advance also; for man, in perpetuating systems, perpetuates only the expression of his former ignorance. The feudal system was the organization of power, because man believed *war* to be the noblest occupation. It was power *organized;* and if it had been *true* that war was man's real occupation, the feudal system was the true system of organization. But another element than *force* began to divide men's credence — *law*. And the form of the feudal system was transformed from the right of the sword to the right of the sheepskin. The sword was bad, but the system was efficient so long as it was spontaneous. The sheepskin was an improvement on the sword; and had the system of the sheepskin gone back to the genuine origin of the system of the sword, it would have resulted in the same efficiency that characterized the power of feudalism. The sword has a right use and a wrong use — it may be in the hand of *justice*, or it may be in the hand of *will*. And the sheepskin also has a right use and a wrong use — it may be the expression of justice, or it may be the expression of *will*. The sword is force, the sheepskin is law; and when men advance from the organization of force to the organization of law, the parchment supersedes the sword, and *injustice* may be done by the one exactly as it was done by the other. It is a higher and more systematic kind of injustice, and so far it is a progress, as fine and imprisonment is an advance upon the torture wheel. The feudal system grew spontaneously, and the elements of its power were in the form of its spontaneous construction. But the form of its construction was not preserved, and feudalism decayed from the very attempt to perpetuate it.

Feudalism became *hereditary;* but neither courage nor skill are hereditary, and hereditary warriors are mummies. The hereditary system transformed the whole genius of feudal society, and the feudal system, as a war organization, had lost its power. The principle of feudalism, as a war system, was to allocate the lands to him who was the warrior; the principle of feudalism, as a parchment system, was to consider him warrior who held the lands.* And when the force organization of society gave way to the law organization of society, the hereditary principle was transplanted into the *legislature*, and men became hereditary legislators. But wisdom is no more hereditary than courage and skill; and the hereditary system of legislation — the parchment feudalism — became as inefficient as the hereditary system of defence — the pennon feudalism. A new element was required, and a new element appeared, to dispute the claims of hereditary force or hereditary law.

The pennon feudalism had a pursuit — war; and the parchment feudalism had a pursuit — pleasure. First, Mars, then Bacchus and Venus, has been the course of semi-barbarous man in all ages. But neither war nor pleasure will satisfy mankind; and man must progress beyond his mere animal desires. A new pursuit began to grow amid the wars and pleasures

* "The companion requires from the liberality of his chief the warlike steed, the bloody and conquering spear, and in place of pay he expects to be supplied with a table, homely indeed, but plentiful."

Note by M. Brotier. — "From hence, Montesquieu (Esprit des Lois, xxx. 3) justly derives the origin of vassalage. At first the prince gives to his nobles arms and provisions; as avarice advanced, money; and then lands were required, which from benefices became at length hereditary possessions, and were called fiefs. Hence the establishment of the feudal system." — AIKEN'S *Tacitus. Manners of Germans.*

of feudalism — *trade*. This new pursuit was a new advance of society, and it introduced a new element in the shape of wealth. It was not merely trade, but trade beginning to be organized and systematized. Trade, like war or pleasure, had always formed part of the occupation of mankind. But feudalism, not content with organizing an army, had organized civil society on the war principle; and parchment feudalism organized society on the principle that the aristocrats were for pleasure, and the rest of the people for labor to supply their pleasures. "Priests are set apart for prayer, but it is fit that noble chevaliers should enjoy all ease and taste all pleasures; while the laborer toils in order that they may be nourished in abundance — they and their horses and their dogs." Trade, however, crept in; and society began to admit a portion of the trade principle. And this, like every thing else, began on false grounds; with privileges, charters, restrictions, exemptions, local boundaries, and a hundred other interruptions to the laws of nature. Trade, however, asserted its claims, and advanced a new element into the constitution of government. The burgesses were tolerated, because they had money and could pay taxes; and gradually the traders have pushed their way against the parchment lords, as the parchment lords pushed theirs against the pennon lords. The *commons* are partly knights who represent proprietors of land, and partly "citizens and burgesses, chosen by the mercantile or supposed trading interest of the nation." And though the commons have never in reality represented the *people* of Britain, but at the most the wealthier traders, the direction of society may be inferred from the relative position of the commons now, and the commons two or three centuries ago. Henry VIII. was a parchment king, whose *will* was *law*. The war lords had fought themselves out in the wars of the Roses, and *as* war lords appeared no more. The commons were a few cringing burgesses, without power. The king was the state, and, to all intents and purposes, the only real power in the state. He did what it has been the lot of few to do — he changed the religion of the nation and confiscated the lands of the church, and, in so doing, laid the foundation of the parchment power of the lords. A few reigns, and the commonwealth passed over; and the lords had found that *law*, and not the sword, was the genuine source of power. The *lords* were now the state, and admitted William of Orange to be the organ of aristocratic domination. This scheme has extended down to the present day; but another change has been going on, showing plainly that the power of the lords is no more permanent than the power of the king. The commons have taken up the power. It is now customarily admitted that the government cannot function without a majority of the commons; in fact, that the king *reigns*, but does not *govern*, and that a majority in the commons is the necessary element for carrying on the operations of the state. The lords have retired in solemn decency, and the knights and burgesses direct the affairs of Britain.

To suppose, however, that this change is *ultimate*, would be contrary to all the teaching of history. Parchment lordship is contrary to the credence of modern times. Men are beginning to believe that he who does not *work* ought not to be supported, as those who *do* work support the whole. The war lord *worked*, and worked hard. He fought, or was ready to fight, and his life was at stake for his wages. He deserved his reward. He was a man who led men; and so long as he was a real war lord, and war was the real pursuit, he was a genuine man, and filled an office for which men were willing to accord him wages. When he became a parchment lord, he still worked. He made laws, and ruled the country. He was to a certain extent necessary, like the bishop, who once worked also, and ruled the church. And in former days, the rule of the church was no more a jest than the rule of the state. It was a *real* office — a thing not of silks and drawing-rooms; but of the translation of the Word of God, and appearance at the martyr's stake when requisite. The bishop *was* a pastor, a real genuine pastor, who had a flock, and cared for it; and even now, if it were possible to reanimate the bishop, and make him again a leader, a genuine *leader of men*, there is no man in the country who could count followers with him. But both have outlived their time. The *commons* are said to rule, and the bishop's voice is heard only in the minor wranglings of sectarianism. True, there are good and pious bishops and archbishops, and their writings, as cultivated *men and ministers*, are excellent. But as *bishops*, they are almost unknown.* The *office* is no longer requisite. And the

* For an account of the revenues of the church of England, incomes of the bishoprics, &c., see Wade's "Unreformed Abuses

parchment lord is also antiquated, because he does not *work.* There is *no* work for parchment lords, no demand in the market, nothing for them to do. Formerly, if there had been no lords, they would have been originated. Society required them, and would pay for them; and, if there had been none, society would have made them, and did make them. There

in Church and State." Some curious facts are there stated regarding the expense at which England supports her ecclesiastical ministrations. It seems that there are 32 cathedral and collegiate churches in England and Wales, with 261 members, (deans, canons, prebendaries, &c.,) and a revenue of £184,123 per annum. For this sum a week-day service is maintained, (in addition to the Sabbath services,) and the congregations are stated to amount to nearly the same number as the officials. Thus:—

Cathedrals.		Officials Present.	Congregations.
Durham,	1	32	18
Peterborough,	1	12	7
Wells,	1	19	22
Carlisle,	1	17	9
Rochester,	1	22	14
Oxford, (!)	1	15	18
Lincoln,	1	24	8
	7	141	Persons, 96

The seven *bishoprics* bearing the above names had the following incomes in 1843:—

Durham, - - - - - -	£22,416
Peterborough, - - - - -	4,060
Bath and Wells, - - - -	4,567
Carlisle, - - - - - -	2,476
Rochester, - - - - -	1,102
Oxford, - - - - - -	2,506
Lincoln, - - - - - -	5,610
Total, -	£42,737

was an *office* which men required to fill; an office that had its labors, its responsibilities, its dangers, and consequently its rewards. But if lords no longer lead, and no longer govern in reality; or if they govern not as lords, but as wealthy members of the state, influencing the election of the commons who *do* govern — their *office* is gone; like the war lords, who were useless when made hereditary, and settled on their estates. The war lords disappeared, and an *enlisted* army of real soldiers took their place. Men who were not *born* soldiers by caste, but who became soldiers by profession, have been universally substituted for the feudal soldiers. The feudal soldiers were inefficient; their *office* was taken up by men who could do the duty better, and against whom the feudal soldiers did not dare to appear. And so with the parchment lords. *Their* office was to make laws, to govern the country, to rule the state. And if they no longer rule the state, but have disappeared from the *work* before the *enlisted* legislators who were not *born* legislators, but *became* so, their office has vanished; and, if history tell true tales of the past, we may rest assured that time will ultimately accord the office to those who do the work in reality. Pleasure lords are too contrary to the spirit of labor which an age of *trade* requires, to be allowed long to occupy the first position. The work of parchment aristocracies is gone from their hands, and *commons* govern; and though titles are harmless in the present day compared to what they were once, there is *maintenance in luxury without labor*, which, in an age of trade, is certain at last to reduce the question to a calculation of profit and loss, measured by money, and to make *trading* rulers act on the result of the balance sheet.

In estimating, however, the historic probabilities of Britain, various considerations must be taken into account. It seems quite certain that the pleasure lords cannot continue to occupy the first position, merely because they have a sheepskin with a few black marks upon it. But *who* is to take their place? The trading community are fast, very fast, pushing out the parchment holders. Land tenures are undergoing alterations. Old families are failing, not from the want of parchments, but from the want of *wealth.* Merchants are now the *notables*, the men of note who express the requirements of the country. But the pursuit of money is no more the ultimate pursuit of man than the pursuit of war or pleasure. The trader, in his turn, must cede the first place to those who express man's higher requirements. Money is a means, not an end; and when those who represent the means have played their part, those who represent something beyond the means will assert their claims, and push the trader from the direction of the state. Man is a rational and a moral being, and his rational and moral nature must ultimately prevail to determine the arrangements of society.

Let us then look at the principles that have determined the past construction of British society. What have been the occupations of the governing class? What in fact has been, in the estimation of society, the highest pursuit of the civil and secular man?

1st. War. Society was constructed on the war principle. War manifested itself first in the form of barbarous war; second, knightly war; and third, national war; and then the war construction of society was finished. The war was then performed, not by the rulers in person, but by a *service;* that is, by men who fought because they were paid for it. The army was not the state, but the servant.

2d. PLEASURE. As one system arrives at its height, and begins, although imperceptibly, to decay, another system, which is destined to supersede it, already has begun to take root and to grow up under the shelter of the old system. The war system gave birth to the political system, and the war leader was the origin of the political ruler. National war gave birth to the national court, and the national court gave birth to courtly pleasures, and the knights who had been field knights gradually became transformed into court knights. As the war system decayed, the court knights superseded the war knights, the accomplishments of the court were held in higher estimation than the accomplishments of the field, till at last the fop was the genuine ruler, and society was constructed on the pleasure principle. Barbarous pleasures grew first, then refined pleasures, till at last the very corruption of manners necessitated a change.

3d. POLICY. Out of the courtly pleasures grew courtly policies. The ambition was now, not to be a warrior, nor a mere court gallant, but a statesman. An age of policy occurred, in which the destinies of nations, and the welfare of whole populations, were sacrificed to the crotchets of statesmen who made great experiments for their amusement. The population, who did the work and got the food out of the earth, had first been sacrificed for the *war* rulers, then for the *pleasure* rulers, and now they were sacrificed for the *policy* rulers. The *balance of power* was one of their crotchets, the *integrity of the empire* another, the *balance of trade* another, and the *protection of trade and agriculture* another. To these gentlemen Britain owes the American war, the French war, the national debt, the corn laws, the customs, excise, (in their present extent of evil,) and a great many other things not less destructive to the laboring community than was the reign of war or pleasure. War killed a man, and to a genuine man there is pleasure in war, — in fighting, contending, striving, and battling, — although at the last he is killed. It was a rude and fierce pleasure, and very destructive to society; but still a man had a chance of fighting, and that was something. But *policy* kills a man without even the chance of the fight, taxes him to expatriation, hunger-fevers him to death with thoughts of murder in his head, and intentions of murder in his heart if he recovers. The reign of policy was, and is, no less destructive to society than the reign of war, and it also must pass away, and is passing away fast. The policy statesman is making way for the trader; and the trader, who also is only a step in advance, and not a finality, is already sheltering the man who will supersede him — the political economist. The trader's day is now, and every day will see the policy and pleasure laws clearing away, because they interfere with trade. Trade is now the genuine pursuit of Britain, as war was once; and as the feudal laws grew and decayed, and have been undergoing a process of abolition, which will not stop till every vestige of them is utterly obliterated both from the the statute book and from the institutions of British society, the trading laws, which are at this moment pauperizing the population, must give way one after another till men discover that God has constituted nature aright, and that the only protection trade requires is protection from violence, and fraud, and state interference.

In endeavoring to fix the periods of war, pleasure, and policy, of course no exact boundaries can be assigned. The one system grew out of the other, and one was developing while the other was decaying. At the same time, it is easy to point out the period when each system was in operation, just as it is easy to perceive the colors in the rainbow, although we cannot exactly determine where the one color ends and the other begins.

The Roman period of British history belongs to the *ancient* world. It has little or nothing to do with modern development. It was the realization of a different system of credence from that which was to take possession of the world. The credence was false, and the system had worn out. The middle of the fifth century, then, was the period when the modern history of Britain commences.

The first period was expressed in *barbarous* war. From the shores of the Baltic, and from the neighboring countries, hordes of barbarous warriors poured forth under the names of Saxons, Danes, or Northmen. They were pirates by profession, pagans in religion, and men of the most dauntless courage, combined with the direst ferocity. Their trade was war, which they carried on relentlessly.

The Saxons settled in Britain, and laid the rude foundations of a civil state. Christianity began to exert its influence; and though the Saxon leaders or kings were for the most part warriors, the people would probably have settled down to peaceable agriculture had it not been for the arrival of new hordes of Northmen, who from the latter part of the eighth century invaded England, and continued the barbarous system of war down to the Norman conquest.

By barbarous war must be understood war which is not conducted according to rules which bind both parties; and this system may be said to have prevailed from the departure of the Romans to the arrival of the Normans.

The Normans introduced *knightly* war. A knight was not a barbarian. He had his laws of chivalry — rude at first, but gradually becoming more precise, more merciful, more fair, and more punctilious of honor. William was a *knightly* leader; neither a barbarian nor a king, but a war chief whose title was the sword, but still the sword of a *regulator* or systematizer.

From 1066 to 1485 was the period of knightly war, and Richard III. was the last of the knight warriors. His successor, Henry VII., was a king — a law or parchment king — a politic prince, who did his best to destroy the war retinues of the barons who had so long distracted the country with their minor dissensions. During this period we have two *types* of leaders, — one at the end of the twelfth century, the other at the beginning of the fifteenth, — namely, Richard I., who was more a knight than a king, and

Henry V., who was a knight fast verging towards a king. Both were warriors, both performed prodigies in the field; but Richard was a knight leader, Henry a king leader. This was the period of *warlike* pleasures, jousts, and tournaments, which prepared the nobles for the court pleasures that superseded them in after times.

The wars now became national, and the individuals who performed the service had little or no connection with the cause of the wars. From this period down to James II., the *king* ruled; and he ruled not in the field, but in the cabinet.

This was the period of courtly pleasures; at first rude, coarse, and sensual, but gradually becoming more refined. The nobles became *court* gallants, and the warlike pastimes gradually died away. The court of Elizabeth was the type of the transition, and the court of Charles II. was the full-developed type of pleasure. Here were courtiers and courtesans in their glory; the first without courage, the latter without modesty, but very elegant and agreeable gentlemen and ladies, there can be no doubt.

England had never been so great as under the dominion of Oliver Cromwell, and Cromwell permitted no court gallants. And had England and Scotland understood their interests, there would have been no Charles II. and no James II. on this side of the Straits of Dover. Twice England has missed her destiny, and suffered for it; once when Wickliffe taught religion, while Wat Tyler demanded the abolition of slavery and the destruction of the feudal system. These were voices which England would not hear;

and England had a Henry VIII. and a Charles II. to do the work.. And once when Cromwell would have organized the state if men would have let him. But they chose rather a king than a republic, and Charles II. abolished the feudal tenures, allowing the *lands* to escape; and George III., in consequence of that alienation, fixed the national debt on the *laborers* of the country. The *third* time that England's opportunity occurs, it is to be hoped that sure work will be made of the evils that remain; and probably that opportunity is not quite so far distant as many imagine.

From the reign of William III. down to the reign of George IV. was the age of *policy.* Whigs and tories now began to rule. They were no longer war lords nor pleasure lords, but *policy* lords. Every thing now became a mysterious matter of policy. The most vague and ridiculous notions were esteemed profound truths, to which as much importance was attached by the nobles of this period, as had been attached to the shape of a frill by the court gallants of the former period, or to the punctilios of knightly war in the fourteenth and fifteenth centuries.

The court women also, like the men, had progressed beyond the mere elegancies of the courtesan, and had become politicians or tools for political purposes. War was now not the pursuit but the engine of the politician; and national wars were engaged in at the expense of the people as matters of *policy.* The court of Anne represented the earlier form of this period; and in it we recognize pursuits essentially different from those of former courts. William had been half a king, half a tool in the hands of the policy aristocracy. The *religion of the people* had by no means been the great motive that led to the introduction of his Protestant majesty, but the *protestantizing of the state*, for the purpose of destroying the despotism of the crown. The monarch now ruled no more, but the *ministers* and the *parties;* and the monarch was the legal instrument in the hands of the parties; in fact, the effigy shown to the people to give validity to the arrangements of legislators and schemers. During William's reign, the policy system acquired its strength, and in Anne's reign it took the direction of the national affairs. Her court, consequently, became the scene of political intrigues, in which she was the puppet, the politicians the showmen, and the people the spectators who paid for the show. "The queen loved her own way, and, with the ordinary infirmity of conscious incapacity, was extremely jealous of any semblance of interference with the exercise of her authority; yet she was the constant slave of favorites, who in their turn were the tools of intriguing politicians. Though her preferences and dislikes had often no better foundations than the predilections of the toilet, it was upon them that the policy of her administration and the destinies of Europe depended. By a chambermaid's intrigue Bolingbroke triumphed over his rival, the earl of Oxford. It was because the queen fondly doated on the Duchess of Marlborough, that her reign was 'adorned by the glories of Blenheim and Ramillies;' it was because Mrs. Abigail Masham artfully supplanted her benefactress in royal favor, that a stop was put to the war which ravaged the continent; it was in great part owing to the influence of the duchess of Somerset, another favorite lady, that the queen did not attempt to recall her brother, the Chevalier St. George. Thus, probably, a feeble-minded princess, influenced only by her waiting-women, determined that the Pretender should be excluded from England, a tory and high church ministry formed, and a Bourbon seated beyond the Pyrenees. Of the twelve years of her majesty's reign, ten were years of fierce warfare, that laid waste the finest countries in Europe. The point at issue between France and the confederate powers was the succession to the Spanish monarchy; whether Philip of Anjou, a grandson of Louis XIV., or Charles Archduke of Austria, the second son of Leopold, emperor of Germany, should inherit the crown of Spain. England exerted her utmost force in this contest, both in men and money, though it was nearly indifferent to her interests whether Austria or France were aggrandized by the acquisition of Spain and America." "But the splendid triumphs of Marlborough and Prince Eugene were an inadequate compensation *for the decay of trade and rapid increase of the public debt and taxes*." This, however, was only the *commencement* of the policy system, which came to its full completion in the reign of George III., who was to *policy* exactly what Charles II. had been to *pleasure;* namely, the complete and full-grown type, who carried the system to its maximum, and indicated to a certainty that a change of system would take place ere long.

The whigs and tories, or *policy lords*, have governed England from the revolution of 1688 down to the present time; but a new system is in preparation, and must soon undergo its development. The policy lords are abandoning the direction of state affairs to men of facts and figures; and these facts and figures are certain in the long run to obliterate the policy system, and to establish the government of *political economy*.

During this period (from the end of the seventeenth century to the present time, nearly) *church and state* was the watchword of internal politics. The altar and the throne were the effigies, church and state was the war-cry, and the clergy and nobles were the priests of the superstition. Every thing was squared upon the plan of church and state policy. Scotland, which had withstood the arms of England, was overcome by state policy, and united legislatively and executively to the state. "This important measure was more popular in England than Scotland, where it was stoutly opposed by Fletcher of Saltoun, the earl of Belhaven, and the dukes of Athol and Hamilton, though the quiet acquiescence of the last with a majority of the Scots Parliament was procured by a judicious distribution of honors and bribes towards the close of the negotiations." This was another step towards the *generalization* of government, which has been going on since the barons were denied the right of private war, and which process of generalization is as apparent in the history of France as in that of Britain.

Another and very important step was the suppression or suspension of the convocation of the church of England; a step which in fact destroyed the ecclesiastical liberties of that church, and made it a branch of the service, like the army. As soon as the convocation revives, a new era will commence for England.

The great reign of policy, however, was the reign of George III., which exhibited the system in full perfection. The policy of this reign appears *now* to be remarkable; but to the actors themselves appeared no doubt very wise and clever, and quite as indubitably *right* as war or pleasure had appeared to Richard I. or Charles II. The first great exhibition was the attempt to coerce the American colonies, "the deluded and unhappy multitude," as the inhabitants of America were termed in the king's speech of 1777. This was a *policy* war; and it cost Britain about one hundred and thirty millions sterling, the interest of which is now taken from the profits of the present laborers. And the policy of the war may be inferred from the fact, that the advantages derived by Britain from a trade with free America increased continually from the moment the transatlantic Britons were allowed to make their own political arrangements. The next piece of policy was the great French war, or series of wars, which was at first a war against popular *democracy*, and latterly a war against imperial *despotism*. The policy rulers of Britain carried on this war at an expense of about six hundred millions sterling; and, to defray the charge, the revenues of this and future generations were sold in perpetuity to Jews and money dealers.

Another piece of policy was the *union* with Ireland *without* Catholic emancipation, and the union of the Protestant Episcopal church of that country with the church of England. The reign of policy, however, has culminated, and a new system may reasonably be expected to supplant it. Catholic emancipation, the reform bill, the emancipation of the negroes, and the repeal of the corn laws, are certain evidences that the reign of mere policy is dying away. Changes of this character, however, do not take place at once; but as new generations grow up in different circumstances, and with different associations, new credences supplant the old, and those new credences grow gradually into realization. The policy system is not dead, only dying. It still retains its power with regard to Russia, the great bugbear of the policy gentry, as if God intended the nations of the earth to progress only as the rulers of Britain would allow them. The Russians are the progressors, the centralizers, the generalizers, the reducers to rule and system; and the Russians are doing that greatest of all state services — destroying the power of the nobles, and subjecting men to *the laws of the state.* Of course, Russia is a despotism, and cannot be otherwise without falling into confusion. There is a period in the history of civilization when the ruler is *necessarily* despotic, as there are evils which can give way only before the influence and beneath the hand of despotism. Despotism alone, whether democratic or autocratic, appears capable of destroying the superstitious ecclesiastical institutions which have descended from darker ages. Henry VIII. was a despot, and, had he not been a despot, he could not have uprooted the papal church and taken away its lands. The French democrats were despots, and they also uprooted the state superstition, and took away its lands. And who knows how soon a Russian despot may destroy the Greek church, and emancipate the whole of the serfs? Organization by all means, and at all hazards, appears the only mode by which barbarous nations can be civilized; and the real evil lies not in despotic power, but in the legal or parchment perpetuation of that power beyond the circumstances that make it arise spontaneously.

And yet of this progressing Russia, (which has already collected the *laws* of the empire, thereby laying the foundation of the ultimate supremacy of *law*, and not of *man*,) the policy rulers of Britain consider themselves bound by *policy* to entertain vague apprehensions, and in consequence to prop up the Mahomedan despotism, which does not progress. It would have been much more rational if England and France had driven the Turks out of Europe altogether. To allow the first geographical position in eastern Europe to remain in the hands of Mahomedans, is perfectly absurd; and if Russia can take possession of it, surely England, with Gibraltar, Malta, the Cape, &c., &c., can have no just ground of interference, except to make sure that the seas are kept open for her merchants. The seas are "the highways of the world," and every nation has a right to require that they shall never be obstructed. Britain has already had two lessons in policy wars, and these might suffice to show their total inefficiency to produce even the end required, setting aside the question whether the end *was* desirable. Notwithstanding the efforts of Britain, America did become independent; and all that Britain obtained was her debt. And, notwithstanding all the efforts of Britain, France rejected the Bourbons, old and young; and all that Britain obtained was a much larger debt. And if the latter effort, which cannot reasonably be expected to be surpassed on any future occasion, was so utterly powerless to arrest the progress of advancing credence, surely the policy system may be laid aside as a mere superstition, destructive to those who act upon its dictates, and proven beyond dispute to be *not* the rule that should guide statesmen in their labors.

But the reign of *policy* is fast drawing to a close; and we must endeavor to estimate its logical successor. Looking to the past, what may we expect the future to be? This is the question for which we have endeavored to exhibit the *principles* of the past; and out of those principles we think there flows a future scheme of progress.

What have been the occupations of the ruling classes of Britain?

1st. War, which was barbarous war so long as the Northmen were afloat.

Knightly war, consequent on the Norman conquest. William was partly a barbarous leader, partly a great baron with his retainers, and partly a knight; or a war leader beginning gradually to grow into a knight. Richard I. was a knight, Henry V. was still a knight with a considerable degree of the court, and Richard III., the last warrior, was more of the courtier than the knight. These are the types or representatives of the war period of society. The nobles, or ruling classes, followed the same kind of development; first, barbarous warriors, then knightly warriors, then barons with retinues, who fought for causes, and then *courtiers*.

2d. Pleasure.* The nobles, from knightly war progressed to knightly courtesy in the former period, and the warlike pastimes at which ladies were present, prepared them for the court pleasures. Queen Elizabeth was a court lady, (still, however, with a smattering of the war system,) and in her court the nobles exhibit the feeble remains of knighthood, and the rapid growth of courtiership. In Charles II.'s time the war knight had become supplanted entirely by the court knight. Court pleasures were the summit of human aspiration for the *rulers* of the state.

3d. Policy. The introduction of a foreign ruler necessarily introduced foreign politics, and the courtiers naturally became schemers and intriguers. The court of Anne presents the pleasure courtier defunct, and the policy courtier assuming the first importance. In George III.'s reign, the policy system had arrived at full perfection; and, if it could have been carried on without costing money, might have gone on perhaps much longer.

Between war, knightly war, courtly pleasures, and courtly policy, there is a *natural* connection. The one grows out of the other. Their order is not *accidental.* Courtly pleasures could never have succeeded imme-

* The question is, What pursuit was esteemed as the *highest* pursuit in which men could engage? and though *pleasure* expresses imperfectly the meaning, there can be no doubt that during this period *court pleasure* held the very first rank, as *war* had previously done, and *policy* did at a later period.

diately on barbarous war; nor could courtly policy have succeeded immediately on knightly war. We have here a *growth*, or expansion, or development, of the pursuits of the ruling classes; and, singularly enough, the connection of one system with another is still preserved in language. The ambiguities of words sometimes involve curious truths; and several words now in use in English are applicable to *two* of these systems. The word *gallantry* may mean gallantry in the *field* or in the *court;* in the former it belongs to the war system, in the latter to the pleasure system; and when court gallantry from ceremonious devotion became transformed into the Charles the Second system, the word *intrigue* expresses the action, and this is also applicable to the *policy* pursuits which followed. Thus:—

Knightly war, Court pleasures,	Gallantry.	Court pleasures, Policy,	Intrigues.*

But the policy system is drawing to a close. The balance of power is an exploded superstition; the balance of trade is nearly exploded; the integrity of the empire is now a matter of little moment; and Canada or the West Indies might govern themselves without costing Britain another one hundred and thirty millions to prevent them; and the protection of trade

* The ambiguous word that connects the policy system with the political economy system is perhaps *measures.* Thus:—

Knightly war, Court pleasures,	Gallantry.	Court pleasures, Policy,	Intrigues.	Policy, Political economy,	Measures.

Where the word *measures* means in the first sense *actions*, and in the second sense *measurements*—that is, the measurements that determine whether the actions are or are not *correct.* The word is actually used in these two senses.

and agriculture are very generally regarded as fallacious impostures, meaning monopoly, labor taxation, and increase of the landlords' rents.

But what system follows *policy* in the natural order of development?

Policy is a very vague word as used by politicians. It had a definite meaning in the abstract, but in the concrete meant any thing that any party chose to advocate. In the abstract, it meant that certain measures, or certain modes of operation, would be *advantageous* to the country. But in the concrete, it meant a war with America, or a war with France, or the exclusion of foreign goods, or the deprivation of *civil* rights because a man held certain *religious* tenets, or the employment of *spies*, or the retention of the negro in slavery, or a host of other measures, all advocated by the ruling classes of Britain as matters of excellent *policy*. But while the policy superstition was in the ascendant, a vast *trade* was growing up in Britain, and traders have an unfortunate habit of regarding profit and loss as measured by money. And though traders are nearly as backward in ascertaining their real interests as agriculturists in abandoning their clumsy implements and adopting an improved system of cultivation, trade, with free discussion, gradually opens its eyes, and discovers that, alas! all this admirable policy has been only a delusion, a creditor by blood, glory, and pauperism, and a debtor to vast sums of gold.

Trade, then, imperceptibly, and almost unconsciously, begins to influence policy, not by denying that policy ought to rule, but by discovering and making manifest that certain acts which were *assumed* to be politic are actually disadvantageous; that they involve loss and not profit, and, consequently, that they ought not to be done. *Knowledge* reduces policy from its flights of eloquence to the investigation of facts and figures,—from its vague and mysterious superstitions to its plain and palpable truths, far less grand, of course, but still *truths;* and truths are powerful when profit and loss are concerned. And thus the dispute between policy and trade is not whether policy ought to direct the affairs of the state, but whether an act propounded as an act of policy really is so or not. Is it *really* advantageous? The policy gentlemen may enlarge on the glory of the British arms, the necessity of preserving the constitution, &c.; but Trade replies, "Exactly. But does what you are pleased to term the glory of the British arms really conduce to the welfare of the country? Does your mode of understanding the constitution really conduce to the welfare of the country? Does your mode of imposing and spending the taxes really conduce to the welfare of the country? for in this case alone can your measures be looked upon as acts of *policy.*"

And thus the moment acts of policy come to be accurately measured, instead of having their value *assumed,*—and this measurement follows quite naturally in the order of progress,—the policy system is defunct, and *political economy,* which has grown out of it by the mere *measurement* of the acts of so-called policy, supersedes it. Policy was a major *without* a minor, or rather with any minor which the statesmen chose to put into the syllogism; but political economy undertakes to furnish the true minor, — not arbitrary, but scientific, — and a consequent rule of political economy takes place by a natural order of development.

And as this method appears so plain and natural, it would seem a fair inference that Britain is now about to see the policy system interred, and to see the political economists take the direction of the country. And that they *will* ere long take the direction of the state, appears beyond a doubt. But how far the government of Britain, upon the principles of political economy, is compatible with the preservation of an aristocracy and a labor taxation, of course remains to be proved. The economists have not *yet* the power, nor *can* they have it till a modification takes place in the representation; but when that modification takes place, — and perhaps few men would give odds that it does not take place in less than fifteen years, — the rule of the policy lords and parchment aristocracy is done. The moment a new change makes the representation more liberal than the present system, and really adapts it to the requirements of the country, that moment does a new era of government open up to Britain, and that moment do the economists naturally enter on the functions of state direction, provided no great accidents happen in the interval.

But neither is political economy the *ultimate*. It is a step beyond policy, as the reign of court policy was a step beyond the reign of court pleasure. But it is logically insufficient. There are questions which it cannot answer, or dare not answer. It must take the *money* management of the state, and determine the mode in which taxes should be levied, as well as the amount of taxes; and, in determining the mode in which taxes ought to be levied, it must come between two parties — the laborers who create the wealth of the country, and the landlords who consume the rents. This position will bring political economy to a stand. The difficulty is insoluble to political economy, and a *new* system must grow, develop, and assume the direction of the country.

Political economy professes to teach *how* value grows, increases, accumulates, and *who* makes it. The latter question, solved by a fair exposition of ascertained facts, first systematized, and then reduced to a law, lands society on the grand question, "To whom does it belong?" With this question political economy, as such, has no concern. It is beyond political economy, higher than political economy, and is what political economy is not — it is *final* in theory. Let political economy be as perfect as any science can possibly be, beyond it there lies the question, To *whom* — to what *persons* — does the created value *belong?* And first and foremost must come the question of the *land.* Suppose, for instance, it should be clearly proven, according to the science of *facts,* (as some have termed economy,) that it would be more beneficial to the whole associated community of Britain to abolish all customs and excises, and all taxes whatever except a *land tax,* which could be collected for nothing, or next to nothing, what would political economy say in that case? Would it abolish all the taxes that interfere with trade, and thereby absorb the rents of the lands, or would it determine that a man with a parchment, who does *not* labor, is to be preferred to a man without a parchment, who *does?* From this dilemma political economy cannot escape. There must be *another* system — one that can solve these questions by rule — not arbitrarily, but scientifically — by a rule that is general, and applicable to all parties.

And this new system is necessarily *politics*, or *the science of equity.*

Political economy, in fact, is the natural preparative for a science of equity. All its questions solved, (and solved in such a manner that the solutions are incapable of dispute, and come to be taught as ordinary matters of ascertained truth,) there yet remains the question, "Who is the *proprietor* of the created value?" And this question arises necessarily so soon as political economy has discovered *who* creates the value. And thus politics, or the science of equity, springs necessarily in chronological order out of political economy; and when economists have directed the state affairs up to those questions which they cannot answer, they must cede the first place to the true politicians, or themselves become true politicians. And when that period arrives, the political evolution is *complete*, and there is the reign of equity or justice.

To sum up the historic probabilities, then, we may present the following table. The producers of food and of articles to exchange against food are *the ruled;* and *the rulers* appear under the respective forms of

THE RULERS.	THE RULED.
Warriors. War on barbarous principles, from the departure of the Romans to the Conquest.	The Cultivators, Traders, Manufacturers, &c., &c.
Knight Warriors. From the Conquest to death of Richard III.	
King and Courtiers. From Henry VII. to revolution of 1688.	
Church and State Policy Rulers. From 1688 to George IV. or William IV.	
Political Economy Rulers. Beginning to assume direction of the state in the reign of Queen Victoria.	

And the order of the systems that have hitherto been pursued by the ruling classes, and of the systems which may be expected in future, is as follows: —

Manifestation.

1. The Barbarous War System.
2. The Knightly War System.
3. The Court Gallant System.
4. The Court Policy System.
5. The Political Economy System.
6. The Science of Equity System.
7. Finally, the Supremacy of Christianity.

Faculties of Mind.

1. Combativeness and Lower Passions — Manual Arts developing.
2. Combativeness and Sentiments — Fine Arts developing.
3. Voluptuousness, with the Mechanical Arts developing.
4. Cunning, with the Understanding developing.
5. Benefit, or Utility, with the Practical Reason.
6. Justice, with the Theoretic Reason.
7. Benevolence, with the Mind developed.

If this scheme be correct, the civilization of man under the influence of Christianity — such as it was after its corruption, and such as it was when reformed by the resuscitation of the Bible — would manifest itself *in the state* in the predominance of

Starting point. — The Lower Passions.
The Lower Sentiments.
The Non-Moral Reason.
The Moral Reason.
Termination. — The Higher Sentiments.

[By non-moral reason, we mean the intellect applied to external nature, or to such of the human phenomena as neither involve man's relation to man, nor the laws that should regulate the interference of one man with another. By moral reason, we mean the intellect applied to the relations of men in the matter of interference, and to the discovery of the laws which should regulate that interference, and also the intellect applied to the relations of man to the divine Being.]

And this scheme, (imperfectly and crudely as we have advanced it,) we maintain, is borne out, first, by the analytic reason analyzing the forms of scientific truth and the order of scientific development; second, by the analysis of the components of man's nature; and third, by the abstract form of history, so far as it has extended. And on these three grounds, if they coincide and mutually support each other, may be projected the natural probability of a period yet to come, when justice shall be realized on earth, to be followed by a period when Christianity shall reign supreme, and call into real and systematic action the higher and nobler sentiments of man.

CONCLUSION.

We have now to offer a few observations on the knowledge that is *logically* subsequent to the science of equity, and which, therefore, may be expected to evolve *chronologically* at some future period. The whole of our argument is based on the consideration, that there is a *logical* connection between the sciences, and that, *therefore*, there is a necessary order in which they must evolve chronologically; and, consequently, that the logical classification of the sciences does actually scheme out in its abstract form the intellectual development of the human race. If, then, we can class the knowledge not yet reduced to scientific ordination, we can project according to a plan (which is not arbitrary) the future phase of man's intellectual *credence*, and consequently form within certain limits an estimation of man's future destiny on earth.

Science exists *in the mind*, and in the mind *alone*. And a branch of knowledge has become a science when its substantive elements are made to function in the blank or abstract categories of the reason, which are identically the same in all human intellect. And on this account it is that science abolishes diversity and restores *unity* of credence. And as there is but one universe for man to know, and but one type of intellect* to apprehend that universe, it follows as a natural necessity, that if man be allowed sufficient time to reduce to scientific ordination *all* the cognizable substantives that exist within the range of intellection, a universal unity of credence will evolve. And this is the magnificent destiny of science. Æsthetic differences there will always be, so long as individuals present a variety of constitution; but differences of intellection there can only be from ignorance, superstition, or error; and science is the obliterator of ignorance, superstition, and error.

The unquestionable tendency of science is to improve the condition of mankind on the surface of the habitable globe; but the past period of scientific evolution has been necessarily employed more in the evolution of *true intellection* than in the transformation of the correct credence into a concrete rule of action, which should bear its legitimate fruits and exhibit the human race in an aspect as yet unknown, and as yet almost universally discredited, notwithstanding the cheering and unmistakable promises of divine revelation. The *light* of science has arisen, and the morning of man's welfare is at hand; but the light is as yet only cold and gray, and the genial rays of warmth that shall bring into life *the good* are only beginning to manifest their power, and to bring into

* The same in essential quality, though not the same in relative quantity.

active being those germs of bounty which God has never withdrawn from the world, but which man has hitherto, in the darkness of his fallen nature, turned to so little avail. Science has as yet only been undergoing its process of *discovery;* but the period of its *application* must ere long arrive, and a new world of human benefit, as different from all that man has yet experienced, must open to the race a world of GOOD, as vast and wonderful as the realm of TRUTH which has opened its portals to the inquiring reason of modern humanity; revealing matter not as a brute material, but as the home of varied forces with which the Creator has endowed it, to work out before the eyes of his creature the operations of created nature. Science is truth, and truth is the fountain of good. The age of truth is now, and the age of good cannot fail to appear.

"Knowledge is not a couch whereon to rest a searching and restless spirit, or a terrace for a wandering and variable mind to walk up and down with a fair prospect, or a tower of state for a proud mind to raise itself upon, or a fort or commanding ground for strife and contention; or a shop for profit or sale; but a rich storehouse for the glory of the Creator, and the relief of man's estate."

If science were merely the reflection in the human intellect of the order of nature's operations, science would make man knowing without making him wise; and if science were only calculated to improve man's terrestrial condition, and to make man rich, science would only make man rich as the brutes are rich. Beneath the outward formula of science there lies the everlasting TRUTH, as beneath the outward forms of nature there lies the everlasting POWER. Science has a higher and a nobler destiny than the mere illumination of the intellect, or the mere increase of man's terrestrial advantages. "The heavens declare the glory of GOD, and the firmament showeth his handiwork." And the summation of all that science can teach, and of all that man's reason can abstract from the sensational apprehension of material nature, is the knowledge of that divine Creator, "who hath measured the waters in the hollow of his hand, and meted out heaven with the span, and comprehended the dust of the earth in a measure, and weighed the mountains in scales, and the hills in a balance."

"Lift up your eyes on high, and behold who hath created these things,* that bringeth out their host by number; he calleth them all by names, by the greatness of his might, for that he is strong in power, not one faileth."

Posterior to the science of equity in the logical order of classification comes *theology;* and consequently, if the sciences evolve in the order of their logical ordination, a period must come when theology — *natural* theology — shall be evolved, and men shall come to a systematic unity of credence on the great question of "*Who hath created these things?*"

We have, therefore, to inquire what kind of theology can be taught by reason, and how the scientific

* This most natural reply to the mere logic of scepticism is said to have been used by Napoleon — in Egypt, if we remember rightly — when the *savans* around him were developing their infidel reasonings. "All very true, gentlemen," he said, pointing to the starry firmament, "*but who made all these?*"

determination of the Creator grows gradually more and more precise with the discovery and reduction to ordination of the various sciences.*

In the first place, we may assume that natural theology is impossible, in its *complete* form, until men have arrived at a knowledge of the natural universe. If the God of nature be inferred from the *works* of nature, it is plainly evident that a knowledge of those works is antecedently requisite before the attributes of God are placed on a sure and scientific basis that commands universal assent.† And if the various sciences

* In taking this view of natural theology, we must remind the reader that we treat only of the manner in which theology grows and expands *in the reflective reason of mankind*, and thereby becomes capable of being taught as a branch of *knowledge*. The question of *individual responsibility* is much more implicated in the moral character of the *dispositions* than in the greater or less perspicuity of the intellectual perceptions; so much so, in fact, that each individual would have been *morally* responsible, even although no man had ever mentioned the name of the divine Creator to his fellow-man. Responsibility is a primary fact belonging to man's *nature*, but *theology* is susceptible of a greater or less degree of perfection, as it becomes capable of being systematically exhibited in a series of propositions *logically* substantiated.

† By natural theology we do not mean that which is accepted by the *church*, which, neither in its origin nor its method, is *natural* theology, but rather the corroboration of the general truths of Scripture from the works of nature; but we mean such a natural theology as shall convince intellect as intellect, and thereby produce a unity of credence for the whole race of man. The question is a very simple one. There either is, or there is not, within the range of natural cognition, the proof, perfectly valid, clear, and satisfactory, of the moral existence of the Creator. If there is, (as can scarcely be doubted, save by those who have entangled themselves in spurious reasonings, which do not go deep enough,) the

are only openings up to the intellect of humanity of the various portions of the natural universe, it is also plainly evident that the sciences have, each one in particular, some light to throw on the great question of the character of the Creator, and that the whole mass of the natural sciences must give, as the grand result, a purely scientific natural theology, beyond which man can go no farther without a *super*natural revelation; and therefore, although revelation be given to guide man *by faith*, and especially to make known to man those manifestations of divine goodness which could not possibly be learned through natural theology, it appears evident that the natural knowledge of God will grow and expand under the development of science, until in the end natural theology comes to the very verge of revelation, and proves beyond a doubt that revelation is exactly what man required to complete his range of knowledge. It might, however, be reasonably advanced, that revelation is not an *accidental* source of knowledge, existing only because man is a

proof must ultimately enlighten the whole world, exactly on the same principle as science enlightens the world. But for this, *time* is requisite. Nor need we be surprised that time should be requisite, when we reflect that even physical truth is slowly accepted by the world. The Newtonian philosophy is, as yet, only accepted by a portion of the world; and even it was met by refutations, "proving it to be false and absurd, both by mathematical and physical demonstration." And if physical truth of this kind expands so slowly, and takes so long a time to overrun the earth, no natural theology could expect to meet with a more cordial reception, but gradually to fight its way with the superstitions, false religions, scepticisms, and mysticisms which enslave the larger portion of mankind.

fallen creature, but that a revelation from the Creator is as really a natural source of knowledge, belonging to this earth and to the human race, as is the world of material phenomena, or the world of mental phenomena. The fall of man did not entail revelation. Revelation was anterior to the fall, and was a portion of man's terrestrial lot. It was a thing not miraculous, but common; and it would appear that the revelation we now have is the substitute for the ordinary *communication* that would have taken place between the Creator and the intelligent beings he had called into existence. That there was a direct communication between God and his human creatures, is plainly affirmed in Scripture. Revelation, therefore, (that is, communication from the world of spirit,) is not to be regarded as *accidental* to the world, but as part of man's lot on earth, quite as much one of man's original sources of knowledge as sensation or intellection.

But setting aside this view, and adhering only to the *traditional element*, we may ask, What became of man's knowledge of God? It has been, of course, preserved in the books of Scripture, and in the minds of a small portion of the human race; but with regard to the great mass of mankind, those not specially enlightened by supernatural means, what became of man's knowledge of God? In every country of the world it has presented itself in a corrupted form. *False* gods, and false views of God, have universally prevailed. Superstition (credence without evidence) has universally destroyed some of the attributes of the true God, and substituted for them some invention of man's imagination. And not only has theology in its general form been corrupted in the intellectual apprehension; but in the practical acknowledgment of God in worship, men have introduced superstitious and erroneous ceremonies, symbols, and offices, which were also corrupt, and, in many cases, absolute abominations.

Against the traditions of false gods and erroneous worship, *science* enters the lists. Science assumes as its first proposition to base credence on evidence, and thereby to evolve *truth* instead of error or superstition.

Consequently science, taking its birth, will invariably manifest itself in *scepticism*. And this scepticism, much as it has been abused, is really and truly a valid process when brought to bear on a *superstition;* and the Christian religion is now valid, because it has stood before every attempt of scepticism, and fairly triumphed over every effort that man has made to impugn the divinity of its origin. In every country, therefore, that has a traditional worship, it is a natural consequence that that worship should be tested by scepticism, whenever it happens that men resolutely apply a scientific method, and proceed to posit truth only when it is substantiated by evidence. Scepticism in its legitimate form is *doubt*, and doubt is one of the great elements of humanity absolutely requisite to place knowledge on a secure basis.

Let us grant then that a scientific method, originating in a country, will naturally come into contact with the traditional elements already prevalent in that country; and also, that it is the property of a scientific method to destroy superstition, and to substantiate truth — first, in its most general form, and then gradually to enter more and more specially on the accurate survey of the universe with which man is acquainted. Truth can have nothing to fear, but every thing to hope, from the most accurate survey that man can possibly take of the region open to cognition.

As an historical fact, the cultivation of science in Britain and France was accompanied by scepticism, far less terrible in the former country it is true, but not the less arising from the prevalence of a scientific mode of grounding credence on evidence.

Let us, then, endeavor to ascertain how a true knowledge of God must naturally *grow*.

1st. Scepticism enters into a contest with traditionalism, and as in every country there has been either a false or a corrupted religion, scepticism (setting aside scriptural reformation, which is not, properly speaking, scientific*) has to achieve the destruction of

* As Mr. Morell has well observed, philosophy *reasons*, but does not *preach*. Thus the advancement of natural theology consists in developing its propositions, and substantiating their *trueness*. A scriptural reformation, on the contrary, consists not merely in the substantiation of propositions, but in the circumstance that men accept the propositions of Scripture as *rules of life*. But although philosophy, in one sense, is purely speculative, we must not overlook the fact, that ethics, while inquiring what is *true*, has for its question, "What ought to be *done?*" And if, from the natural relations of man to man, there arises a system of human ethics, (or rules of action,) so, if the existence of God be established by a purely scientific method, must there necessarily rise a system of *theological* ethics, establishing in general terms what ought to be the conduct of the human creature in reference to the divine Creator. This branch, which the great Dr. Chalmers expounded under the name of "ethics of theology," we have termed ***Dikaistic***, (see

superstition; but in place of superstition it has *nothing* to substitute.

2d. That man should permanently refrain from a theological credence is out of the question. There is either nothing whatever, or there is some permanently enduring something that was anterior to man, that underlies all the operations of nature, and that constructed, and continues to construct, all the varied mechanisms, physical and mental, with which man is acquainted; and this permanent element which man posits, in accordance with the laws of his reason, is what is meant by God. God, therefore, has a necessary existence to the human mind; and the main question is not, Whether there is an eternal and all-pervading power; for man cannot conceive that there is not; but, What is the character of that immortal Power that sustains the universe? what, in fact, are the attributes of God?

And in the growth of these attributes, that is, *in the addition of predicate after predicate* to the substantive idea, lies the process by which a natural theology, purely scientific, must ultimately be developed, and actually command the human credence in the same manner as any other truth.

The first positing of the theological idea is, *logically*, universal existence in space and immortal existence in time. This is the first step towards a scientific

table in the Appendix,) from δίκαιος, *righteous;* and it should answer the question, "How ought man to act, rightly or *righteously?*" It is plain, however, that from the fall of man, dikaistic cannot *satisfy*, but only direct, in *general* terms, to the fountain of divine satisfaction. It is a perfectly valid branch of knowledge, but altogether inadequate for man's fallen necessities.

theology purely rational and objective; and it is absolutely necessary that it *should* be objective, otherwise we abandon the scientific method, and launch into mysticism. An infinite and immortal substance may be termed that portion of natural theology which is furnished by the mathematical contemplation of the universe.*

* Historically, the celebrated argument of Samuel Clarke comes under this head. Another, and well-constructed argument, is that of Moses Lowman. Neither of these arguments is pure; both authors attempting to prove more than can be proven by their *method.* An *à priori* argument cannot prove *a fact*, only a rational necessity. Geometry does not prove that there *is* space; it only proves what the relations between the forms of space *must* be. And so an *à priori* argument in reference to theology cannot prove that there *is* existence, but only what the rational necessities of the forms of existence must be in the human apprehension. The form of this argument may be concisely expressed as follows:—

1. Major. If there be existence actual, there must be existence necessary.
2. Minor. There is existence actual.
3. Conclusion. There is existence necessary.

The major proposition is an abstract conviction of the human reason, and is *à priori;* and, in fact, all *à priori* propositions should be announced in the hypothetical form.

The minor is derived from *experience*, and consequently the argument is not *à priori.*

To extend the argument, it is necessary to discover what the characteristics of the *existence actual* really are, and thereby to infer, by a reflex process, the attributes of the *existence necessary.* The *growth* of the theological argument depends on the qualification and quantification of the actual existence known to man; and, therefore the scheme of natural theology depends on the extension of the sciences. But then again, experience cannot discourse of *infinite* attributes, and reason must, *à priori*, determine the infinity of the attributes, although reason could not possibly determine the existence of the attributes without experience. And thus reason and

The universality in space and the immortality in time being posited, the general groundwork is laid for the addition of predicates; and these must be derived from the world of material function. The physical sciences must contribute to transform the abstraction into something farther removed from negation.

The next attribute is *power*. And this addition of power very possibly produces *pantheism*. The idea has now become an infinite and immortal *power*. And further than this, no physical or metaphysical argument can legitimately extend. Another region must be surveyed before science posits indubitably other attributes which shall transform the *power* into *intelligence;* and thus the theology of nature will receive a new extension. Physical science, as such, can afford nothing but an all-pervading power; and if man were never to go beyond the physical sciences, the scientific world would remain (that is, without revelation) at the natural theology of *pantheism;* and, historically, pantheism is now succeeding the continental scepticism.

It has usually been supposed that the contemplation of what is called *design* in the works of creation *proves* the existence of an intelligent designer. This argument has been so commonly advanced, and is supposed to be so perfectly valid, that it appears almost a philosophical heresy to call it in question.

experience gradually and systematically construct an argument; reason furnishing the metaphysic of necessity, and experience the concrete of reality. Reason is the operation of weaving, and experience the material woven; both are necessary to produce the fabric.

Let us examine, therefore, whether this argument, as hitherto advanced, is really conclusive. It may, perhaps, be necessary to observe the fact, that this argument has *not* convinced a large portion of the scientific world; and, if there be nothing more conclusive, it is evident that such natural theology, taken *alone*, has failed.

We must remind the reader that we are by no means engaged in an attempt *to prove the existence of God;* but only to trace the mode in which the *idea* of God arises necessarily in the human reason as actually involved in the spectacle of nature, thoroughly understood; and, therefore, we only endeavor to estimate *how much* is really and truly furnished by one method, and how much is furnished by another method. And we affirm that neither the mathematical nor the physical contemplation of the universe can *legitimately* introduce any term into the conclusion which is not a term of mathematics or a term of physics, except those general terms of metaphysic which are anterior to both. And by general terms of metaphysic we mean those which express abstractions and relations, without in the least affirming whether there are or are not any *realities* which coincide with the abstract terms. The office of metaphysic is to furnish *abstract categories* (substantial and propositional) into which *experience* must locate realities; and if we introduce terms which are neither *abstract* nor yet furnished by physical (sensational) experience, we have an illicit process, and, consequently, an inconclusive argument. And though the argument of *design* is satisfactory to those who are *already* believers, (as illustrative of the divine wisdom,) we must remember that a great difference exists between an exposition of God's wisdom and a proof of God's existence, so conclusive in itself that it commands the assent of intellect, as intellect.

That there *is* a proof of God's existence, and of his power and wisdom, so perfectly conclusive that it shall command the assent of the reason of mankind, we have no possible doubt; but that such an argument can be drawn from physical science (farther than *power* is concerned) we by no means admit; inasmuch as the term *intelligence*, necessary to substantiate the personality of God, belongs neither to metaphysics, nor to mathematics, nor to physics.

All metaphysical dogmas must confine themselves to abstract terms, abstract divisions, and abstract relations. Such are the following: —

Existence, non-existence, necessity, contingency, creation, created, substance, attribute, cause, effect, condition, change, &c. And whenever these terms are used *concretely*, and not abstractly, we have left the realm of metaphysic. This metaphysic underlies all human knowledge whatever, and is in reality nothing more than *the necessary form of thought.* Into this necessary form of thought, the mathematical substantives — identity, equality, number, quantity, space, and force — are located, and the mathematical sciences arise. And again, into the blank categories of the mathematical propositions the facts of sensation are located, and the physical sciences arise. But as the physical sciences do not involve *objective intelligence*, but only the objective conditions and functions of matter, it is plainly evident that a conclusion which involves *intelligence* can never be drawn from the bare contemplation of matter; and that, therefore, there must *first* be the contemplation of *mind*, and the discovery of the laws of mind, before we can posit legitimately the *intelligence* of that power which pantheistic physics posits as universal.

The argument that there is *design* in the works of nature is, properly speaking, *not* physical, but physico-psychological; and the bridge that connects the all-pervading *power* with *mind* is as follows: —

In the works of nature, and the operations of nature, man intuitively perceives by his reason a *power* or *force;* and the primordial force, if we make nothing *objective* but matter, necessarily lands us in *pantheism*, which is at present the theological credence of a large portion of the scientific men on the continent. And out of this pantheism there is no scientific exit until *mind* is made objective, and the facts of mind are brought to bear on the facts of physics; so that what was before only a primordial *force* becomes an intelligent *agent*, of whom *power* is the attribute.

In the world of matter, two phenomena are apparent. *First.* The performance of a function. This supplies the material from which man intuitively posits power or force. *Second.* The adaptation of the physical conditions of matter for the achievement of certain ends. This is the portion that has been called *design;* but as design *implies* a designer, the term is illegitimate until it has been determined what a designer is, and what the term design is really employed to signify. If we assume a designer because there is design, we have assumed only a truism; but we have forgotten to establish the most essential proposition, namely, that the adaptation of means to an end *is* design. Every *merely* physical argument to prove the intelligence of the primordial force will split on this rock; and it is absolutely necessary, therefore, for man to progress beyond matter science before natural theology can be other than pantheism. Pantheism is the theology of physical science; and if there were no other science beyond physical science, pantheism would be the last final form of scientific credence.

Let us, however, still bearing in mind the division of the sciences into

The mathematical sciences, (or *notion* sciences,)

The matter sciences,

The man sciences,

— Let us ask *how* the primordial force of pantheism is legitimately transformed into an attribute of an intelligence.

Let *a designer* stand for an intelligence who is possessed of power, and who intentionally adapts means to an end. Design, therefore, will stand for *intentional* adaptation; and from the contemplation of *man* we are enabled to make the above definitions without transcending the realm of experience. When we have made *man* objective, we can affirm, "man can design;" and when we contemplate the *product* of man's design, we find it expressed in the terms, "adaptation of means to an end," where neither of the terms are psychological, but such as are used legitimately in physical science. And when, on the other hand, we find in nature the adaptation of means to an end, we *infer* design and a designer, because the only circumstances within our experience in which we can trace the origination of adaptation are those in which human *mind* is implicated.*

And thus what was at first an omnipresent and immortal *substance*, and afterwards an omnipresent and immortal *power*, becomes transformed into an omnipresent and immortal *intelligence*. And this *growth* of the theological idea is borne out by the chronological fact, first, Spinoza, Clarke, Lowman, &c., then Paley, Chalmers, and the Bridgewater Treatises.

But an intelligent and all-pervading mind, although possessed of even infinite power and infinite wisdom, is still insufficient. There are facts in nature which

* The word *design*, like hundreds of other words, is subject to an ambiguity of so common a character, that it is apt to be overlooked. In one sense it is used *subjectively*, in another sense it is used *objectively*. In its subjective sense it means a *mode of action*, in its objective sense it means a *product of action;* and when man observes the character of the product resulting from his own mode of action, and recognizes in the objective universe *products of an analogous character*, he transforms the objective idea of those products into a subjective form. And this transformation of the objective into the subjective, is in fact the whole secret of the progression of science. When the mathematical sciences are *studied*, they are objective; but when they are *used*, they are transformed into the subjective form, and become *powers of operation*. Every science, when its laws are discovered, becomes thus transformed into a subjective power of operation — that is, into an *art;* exactly as a proposition in any one science is first considered objectively as to its truth or falsity, and afterwards used subjectively for the purpose of determining the truth or falsity of a subsequent proposition. This metamorphosis is one of the most beautiful considerations in the whole realm of reasoning.

power taken as power, and wisdom taken as wisdom, will not account for. Not only is man, when made objective, found to be possessed of an intellectual capacity which enables him to design, and of a power which enables him to execute, but also of a moral nature which lays on him the imperative obligation of designing certain ends, and of refraining from designing certain other ends. And as *man* is as much a portion of nature as is *matter*, we must have a productive power of such a character as would *account* for this moral nature of man, and to have this we must have the transformation of mere natural theology into *moral* theology. And although this moral theology is not yet universally admitted by men of science, it follows so plainly and evidently from the preceding method that it cannot fail to evolve.

Let us then reinvestigate the process according to which a purely scientific natural theology must grow. Natural theology is strictly *a science;* and this science must be classed as the last and highest of the direct sciences. In so far as it is an intellectual dogma, only discoursing of *truth*, it is a direct science, quite as much so as dynamics, which treats of the laws of *force*, except only that dynamics treats of the laws of mechanical force, and thereby explains logically (that is, in *three* propositions, one of which follows as the *conclusion* of the other two) the mechanical functions of matter; while theology must furnish such a major power as shall account for *all* the cognizable phenomena within the reach of human cognition. And thus exactly as man's knowledge of the universe, both material and mental, grows and expands in the form of science, so must the idea of God grow and expand also, until the whole of the possible sciences are completed, and man comes to the universal *application* of truth.

We have then to glance once more at the order of human knowledge, and here we must remark on the groundwork of the mathematical sciences.

In the mathematical sciences the object-noun is an abstraction. Number, quantity, and space are abstractions.

These abstractions are divided into *forms* or partial numbers, partial quantities, and partial spaces.

And these forms are made *to function* by the application of the subjective axioms of the reason. These subjective axioms are taken for granted as true, anteriorly to any consideration of the actual matter of the mathematical sciences.

But these subjective axioms, or universal and purely abstract propositions, when considered as *objective*, belong to the region of *metaphysic*, and, therefore, metaphysic is the groundwork of all scientific knowledge. And metaphysic furnishes to mathematic the synthetic propositions purely *à priori*, and perfectly abstract, which enable the substantives of mathematic *to function.* That is, in fact, the substantives of mathematic are located in the blank propositions of metaphysic, and the mathematical sciences are produced; in the same manner as the facts of sensational observation are afterwards located in the propositions of mathematic, (that is, of number, quantity, space, and force,) and the physical sciences, properly so called, are produced.

The order of human knowledge, therefore, is, logically, —

Metaphysics, which furnishes the abstraction and the axiom to mathematics.

Mathematics, which furnishes the computing power to physics.

Physics, which furnishes the correct rule of the arts to political economy.

Political economy, which furnishes the correct *mode* of action to politics.

Politics, which furnishes the correct *mode* of action to theology.* [Politics, the science of equity, determines what is *just;* and *theology* brings the just into *operation.*]

Theology, which furnishes the ultimate rule of action for mankind, and leads his hopes towards *immortality.*

* It must be remembered that theology would not be of *practical* avail unless man were a *moral* being — that is, an *accountable* being. The existence of a great First Cause might be substantiated by valid evidence; but to make man *accountable* to the First Cause requires a separate process of proof, and this proof is found in the moral nature of *man;* and the moral nature of man is indubitably substantiated the moment moral science is achieved. So that moral science furnishes to speculative theology its moral element; and though politics confines itself to the minor question of man's accountability *to man,* it transmits to speculative theology the incomparably greater proposition, *that man must also be accountable to God,* which proposition a merely speculative theology could not prove, as it confines itself to the question of God's existence. The divine attributes could not be proven in their *moral* form, unless *man* be first admitted to be a moral being. Hence the advantage of a system of *natural* morals, which, if once substantiated, must forever uproot the argumentations of the sceptic.

These are the direct sciences which are *objective;* and this is not only the order in which they must be classed, but the order in which they must necessarily be evolved in the history of human evolution.

If we take the sciences in this order, it is plain that science reads the universe *backwards*, beginning at the most ultimate abstractions, and gradually becoming more and more real, more and more directly applicable to the great requirements of the moral man. And if we consider science to be "the universe seen by the *reason*, and not merely by the senses," we see that this inverse order is absolutely necessary, because the reason must master the most universal forms *first*, and afterwards those that are more special in their order. But while metaphysic, and next to it mathematic, is the genus of science which presents the greatest possible *extension*, it is that which presents the least possible *comprehension;* and on the contrary, natural theology, considered as a mode of thought, presents the greatest possible *comprehension*, really involving all the other sciences whatever.

And this being the case, natural theology *grows* (in the mind of man) exactly as the anterior sciences are perfected; and thus the final ultimatum of all scientific cognition, when perfected in its whole sphere, is the teaching of natural theology. And on this account it is, that the prevalent natural theology, wherever it is scientific, will always assume the form of those sciences which have been last laid open to the intellect. So that it need excite no surprise, that at one period of man's evolution we should see the metaphysical attributes developed; at a subsequent period, the mathematical attributes; at a subsequent period, the physical attributes, (power, &c.;) at a still later period, the intellectual attributes; and finally, the *moral* attributes. But this progressive development is nothing more than the progressive development of man's *knowledge*, the Divine Reality remaining always the same, however darkened or however enlightened *man* may be; so that at the last, natural reason, by a purely scientific process, will have seen in the universe, not an aggregate of functioning *matter*, nor a pantheistic power, nor a mere intelligence possessed of power, but an INFINITE CREATOR, infinite in his *moral* attributes; that is, infinitely *holy;* to whom the whole human race is accountable for every thought, and every word, and every action.

And thus natural theology, opening up to the reason of mankind, one after another, the attributes of God, will at last land the race on the very threshold of divine revelation, which alone can solve the moral difficulty of a *reason*, which points infallibly in one direction, and a *fallen nature*, which tends infallibly in another. When political economy shall have done her work on earth, and taught men how to evolve the maximum of material good, and when equity shall have taught men to construct society in accordance with the principles of justice, the reason of mankind will still go onward, and the higher and nobler good, the aspiration after immortality, will still beckon on humanity; and earth, transformed by truth, harmoniously reverberating from nature to reason, and from reason to revelation, shall at last rejoice in the universal knowledge of Him whose kingdom is everlasting.

Let us then concisely review the growth of the theological idea, and examine how much each genus of science contributes.

All science is the knowledge of BEING, and each particular science discourses of the *mode* of being, or of the manifestation of being.

1. Metaphysic.	Posits the universal mode in which the human mind views being. Its contribution to theology is the division of being into *necessary* and *contingent*, *substance* and *attribute*, *cause* and *effect*, &c.
2. Mathematic.	Introduces *space* and *quantity*. The idea now becomes a substance having no limits in space. (Infinity.)
3. Dynamic.	Introduces *power*. And as *space* is the *static* condition of the universe, so *time* is the dynamic condition. The idea becomes non-limited in *time*, (immortal;) and the substance is a *power* without limits in time or space.
4. Physic.	Introduces *construction*, or the adaptation of condition to the achievement of an end. The power now becomes an infinite constructive power. (Pantheism.)
5. Economic.	Introduces *intentional design* in construction. The idea now becomes an *intelligence* infinitely powerful and infinitely wise.
6. Politic.	Introduces *justice*. That is, treats,

not of the mode of producing an end, but of the end that ought to be produced. The intelligence now becomes a God of infinite justice.

Such is the direct mode in which natural theology is produced; but it is plainly evident that if man were to stay here, he has nothing whereon to ground his *hopes*. A God of infinite justice, no man who ever lived on earth would or could desire to stand before. Justice is exactly that attribute which, while it clothes God with righteous majesty, fills man with reasonable terror. Man is not only an intelligence who comprehends, but a voluntary agent who acts; and no man who ever lived would desire that his actions should be weighed in the balances of justice, and that he himself should abide by the award. Between the dictates of man's reason and the history of his actions there is a *discrepancy*. Man, in fact, is a *fallen* being; and science, while it enlightens him, cannot obliterate his crimes. Natural theology, then, while it solves the mystery of the *natural* universe, can never solve the mystery of the *moral* universe. It may establish man's responsibility, but in so doing it as indubitably establishes his *criminality;* and thus when natural theology shall have achieved its highest point, and blazoned forth the moral attributes of God, it will, at the same time, have heralded man's *condemnation*, and pronounced irrevocable judgment on the race.

And thus the final destiny of natural theology (which really comprehends *all* science *) is only to

* Man, in evolving the sciences, reads the universe *backwards*, and *terminates* at natural theology. Thus natural theology is, in

lead man at last to the divine message of *mercy*—to the glad tidings of forgiveness and reconciliation. And thus, also, as the sciences evolve chronologically in the same order that they are logically classified, the ultimate end of human study, and of all man's intellectual achievements, is only at last to prove beyond a doubt the absolute necessity both of a revelation and of a means of redemption, of which God is the author. And therefore, as we have pursued exactly the same method in evolving the sciences to come which explains the evolution of those already ordinated, there is a *natural* ground for anticipating not only a millennium of *justice*, in which all man's political arrangements shall be made in accordance with the dictates of enlightened equity, but beyond that period a millennium of *Christianity*, when the burdened heart of humanity shall return to the true waters of life, and drink from the immortal streams of Truth.

Having thus endeavored, in a concise manner, to exhibit the mode in which natural theology must necessarily be evolved, both logically in the reason and chronologically in the history of mankind, we may

the first place, or in the process of its formation, an *inference*. But when the sciences are completed, and man reverses the order of knowledge to make it correlative with the order of reality, all the operations of nature, instead of being viewed as the *proofs* of God's existence, are viewed as the operations of the Divine power and wisdom. And thus, though all knowledge may be viewed as leading to God, all reality (save the moral determinations of voluntary agents) must be viewed as *flowing from* God; so that a knowledge of God and of the divine operations would really comprehend all science whatever.

attempt to estimate the present position of natural theology, and to account for its present unsatisfactory character.

1st. *Revelation* is given to guide man correctly, under *all* circumstances of his scientific knowledge. If man be ignorant of science, revelation is in itself the divine record of that *truth* which it behoves man the most to know. Revelation solves the *moral* mystery of the universe, and points out to man the one thing needful — namely, how man can attain to an immortality of purified soul and blissful existence. And let science progress as it may — let man's knowledge become as extensive and as accurate as it ever could by any possibility — *revelation* is still and always *supreme*, always infinitely greater than any possible increment of natural knowledge. Revelation has an absolute and infinite truth for the most ignorant, and it has also an absolute and infinite truth for the most enlightened.

2d. Between natural theology, which is *purely* scientific, (that is, such as would have arisen had there never been a revelation, and consequently no traditional idea of Deity,) and such natural theology as first takes its major propositions from Scripture, and then proceeds to illustrate them from nature, there is of course a difference so great, that the two, although passing under the same name, are not even comparable. Natural theology is as different in its *method* from *scriptural physics*, or *scriptural metaphysics*, or *scriptural morals*, as is geology from the scriptural account of the creation. The two can never be legitimately compared until the natural science is *completed*, exactly as geology can never be legitimately compared with Scripture until men of science have agreed what geology actually *does* teach.*

3d. Natural theology, purely scientific, is an attempt to solve the mystery of the universe by the natural powers of the human intellect. It is, therefore, an attempt to posit such a *major* as should account to the reason *for the whole facts of cognition.* And consequently every realm, and every branch of cognition, does necessarily bring its *contribution* to natural theology. It is true that any branch of cognition may be considered in its separate isolation, and investigated in its internal detail alone; but as all branches of cognition actually do meet in the one *universe* with which man is acquainted, "What is the one major *substance* of that universe that makes matter to *be;* and the one major power of that universe that makes matter to *function;* and the one major intelligence that makes mind to be; and the one major moral Ruler, who makes mind to function towards a definite end?"

Had the universe been a blank space, and man only a disembodied reason capable of contemplating that space, but incapable of making himself and his own mental operations *objective*, he would only have posited an infinite and invisible space. Had he been presented with such a physical universe as really exists only *at rest*, but still been disembodied and capable only of contemplating the material world existing in space, he would have posited substance, quality, and condition,

* At the same time, an *objection* from one science may be fairly met and triumphantly overthrown by an *argument* from the same science.

and drawn the line of distinction between the infinite substance and the finite manifestation.

Had the physical universe begun to *function*, (move,) he would have posited *power;* and had the functions been regular, or apparently in accordance with the relative *conditions* of the various portions of matter, he would have posited *constructivity* as well as *productivity.*

And if he were then endowed with *a body*, and with the power of reflection on his own existence and his own operations, he would have posited a *mental* power and *mental* construction. And if he found within his intellectual nature a reason for acting in one direction rather than another, and a conscience which laid on him the *duty* of obeying his reason rather than his passions, he would posit a *moral* intelligence with all the preceding attributes. But then it must be remembered, that if in his ignorance he failed at first to apprehend the unity of design presented by the actual construction of the physical universe, he would posit as many different powers as there appeared to be different qualities of forces, and would endeavor to unite these secondary powers in some higher unity, so as still to make the facts of experience coincide with the dogmas of his reason. And thus, though he would posit *power* in the general, he would require to elaborate the sciences of the powers of nature before he was in a condition to speak of the *character* of the major power.* And so with *morals.* Man may, it is

* "A considerable portion of the qualitative properties of matter — or, to speak more in accordance with the language of natural

true, posit a moral deity in the general, and speak of punishments and rewards, instead of mere *occurrences;* but what he never can determine, until he has admitted the first propositions of moral science, is the *character* of the moral Ruler of the universe.* This character may be taken from revelation, or it may be *assumed;* but *proven*, in the same manner as any other portion of science, it never can be, till moral science is actually achieved and taught as a branch of knowledge. If, then, *moral science* has not yet been evolved, but is only in course of preparation through the evolution of political economy, it is plainly evident that all speculations as to the moral character of the Deity are not to be ranked as *natural* theology.†

philosophy, of the qualitative expression of forces — is doubtless still unknown to us; and the attempt perfectly to represent unity in diversity must, therefore, necessarily prove unsuccessful." — HUMBOLDT'S *Cosmos*, chap. i. 63.

* It must be distinctly remembered, throughout this argument, that those who *do* admit man to be a moral being have all the elements of a genuine natural theology, and are imperatively bound by its conclusions.

† We speak, of course, not of such natural theology as is elaborated by the Christian, who has the problem of the universe solved for him by revelation, but of such natural theology as should convince *the world* in the same manner as a correct system of astronomy convinces the world. When *the fact* of God's moral existence is made perfectly indubitable to the Christian through revelation, he can easily corroborate his belief by perceiving the marks of the divine hand in all the works of nature. But it must be remembered that the very question of *natural* theology is this very fact; and if the fact is really involved in the phenomena of nature, (as no doubt it is,) the scientific world may ultimately find

If natural theology be an inference from the whole realm of knowledge, it is plain that if a portion of that realm, and this the most important portion, has not yet been accurately surveyed, natural theology must necessarily be *incomplete;* and as it is plainly apparent that *moral science* has not yet been reduced to ordination, nor can be so reduced till political economy is developed as a teachable branch of knowledge, it is also plain that *moral theology*, which depends on moral science, is still incapable of assuming a scientific form.

And this we imagine to be the present position of science and natural theology. Natural theology, at present, is little more than constructive pantheism — the universal prevalence of a power that constructs

itself *absolutely obliged* to admit the fact, and the sceptic will be regarded in much the same light as one who should deny the Newtonian theory of planetary arrangement. But for *this* natural theology, *moral science* is absolutely requisite. The French philosophers of the last century denied that *man* was a moral being, and the English sensationalists of the present day maintain the same proposition. And if the proposition were *true*, moral theology would be not only impossible, but absolutely unintelligible.

But if moral science were once made, (and it *can* be made if man be a moral being,) such a proposition would be universally rejected as untenable; and it would become a matter of indubitable truth, not only that man was an *accountable* being, but that there must necessarily be a great moral Being to whom humanity is to render account. And as this truth is involved in man's rational contemplation of the universe, the whole world, if it continue to progress in knowledge, must necessarily come to it at some period or other. But this natural theology cannot evolve for the *world*, until moral science has been so perfected as to be beyond the reach of question.

and operates being, in fact, the theology of the scientific world. Nor, unless the scientific world accepts revelation, can natural theology assume a higher character until *moral* science be achieved, and then moral theology must follow. If it still be a matter of dispute among men of science, whether *man* be a *moral* being, or only a politico-economical being, it is perfectly evident that science has no groundwork for the establishment of a *moral universe;* and if the universe within the range of cognition be assumed non-moral, there can be no reason for substantiating a *moral cause* as the originator and director of the universe. Nor are we to admit mere assumptions, and presumptions, and speculations, as science in the world of morals any more than in the world of matter. Either it is true that a definite rule of moral action can be discovered by the reason, or it follows of course that rules of action are not naturally *imperative;* and if they be not naturally imperative, it can only be a superstition to consider them as obligatory. So that the possibility of moral science must be granted, or else we must grant the non-imperative nature of all moral rules whatever; for certainly the logical destruction of natural morals would entail the destruction, not only of all actual revelation, but of all possible revelation. If there be no natural reason which lays on man an imperative obligation to act *rightly*, there can be no reason for acting in accordance with a divine rule which *specifies the items* of which that *rightly* consists; and as revelation does not reveal man's moral *nature*, but only his moral *condition*, and the mode by which that condition can be amended, it is plain that if man's moral *nature* be rejected, (as it really is by the sensationalist,) the revelation is incapable of reaching him, and must ever remain unintelligible to him.

But then, on the other hand, sensationalism is only a *partial* view of the phenomenon. Sensationalism considers not man, but the product of man's action; it treats not of *mind*, but of the conditions of *matter;* and as the universal consciousness of humanity is against a mere material contemplation of the universe, inasmuch as each man finds himself capable of *acting*, and of understanding reasons for acting in one mode rather than another, sensationalism must be viewed only as the philosophy of the world *physical.* And as the world physical is only the unintelligent object, sensationalism is only the philosophy of the unintelligent object; whereas the intelligent subject (*man*) offers an entirely new region of investigation, and superadds various *qualitative* predicates, which extend knowledge into an entirely different sphere, and consequently transform sensationalism first into intellectualism, and ultimately into moralism.

The physical world, when considered *objectively* and *exclusively*, (as it is in physical science,) does not present within the field of contemplation *the operation of mind.* For this we must turn to *man*, and, having evolved the laws of physical operation, the laws of *man's* operation fall next to be considered. And human action falls to be considered logically in the following order: —

1. Action upon the material world, for the direct purpose of producing an effect upon the material

world. This involves the laws of the *arts*, which laws are drawn from the physical sciences.

2. Action upon the material world, for the purpose of producing an effect on man. This involves the laws of political economy, which laws are drawn from an induction of observed facts, as to what effects have been ascertained to follow certain modes of action.

3. Action upon man without forcible interference, for the purpose of producing an effect on man. This involves the laws of *social* action, but only such social action as does *not* involve constraint or interference against the will of the party operated upon.

4. Action upon man by interference or forcible control. This involves the laws of justice.

Such are the *modes* of human action, and the laws of these modes must be evolved in this order. First, the arts, (mechanical, chemical, agricultural, &c.;) then political economy, which treats of the *production of wealth;* then social science, which treats of the *distribution of wealth, the public health, the public education, the public recreation,* &c.; and, last of all, politics, which treats of the laws which should regulate interference, (legislation, government, &c.)

The two last of these divisions *alone* are entitled to the name of *moral* science, which lays down the laws of human *duty*. Anteriorly to the consideration of man's action on man, the concept of *duty* does not arise. Justice is the rule regulative between man and man; and the consideration of man's relations to man is the *first* period at which moral science makes its appearance. In chronological evolution, the scientific world is only attempting to complete the second division, (political economy,) and to break up the ground of the third division, (social science.) The fourth division is, as yet, almost unattacked, and in practice is a mere *superstition.*

Now, natural theology can never legitimately go *beyond* those branches of science which have been evolved and reduced to scientific ordination. And every attempt to make a more complete theology than science really warrants, only produces *scepticism* on the part of those who find an inconclusive argument advanced as a demonstration. Moral theology, strictly and purely scientific, is at present *impossible*, (that is, impossible *for the world;*) and impossible, because moral *science* has not yet made its appearance, and because moral theology depends on moral science, and is an inference from it. In Britain, of course, Scripture is the source of theology, and moral theology is derived from the written revelation. But, on the continent, *philosophy* is the theology of the great mass of thinking men; and *their* theology, derived from the revelation of nature, does actually follow the development of science. And as scepticism was first posited with its negation, and then pantheism with its most general affirmation, and now, instead of a mere power, an intelligent power is beginning to be seen as absolutely necessary to explain the phenomena of nature, we may rest assured that, with the development of social and moral science, (which cannot fail to undergo their evolution in their order,) there will arise necessarily a moral theology, and the world will be indoctrinated with the theory of a moral Deity.*

* "Now, this moral theology has a peculiar advantage over the speculative, that it leads infallibily to the conception of a single *all*

Now, this consummation of science, although of course *still* insufficient, is most earnestly to be desired, not because natural theology can ever be a *substitute* for the written Word, but because a true natural theology may be the great preparative for the universal acceptance of the written Word. Eighteen hundred years have elapsed since the Creator of mankind appeared on earth to proclaim the doctrine of human restoration; and yet three fourths of the world are unacquainted with the truth. Even in those countries where the Christian religion has been accepted, no such improvement of man's condition has followed as would at all justify the supposition that the gospel

most perfect and *reasonable* First Being, whereunto speculative theology never directs us from objective grounds, and much less could be able to convince us of the same. For we do not find either in transcendental or natural theology, howsoever far reason therein may lead us, any sufficient ground for admitting a single Being only, which we presuppose for all natural causes, and upon which we had, at the same time, sufficient cause for making these in all respects dependent. On the contrary, if we consider from the point of view of moral unity, as a necessary law of the world, the cause which alone can give to this the adequate effect, and consequently, as to ourselves, obligatory force, it must then be a single supreme *will* that comprehends within itself all these laws. For how would we find, under different wills, perfect unity of ends? This will must be omnipotent; so that all nature, and its reference to morality in the world, may be subjected to it — omniscient, so that it may cognize the internal of sentiments, and their moral worth — omnipresent, so that it may be ready immediately for all the necessities which highest optimism demands — eternal, so that at no time this harmony of nature and liberty be wanting." — KANT'S *Critic of Pure Reason.*

See, also, some noble passages in Samuel Clarke's "Evidences," appended to his "Demonstration."

has ever yet borne its legitimate fruits. The truth has been *preserved;* but most assuredly it has yet to achieve far more for the whole race of man than it has ever yet achieved for any one community. And, again, when Luther's repetition of the fundamental truth of Christianity (justification by *faith*) held out a promise of good, the good was gradually sacrificed to *political* superstitions; and the reformation failed to achieve more than a partial, and very partial, benefit to the world. In Germany, the church became rationalistic; in England, Erastian, sectarian, schismatic, rationalistic; and, lastly, there has come a sickly tendency to Roman paganism and idolatry. In Scotland, *moderatism* assailed the church; and for a long period the majority of the ministers were rather moralists than Christians. And this rationalistic, moralist, or moderate exhibition of Christianity is only a *national* diversity of the same fundamental reality — namely, a return to an imperfect theology of nature. In fact, the history of the reformation is rather the history of the dissolution of the papacy, which constructed the church on *false* principles, than the history of the restoration of the church constructed on *true* principles. And it would seem almost an inference from the past history of ecclesiastical Christianity, (we speak in no respect of spiritual religion,) that the Christian church, as one association, offers little prospect of being reunited until *civil* society has discovered the true principles of civil association, and founded the social institutions of mankind on the demonstrative principles of equity.

But while the written Word has not hitherto achieved a condition of society such as its principles would dictate, and such as, without doubt, it will one day achieve for man, we must not overlook what it *has* achieved. It has not yet achieved the Christianization of mankind; but *it*, and it as the major cause, has achieved the civilization of mankind. And this civilization has been the slow and gradual acquisition of natural truth, and the reduction of that truth to practical operation.

Now, if it be true that all human science ends in *morals*, and that natural theology follows the development of science, (and it can never legitimately be in advance of science,) then natural theology will come ultimately to be a purely scientific *moral* theology, and will thus be brought to the point where man *identifies* the God of nature with the God of Scripture. And thus the long-lost unity will be once more restored, and the enlightened reason of mankind, reading aright the revelation of the true God in the cosmos of creation, will see — not in doubt nor in darkness, but in the full daylight splendor of its own inherent majesty — the divinity of that gospel which opens up the heaven of the moral universe, and spreads before the full-grown intellect of man the eternal joys of a purchased immortality.

"Truth, indeed, once came into the world with her divine Master, and was a perfect shape most glorious to look on; but when he ascended, and his apostles after him were laid asleep, then straight arose a wicked race of deceivers, who, as that story goes of the Egyptian Typhon with his conspirators, how they dealt with the good Osiris, took the virgin Truth, hewed her lovely form into a thousand pieces, and scattered them to the four winds. From that time, ever since, the sad friends of Truth — such as durst appear — imitating the careful search that Isis made for the mangled body of Osiris, went up and down, gathering up limb by limb still as they could find them. We have not yet found them all, lords and commons, nor ever shall do till her Master's second coming. He shall bring together every joint and member, and shall mould them into an immortal feature of loveliness and perfection."

APPENDIX.

THE CLASSIFICATION OF THE SCIENCES.

Having assumed, as the basis of our argument for the progression of humanity, *the consecutive evolution of the sciences, and their logical dependence on each other*, we have endeavored to present the sciences in a tabulated form, which, if correct, should present the *logical* order in which they must be *classified*, and the *chronological* order in which they must be *evolved* by the human race. To have exhibited the chronological evolution of the sciences, would have required a separate dissertation, for which we have not space in the present volume; but if the reader will consider the progress of science from the days of the schoolmen down to the present day, he will find that the following table, which is merely logical, might be exhibited, in fact, as chronological. For that purpose, however, each science would have required to be divided into its separate portions. Thus, acoustics would require to be divided into its *mechanics*, or the doctrine of its motions or vibrations, and its *music*, or the doctrine of its tones. And, again, optics would require to be divided into its *geometry*, or the doctrine of its reflection, refraction, &c., (in which it is unnecessary to consider the *motion* of a distinct fluid;) into its *mechanics*, or the doctrine of its motion; and into its *chemistry*, or the doctrine of its agency on other substances. These various portions are perfectly distinct, (as distinct as the mechanics of solid matter from the chemistry of solid matter;) and consequently, in the history of evolution, it is to be expected that the one portion will evolve before the other, although all may be assembled under the same name.

Again, this mode of viewing the progressive evolution of the sciences explains at once the controversy between the Baconians and the Aristotelians. Many tirades have been levied against Aristotle and his followers, by those who appear altogether incapable of comprehending his method. Aristotle's method was absolutely necessary, (meaning thereby the *deductive* method of reasoning;) and it was perfect, so far as the mathematical sciences extended. Without Aristotle, there could have been no Bacon. Both were requisite. The first developed the general form of all reasoning, and the second applied the form to the phenomena of matter. But the *deductive* mode is only one of the phases of reasoning; and the Baconians, overlooking the fact that the deductive mode was the only mode applicable to mathematics, imagined that they had invented a new method, when they had only inverted the method which Aristotle had bequeathed to them. For, in fact, between the deductive method and the inductive method there is only this difference, that in the former we begin with the major and minor premises, and *deduce* the consequent; whereas, in the inductive method, we begin with the minor premiss, (the observed conditions,) and the consequent, (the attendant phenomena,) and from these *infer* the major premiss; that is, the law or generalized fact. Aristotle was as necessary as Bacon; and though the Baconians of the present day do not perceive it, they are exactly in the same position with regard to *moral* science that the Aristotelians were in with regard to matter science. The sensationalist Baconians, who endeavor to make moral science by a mere induction of facts, are as much out of their province as the metaphysicians, who endeavored to make physical theories by ratiocination. A third method is now requisite, and then the scheme of knowledge will be completed. Aristotle, Bacon, and the man to come,* will have exhausted the whole doctrine of *method.* But each is necessary in his place; Aristotle to give the method of the mathematical sciences, (and also, let it not be forgotten, the method of the physical sciences when once they *are* discovered;) Bacon, to give the method of the physical sciences, (in the process of discovery;) and the man to come to give the method of the *man* sciences. But even in the man sciences there can be nothing to transcend the method of Aristotle, as there really was nothing in the *Baconian* method to transcend the method of Aristotle. Aristotle gave the

* To Kant this position may perhaps be ultimately assigned, but even in that case he would be the *man to come*, as he has not yet been acknowledged as the author of the terminal method, which must exhaust the realm of cognition. It is questionable whether any future writer will ever be able to transcend Kant; but at the same time it is also questionable whether the critical method can be fully achieved before the whole of the sciences are evolved.

blank *forms* of reasoning, and Bacon pointed out the mode of putting *real* facts into the minor propositions of the syllogisms. And whenever man science is fully made, it also will be only a filling in of real truth into the blank formulæ of Aristotle, who, although for a time degraded from his high position, will again hereafter be esteemed as the genuine founder of scientific method. When physical science, passing through the phase of *induction*, which is the process of discovery, shall have fairly established the great major propositions of the physical world, the method of Aristotle will once more be applicable, and his name will again be revered as second to none in the grand phenomenon of man's intellectual development.

If, again, it be true that man evolves the sciences in a certain chronological order, we learn to appreciate more correctly the various labors of those great men whose names symbol the respective eras of development. Thus Aristotle might lay bare the universal doctrine of method, and after-ages might have little to improve upon his labors. His *logic* might be exhaustive, and no future writer might be able to say that he had seen more completely than Aristotle into the universal form of science. But if (as we affirm) logic is the first and most general of all the sciences, the genuine origin of all systematic reasoning, then logic necessarily falls to be classed *first*, and Aristotle might develop logic, while his opinions on all other branches of knowledge were empirical, incomplete, superstitious, or erroneous. His logic might be perfect while his politics would be little else than a tissue of assumptions.

But the most important consideration connected

with the following scheme of classification is the logical dependence of one science on its antecedent science. And this dependence manifests itself in the fact, that the one science applied to the forms of the next fundamental noun-substantive, actually becomes the *next* science. Thus, logic applied to number becomes arithmetic; arithmetic applied to quantities, becomes algebra; algebra applied to spaces becomes geometry; and geometry applied to force becomes statics.

This process cannot possibly be reversed. It is not arbitrary, but necessary. It belongs not to a mode of classification which might serve a temporary purpose, but to a general mode of classification which would always impel man as man to arrange the sciences in this order, and in no other, because no other is permanently possible. Not that we have succeeded in arranging the physical sciences in an order altogether unobjectionable, but that we have exposed the principles of classification which must ultimately prevail when the doubts and difficulties now connected with the physical sciences shall have been cleared away, and the relations between electricity, chemistry, and magnetism been so simplified, as to enable lines of demarcation to be drawn with a precision which the mere logician would not now be justified in attempting.

Those who are familiar with logic (and happily that science is gradually regaining its position) will perceive that the fundamental nouns-substantive of the sciences are classed on their *extension* and *comprehension*, the extension diminishing exactly as the comprehension includes more and more qualities or predicates.

And this circumstance affords a high presumption that the order is not arbitrary, but the genuine order of nature.

Science, in every case, involves *reasoning*, and where there is not reasoning (as in the descriptive sciences) there is only *classification*, which is the preliminary of science. But, anterior to reasoning, there are the fundamental and universal propositions of human credence, which belong to ontology or metaphysic. And ontology furnishes *the axioms* to the mathematical sciences, which axioms render deductive reasoning possible.

Ontology posits what Kant has accurately termed a *synthetic proposition;* and this synthetic proposition, next to the *abstraction*, is the very foundation of all science whatever. True, the sensationalists have endeavored to obliterate this synthetic proposition; but the current of human credence is rapidly returning to a more genuine estimation of the real character of the phenomena of thought, and the fundamentals of belief (never capable of being rejected *in fact*) may ere long be expected to undergo an examination which shall place them beyond dispute.

But another consideration may be made with regard to thought. Two methods of studying thought are open to mankind: first, the psychological; and, second, the critical. The psychological assumes the power of man to make thought itself objective, to study it, classify it, and reason with it; the ultimate appeal being to the human consciousness. This method is ever open to objection. The intellectualist may posit *substance*, and *cause*, and *power*, and appeal for the confirmation of his doctrine to the consciousness of mankind. The sceptic at once asserts the *subjectivity* of the concepts, and uproots the very possibility of proof. True, he says, there is a substance, but that substance is *in thought;* and a cause, but the cause is in thought; and a power, but the power is in thought. And thus the intellectualist is reduced to the mere reiteration of his dogma—a dogma which, so long as he confines himself to the criterion of *consciousness*, is no more than an assertion of his own mental experience or conviction.

Far otherwise with the *critic.* The critic takes his stand on the immovable basis of *science*, and, leaving all questions of consciousness or of mental operation, he makes the whole range of the sciences objective, and asks what thoughts they have posited, and what methods they have pursued. He leaves it to every science in particular to determine what is *true* and what is *false* in each region of inquiry; and, when science has achieved her office, he culls the first and fundamental truths of each science, and says, "These are indisputable; and, if you question them, you must fight your battle with the *world of science*, which has established and authenticated these propositions." And thus when he speaks of *power*, he appeals not to *consciousness*, but to the *science of dynamics*, which treats especially of power, and performs with that substantive operations which could not be performed without it.

The sciences are all direct and spontaneous, and their office is to determine what is *true.* In geometry, for instance, the axioms are spontaneously true; and geometry never does, and never can, inquire into the objectivity or subjectivity of her fundamental propositions. They are true *necessarily*, because no effort of man can conceive them otherwise. And when they have been accepted on these terms by geometry, they are handed over to the critic; whose office is not to determine what axioms are *true*, but to examine *what they consist of*, what is their form, their *meaning*, and their function.

And as the sciences, when completed, will involve every substantive that can enter philosophy, and every proposition that could give rise to a question on the reality of knowledge, critical philosophy will thus become the genuine doctrine of *thought;* not inquiring into *the truth* of the thought, for that is the office of science, but into its *form* and mechanism. And thus philosophy would be at once the genuine *scientia scientiarum*, and the genuine exposition of the laws of human thought, based on the whole range of science, and appealing to ascertained knowledge for the substantiation of her fundamental truths.

If psychology have any truths to advance, they must be advanced as scientific, and not philosophic truths. Philosophy cannot acknowledge them till they have been *already* established beyond dispute; and then philosophy uses them for a purpose altogether distinct from the purpose of science. Science, making its realm of investigation *objective*, inquires what is true in the *object*, and this object may be man as well as matter. But when science has made her truth, and achieved her independent inquiry, philosophy accepts the truth, and endeavors, with the whole mass received from the whole category of the sciences, to read aright the phenomenon of knowledge; and, linking the object with the subject, to complete the circle of cognition, and, it may be, to project some reasonable anticipation of the future destiny of humanity.

The last of the direct sciences is *theology*. Theology completes the range of spontaneous science, and closes the book of science, properly so called. But beyond theology lies critical philosophy, which reflects on the whole course of knowledge, and examines the method that has been pursued. And this critical philosophy can never be achieved till the whole of the sciences are complete — complete, not in having made manifest every truth which they quantitatively contain, but complete in having posited their fundamental propositions, and acknowledged the method by which they evolve truths of a certain specific quality. And if this be the case, it is plainly evident that critical philosophy has yet to undergo a new expansion; in fact, that so long as there remains one qualitative science to be reduced to ordination, critical philosophy is only *partially* possible. Moral science and natural theology must be truths for the world, before critical philosophy can sum up the whole facts of cognition, and pronounce judgment on the cosmos of man's knowledge.

But what is the lesson that philosophy can teach — the last problem of man's inquiries upon earth?

In this philosophy there may lie involved the stupendous fact of a mystery insoluble to the reason — a mystery that has borne down humanity, and baffled the mightiest efforts of the intellect. Ever and ever there comes back the appalling consciousness of "a reason that points infallibly in one direction, and a fallen nature that tends infallibly in another." Science is here utterly helpless to inform; and philosophy, while recording the fact, weeps over the hopeless mystery. *Man* cannot solve the mystery. And thus philosophy, reading the whole realm of knowledge, and beholding all that the intellect can teach, lands at last on the shore of that ocean where a higher than man must guide — where the horizon is infinity, and where she might gaze forever on the lost regions of illimitable space. That ocean *philosophy* cannot traverse. Reason cannot survey the infinite. Time, and earth, and man's knowledge are all behind; and before is the infinite ocean of immortality. And here philosophy must end with a pathless ocean and an insoluble mystery. Her work is over — finished. She has no compass to guide on the trackless waters — no beacon to direct her. The loadstar of heaven must appear, and Faith, giving the hand to reason, may lead by the records of eternal Truth.

Nor is this faith itself *unreasonable.* It is not mysticism nor superstition, but credence of *a matter beyond the realm of reason,* by means of *an evidence within the bounds of reason;* reason being judge of the *evidence* which authenticates the *matter.*

And thus the last final lesson that philosophy can teach, and which one day it will teach the world, is, that there is an insoluble mystery within the region of cognition; and that, consequently, the only hope of *knowledge* is in a revelation from that divine Creator and Preserver whose moral existence has been proven by natural theology. And this indeed is the true province of philosophy, her great work, her terrible achievement, save that there is hope from on high. She lands, indeed, at last on the shore of a boundless ocean; but in so doing she bequeaths to man the last record of her teaching — that in revelation *alone* can be found the truth that humanity requires.

CLASSIFICATION OF THE SCIENCES.

All science presents itself under the following aspect: —

1. The substantive.
2. The relation between two substantives.

This is called the proposition.

Two propositions must in every case be given before there can be *reasoning*.

3. The evolution of a new relation from two propositions given. This in its complete form is called the syllogism.

This is the universal *form* of science, and it first appears in *logic*, which is the most abstract form of all science.

The evolved relation is always a *new* relation, being the relation between one of the substantives of one of the given propositions, and one of the substantives of the other proposition.

A perfect syllogism presents itself under the following general form: —

Major Premiss.	The whole of B is C.
Minor Premiss.	The whole of A is B.
Consequent.	The whole of A is C.

In the deductive sciences, (the mathematical sciences always, and the physical sciences when their laws *are* discovered,) the evolved relation is the conclusion or consequent of the syllogism.

In the inductive sciences, while undergoing their process of discovery, the evolved relation is the major premiss, which then becomes sufficient for deductive reasoning in new cases.

Every single science consists of a *nomenclature*, a *classification*, and a system of *syllogisms;* that is, of a system of propositions connected together by the law of reason and consequent.

A *classification* is improperly termed a *science;* it is only a *portion* of a science, the propositions which are isolated in a classification requiring to be connected by the law of reason and consequent, before science properly so called is achieved.

In the physical sciences, matter invariably appears as a *power*, or force, or agent, or as acted on by a power, or force, or agent; whereas in the mere classification it is *a substance.**

In mechanics, matter is viewed as a power capable of acting on other matter, without producing a change in the qualitative powers of the portions of the matter operated upon.

* Unless matter be conceived as a *power*, (a power located or conditioned,) there cannot be *science*. There might be a knowledge of facts, but the facts must be connected by the law of reason and consequent, before the facts will function in science; and they can only be connected by the law of reason and consequent by making matter an agent, or power. But though *some* matter is always present as a power, there may also, in the same syllogism, be matter present as a substance — that is, as an object acted on by the agent; while for the moment the *reaction* of the object on the agent is not taken into consideration.

As every major premiss represents a *power*, every minor premiss

In chemistry, matter is viewed as a power capable of producing a change in the qualitative powers of every portion of the matter operated upon.

In political economy, matter is viewed as a power, (called value;) which power is the power of exchanging against other articles, or against services: or it is viewed as a power capable of *producing* articles of value. In political economy, man himself is viewed as a power capable of producing value, or consuming it.

In politics, man is viewed as a conscious power, capable of acting equitably or unequitably towards his fellow-men.

Power, and not *substance*, is the essence of all physical science; and the object of research is the discovery of the exact specification of the powers of nature in their most general form, so that those powers shall function in the syllogism, and produce logical consequents which shall coincide with the observed consequents wherever the verification can be made.

All science exists in *the mind*, and it is only as the substantives of the sciences are made to function logically in human thought that science is really achieved. Science, then, is a form of *thought*, and when evolved

a *classification*, and every consequent a *produced phenomenon*, matter may appear in the major as a power, and in the minor as a substance, thus: —

Major. Matter acting, (a power.)
Minor. Matter acted upon, (a substance.)
Consequent. Produced phenomenon.

Dr. Thomas Brown, in advocating the *substantial* claims of matter against the *potential*, appears to have overlooked the fact, that we know as little of *substance* as of *power*. Both are relative terms; and if the one be obliterated, the other, by a parity of reasoning, ought also to disappear.

it is the same for all human intellect; so that it involves in itself the unity of human credence, in opposition to the diversity of error, superstition, or mere opinion.

First.

The foundation of human knowledge is *Ontology.*

Ontology furnishes — 1st. *The abstraction* or substantive of the science; and, 2d. *The axiomatic proposition,* or necessary *relation* which renders reasoning possible. Ontology is not a *science,* but is the necessary preparation for all the sciences. The mathematical sciences derive their *axioms* from ontology. Ontology presents itself in the form —

A. The abstraction or substantive posited.

A is B. The relation or proposition. The synthetic proposition of Kant, which becomes the axiom in mathematics.

Science.

Science originates when we apply a rational method to the object of intellectual perception, rejecting all human authority and all human superstition.

The universal form of science is *Logic.* Logic furnishes the laws of identity and equality, and its process is called *reasoning.* Logic presents itself in the form —

A is B; B is C; *ergo,* A is C: the law of identity.

A is part of B; the whole of B is part of C; *ergo,* A is part of C: the law of equality.

The doctrine of identity and equality is therefore the first science, and the sciences range themselves in the order given in the accompanying table: —

THE REGION OF KNOWLEDGE.		THE REGION OF REALITY.
METAPHYSIC; or, Formal Intuition.		
The necessary and universal forms of thought, *i. e.*,	Ontology or Metaphysic in spontaneous operation.	
SCIENCE; or, Formal Apprehension.*		
I. Formal Science.		
THE CATEGORIES.	THE SCIENCES.	
Identity Equality	Logic, or Syllogistic.	
II. The Mathematical Sciences.		The firmament of Space, the knowledge of which involves geometry and the anterior sciences.
Number Quantity Space	Arithmetic. Algebra. Geometry.	
III. The Force Sciences.		The Heavenly Bodies, the knowledge of which involves the force sciences and all the anterior sciences.
Forces, *neutralizing each other* Forces, *producing motion*	Statics. Dynamics.	
IV. The Matter Sciences, or powers conditioned.†		
INORGANIC.		
Force, *conditioned in* Solids Liquids Aeriform fluids	Mechanics. Hydrodynamics. Pneumatics.	The Earth and its Atmosphere, the knowledge of which involves the inorganic sciences and those which precede them.
Sound	Acoustics.	
Light, Heat — Imponderables.	Optics. Thermology.	
Magnetic Force	Magnetism.	
Affinity of Solids, Liquids, Gases, Light, Heat, according to their *chemical* classification	Chemistry.	
Electric Force	Electricity.	
ORGANIC.		
Life or Vital Force	Vegetable Physiology. Animal Physiology.	The Vegetable Kingdom. The Animal Kingdom.
V. The Man Sciences, or Mind Sciences.		The Human Race, the complete knowledge of which would involve *all* the sciences, without exception.
Utility Equity Accountability	Political Economy. Politics. Theology (natural.)	
PHILOSOPHY; or, Formal Reflection.		
Critical Philosophy Ethics of Theology Expectation of a Future Life	Critic Dikaistic. Elpistic.	The Creator, posited by the reason in natural theology.
REVELATION.		The Divine Creator, made known by personal communication

* GENERAL FORM.

Major	. . . .	The General Proposition.
Minor	. . . .	The Specified Condition.
Consequent	. .	The Resulting Proposition.

† GENERAL FORM.

Major . .	Agent . .	The Qualitative Power.
Minor . .	Object . .	The Classified Matter.
Consequent	Phenomenon	The Resulting Function.

A more uniform nomenclature might, however, be attempted in the following manner:—

1st. Primary Knowledge, necessary and universal. Ontologic.

2d. Science.

Logic or Syllogistic.
Mathematic.
Dynamic.
Physic. (A term absurdly applied in Britain to drugs and drugging.)

Mechanic Magnetic Chemic Electro-Galvanic	Of all the various forms or manifestations of matter with which man is acquainted, classified specially in each science.

Organic,—
Botanic.
Zoölogic, (including man as an animal.)

Anthropologic, or Man science.
Artistic, (Arts and manufactures, &c.)
Economic. (Production of wealth.)
Socialistic. (Distribution of wealth and welfare of the community.)
Politic.* (The laws of equity.)

* The term *ethic* is objectionable, *ethos* meaning a manner or custom. On the contrary, if it be true that man ought to be a citizen or member of a state, and not an isolated individual, the term politic may properly apply to the rules that should regulate men as citizens; that is, in their actions towards each other, and to the sys-

Theologic.* (The divine Creator of man and the universe.)

3d. Philosophy.

Critic.	What have I known?	See Kant, Canon of Pure Reason. Sect. 2.
Dikaistic.	What ought I to do?	
Elpistic.	What may I hope?	

Seeing that man is a fallen creature, and that there is an insoluble mystery within the region of cognition, the two latter questions can never receive a satisfactory answer from natural knowledge. Revelation *alone* can answer them.

If we view knowledge as *necessarily* evolving, both logically and chronologically, in the above order, the scheme ought to explain the *generation* of science; that is, the mode in which one science grows out of, and is produced by, another. And to effect this explanation, we have only to arrange the sciences as consecutive, so that one science *applied to the classification* (or classified substantives) of the next science should *produce* the next science; remembering always that

tem of truth on which those rules are founded. It must be remembered that man is *by nature* either a politic being or *not* a politic being; and very important consequences follow in either case.

* In the previous table we viewed theology from the point of view of *man's accountability;* but *when* that view has been taken, theology must, of course, be erected into a genus by itself, and as *comprehending* all the other sciences. In looking upwards from *man*, the divine *Judge* is alone apparent; but in tracing the universe from God, the whole universe appears as his handiwork. Both of these modes are legitimate, but each gives rise to a separate series of considerations.

each science introduces a new concept, a new nomenclature, and a new series of *classified substantives*, which are made to function in the mind by the laws of the previous science.

Thus, *ontology* gives the laws to *logic*, while *logic* gives the laws to *arithmetic*, *arithmetic* to *algebra*, and so on.

Abstraction gives the substantives to *ontology*, and ontology gives the universal forms of rational thought, (or of knowledge;) and these, applied to the classified terms of logic, evolve the *process of reasoning;* and the process of reasoning applied to classified numbers gives arithmetic; and so forth. Thus: —

Ontology.
Ontology, Logic.
Ontology, Logic, Arithmetic.
Ontology, Logic, Arithmetic, Algebra.
Ontology, Logic, Arithmetic, Algebra, Geometry.
Ontology, Logic, Arithmetic, Algebra, Geometry, Statics.

This table would extend as far as the *mechanics* of sound, light, and heat; and if electricity (or any *power* by whatever name known) should come to be viewed as the *cause* of magnetic, chemic, and electric phenomena, the table would then extend to physiology, the last of the purely physical sciences, after which *intelligence* appears. A new region is then entered on.

On analyzing a science into its general elements, a correlation is observed to exist between *the operations of nature* and *the operations of the human reason.*

Every function *in nature* is conceived under the conditions of —

An agent, an object, a phenomenon;

or concretely —

Force, matter, motion;

whereas the function, when transformed into language, presents itself in the form —

A major, a minor, a consequent;

the syllogism in the reason being the representative of the function in external nature. But as it is the rational apprehension of the function, and not the function itself, which constitutes *science*, every individual science will present itself as ordinated on the plan of major, minor, and consequent. And as each science may be viewed in its general or *speculative* truth and in its *practical* application, each science may present itself as a series of *double* syllogisms, where the consequent of the speculative portion becomes the major premiss of the practical portion. The following scheme will be sufficient to illustrate this point, taking one example from the mathematical sciences, one from the physical sciences, and one from moral science. In a special treatise the subject might be pursued to a much greater length.

Speculative Geometry.

Major. The axioms.
Minor. The specification of spaces, (definitions.)
Consequent. The function of lines, &c.

Applied Geometry.

Major. The function of lines, &c.
Minor. The specification of concrete conditions.
Consequent. Concrete determination of spaces.

In *commerce* again, this consequent becomes the *major* premiss of a new syllogism, *e. g.*:—

Major. Concrete determination of spaces, (so many acres of land.)
Minor. Rate of value, (so much per acre.)
Consequent. Concrete determination of value.

This is the process that connects the very highest and most ultimate abstractions with the most immediate and concrete matters of practical life. It is also the process which constitutes *the chain of proof* in any particular science, the proven conclusion being transformed into an admitted major, for the purpose of evolving a new consequent.

Speculative Mechanics.

Major. General laws of force.
Minor. Specification of particular forces.
Consequent. Action of particular forces.

Real Mechanics, (Astronomy, for instance.)

Major. Action of particular forces.
Minor. Specification of the conditions of matter.
Consequent. Action of matter.

Reading this last syllogism from the bottom upwards, it becomes an *inductive* syllogism, the *forces* being *inferred* from the actions of matter and the conditions of matter. The consequent, again, might become a major in another syllogism; for instance, in the determination of a ship's latitude, *e.g.*: —

Major. Action of matter, (motions of the heavenly bodies.)
Minor. Observed conditions, (sun's apparent altitude.)
Consequent. Latitude of observer.

This syllogism, of course, involves numerous details and special considerations. Its consequent, again, becomes available in a new reasoning, either by itself, (as in running down a port or island in the same latitude — a common practice among elementary navigators,) or combined with the determination of the longitude. Thus, (the mariner knowing himself to be east or west of his port,) —

Major. Latitude of observer.
Minor. Latitude of desired port.
Consequent. Course to be steered.

So that a few general syllogisms, with their propositions properly filled with the specific details, lead from celestial mechanics to practical navigation.

Speculative Politics.

Major. The axioms or general laws of equity.
Minor. Specification of particular actions.
Consequent. Moral value of actions.

Politics applied as a Rule of Action.

Major. Moral value of actions.
Minor. Specification of the conditions of men.
Consequent. Concrete actions that *ought* to result.

Politics realized in Legislation.

Major.	Concrete actions that ought to result.
Minor.	Concrete actions that do or may result.
Consequent.	Legal prohibition, restriction, &c.

In the foregoing table of the sciences, neither astronomy nor geology appears. Astronomy is not in itself a science, but a real illustration or example of the science of mechanics.*

The qualitative forces of all *real* matter have to be *inferred*, (and herein lies the method of induction;) but *when* inferred, the substantives are viewed as functioning under the influence of laws which are more general than any real or concrete manifestation with which man is acquainted.

* When, however, knowledge is classified on its *objective* elements, (which exhibit the real operations,) the realm of nature may be divided into its physiologies, and these are viewed as existing in time and space. The division would then be into —

1. Astronomy, or the physiology of the siderial universe.
2. Geology, (in its most extensive signification,) or the physiology of the terrestrial world.
3. The vegetable world.
4. The animal world.
5. The human world.

But, as astronomy and geology present certain *concrete* conditons, concrete arrangements, and concrete functions, it seems more simple to reserve the term *science* for a knowledge of the principles according to which the functions are supposed to take place, and according to which other concrete functions would have taken place, had the conditions been other than they are. By this arrangement, the sciences would form the *major* premiss of a great syllogism; the *conditions* of the various substantives of nature, the *minor* premiss; and the *history* of real events or functions, the *consequent.*

Science is an attempt to make the conceived substantives of nature function in the human *mind* correlatively with their real functions; so that from the observed conditions of to-day, the reason may predict what the conditions of to-morrow will be — nature performing the real operations, and reason performing the rational computation. And if the *rational* operation be correct, — that is, coincident with the real operation, — the sensations of to-morrow will confirm the method, and authenticate the rational process of the *thought*.

But if astronomy be viewed as only a stupendous art, or real operation done, it follows, according to the same mode of viewing, that the qualitative characteristics of matter revealed by chemistry must also be assembled in a *classification*, and be viewed as functioning under the influence of a *general* power; and if magnetism, chemistry, and electricity could be absolutely *identified*, — on which, of course, we can offer no opinion, having only to do with the method of classification, — then chemistry would recede from its position as a *science*, and take up its position as the *classification* of the science of electricity. But these points must all, in the first place, be satisfactorily determined by the men of science, from whom the logician receives the materials that require to be schematized.

When the whole of the sciences are evolved, *critical philosophy* becomes possible in its complete form, being always possible so far as science has actually extended, and no farther. Critical philosophy is the final termination of man's intellectual labors on earth.

It consists in the reflex consideration of the scheme of science, and critically examines the mode in which human intellect, constituted as it is, has been able to evolve and develop the sciences. Critical philosophy pronounces nothing on the truth or falsehood of the sciences, but on their *form*, their *order*, their *relations*, their *classification*, and their *functions*. The whole scheme of natural knowledge being completed, the last inference that can be drawn from the consideration of the whole, is the prospective destiny of man; and the scheme of natural knowledge will thus be brought to the verge of that region where revelation alone can speak authoritatively, and solve those questions which are insoluble by the unaided reason.

NOTE A.—p. 140.

In political economy, land, labor, money, &c., may all be reckoned as *raw material*, out of which the ultimate *value* is produced. The agriculturist inquires how *corn* is manufactured, but the economist inquires how *value* is manufactured.

NOTE B.—p. 160.

While we hear so much of the horrors of the French revolution, it is singular that we hear so little of the horrors that caused it. The most infamous injustice, systematically established by law, seems to excite little or no indignation; while the popular reaction consequent on that injustice—although only a consequence flowing from the laws of human nature—is branded with every epithet that language can supply. Surely, this is a most unphilosophical method of studying history. The condition of France after the revolution was incomparably better than its condition previous to that great outbreak; and though the passage was a stormy one, (from the total absence of religion among the people,) France gained as much in thirty years as it would have taken centuries to achieve had the sword not been appealed to. The condition of the law in France before the revolution, as contrasted with its present condition, is exhibited in the following quotations:—

" The ancient laws of France were a mixture of the civil, feudal, and canon law. Partly they were the doctrines of the authorities on the civil law, and partly they were the ordinances issued by the various monarchs. By far the greatest portion, however, in bulk, consisted of the peculiar feudal customs of the various provinces. In these the feudal system was sometimes retained in so high a state of purity, that the collectors of provincial customs are esteemed excellent authorities on the subject. But it was not merely in each province that there was a local custom. The power of the crown, or any other paramount legislature, was so feeble, that wherever an assembly of men were held together by one common tie, as where they were co-vassals of one lord or members of the same civic community, they had, in some measure, a code of laws of their own. The royal codes, which existed on a large scale, are estimated at about 300; but of the number of inferior local customs it would be impossible to make an estimate. Voltaire observes, that a man travelling through his country has to change laws as often as he has to change horses, and that the most learned barrister in one village will be a complete ignoramus a few miles off. The seignorial courts were divided into three grades, according to the extent of the penal authority exercised by them. The principal courts of law were the parliaments of the respective provinces. Seats in them were generally held by purchase, or were in the hereditary succession of great families, who thus constituted a species of professional nobility. The decrees of these bodies were often baffled or reversed by the royal authority, exercised in the well-known form of *lettres de cachet.* These alterations of the decisions of the courts, however, were performed not as a judicial revision, but by the simple authority of the king; and thus the parliaments, being subject to no judicial control or responsibility, adhered but slightly to fixed rules of law, and often acted according to their own will and discretion. The jury, even so much of it as may have existed under the old feudal form, had entirely disappeared, and proceedings were conducted in secret. *Criminal investigations, instead of terminating in a conclusive trial, as in England, were protracted through a lingering succession of written pleadings and secret investigations, from which the accused could never calculate on being free.* The torture was extensively employed, but in the general case only when there was as much circumstantial evidence as would justify a conviction in this country.

"The whole of this system was swept suddenly away before the tide of the revolution."

PRESENT STATE OF THE LAW.

"To an unlearned person in this country it is a much easier thing to know the law of France, on any particular point, than the law he is living under. If an English lawyer is asked a question, his answer involves references to commentaries, decisions, and statutes innumerable; but, in the general case, the answer of a French lawyer bears simple reference to such a paragraph of such a code." — *Chambers's Information for the People*, No. 44, *New Series.*

France, by her revolution, achieved two of the greatest reformations that could possibly have been devised for the welfare of the country — two vast and permanent social changes, which continue to diffuse benefits of the best and most important character. The first was the revision and codification of her *laws;* the second, the emancipation and re-distribution of her *soil.* The change in the laws was a change from darkness to light — from death to life — from corruption and impurity to comparative spotlessness and impartiality. In this change the France that survived the revolution reaped a rich inheritance of good — an inheritance which no mere change of dynasty could permanently deprive her of; and it would have been well for England if she also had framed a homogeneous system of codified laws, with provisions at once equitable and intelligible. It is, of course, true that no mere code of laws can entail the good that depends on the moral and intellectual improvement of the population; but it is also true that many disadvantages necessarily arise where the civil arrangements of a community are regulated by an indefinite multitude of statutes, and an antiquated system of administration. In England, the improvement of the laws has been sacrificed to the interests of the lawyers.

www.ingramcontent.com/pod-product-compliance
Lightning Source LLC
LaVergne TN
LVHW010740120826
845150LV00009B/520

* 9 7 8 1 4 2 5 5 5 9 1 2 0 *